Advance Praise for *Hermeneutics of Hymnody*
A Comprehensive and Integrated Approach to Understanding Hymns

"This is an impressive book. It succeeds in its aim of integrating different approaches to the hymn form (musical, literary critical, theological, etc.) in a way that marks a genuine step forward in our understanding of the way in which hymns work on our minds and hearts. It has a wide range of reference, from ancient to modern, and a judicious assessment of what Professor Gray calls the 'polyphony' of hymns."
—J. R. Watson, Emeritus Professor of English,
University of Durham, UK
General Editor of *The Canterbury Dictionary of Hymnology*

". . . a monumental study of hymnody's whole and parts . . . ."
—Paul Westermeyer, Emeritus Professor of Church Music
St. Olaf College, Luther Seminary, St. Paul, Minnesota

". . . Simply put, there is no other volume that does for the study of hymns what this one does."
—David Music, Professor of Church Music
Baylor University

". . . a fascinating and profound work."
—Harry Eskew, Emeritus Professor of
Music History and Hymnology
New Orleans Baptist Theological Seminary

"This book calls for hymns to be taken seriously. It could be read beneficially by authors and composers as well as hymnologists. . . . It uses as examples a huge number of texts of very varied styles though these are always essentially Christian and Trinitarian. Historically it reaches from the time of the early Church to the opening years of the twenty-first century with the likes of Thomas Troeger pointing us to a future, which beckons us to transform our writing without distorting its content. This is not a light nor an easy book, yet it is beautifully written."
—Andrew Pratt, Hymn Writer and Editor of the
Bulletin of the Hymn Society of Great Britain and Ireland

"Scotty Gray has given an important gift to all of us who love hymns. I learned many new things from his impressive interdisciplinary approach to hymnody. But even more, I was inspired anew by the way that hymns, as the spiritual and theological memories of the church in poetic form, are indispensable resources for strengthening the life and witness of the twenty-first-century church."

—Richard J. Mouw, President Emeritus
Professor of Faith and Public Life
Fuller Theological Seminary

". . . an informing and timely contribution to the bibliography."

—Carlton Young, Emeritus Professor of Church Music
Candler School of Theology, Emory University

". . . a remarkable exploration of the life of congregational song, from its genetic makeup to its vocation. With scientific precision and artistic perception, he unfolds the identity and employment of hymns. . . . Drawing on remarkable breadth of bibliography, experience, and insight, Scotty Gray offers the reader a thoughtful and useful methodology."

—Paul A. Richardson, Professor of Music (retired)
Samford University, Birmingham, Alabama
Former President of the Hymn Society in the United States and Canada

"This unique interdisciplinary study of hymnody belongs in a wide range of libraries—seminary, university, and public. . . . impressive scope and intriguing content."

—Linda W. Corman, Nicholls Librarian & Director
John W. Graham Library, University of Trinity College
Toronto, Ontario, Canada

". . . an inspired plea to make use of the treasure of hymnody, nurtured by familiarity with and profound analysis of hymns ranging from the fourth century to contemporary, hymns of a high aesthetic quality, which give emotional support and support faith. The essential and interdependent concert of multifaceted approaches to unfurl and present the rich potential of hymns is paradigmatically and convincingly executed. Hopefully, this plea will foster the understanding of all in church ministries on the values of attentively prepared congregational singing."

—Elisabeth Fillmann
Academic Staff Member of the Gesangbuchbibliographie
Member of the Executive Committee of the
Internationale Arbeitsgemeinschaft für Hymnologie

"Any person who is responsible for choosing the texts and tunes that are placed on the lips of their worshiping community each week owes it to that community to thoughtfully contemplate this book."

—Robert J. Batastini, FHS
Past President of the Hymn Society in the U.S. and Canada
Retired Senior Editor, GIA Publications, Inc.

". . . insightful, comprehensive coverage of the topic . . . welcome and timely. . . . a valuable resource. . . . reminder for composers, worship leaders, and worshippers, to pursue enduring and edifying expressions that are permeated with spirit, heart, truth, skill, and understanding."

—Grant Eaton, Head of Music
Hope Christian College
Adelaide, South Australia

"The faith once for all delivered to the saints is not so much confessed as it is sung, a truth often observed but scarcely expounded in such breadth, detail, and fervor as Scotty Gray does in *Hermeneutics of Hymnody*. Professor Gray, a seasoned practitioner of the discipline—hymnology—takes the reader on an enriching and surprising journey, mapping out the ancient meaning of 'interpretation' (hermeneia) and visiting all aspects of the Christian hymn: the Bible, theology, liturgy, poetry, music, history, culture, and practice. In contrast to many books on interpretation, this volume spares the theory and engages the matter, dozens of texts and tunes examined and illustrated. Well-balanced, widely-read, deeply-devoted, and sure-footed guide, Gray the interpreter has rendered a wonderful service to the church and has provided a rewarding resource for pastors, students, and worship leaders."

—Bruce Corley, President Emeritus
Carroll Theological Institute, Senior Fellow
Professor of New Testament and Greek

". . . this book focuses on the interpretation of biblical witness and theological thought as captured in the singular genre of hymnody. Understanding who we are as worshippers requires the careful examination of and reflection on what we sing. This volume helps immensely in this process."

—C. Michael Hawn
University Distinguished Professor of Church Music
Perkins School of Theology, Southern Methodist University

Smyth & Helwys Publishing, Inc.
6316 Peake Road
Macon, Georgia 31210-3960
1-800-747-3016

Library of Congress Cataloging-in-Publication Data

Gray, Scotty Wayne, 1934- author.
Hermeneutics of hymnody : a comprehensive and integrated approach
to understanding hymns / by Scotty Gray.
pages cm
Includes bibliographical references and index.
ISBN 978-1-57312-767-7 (pbk. : alk. paper)
1. Hymns--History and criticism. 2. Music--Religious aspects--Christianity. I. Title.
ML3086.G74 2015
782.27--dc23

2015024116

HERMENEUTICS OF HYMNODY
A Comprehensive and Integrated Approach to Understanding Hymns

Scotty Gray

We cannot fully understand a language, a person, or a text, unless we understand its parts, but we cannot fully understand the parts unless we understand the whole. Thus at each level we are involved in a hermeneutical circle, a continual reciprocity between whole and parts; a significant "text can never be understood right away . . . every reading puts us in a better position to understand since it increases our knowledge."

—M. J. Inwood, "Hermeneutics,"
The Oxford Companion to Philosophy

To Frances, June, Lynne, and Amy

Acknowledgments

My own love of hymnody began with my father and mother, Herman and Frances Gray, and the experiences of singing and playing hymns with them at home and in church. The experiences were continued with my wife, June, and our daughters, Lynne and Amy, as we sang hymns in church, in the car, at home in the States and in our travels, churches, hotels, pensions, and dwellings during our years in Europe. Dr. Albert Venting, my first professor of hymnology at Baylor University, instilled in me a deep interest in and love for hymns and hymnology.

Because this is an interdisciplinary study, it was considered important to subject the manuscript to the critical opinions of persons in a wide range of perspectives—men and women who are scholars and practitioners (editors, authors and composers, university and seminary professors, librarians, and presidents); persons of various denominational perspectives (Anglican, Lutheran, Presbyterian, Methodist, Baptist, Mennonite, Roman Catholic); and persons from several countries (United States, Canada, Australia, England, Ireland, and Germany). I express appreciation especially to the following readers who offered valuable observations and suggestions:

J. R. Watson, Emeritus Professor of English, University of Durham, UK and General Editor of *The Canterbury Dictionary of Hymnology*;

Paul Westermeyer, Emeritus Professor of Church Music, Cantor, MSM Director, St. Olaf College, Luther Seminary, St. Paul, Minnesota, and former editor of *The Hymn*, the journal of the Hymn Society in the United States and Canada;

Harry Eskew, Emeritus Professor of Music History and Hymnology, New Orleans Baptist Theological Seminary and former editor of *The Hymn*.

Richard J. Mouw, President Emeritus, Professor of Faith and Public Life, Fuller Theological Seminary;

Carlton Young, USA Editor of *The Canterbury Dictionary of Hymnology*, former director of the Master of Sacred Music Program, Perkins School of Theology, Southern Methodist University, Dallas, Texas, and Emeritus Professor of Church Music, Candler School of Theology, Emory University;

Andrew Pratt, Editor of *The Bulletin of the Hymn Society of Great Britain and Ireland*;

Linda W. Corman, Nicholls Librarian & Director, John W. Graham Library, University of Trinity College, Toronto, Ontario, Canada;

Paul A. Richardson, Professor of Music (retired) Samford University, Birmingham, Alabama and former president of the Hymn Society in the United States and Canada;

Grant Eaton, Head of Music, Hope Christian College, Adelaide, South Australia;

C. Michael Hawn, University Distinguished Professor of Church Music, Perkins School of Theology, Southern Methodist University;

Bruce Corley, President Emeritus, Carroll Theological Institute;

C. L. Bass, Distinguished Professor Emeritus of Music Theory and Composition of Southwestern Baptist Theological Seminary;

Robert J. Batastini, FHS, Past-president of the Hymn Society in the U.S. and Canada, retired senior editor, GIA Publications, Inc.;

and

Elisabeth Fillmann, reference person for the Gesangbuchbibliographie and member of the Executive Committee of the Internationale Arbeitsgemeinschaft für Hymnologie.

I express appreciation to Janet Copeland for her careful input of data in the early stages and attention to style and formatting in later stages.

I express deep appreciation to persons at Smyth & Helwys Publishing— Keith Gammons, Executive Vice President, and especially to my editor, Leslie Andres, whose professional and personal attention was welcomed at every step. She was unfailingly prompt, efficient, effective, and gracious in her guidance and went the second mile on more than one occasion.

Special appreciation is expressed to David Music, Professor of Church Music at Baylor University, Director of Graduate Studies in the School of Music at the time, and who served as editor of *The Hymn*, for his encouragement, his careful reading of manuscripts, and his detailed and valuable observations and suggestions that come from his deep understanding of the discipline of hymnology.

Scotty Gray
October 1, 2014

Contents

List of Figures

Preface

This work presents a comprehensive and integrated hermeneutics of hymnody, giving attention to the biblical, theological, liturgical, literary, musical, practical, historical, biographical, and sociocultural aspects. The writing began in Rüschlikon, Switzerland, on the west shore of Lake Zürich during a sabbatical leave and grows out of more than thirty years of teaching hymnology in a graduate theological seminary, almost sixty years as a church member singing in and leading congregations, several years as a minister of music, numerous visits to churches of many denominations in several countries, and a lifelong love for this basic form of Christian literature. The writing also grows out of a deep concern that both the singing of hymns and the study of hymns are deteriorating into narrow (sometimes shallow) approaches to this great body of Christian literature. While there is currently a healthy exchange of knowledge in the meetings and writings of scholars in the field of hymnology, what is missing is the integration of that knowledge and its application to the study and singing of hymns. This work presents a holistic approach to the interpretation of hymns.

Each week, in various liturgical and cultural contexts across the world, millions of people participate in hymn singing as an active, enjoyable corporate experience. In most congregations, many hymns are repeated over the course of years, months, or even weeks. The vast and unique body of hymns of the Christian church is among the most powerful means for understanding and expressing the Christian faith and for shaping peoples' theological understanding. Hymns can communicate biblical and theological truths in memorable ways through beautiful language, poetic devices, meter, rhythm, and rhyme. When combined with melody, rhythm, harmony, timbre, and musical form, they can stimulate and convey profound thoughts and feelings. No other aspect of congregational church life has at its disposal this particular powerful combination of features. It is little wonder that God's word gives so much attention to the singing of his people and to the admonitions, especially in the Psalms and the Epistles, for God's people to "sing praises to the LORD with the lyre . . . and the sound of melody" (Ps 98:5)[1] and to "be filled with the Spirit, speaking to one another in psalms and hymns and spiritual songs, singing and making melody with your heart to the Lord" (Eph 5:18-19).

Yet there are ample reasons for considering that most individual Christians and congregations have generally failed to realize the great potential of this basic form of Christian literature. It may be argued that theological educators have not found ways for pastors and musicians to develop together the knowledge, attitudes, and skills necessary for their understanding of the multi-faceted nature of hymns (biblical, theological, liturgical, literary, musical, historical, biographical, sociocultural, and practical) and have not trained ministers in leading parishioners into a deeper understanding of the songs they sing each week.[2] Hymnology, at its best, is an interdisciplinary study involving the arts of literature and music as well as the fields of biblical studies, theological and philosophical thinking, liturgics, pastoral ministry, history, and sociology. There is much work to do in order to better integrate learning and to create an academic environment in which faculty and future ministers are eager for vigorous conversatons that will open new vistas and hone thinking in one's own discipline. Many of us who have been involved in church music for the last decades have too often failed to help our people, especially our children and youth, understand, appreciate, enjoy, and express the truth and beauty of hymns in their multiple facets.

I make no claim to be an authority in the diverse areas of this study, but the book was prepared because many specialized studies do not treat the multiple dimensions of hymnody in a comprehensive way or wrestle with the vital interaction of these facets. The true meaning and beauty of fine hymnody is often found in such interaction.

This book stems, in part, from my increasing disappointment in the neglect of the facets of hymnody in churches. It is also a result of the influx of many texts written by those who possess little biblical, theological, literary, or liturgical training or insight and the invasion of music often provided by people with little musical training, musical sensitivity, or understanding about text settings for congregations. To me, this impoverishes congregational church music and leads to an influx of the mediocre. The church must not resort to drawing from the vast body of hymns (contemporary or traditional) that lack true biblical basis and have shallow theology, trite poetry, and unimaginative music.

Some current church music seems superficial, entertaining, and commercial, lacking the larger spectrum of the Christian gospel and without language or music that will bear continued use. There are pieces that appear conceived and perceived, visually and aurally, as a performance directed primarily to an audience. Some current forms with appropriate texts focus on limited aspects of the Christian faith, expressing the Scriptures in ways that distract from their meanings, often with melodies that do not lend themselves to congregational singing or trite melodies that become wearisome. The problem is not new. Ralph Vaughan Williams, musical editor of the 1906 *The English Hymnal*, asserts, ". . . unfortunately, many of the tunes of the present day which have become familiar and, probably merely from association, popular with congregations are quite unsuitable to their purpose. More often than not they are positively harmful to those who sing and hear them . . . tunes, which are worthy neither of the congregations who sing them, the occasions on which they are sung, nor the composers who wrote them. . . . It is indeed a moral rather than a musical issue."[3]

Much contemporary church music, some of it called "praise and worship," is well intended and often contributes at certain points in the pilgrimage of faith. There is certainly a significant place even for the relatively short, spontaneous, emotional Christian expression that characterizes contemporary church music as a complement to more developed, carefully reasoned expressions of a wide spectrum of Christian doctrines. The danger is that people will stay in one intellectual, emotional, aesthetic, and even spiritual realm and fail to mature into broader, deeper, finer expressions of the Christian faith. This danger looms for everyone, whatever their depth, breadth, and quality of experience or their particular expression of faith. Worship leaders face a challenge in choosing hymns for diverse congregations and sometimes make judgments about hymns with little understanding of the diverse styles, forms, and contexts. Whatever our experiences and perspectives, we must grow in Christian discipleship, and we should not ignore nor despise those who are different from us. We must learn from each other and contribute to each other.

Much in the contemporary "choruses" has an immediate appeal to many people, but much of it probably fails to contribute much to true Christian growth. Jeremy Begbie addresses forcefully a major weakness in much of contemporary music:

> . . . much of the music currently employed in Christian worship deploys remarkably little in the way of delayed gratification. Admittedly, a congregation must be able to grasp quickly new hymns and songs if music is to enable and release their worship, but . . . rather too often goals are

reached directly and predictably with a minimum . . . of delay . . . . Could we be witnessing here a musical articulation of the tendency in some quarters of the Church to insist on immediate rewards and not to come to terms with the (potentially positive) realities of frustration and disappointment? One of the most significant challenges for any composer for worship today is to offer music which can reflect the conviction that intrinsic to salvation is a process of learning in which we are led towards goals by paths which are not easy, straightforward or expected.[4]

Some contemporary church music is not so much contemporary as temporary and in its very ephemeral nature it may not only fail to contribute to Christian growth and depth, but may leave many (especially the young) with impressions of a shallow, passing, faddish kind of Christian faith. In the worthy interest of relating to our culture, the church has often succumbed to the unworthy practice of increasingly accepting texts and music that may be distorting the Christian message: a misdirected concession to contemporaneity that will haunt the church for years to come.

It must also be confessed that much traditional hymnody has more than its share of poor biblical bases, shallow theology, trite poetry, and unimaginative music and that much singing of traditional hymns lacks the admirable spontaneity and exuberance that typifies some contemporary church music. "Traditional" church music can learn from the best of the contemporary with its newness, freshness, and difference from what has too often become a worn and meaningless tradition. A more holistic hermeneutics of hymnody can help address weaknesses in both contemporary and traditional congregational singing.

Much contemporary Christian music has become widely popular. Bert Tosh, senior producer of Religious Programmes, BBC Northern Ireland, noted in a conference address to the Hymn Society of Great Britain & Ireland in 1990 that the "praise and worship" song, "In Christ Alone My Hope Is Found" by Keith Getty and Stuart Townend, "has been described as the most popular worship song ever."[5] There are occasions when "praise and worship" music and traditional hymnody, certainly evangelical music, are showing mutual influences. Gesa F. Hartje made a perceptive examination of technological, sociological, and theological similarities between contemporary "praise and worship" and evangelical hymnody (gospel song).[6] Both, in their "simple" and repetitive music, emphasize knowing/learning the music, which occurs even outside the church. Both use music as an enduring devotional companion that forms a shared ecumenical community. Both shape theology and have a small minority of songs that survive. Both are a counterbalance to the often emotion-deprived traditional hymns.

Some "praise and worship" music is showing more hymn-like characteristics in the spectrum of subject matter and in the more developed, less repetitive texts. Also, the interpretation depends on the manner of singing. Some praise and worship events include texts and tunes of traditional hymns but with new harmonies, rhythms, and accompaniment media. This is fortunate, and some of the trends in praise and worship music may serve to give it more permanence and enrich "traditional" hymnody. On the other hand, it has been observed that

> the worship-song . . . often carries some of the seeds of its own decay. . . . part of the very nature of the worship-song, that it is existential, ephemeral, disposable almost, written for the hour, so that, like the rose, it blooms and dies? Am I mistaken to think that such performance-oriented music, by its very nature reflects the culture of the popular secular music of its day? And I remember that he who marries the spirit of the age will be a widower tomorrow.[7]

This book attempts to present foundations for a sound, comprehensive, and integrated understanding of hymnody and more objective criteria for evaluating hymns and tunes of whatever style. Well-written, well-chosen, and well-sung hymns, regardless of style, offer more for the whole person. Christ identified the greatest commandment as being to "love the Lord your God with all your heart, and with all your soul, and with all your mind, and with all your strength" (Mark 12:30). "All" may be a different amount or quality for different people, but it is the same percentage. Hymn singing at its finest should endeavor to speak to and for all the heart, the soul, the mind, and the strength. Michael O'Connor expresses it well: "Singing enables praise because it involves the whole person: it is at once mental, emotional, and muscular, a work of the spirit and a work of the flesh, a work of individuals and a work that fosters fellowship."[8]

The great flow of twentieth-century Christian hymnody is also being fed with rich new streams of carefully written texts and tunes by devout and skilled writers, and the church must continue to seek vibrant, current expressions of faith. A wealth of fine traditional and contemporary hymnody is accessible to the average Christian, but the realization of the full potential of hymnody demands more of the minds and hearts of those who create, who choose, and who sing the literature. Judgments about creating, choosing, and using congregational music in the ministries of the church require consideration of the multiple, interrelated dimensions of hymnody. Even those less familiar with the church and the Christian faith can appreciate many of the finest hymn texts and the music associated with them. With proper exposure and education, the enjoyment of fine hymns will continue to deepen as people mature.

A major challenge remains in educating ministers and parishioners in a renewed appreciation for the importance of hymns, in a sound hermeneutics of hymns, and in a new commitment to a deeper understanding of this basic literature of the church. When churches realize the great potential of hymnody, meaningful congregational singing will serve both as an expression of worship and an impetus for a revitalization of deeper worship. After all, worship is the most basic duty and delight of Christians, the rich wellspring for the other ministries of the church.

Notes

1. Unless noted otherwise, scriptural references in this work are to the *New American Standard Bible* (NASB).

2. I offer my perspective with the experience of thirty-five years in graduate theological education, more than ten of which were at the executive level of administration, and out of decades of involvement with national accrediting agencies, serving on and chairing accreditation site visits to multiple graduate theological institutions.

3. Ralph Vaughan Williams, Musical Editor, "Preface, The Music," *The English Hymnal with Tunes* (London: Oxford University Press, 1933) viii–ix.

4. Jeremy S. Begbie, *Theology, Music, and Time* (Cambridge: Cambridge University Press, 2000) 105–106.

5. Bert Tosh, "Producing 5,842 Hymns," *Hymn Society of Great Britain & Ireland Bulletin* 19/5 (January 2010): 161. The text and tune of "In Christ Alone" are discussed in chapter 6.

6. Gesa F. Hartje, "Keeping in Tune with the Times—Praise & Worship Music as Today's Evangelical Hymnody in North America," *Dialog: A Journal of Theology* 48/4 (Winter 2009): 364–73. (This is a theme-based issue on "Theology and Hymnody," Gettysburg, Lutheran Theology Seminary.)

7. Timothy Dudley-Smith, "Hymns and Songs in Christian Worship: Past, Present—and Future?" *Hymn Society of Great Britain & Ireland Bulletin* 19/5 (January 2010): 179.

8. Michael O'Connor, "The Singing of Jesus," *Resonant Witness: Conversations between Music and Theology*, ed. Jeremy S. Begbie and Steven R. Guthrie (Grand Rapids MI: William B. Eerdmans Publishing Company, 2011) 452–53. See Thomas Aquinas, Summa Theologiae, II-IIae, q, 91, a. 1 and 2.

CHAPTER 1

Prelude to the Fugue: An Approach to a Comprehensive and Integrated Hermeneutics of Hymnody

The Importance of a Comprehensive and Integrated Hermeneutics of Hymnody

Hermeneutics is the art, theory, and practice of interpretation, primarily the interpretation of written texts, especially religious, literary, or legal texts, though the term has been adopted for interpretation in other fields such as musical aesthetics.[1] Basic concepts of hermeneutics serve the interpretation of literature in general and biblical interpretation in particular, calling the reader to look deeply into the language to see that *what* a text means is intricately bound up with *how* it means. The present book begins with a belief in the vital interaction of the multiple dimensions of fine hymnody and with a desire to help Christians to recognize in a more complete way the enormous potential of this basic Christian art form.

After the Scriptures, hymns are commonly considered to be the most basic and familiar form of Christian literature. The Scriptures, as the word of God, require proper interpretation (hermeneutics). Hymns, as companions to the Bible that contain interpretations of the Scriptures and theological teachings, and as songs that occupy a significant role in corporate Christian worship across the world each week, also require careful interpretation—a comprehensive and integrated hermeneutics. The comprehensive and integrated approach of this study is similar to a seven-voice fugue in which each voice (biblical, theological, liturgical, literary, musical, practical, and historical/biographical/sociocultural) has a vital role and also a significant relationship to the other voices.

A hymn, at its best, is considered here to be a well-conceived, well-written poetic statement in strophic form. It is borne out of personal Christian experience; consistent with biblical theology; suited for personal or corporate expression of and in the Christian ministries of worship, discipleship, proclamation, and service; intended to be chosen prayerfully and carefully; set to a hymn tune and to be sung with spirit (1 Cor 14:15) and with understanding. A hymn tune, at its best, is a well-conceived, well-written strophic melody with temporal, harmonic, and formal artistic merit that is composed to provide musical expression of a hymn text through congregational singing of the stanzas, often with instrumental accompaniment.

The finest hymns from every period of Christian history are biblically based expressions of Christian truth that deal significantly with the most profound issues of human existence. They are suited to the wide spectrum of liturgy; cast in clear, beautiful, powerful, and memorable language; set to music that beautifully and memorably conveys the text; and, properly chosen, speak to and for millions of Christian worshipers. Given these multiple dimensions of hymnody, a hermeneutics of hymnody must consider not only each dimension but also their vital interaction. A valid hermeneutics must be comprehensive and integrated, must employ sound hermeneutical principles, and must provide through critical scholarship not only an academic interpretation and understanding of the text but also an avenue for a diverse spectrum of singers to experience and live out the text.

Cleanth Brooks and Robert Penn Warren affirm that

> . . . a poem [hymn], insofar as it is a good poem [hymn] is an organic unity in which all the elements are vitally interfused. We may abstract rhythm or imagery, for discussion, but we know that we are making an abstraction and the thing we abstract is really an aspect of a whole. We make the abstraction, we study the aspect, merely in order to understand better the whole in its complex interrelations—to experience more deeply the whole in its wholeness.[2]

A sound hermeneutics of hymnody requires that we understand the whole in all its complex interrelations. It must be a comprehensive and integrated hermeneutics.

A sound hermeneutics of hymns is necessary not only for realizing their enormous potential but also for understanding them and avoiding theological error. Bassanio, in act 3, scene 2 of Shakespeare's *The Merchant of Venice*, says "In religion, what damned error but some sober brow will bless it, and approve it with a text, hiding the grossness with fair ornament." The "fair ornament" of music, with its enormous power to influence thoughts and feelings, carries the unusual dangers of hiding "damned error" and makes necessary a carefully thought-out hermeneutics. More positively, sound hermeneutics can focus attention on the deeper truths and beauty of a text.

One of the most inspiring and important examples of hermeneutics occurred on the afternoon of our Lord's clearest validation of his divinity and seal of our salvation. It happened during Jesus's conversation with two people on the way to a town called Emmaus "about seven miles from Jerusalem." We know little about these people or the town, but we do know that Jesus "explained to them the things concerning Himself in all the Scriptures" and that the two exclaimed, "Were not our hearts burning within us while He was speaking to us on the road, while He was explaining the Scriptures to us?" (Luke 24:27, 32, NASB). The two returned to Jerusalem to tell the apostles of their experience, and "While they were telling these things, He Himself stood in their midst . . . . Then He opened their minds to understand the Scriptures" (24:36, 45). These experiences represent hermeneutics at its finest—the interpretation of the most important thing in the world by the most important person in history. Though the hermeneutics of hymnody pales beside this event, it takes new meaning and vitality in sharing the commonality of explaining the things about Jesus, who is the theme of Christian hymnody.

Much of the writing in hymnology has been concerned to a large extent with the historical and biographical dimensions. This is often true of companions or handbooks to hymnals where major attention is given to provenance, the early appearances and forms of texts and tunes, something of the author or composer, and perhaps a brief mention of an obvious scriptural reference. Little attention is given, however, to an interpretation of the text and tune that would contribute to the worshipers' understanding and singing of the hymn.[3] This study is devoted to a more comprehensive and integrated hermeneutics of hymnody for scholars, teachers, and serious students. It is hoped that much in this study will be of interest to hymn writers and hymnal editors as well as to worship leaders, ministers, and the singers of hymns in the many and varied theological and liturgical traditions. "Comprehensive" means that each major dimension of hymnody is addressed in some depth and that consideration is given to the larger context of each dimension. "Integrated" means that the facets of hymnody do not move in isolation; instead, each facet has a connection to each of the other facets. This holistic approach is intended to be a paradigm for the study of any type of English-language hymn or body of hymnody of any denomination, worship tradition, writer, historical period, theological position, or any combination of these. Those who write hymns, compose hymn tunes, study hymns, compile hymnals, select hymns and tunes for the ministries of the church, and read and sing hymns can benefit from a deeper understanding of the multiple facets and their interrelations.

J. R. Watson remarks wisely, "I suspect that the whole matter of hymn singing is much more complex than we think it is."[4] Fine hymns are multi-faceted, and the facets are interrelated. The naïveté of much hymnody does not justify a simplistic approach to fine hymnody. Tracing any one or two of the themes in this polyphony of dimensions can be a fascinating and informative experience. While most of the individual themes have been well traced, little attention has been given to the full complexity of these themes and their rich counterpoints.

Of the millions of people across the world each week involved in some form of hymn singing, actively participating or listening, probably a small fraction begin to grasp the breadth and depth of this ancient form of expression that deals with the profound issues of life and continues to exert such a powerful influence on the individual Christian, on the Christian church, and sometimes even on society and cultures within a society.

Those millions of people love hymns for many different reasons. Some love hymns for the profound insights into Scripture, the revelations of theological truths, the associations with deeply meaningful spiritual moments in life, and the beautiful literary and musical expressions of thoughts and feelings that are common to all Christians. Some, of course, love hymns because of a turn of phrase or the tune or because of an association with some pleasant experience. Alexander Pope, in his 1711 *Essay on Criticism*, speaks of "these tuneful fools . . . to please their ear, not mend their minds; as some to Church repair, / Not for the doctrine, but for the Musick there."[5] He speaks of the shallowness that often characterizes hymnody. Sometimes hymns are loved in spite of the possible absence of any sound biblical, theological, or literary qualities; in spite of literary triteness and poor theology; or (God forbid!) even in spite of heretical theology (some "damned error").

Christian thinkers have, for centuries, recognized the contributions of hymns to the experience of worship, the education of believers, the proclamation to unbelievers, and the ministry to the mental, emotional, physical, or social well-being of people. Many leaders have agreed with the oft-quoted statement, "Let me write the hymns of the church, and I care not who writes the theology." This immense power of hymnody is bound up in the vibrant interrelatedness of its multiple facets.

The power of fine hymnody has often been neglected because of the nature of the form (concise and congregational) and because of the triteness of poor hymnody. Hymns are so concise, and so many are biblically impoverished, shallow in theology, and devoid of literary beauty that many people ignore the form altogether. J. R. Watson stated that one aim of his book, *The English Hymn: A Critical and Historical Study*, was "to remove the prejudices of literary critics who have been too easily inclined to see the hymn as a second-rate art form."[6]

Sound hermeneutics is concerned with addressing the profound responsibility of any Christian to understand hymns more fully as they express our worship and shape our theology (both historically and today). The sad lack of understanding about the breadth and depth of Christian experience found in hymns may remind one of Allan Bloom's comments about our society: "We are like ignorant shepherds living on a site where great civilizations once flourished. The shepherds play with the fragments that pop up to the surface, having no notion of the beautiful structures of which they were once a part."[7] Hymns, at their best, present majestic biblical truths and profound theological insights in language that has clarity, beauty, brevity, forcefulness, and memorableness. At the same time, great hymns speak to and for worshipers who are often largely untrained in matters of Bible, theology, or the subtleties of language. Many hymn writers (and, we might add, preachers!) fail to navigate successfully through the biblical, theological, and literary waters of a vital, changing, and largely uninformed society. This is precisely why the noble themes of Christianity are usually best presented by committed, skillful Christian writers who can cast the great biblical and theological truths into clear, beautiful, forceful, and memorable expressions that have the almost impossible quality of speaking with immediacy and yet bear repetition and continue to stimulate deeper thoughts and feelings. There is then the responsibility of committed Christians to understand what has been presented.

In an age of hectic rush, prevalent noise, small attention spans, and shallow thinking about the important matters of life, the hymn provides opportunities for meditating privately, for singing with fellow Christians, for experiencing beauty, for confronting profound truths about the meaningful issues of life, and for finding and meeting challenges for Christian living. A fine hymn calls for careful attention to details, to the subtleties of poetic language, to biblical allusions, to theological insights, and to the beautiful interplay of these subtleties.

This form of literature deserves a more comprehensive and integrated understanding, interpretation, and evaluating than it has traditionally received. The complexity of hymnody exists in part because of the multitude of significant elements that constitute this "simple" art form and because of the complex diversity of persons involved: the author, composer, editor, worship leader, and those in the diverse body of worshipers—each of whom would do well to have some understanding of the total, interrelated experience. It is unreasonable to expect each person to have the same depth of understanding, skills, or appreciation of every dimension, but it seems reasonable to expect of deeply committed Christians the desire for a more meaningful involvement in this part of the Christian experience, which from the beginning of Christianity through our own day has been such a rich source of biblical understanding, theological insight, and such a powerful medium for the expression of our worship of God.

In the deceptively brief, simple, accessible hymn, there is an unbelievable wealth of biblical, theological, liturgical, literary, musical, and historical material waiting for an ever new understanding, appreciation, enjoyment, and application in our lives.

The hermeneutics of hymnody offered here presents a rational and systematic discussion of principles and procedures for understanding the multiple and interrelated facets of hymns and for forming approaches to the critical and objective evaluation of hymns.[8] A comprehensive understanding of a hymn through the consideration of the following broad principles is a beginning for truly experiencing a hymn in which the singer/reader internalizes it and gives expression to it in reading or singing. The principles are also a beginning for interpreting and evaluating a hymn in clear, concise language that is understandable even to those outside the church.

1. The *biblical* principle of a hermeneutics of Christian hymnody focuses on determining how consistent the hymn is with biblical teaching and how the Scriptures are used: quotation, metrical version, paraphrase, or allusion. Accepted principles of biblical hermeneutics are necessary for the application of this principle.[9]

2. The *theological* principle considers the doctrines of the Christian faith that are expressed in the hymn, the perspective from which they are addressed, and how they are expressed.

3. The *liturgical* principle considers the use of the text and tune in the context of worship and other ministries of the church.

4. The *literary* (*linguistic/grammatical*) principle considers structures and the variety and nature of the forms and types of literature, including figures of speech and thought. This principle also considers the original language (a principle borrowed from biblical hermeneutics) when hymns are translations and acknowledges that there is a responsibility to understand the author's original meaning whether from another language or from an edited version.

5. The *musical* principle considers the interrelated temporal, melodic, harmonic, textural, formal, and timbral aspects of the hymn tune and how they relate to the text.

6. The *historical, biographical, sociocultural* principle focuses on understanding the historical, biographical, cultural, and social background of the writer and the writing, the author's original meaning, and the sociocultural context in which a hymn may be used today. The singer has this responsibility to the author, even if the singer understands or uses the text to mean something different, as may happen in a hymn written from a specific liturgical context and from a specific doctrinal perspective. This principle considers also the place of the text in the larger body of hymnody and in the author's total output. The examination of these contexts may aid in evaluating and correcting one's own subjectivity.

7. The *practical* principle considers the roles of spiritual commitment, education, choice, logistics, and performance in the experience of hymn singing.

8. The *principle of interrelatedness* acknowledges that none of the principles functions alone. Each in some way relates to the others.

The Case for Interrelatedness

In our age of specialization, there is often a neglect of the interrelatedness of elements. This has too often been the case in hymnology. However, the idea of the interrelatedness of much of human activity is ancient. C. S. Lewis has reminded us, "In earliest times theology, science, history, fiction, singing, instrumental music, and dancing were all a single activity."[10] There has long been a concern for the relatedness and even unification of the many branches of knowledge. The thirteenth-century English natural philosopher, Roger Bacon, affirmed, "All sciences are connected; they lend each other material aid as parts of one great whole, each doing its own work, not for itself alone, but for the other parts."[11] Alexander von Humboldt (1769–1859) considered all natural phenomena and physical sciences to be interrelated—an "Einheit" or unity. Friedrich Schiller (1759–1805), the great German dramatist, poet, and literary theorist, notes in his introductory lecture (*Jenaer Antrittsrede*) at Jena University on May 26, 1789,

> In the same way that a pedantic scholar carefully isolates his learning for all others, [the philosopher] seeks to broaden its realm and to re-establish its association with other areas of learning—I say re-establish, because only abstract reason has created these boundaries, has separated these learnings from each other. Where the pedantic scholar separates, the philosophic mind unites. The philosopher has convinced himself early on that in the realm of reason, as in the world of the senses, everything seeks the other, and in his strong desire for a concord of learning he cannot be content with fragments.[12]

The interrelatedness of all the arts[13] was the concern of art historian and musicologist Curt Sachs, whose purpose in his *The Commonwealth of Art*, was "to show that, and how, all arts unite in one consistent evolution to mirror man's diversity in space and time and the fate of his soul." He declares, "The commonwealth of art, the life and the concurrence of all individual arts under a common law and fate, is not a vain, utopian wish, to be realized only in a distant future. It has been a reality, an inevitable fact from the very outset of civilization."[14]

Leonard Bernstein, at the beginning of his first Norton Lecture in 1973, spoke of the importance of interdisciplinary inquiry, saying that "the best way to 'know' a thing is in the context of another discipline,"[15] and he devoted his lectures to the relationships between music and language, speaking of linguistics, aesthetic philosophy, and acoustics as well as music history.

The larger academic world has seen an increasing interest in interdisciplinary studies. In what has been an age of specialization, there is now renewed interest in other disciplines growing from the recognition of a need for dialogue regarding common elements of content and methodology. There has been, in the last few decades, a significant movement toward more holistic approaches within the major disciplines, toward more synthesis in inquiry, and toward interdisciplinary studies. Stephen Hawking, one of the great thinkers of our time, has spent his life pursuing a Theory of Everything (TOE) to explain and link all physical phenomena. He said, "My goal is simple. It is a complete understanding of the universe, why it is as it is and why it exists at all."[16] Physicist Robert B. Laughlin, co-winner of the 1998 Nobel Prize in Physics and author of *A Different Universe: Reinventing Physics from the Bottom Down*, writes, "I think a good case can be made that science has now moved from an Age of Reductionism to an Age of Emergence, a time when the search for ultimate causes of things shifts from the behavior of parts to the behavior of the collective."[17]

The Pulitzer Prize winner and Harvard professor of science Edward O. Wilson makes a similar observation in his 1998 book, *Consilience: The Unity of Knowledge*: "As the century closes, the focus of the natural sciences has begun to shift away from the search for new fundamental laws and toward new kinds of synthesis—'holism,' if you prefer—in order to understand complex systems."[18] Wilson also affirms that "We are approaching a new age of synthesis, when the testing of consilience is the greatest of all intellectual challenges."[19] More specifically, he asserts that "The greatest enterprise of the mind has always been and always will be the attempted linkage of the sciences and humanities."[20] Beyond the commonwealth of the arts and beyond the current theories of modern physics about the unification of all the forces of nature, E. O. Wilson also asserts a unity of all knowledge: "the deliberate systematic linkage of cause and effect across the disciplines"[21] that "extends to other fields of science as well, and in the minds of a few it reaches beyond into the social sciences, and still further, . . . to touch the humanities."[22] By "humanities," Wilson means "particularly the creative arts"[23] and devotes, in his study of the unification of knowledge, a full chapter to the arts and their interpretation—literature, visual arts, drama, music, and dance.

In spite of these profound movements toward the synthesis of knowledge, the unification in and among the sciences, the integration of the sciences and humanities, and the prevalence on interdisciplinary studies, the understanding and study of hymnody remains largely fragmented. Much of hymnological study dwells on isolated aspects of hymnody, especially the historical and biographical. In-depth studies into each of the individual and diverse aspects of hymnody are crucial and must continue. There needs, however, to be more dialogue between and conversations among those skilled in the various disciplines that are part of hymnody. There is no extended work that treats in any depth the multiple dimensions of hymnody in an integrated, orderly manner showing how these dimensions are vitally interrelated.[24]

The Challenge of a Comprehensive and Integrated Hermeneutics

One obvious reason that most hymnody studies do not treat the multiple facets and their interrelatedness is that most of us do not have the necessary skills in the diverse, though related, disciplines. While this author certainly does not claim expertise in all of the diverse fields of hymnology, the attempt is made to treat the multiple facets of hymnody in a comprehensive way and to wrestle with their vital interaction in order to find the true meaning and beauty of fine hymnody. Those with expertise in each area have seemed disinclined to explore deeply the other areas. Consequently laypersons and many specialists have been deprived of the larger truth and beauty that is inherent in this basic form of Christian expression.

Another reason for the lack of an interrelated study of and writing about hymns is that it is difficult to present the complexity and simultaneity of the many diverse but related dimensions. Prose, unlike music, does not lend itself to polyphony. Hymnody is complex, and discussing it is complex. Gustave Reese, in the preface to his *Music in the Renaissance*, notes, "If there were such a thing as polyphony in prose, it would obviously be a godsend to the writer of history, whatever it might be to the reader."[25] This absence of "polyphonic prose" has been a bane especially to writers of history and of complex analyses. Dealing with a topic that involves multiple disciplines often functioning simultaneously (as does hymnology) and addressing readers who have knowledge and skills in some areas and much less expertise in others (as do I) is indeed a daunting task. But it is my conviction that there is a place for a more comprehensive and integrated approach to hymnology. Because the excellent works on hymnody do not address all of its dimensions or attempt to show their vital interrelations, an attempt is made here to emphasize and illustrate this polyphony and often to refer to and quote from a variety of sources.[26] Some readers may find some of these references and quotations to be obvious. Others may find the same references and quotations to be esoteric. It is hoped that this effort will encourage more interdisciplinary conversations among the scholars, teachers, ministers, and serious students of hymnody for whom this book is intended.

There is in fine hymnody a beautiful "polyphony" in the interaction of the aspects of imaginative, creative language as it shapes words, sounds, meanings, patterns of rhyme, meter, rhythm, tones, imagery, ideas, and allusions that cause our thoughts and feelings to soar to heights and plumb to depths that we long to experience and express. We often sense these multiple aspects as a single experience or as some interrelatedness of experiences. If we desire deeper worship and strive to understand hymnody better for learning, teaching, reading, or singing, we must seek to know how the various "voices" interact and how intricately they are interwoven, and recognize how difficult it can be to discuss the complexity. In the present work, I have attempted to deal with this "polyphony," the vital interaction of these dimensions, and to provide a better understanding of the parts and consequently the whole. Lacking the "polyphony in prose," the attempt is still made to describe those various lines and their simultaneity and to show how they work in beautiful counterpoint. In his violin and cello sonatas, Bach achieves, by register, rhythm, dynamics, articulation, and phrasing, magnificent "accompanied" single-line melodies—a virtual single-line polyphony. Medieval Gregorian chant, sung in the live acoustical environments of the great cathedrals, often achieved in the reverberations of their single-line melodies a subtle homophony and even polyphony. Perhaps, then, there is even in "monophonic" prose the possibility of conveying some simultaneity and even "polyphony" of the vibrant interactions of the dimensions of hymnody.

The vibrant interactions, the interrelatedness of the dimension of hymnody is much more than a simultaneity of aspects. In Christian theology of the early Church Fathers, the Greek term "perichoresis" (περίχορεύω περιχώρησις) was used to refer to the co-indwelling or co-inhering in which the distinctive identity of each person of the Trinity is maintained while, at the same time, each person of the Trinity shares in the life of the other two. Something of this concept is implied here in the term "interrelatedness." Each dimension of hymnody discussed here has a distinctive identity that is maintained in the interpretation of a hymn. A distinctive synergy often blossoms when the interrelatedness of the dimensions is realized.

There are, beside polyphony, many other possible metaphors for the interrelatedness of the dimensions of hymnody. It may be compared to a rich and varied tapestry with many threads and strands where myriad colors, shades, and textures are woven into a meaningful expression of lines, design, and form. The use of the weaving metaphor is seen when Frank Baker, speaking of Wesley's nativity hymn, "Let earth and heaven combine," says the hymn "illustrates what Dr Davie describes as the threading of Latinisms on the staple Anglo-Saxon of his diction so that both 'criss-cross and light up each the other's meaning . . . .'"[27]

Harold Bloom notes in his book *Genius: A Mosaic of One Hundred Exemplary Creative Minds*, "print demands a sequence," and he uses a visual/temporal metaphor to describe the intent of his "book to be a kind of mosaic-in-perpetual-movement."[28] The dimensions of a fine hymn flow in sequence, and many aspects of these "mosaics" of sound flash simultaneously into our minds and demand to be examined. It may remind one of the facets of a gem when turned. Separating these layers for discussion may deprive us temporarily of the simultaneity that comes from the fusion of a profound biblical teaching, an insightful theological concept, a beautiful literary figure, a meaningful liturgical context, and an expressive musical setting. On the other hand, separating the facets may help us to understand more fully and appreciate more deeply the sparkling simultaneity of their fusion when we see them together.

Unlike tapestry, mosaics, and the facets of gems, hymnody is a temporal or lively art. It moves, unfolding in the dimension of time and with simultaneity of the dimensions as well as sequence of the dimensions.[29] There is, for a comprehensive and integrated hermeneutics of hymnody as proposed here, a particular value in the analogy to polyphony or counterpoint in music. As aspects enter, other aspects continue in counterpoint. In this intricate polyphony, the various voices ebb and flow in their relationships and importance, always forming their part in one vitally integrated interpretation. Each facet and the various combinations of facets of a hymn may unfold almost simultaneously. There are times when one facet may be more important than another; there are times when one or more facets may be less obvious or even "silent"; and there is, admittedly, frequently more than one way to interpret the text and the music. Each of the finer hymns has its own configuration of facets that must be considered.

An attempt has been made to show in a cumulative way something of the interrelations of the various dimensions. First, each chapter includes an explanation of how one facet or "voice" functions in a hymn, but also explains something of how that "voice" of the "fugue" relates to previously discussed facets or "voices" and, at times, how it relates to subsequent voices. Each chapter concludes with a cumulative and interrelated interpretation of a hymn. The texts range from the fifth century through the twentieth century and come from Roman Spain, Germany, France, Taiwan, Mexico, Africa, England, the United States, and Canada. The hymn tunes are from the thirteenth century through the twenty-first century and come from Roman areas, Germany, England, France, Mexico, Taiwan, Africa, and the United States. The attempt is to present the dimensions or voices sequentially, cumulatively, and in ways that honor the simultaneity of their relationships. Because of the cumulative approach, the chapters are not of equal length. The early chapters deal with what may be considered, in the broadest way, the content of hymns: the biblical, theological, and liturgical dimensions. The following chapters deal with how that content is conveyed: the literary and musical dimensions. The next chapter deals with the contexts: the historical, biographical, and sociocultural dimensions and the focus is on some aspects that are often neglected in historical studies. The chapter on the practical dimensions of hymnody concentrates on general principles for the applied art of hymnody.

It is precisely the simultaneity and interaction of the facets, the "polyphony," that provides such a beautiful quality of finer hymnody and creates such difficulty in discussing it. There is a profound and distinctive beauty and power when biblical truths, theological implications, and liturgical applications are expressed in appropriately captivating rhetorical figures, rich in rhythms, rhymes, meters, and images; when these are associated with music where rhythm, melody, harmony, timbre, texture, and form sensitively express the text; when the hymn is understood in its larger, historical, biographical, and sociocultural contexts; when both text and music have been carefully and prayerfully chosen for a particular ministry or liturgical purpose; and when the hymn is sung with "the spirit and the understanding." This is hymnody at its finest!

In the final analysis, a work of art is admittedly its own best interpretation, but conservatories, studios, and universities do exist and study, analyze, and explain works of art. There is need for both analysis and synthesis. Seamus Heaney notes in the introduction to his translation of *Beowulf,*

> It is one thing to find lexical meanings for the words and to have some feel for how the metre might go, but it is quite another thing to find the tuning fork that will give you the note and pitch for the overall music of the work. Without some melody sensed or promised, it is simply impossible for a poet to establish the translator's right-of-way into and through a text.[30]

The same challenge Seamus Heaney acknowledges for the translator is often the challenge for those who seek to "translate" or interpret a fine hymn. In the multiple dimensions of a fine hymn, one must seek "the note and pitch for the overall music of the work" and then "establish the . . . right-of-way into and through a text." This is best found in understanding the polyphony of the interrelated dimensions of "voices." The contrapuntal lines of fine hymnody yield rewards to those whose wish to trace the interwoven dimensions and seek to understand better the hymn as a whole, experiencing it much as one sees or hears in a well-created contrapuntal musical composition how each line complements the others. The highest reward is ultimately the deepened, broadened, enriched expression of our worship to God.

The analysis and description of "what" and "how" hymns mean, which is required in a comprehensive and integrated interpretation of hymns, can be a perilous journey for both guide and fellow travelers. This is true of the interpretation of all art. It is a journey that many people choose not to take at all. One is reminded of William Wordsworth's lines: "Our meddling intellect / misshapes the beauteous forms of things—We murder to dissect."[31] One is also reminded of J. R. R. Tolkien's distain of excessive attention to "sources or material" when he wrote in *The Monsters and the Critics*,

> In George Webbe Dasent's words [from his translation *Popular Tales from the Norse*] I would say: 'We must be satisfied with the soup that is set before us, and not desire to see the bones of the ox out of which it has been boiled.' . . . By 'the soup' I mean the story as it is served up by its author or teller, and by 'the bones' its sources or material—even when (by rare luck) those can be with certainly discovered. But I do not, of course, forbid criticism of the soup as soup.[32]

There are also Robert Louis Stevenson's remarks in "The Art of Writing," that "there is nothing more disenchanting than to be shown the springs and mechanism of an art."[33] He does, however, go on to say, "those disclosures [of analysis] which seem fatal to the dignity of art seem so perhaps only in the proportion of our ignorance; and those conscious and unconscious artifices which it seems unworthy of the serious artist to employ were yet, if we had the power to trace them to their springs, indications of a delicacy of the sense finer than we conceive, and hints of ancient harmonies in nature."[34]

It may be that the disenchantment with analysis comes, in part, because of the analogies and not the analysis. Admittedly, ox bones, springs, and mechanisms may not always be enchanting. However, for the archaeologist the discovery and analysis of bones may provide new understanding and real delight, and the lover of fine watches may be fascinated with the springs and mechanism. For the lover of great art, there may be delight in someone's sharing their insights into techniques and meanings of the paintings in the gallery. For one wandering a great river, moving in the dimension of time, there can be something enchanting about being shown the beauty of the rivulets and streams that flow into a powerful river, to see their origins in the hills, enjoy the scenery along their banks, trace their flows into the currents of the river, and know the history along its course to the great ocean.[35] While there may be a real joy in knowing better the river and a true delight in experiencing each of the rivulets and streams, this analogy might also provide lessons in seeing the lack of depth of a small river and the shallowness of little streams that follow the paths of least resistance and finally dry up, in contrast to the streams and the great river whose power forges fresh channels and takes us into new areas of experience.

Obviously, any analogy breaks down at some point. The effort here is simply to show that in hymnody we are dealing with a complex, living, moving phenomenon, a historically vital and powerful force, a confluence of many streams, a blending of many voices that continues to have great potential and that, by a careful look, might enthrall, bless, and delight us all the more and become a means of a fuller, deeper expression of worship.

An Objectivity of Truth and Beauty in Hymns

A comprehensive and integrated hermeneutics of hymnody can be an important response to subjectivity in thinking about hymnody—the concept that you cannot dispute taste and that beauty is only in the eye of the beholder. In the postmodern world, people often think that not only beauty but even goodness and truth are relative and subjectively determined. It is hoped that this systematic look into the interactions of the dimensions of hymnody will provide a more solid and objective basis for the evaluation of hymns, hymn tunes, and their use in the ministries of the church.

In hymns we are often dealing with biblical concepts, theological insights, and some of the most profound themes of human existence; it behooves us to act with discernment. There are generally accepted principles of biblical interpretation and theological truth, and some generally accepted objective aesthetic standards of literary and musical judgment among people who are most versed in these fields. The meaningful worship of God should be the ultimate purpose of hymn singing, and it may be said, with deference to the Shorter Catechism, that the chief end of hymns and the careful interpretation of them is to provide means for us to glorify God and enjoy him forever. This should cause us to seek sound, objective criteria for understanding and judging this medium of our expression.

The concepts of "art," "artistic merit," "aesthetics," and "beauty" have been and continue to be concerns of profound philosophical thought among scholars. They also cause debate even in popular and uninformed circles. For too many of those involved in the musical and textual dimensions of hymnody, especially those who sing hymns, the matter of artistic quality is simply dismissed by statements equivalent to "*de gustibus non disputandum est* (taste is not disputable)," "I know what I like and I like what I know," or "beauty is in the eye of the beholder." Taste *cannot* be disputed if we use only the definition of taste as in "That is not my taste." Taste *can* be disputed if we use the definition as in "She is a person with taste." The former is preference. The latter is discernment.

Discernment, as opposed to simple preference, moves beyond what is immediate or simply pleasing. Not unlike loving God in the way Jesus commanded, "with all your heart, and with all your soul, and with all your mind, and with all your strength" (Mk 12:30), truly significant, meaningful, lasting experiences require not only emotional but also spiritual, mental, even physical commitment to discerning and seeking long-term values. When those who create or who use hymns simply cater to immediate, "popular" taste or preference, they may prevent the cultivation of what is of true value and more lasting. Plato observed,

> The ancient and common custom of Hellas, which still prevails in Italy and Sicily, did certainly leave the judgment to the body of spectators, who determined the victor by show of hands. But this custom has been the destruction of the poets; for they are now in the habit of composing with a view to please the bad taste of their judges, ... (*Laws*, II, 658B)

Discernment in the arts moves beyond preference and implies intentional, thoughtful, clear perception. It also requires objectivity based on broad experience with and a deep study of a range of artistic creations, along with an understanding of some fundamental principles of art. It is probable that the spheres of "discernment" and "preference" are larger than either camp may think, and the spheres may even overlap. It is hoped so.

Subjectivity and taste as preference are important and characterize all of us. The call for objectivity and discernment can lead, ultimately, to the enhancement of personal feelings and opinions. If beauty is in the eye of the beholder, there is still for Christian beholders some responsibility for what they behold and how they behold it, some responsibility for openness to and even an interest in broadening and deepening taste or preference. Christian discipleship assumes growth, to some degree, in every area of life.

While all Christians cannot be expected to have a truly broad experience or deep study of artistic matters, such insights still merit attention. The Christian at any level of understanding has a responsibility for seeking a deeper experience with and a greater expression of our Christian faith.

It must be emphasized that discernment, a growing awareness and appreciation of broader and deeper aspects, in no way lessens one's enjoyment. On the contrary, the enjoyment can be broadened, and a person gains a preference for increasing discernment. Roger Scruton, speaking of discernment and critical judgment, wisely observed,

> . . . as the quantity of communication increases, so does its quality decline; and the most important sign of this is that it is no longer acceptable to say so. To criticize popular taste is to invite the charge of elitism, and to defend distinctions of value—between the virtuous and the vicious, the beautiful and the ugly, the sacred and the profane, the true and the false—is to offend against the only value-judgement that is widely accepted, the judgement that judgements are wrong.[36]

The deeper biblical, theological, and liturgical truths are often available to the maturing disciple in the weekly singing of hymns. The responsibility is not an odious task but rather a joyous privilege where one longs for and delights in new truths and perhaps even in the literary, musical, and practical garments in which they are clothed. This moves the maturing disciple well beyond personal preference toward discernment.

"Deliberate mediocrity is a sin and a heresy" is a familiar statement of the Quaker philosopher Elton Trueblood. There is no place for deliberate mediocrity in any area of a Christian's life, especially not in the worship of God. Our Lord identified the first and greatest commandment as being to "love the Lord your God with all your heart, and all your soul, and all your mind, and all your strength" (Mark 12:30). For each of us, the "all" is the same percentage, but it may be a different amount as our Lord taught us in his observations about the widow's mite (Mark 12:41-44). We must be careful not to distain the "widow" if the "mite" of her musical offering is "out of her poverty"; it may actually shame those of us whose musical offering is only "out of our abundance."

In the congregational singing in worship, we have the responsibility of "deliberate integrity" to probe what is our optimum spiritual, mental, emotional, and physical involvement. It can and should be a joyous and liberating experience. Isaac Watts says in his paraphrase of Psalm 147 that in our praise, God's "nature and his works invite to make this duty our delight." The maturing disciple should always be moving from the sin and heresy of mediocrity, trying to discern, beyond one's own personal preference, objective truth and beauty.

Elton Trueblood, in his *Philosophy of Religion*, discusses in some detail several relevant considerations regarding the objectivity of beauty that can apply to hymnody. These are his major considerations: (1) "the significant remainder [of aesthetic enjoyment] which fashion could not explain"; (2) "people do argue about aesthetic judgment and the subjectivists argue as much as anybody else"; (3) "we habitually distinguish between what people actually think beautiful and what they would find beautiful if their area of awareness were deepened and broadened, people do change their tastes with developing maturity, in ways which we can hardly interpret as other than progressive ways"; and (4) "aesthetic judgment actually gives far more evidence of permanence than superficially appears. . . . there is far more agreement in aesthetics than there is in science."[37]

The Harvard biologist Edward O. Wilson becomes almost poetic in challenging his readers in the pursuit of objective truth.

> Might it be possible then to take the final step and devise an unassailable definition of objective truth? Perhaps not. The very idea is risky. It smells of absolutism, the dangerous Medusa of science and the humanities alike. Its premature acceptance is likely to be more paralyzing than its denial. But should we then be prepared to give up? Never! Better to steer by a lodestar than to drift across a meaningless sea. I think we will know if we come close to the goal of our predecessors, even if unattainable. Its glow will be caught in the elegance and beauty and power of our shared idea and, in the best spirit of philosophical pragmatism, the wisdom of our conduct.[38]

This scientist's pursuit of objective truth has led him even into the humanities and especially the creative arts. In his chapter "The Arts and their Interpretation," he identifies "two questions about the arts: where they come from, in both history and personal experience, and how their essential qualities of truth and beauty are to be described through ordinary language."[39] The first question is not our concern here. The second one is.

Content and Form

The relationship between the message and the medium, content and form (the what and the how), has long been a focus in the Christian faith. On two different occasions (once speaking to his disciples and once referring to his Father's own commandment to him), Jesus speaks of both what is said and how it is said—"what to say or how to say it" (Matt 10:19 NIV), "what to say and how to say it" (John 12:49 NIV). Constantly in our Lord's teaching and preaching there is evidence that he is concerned with how he says his message. He expressed truth with a beauty and force and memorableness that have for centuries captured the imagination of even unbelievers. Those most convinced of the nobility of the theme of Christian faith are often those who strive most for skill in communicating the theme. The great Christian writers and speakers have been aware not only of the message of our Lord but also of how he expressed that message. This study is a look at *how* a hymn means and not only what it means.[40] Edmund L. Epstein in his work *Language and Style* states that "Style is the regard that what pays to how."[41] How concepts of God are expressed greatly influences our understanding of what is said—the meaning of the texts. Cambridge University literary critic George Steiner offers this statement, which is profoundly important to the thrust of my study:

> any coherent understanding of what language is and how language performs, . . . any coherent account of the capacity of human speech to communicate meaning and feeling is, in the final analysis, underwritten by the assumption of God's presence. . . . It is a theology, explicit or suppressed, masked or avowed, substantive or imaged, which underwrites the presumption of creativity, of signification in our encounters with text, with music, with art. The meaning of meaning is a transcendent postulate.[42]

It must be emphasized that there is great truth in the Latin dictum *ars est celare artem*, "true art is to conceal art." The moment a device or technique of "how" is recognized as such or dwelt upon by the reader/singer or hearer, the "bones" or the "springs and mechanism" become a distraction from what is really important and are in conflict with the reason the technique was used. As Frank Baker so aptly described it, "the machinery tends to creak."[43] The finest, most creative authors are probably often unconscious of the devices or techniques that they frequently, innately, and effectively employ. The purpose of discovery, classification, and analysis of the devices and techniques used in hymnody is ultimately to help us to understand and appreciate better the content, purpose, and meaning of the hymns and to use them more meaningfully.

There is much truth in Tolkien's and Stevenson's hesitancy about bones, springs, and mechanism, but it may be even more disenchanting when the aspects of an art that might contribute to its appreciation are overlooked or even ignored. There may be moments when insights into an art can not only be interesting but can also contribute perceptions that will profoundly deepen the understanding of the art, enhance the ability to grasp and retain the meaning of the work, and enrich the purpose of the experience.

I have confessed that I shall occasionally venture into subtleties or nuances of hymns that the average reader or singer might not care to understand, but I hope that most readers, and especially the maturing Christian, will be sensitized to the inner working of the various aspects of hymns and desirous of continually probing into their deeper meanings. More than almost any form of poetry, hymns enjoy (or suffer from) repeated use, but the finest hymnody can continue to disclose new truths and beauties to those who learn to recognize the subtleties of the dimensions and their vital interaction.

It must be confessed again that, when asked either what a hymn means or how it means, one may respond as Robert Schumann did in a possibly apocryphal story. It is said that after the great composer played one of his new piano compositions for a group of friends and was asked to tell them about it, he sat down and played it again. In the final "analysis," the good hymn is ultimately its own best explanation of both what it means and how it means. It can only be hoped in this study that those who read and sing hymns will be more *sensitized* for understanding and appreciating the hymn—if not the first time it is "played" then when it is "played" again. My goal is that this study may contribute to the reader's more thoughtful, prayerful use of hymns in private and family devotion and in corporate worship of God.

The Voices in the Fugue: A "Polyphonic" Hermeneutics

The intricate polyphony of the facets of fine hymnody expresses profound issues of human existence—humanity's relation to God and to other people. This intricacy and profundity must be expressed to and for singers who, in many cases, have little in-depth understanding of the dimensions of hymnody. The biblical, theological, and liturgical contents are conveyed by the literary and musical expressions, brought to life through practical preparation and "performance," and often enhanced by some understanding of the various contexts of the hymn. Truly understanding a hymn must include both what it means and how it means. A comprehensive and interrelated hermeneutics of hymnody contributes to this understanding. Such a holistic hermeneutics requires attention to each of the facets, but the distinctive nature of each hymn determines the order in which the facets are approached, the degrees of depth required for each facet, and how the facets relate to each other. This hermeneutics may be illustrated to some degree by an interpretation of Bishop Timothy Dudley-Smith's[44] "The stars declare his glory" and its musical setting by Richard Proulx.

The stars declare his glory,[45] based on Psalm 19

The stars declare his glory;
        the vault of heaven springs
mute witness of the Master's hand
        in all created things,
and through the silences of space
        their soundless music sings.

The dawn returns in splendour,
        the heavens burn and blaze,
the rising sun renews the race
        that measures all our days,
and writes in fire across the skies
        God's majesty and praise.

So shine the Lord's commandments
        to make the simple wise;
more sweet than honey to the taste,
        more rich than any prize,
a law of love within our hearts,
        a light before our eyes.

So order too this life of mine,
        direct it all my days;
the meditations of my heart
        be innocence and praise,

my Rock, and my redeeming Lord,
    in all my words and ways.

History, Biography, and Socioculture

"The stars declare his glory" was one of four hymns written at Sevenoaks in April 1970 while Dudley-Smith served as Secretary (Chief Executive) of the Church Pastoral-Aid Society. He says, ". . . the 1970s provides a kind of roll-call of a troubled world."[46] It is enlightening to see something of what the hymnwriter calls to our attention about the historical/sociocultural context at the time of his writing this hymn:

> For the IRA, what began with the burning of the British Embassy in Dublin concluded with the assassination of Earl Mountbatten of Burma and his fourteen-year-old grandson. Across the world the war correspondents constantly reported from Vietnam, Lebanon, Cambodia, Angola, Uganda, Iran, Afghanistan, Rhodesia and South Africa. Bangladesh emerged as an independent nation and India as a nuclear power . . . ; Richard Nixon resigned, the first US president ever to do so; Archbishop Janani Lumum was murdered by Idi Amin's military dictatorship; . . . . World oil prices quadrupled . . . . UK inflation reached 25 percent in 1975, and remained continuously in double figures until 1981. . . .
>
> In Britain the relentless growth in unemployment contributed to the social and moral disintegration which was among the fruits of the previous decade. The Divorce Law Reform Act of 1971 saw the statistics for divorce suffer a sixfold increase between 1963 and 1980. Similarly, by the end of the 1970s "there were 140 thousand registered abortions a year and more than a million lives had been legally extinguished before birth over the previous decade."[47] Alarming growth was also evident in the abuse of drugs and alcohol, the spread of pornography[48] . . . and the gulf in living between the rich and the poor. . . .
>
> [M]ost organized religion was steadily diminishing. In 1976 (according to Adrian Hastings' calculations) one Anglican church was being demolished every nine days.[49] Along with this went a growth in pluralism, reflecting an increasing immigrant population in the UK. William Carey has always been honoured as a pioneer of the British missionary movement, yet by the 1970s the Carey Memorial Hall in Leicester was in use as a Sikh temple.[50]
>
> In America a Gallup Poll had designated 1966 as "the year of the evangelical";[51] and through the 1970s "it was becoming increasingly apparent that, while mainline churches were losing members, distinctly

evangelical bodies were gaining them."[52] A 1976 Gallup Poll found that 34 percent of Americans saw themselves as "born again"—and eight years later the proportion had risen to 40 percent.[53]

At the beginning of this decade of "a troubled world," Dudley-Smith's hymn, like the psalm on which it is based, draws us to "a celebration of nature and Scripture."[54] The world was, in this decade, also a world of some hope celebrating discoveries in the sciences, advancements in medicine, and writings in philosophy and religion. In the arts and literature, perhaps more closely influencing hymnody were the work of Solzhenitsyn, Saul Bellow, Eudora Welty, Ernest Hemingway, Neil Simon, John Dos Passos, E. M. Forster, and a host of other figures in literature and theater. In the visual arts, works of art valued at over $38 million sold during the 1969–1970 season at Sotheby's in London. The world of music saw the likes of Pablo Casals, Otto Klemperer, Elvis Presley, Burt Bacharach, Eugene Ormandy, Benjamin Britten, Hans Werner Henze, Duke Ellington, Igor Stravinsky, and scores of others. It was the beginning of a decade of diverse and momentous people and events.

Church life and hymnody in particular were increasingly experiencing some significant influences at this time. Carlton Young, in a nicely concise survey,[55] points out some of the salient characteristics of British hymnody in the decades following the "hymnic explosion" that began in that country in the early 1960s. These characteristics were firmly in place at the time of Dudley-Smith's writing of "The stars declare his glory":

1. The language of the church and hymnody moved from the King James Version of the Bible and the *Book of Common Prayer* to "metaphors and descriptions found in more recent translations of the Bible"; from sexist to more inclusive language; from traditional forms of address of God to terms more readily understood by the average person.
2. The concept of the church was portrayed in terms of our being sent into the world as pilgrims and servants responsible for humanity and the environment.
3. Aspects of twentieth-century science and technology began to appear in hymns.
4. Hymns began to reflect a concern about the destruction, violence, and promise of contemporary urban centers.
5. World peace and ecology were addressed more in hymns.

6. Hymns addressed the issues of Christian unity and reconciliation.

7. Churches and hymnal committees began commissioning hymns about Christ's baptism, ministry, transfiguration, passion, and resurrection as well as about the Holy Spirit, the city of God, personal healing and wholeness, and the Bible.

8. Hymn tunes began to be composed in a wide range of musical styles including pop, folk, and mid-twentieth-century compositional techniques.

9. Important supplements and hymnals appeared during this time.

10. The study of hymnody received a renewed impetus, especially in the work of hymnologist Erik Routley.

11. Young calls attention to Robin A. Leaver's observation about two significant influences in addition to the "hymnic explosion": (a) the charismatic movement that influenced practically all mainline denominations and (b) the ecumenical movement.

There is in the midst of this historical, sociocultural milieu a personal, biographical dimension in that Dudley-Smith considers this hymn a favorite among his own hymns[56] and a hymn based on one of his favorite psalms. It is well established by those most knowledgeable in the field of hymnody that Timothy Dudley-Smith is one of the most significant hymnwriters of our generation. Many have known and, in the years ahead, many will come to know him through his hymns that express to us and for us thoughts and feelings that unfold in new biblical, theological, liturgical, and literary insights as his hymns are read and sung. Many who read and sing carefully and with a growing Christian experience, insight, and maturity will recognize him as a skillful writer of the noble themes of God's work in the world.

In January 1991, Bishop Dudley-Smith was awarded by the Archbishop of Canterbury a Lambeth Degree. The degree, awarded in Lambeth Palace Chapel, was an MLitt with special reference in the citation to services to hymnody. In 2003, he became an Honorary Vice-President of the Hymn Society of Great Britain and Ireland, and in the same year he was appointed as an Officer of the Order of the British Empire (OBE) "for services to hymnody." In 2009, the University of Durham awarded him an Honorary DD. In 2011, the Royal School of Church Music, Salisbury, United Kingdom, bestowed on Bishop Dudley-Smith a Fellowship, its highest honor.

His hymns have been translated into Chinese, Danish, Estonian, French, German, Japanese, Korean, Latvian, Norwegian, Spanish, Swedish, and Welsh and have appeared in more than 250 hymnals throughout the world. Several of his hymns are firmly established in the minds and hearts of many twentieth-century worshipers. In a 1976 broadcast, Sir John Betjeman, poet laureate of England, spoke of Dudley-Smith's hymn "Tell Out, My Soul" as "one of the very few new hymns really to establish themselves in recent years."[57] The *Hymn Society Bulletin* of the Hymn Society of Great Britain and Ireland, following the July 1987 Westminster Abbey hymn sing, referred to Timothy Dudley-Smith, whose work "has a dignity scarcely matched in contemporary English hymnody."[58]

The hymns of Timothy Dudley-Smith have been used for the Enthronement Service of the Archbishop of Canterbury in 1991, for the Lambeth Conferences of Anglican bishops, for the Queen's Golden Jubilee in 2002, and for the papal mass of the visit of Pope Benedict XVI to Washington, DC, in 2008.

While it is generally and rightfully considered that an artistic creation should stand on its own merit, one's appreciation and understanding of works are often enhanced by some familiarity with their creator. Any biographical account here of the life and work of Dudley-Smith would be too brief and not adequately convey the warmth, breadth, or depth of this great hymnwriter. Some dimensions of the man have been experienced in part by some of us in Rectory Meadow, his home at Bramerton in Norwich, in the Diocese of Norwich where he ministered, in the Norwich Cathedral where he often served both as Archdeacon and later as a suffragan bishop, and in his retirement home in Salisbury. A deeper appreciation of the writer came in times with his family at Seacroft, his summer retreat in the quiet, little village of Ruan Minor in Cornwall, as he and I hiked the rocky cliffs and walked the moors and beaches, washed dishes together at Ruan Minor, or sat on a rock wall in Penzance eating a Cornish pasty. Conversations during meals, strolls on the moors and beaches, or tea together all revealed a man of insight, of warmth, of many interests, of high regard for individuals; a man with a deep reverence for God's word and his own call to ministry; and a skillful writer with a personal relationship with the Christ, the noble theme of whom he skillfully writes.

Some of Dudley-Smith's finest texts deal with God's creation or with God's word, and some of the very finest deal with both, as does "The stars declare his glory." Creation and nature are frequent themes in Dudley-Smith's hymns, primarily because of his recognition of God's creating hand all around him and perhaps partly because of his close touch with nature in his beloved Cornwall. In many of these hymns, he sees the redeeming work of God reflected in the creating work of God.

The Bible

Almost without exception, Dudley-Smith's hymns, whatever their specific historical/cultural context, have biblical references or allusions.[59] "The stars declare his glory" is one of Dudley-Smith's many metrical psalms. It is based on one of his favorite psalms, Psalm 19, as is his "O God who shaped the starry skies" that was written twenty-three years later. Derek Kidner notes that this psalm speaks of "the eloquence of nature and the clarity of Scripture."[60] The hymn follows carefully the flow of thought of the psalm with the first stanza of the hymn reflecting verses 1-4, the second stanza reflecting verses 4-6, stanza 3 reflecting verses 7-13, and stanza 4 a prayer like the final verse of the psalm. The hymn is a beautiful metrical setting of Psalm 19 for a congregation, even in a troubled world, to unite their minds, hearts, and voices in praise of God's creation and his word and to do so using a text based closely on that word.

Theology

Theologically, Dudley-Smith would, as does John Stott, consider himself "an Anglican evangelical Christian,"[61] where "Christian" comes first, "evangelical" comes second as the adjective denoting a biblical standpoint in theology, and "Anglican" names the denomination of both his baptism and ministry. But Dudley-Smith's hymns, while reflecting a biblical theology based on the evangelical principle of "sola scriptura," speak to and for the larger Christian community.[62] Dudley-Smith describes Psalm 19 as "a celebration of nature and Scripture,"[63] and he designates the hymn for the themes of "Creation; God's providential order; the Bible; praise and worship."[64] Of his "O God Who Shaped the Starry Skies," also based on Psalm 19, he says, "The main thrust of the text, as of that [second] part of Psalm 19, is that the 'same creative word' which brought forth our world at the beginning may be at work in the new creation of the Christian heart."[65]

Liturgy

An awesome sweep of creation and providence is voiced in the opening sentence of "The stars declare his glory," which forms the whole of the first stanza, and again in the sentence that forms the entire second stanza. The third stanza moves to the wisdom, sweetness, richness, love, and light of the Lord's commandments, "a law of love within our hearts, a light before our eyes." The final stanza is a prayer "that he who orders the heavens and gives the stars their laws will also direct and order the lives of his children."[66] These basic, important theological concepts are vitally interrelated with and founded on the Scriptures and speak to "a troubled world" at the beginning of the decade in which they were written and also to our own troubled world.

Dudley-Smith's identification of the theme of this hymn as "Creation; God's providential order; the Bible; praise and worship" emphasizes the biblical, theological, and liturgical facets of the hymn. The hymn is appropriate for a multitude of different weekly services and for many special occasions in most Christian traditions. It expresses great biblical truths and profound theological concepts suitable to either public or private worship[67] in the meaningful flow of the church year, the season, the particular Sunday, and the place in the service itself. In Lectionary B of the *Book of Common Prayer*, which is so much a part of Dudley-Smith's worship tradition, Psalm 19 is indicated for the Sunday closest to September 28. Used in the Daily Offices or The Holy Eucharist, this hymn can be both a powerful expression of adoration of God's majesty and a strong affirmation of God's creative power in nature and in his word. The hymn is also a fine evangelistic expression in its movement from God's general revelation of himself in nature to God's specific revelation of himself in Scripture. In public worship and certainly in one's private devotion, this is a great hymn of assurance of God's presence in all of his creation and of his speaking to us in his word.

Poetry

The biblical, theological, liturgical counterpoint finds expression in this hymn through a wealth of literary skills. None calls attention to itself, but all serve the meaning and momentum of the text. In this hymn is an imaginative, creative language that shapes diction, grammar, syntax, sound, tone, voice, meter, rhyme, speed, movement, mood, rhetorical figures, rhythm, form, and the interrelations of these to give expression to the biblical and theological concepts so basic to liturgy, to communicate thoughts and feelings of the faith, and to inspire the mind to soar above the limits of discursive prose. The beauty, power, and memorableness of such hymnody can contribute significantly to expressing to and for the worshiper the breadth and depths of thoughts and feelings that are a part of the Christian faith. Dudley-Smith recalls that in this hymn was "the solution of a number of technical problems in a manner more satisfying than one can often hope for."[68] The solution to the technical (literary) problems is likely a significant reason this is one of Dudley-Smith's finest hymns and one of his favorites among his own hymns.

The beautiful opening stanza of "The stars declare his glory" contains the expressive oxymoron "soundless music" wrapped in a meaningful alliteration of sibilants celebrating the silences of space. Within the first five words there sparkle three brilliant "r" sounds that add to the visual image and meaning.[69] Then comes the awesome sweep of creation and providence in one opening sentence of the first stanza. The short statement about the stars is followed by a long, five-line statement about all of heaven. The strong verbs "declare," "springs," and "sings" propel the mind into the stillness of night, the "vault of heaven," and "the silences of space." The declaration of God's glory, "the witness of the Master's hand in all created things," and the stars' "song" are paradoxically proclaimed through the "mute witness," "the silences of space," and "the soundless music." What begins as a declaration of God's glory and an affirmation that "the vault of heaven springs" is suddenly hushed in the "mute witness," "the silences of space," and the "soundless music," all conveyed through the masterful use of sixteen smooth, powerfully depictive sibilant "s" sounds in the one-sentence opening stanza.[70]

The descriptive negatives, the stillness of space, and the silences of night give way in the second stanza to the brilliance of dawn and the brightness of day. The words "burn and blaze" with the "splendour" of "dawn" and "the rising sun . . . that writes in fire across the skies" are set aglow by the four carefully placed brighter "i" vowel sounds and the twelve brilliant "r" sounds in this one stanza. The third stanza moves, like the psalm, from the "celebration of nature" to the "glory of Scripture" with the alliteration of God's "law," "love," and "light" and the use of metaphors of "honey," "prize," "law," and "light." It is a central message of the psalm and of the hymn that the God of all creation has deemed it good to reveal himself to humanity, to grant humanity his life-changing law that is at the same time pleasant for one who is receptive. There is in this stanza the keyword of Christianity—love, which must be reflected to God and to one's neighbor. For the Christian, the law is the "law of love within our hearts, a light before our eyes."

As does the psalm, the hymn ends with a prayer asking, as Dudley-Smith explains, "that he who orders the heavens and gives the stars their laws will also direct and order the lives of his children."[71] The personal mood seems to be enhanced by the pleasant long "a" sounds of the rhyme and the prevailing and assuring "m" sounds. The personal, even intimate note in this final stanza is also conveyed with six of the seven meditative "m" sounds connected with personal pronouns, and the significant word "my" is implored in the middle of lines (mesodiplosis) and at the beginning and middle of lines (mesarchia). A majestic tempo of cross rhyme (abcbdb) and the 76 86 86 meter lend a breadth to the text that is appropriate to the themes and moods. Counter rhythms of short clauses and long, sweeping sentences; the very sounds of the words and the reiterations of those sounds; and the unobtrusive uses of anaphora, alliteration, metonymy, mesarchia, mesodiplosis, personification, paradox, and metaphor inspire the mind to soar above the limits of discursive prose and to sense, in some small way, the grandeur of both God's creation and his word.

Music

Humanity has sought, within its limitations, the highest expression of thoughts and feelings, and when those exceed the boundaries of language, we often turn to music. Some of the most profound thoughts and deepest religious feelings of humankind in all of history and in every culture have found their way into musical utterance in some form of cantillation, chant, metrical psalmody, chorales, or hymns.

The relationship between the words and the music is, obviously, a crucial aspect in the interpretation of a hymn. Each must have its own value, and the wedding of the two is a more complex relationship than the traditional considerations of only mood and meter. We cannot, because hymn singing is basically congregational, expect from this union all the subtleties of an art song. However, there is much to commend the solo singing of certain hymns or stanzas of hymns that will allow the congregation to hear a sensitive interpretation of the text and music and might encourage more intelligent congregational singing. It is likely that there could be more spiritual and mental participation in intelligent listening than in the inattentive routine that too often characterizes much of congregational singing. Authors of hymns and composers of hymn tunes do speak of the textual/musical relationship between certain phrases and certain words. Some of the more sensitive congregants may respond to a certain level of subtlety, and, for others, some sensitivity to the finer levels of hymnody may be cultivated in a presentation by a vocal soloist, a choir, or an organist.

The biblical, theological, and liturgical content in "The stars declare his glory" is provided with a musical setting in Richard Proulx's ALDINE, composed in 1983 for this text. The American-born Proulx studied at the Royal

School of Church Music in England and was known as an organist, educa-
tor, and composer of more than 300 works including sacred and secular
choral works, song cycles, two operas, instrumental compositions, organ
works, and diverse forms of congregational music. He also served as a consultant for numerous hymnals. His setting of Dudley-Smith's "The stars
declare his glory" is sensitive in its temporal, melodic, harmonic, and formal
aspects to the biblical, theological, and literary facets of the text and is a
hymn tune suitable in many liturgical contexts. The singable, diatonic
(except for one climactic note) melody is sparse in its rhythmic figures with
only four, but they are used judiciously, sensitive to enjambments of the
text, and beautifully balanced with the melodic contours. This kind of economy of musical materials is appropriate for hymn tunes. The use of fresh
harmonies moves beyond those of traditional nineteenth-century hymnody,
and there are only some two beats in the entire hymn tune that are absent
a "traditional" dissonance formed by a passing tone, neighboring tone,
appoggiatura, suspension, retardation, or pedal tone, all yielding a constant
eighth-note movement to every beat of the tune except the first. The first is
a tense, dominant 13th chord that "resolves" to a dissonant, accented passing
tone that inaugurates the constant momentum. This propels each musical
and textual phrase into the next, honoring the enjambments that are part
of the single sentence that makes up each stanza. Following the modified
repeat of the opening musical phrase there is, for the text "and through the
silences of space," a change of rhythm, a lovely movement to a minor dominant chord (with the only chromatic tone in the melody clearly anticipated
in the accompaniment), that is the musical apex of the tune and provides a
tonic, agogic, and dynamic accent on important words in each stanza—
"space," "skies," "hearts," and "Lord"—from which the music then floats
down with the text "their soundless music sings" in the first stanza. There
are expressive melismas on the words "silences" and "soundless," and, in a
symmetry seen often in Dudley-Smith's writing, these accommodate the text
of the remaining three stanzas.

Figure 1. Words: "The stars declare his glory," Timothy Dudley-Smith (b. 1926). *A House of Praise*. © 1981 Hope Publishing Company, Carol Stream, IL 60188. All rights reserved. Used by permission. Music: ALDINE, Richard Proulx (1937–2010). © 1985 by G.I.A. Publications, Inc. 7404 S. Mason Ave., Chicago, IL 60638 www.giamusic.com. All rights reserved. Used by permission.

Practical Application

Erik Routley once suggested, "A hymn . . . is not really a good hymn until it has been well written, well chosen, and well sung."[72] "Well written" might be applied to the biblical, theological, liturgical, literary, and musical facets. "Well chosen" and "well sung" are the practical facets that facilitate a rich, meaningful experience with hymns and demand attention to a multitude of matters that may, in the most general way, be grouped under five broad headings: (1) spiritual commitment to the fullest possible understanding and use of hymns; (2) education of the congregation to the importance, possibilities, and manner of hymn singing; (3) planning of worship and the choice of hymns and hymn tunes; (4) attention to logistical matters of physical facilities; and (5) "performance" of the hymn—attention to the tempo, dynamics, media, and phrasing.[73]

Proulx's setting lends itself to subtle varieties of media, tempi, and volume that can reflect the meanings and moods that are different in each stanza and that can be enhanced by an organist's sensitive registration and playing. The opening stanza might be sung by a soloist, the second stanza by the choir, and the two final stanzas with their resultant phrases, "So shine the Lord's commandment . . ." and "So order too this life of mine . . . ," sung by the congregation. Singing in this way could introduce the congregation to the melody, demonstrate how a hymn might be sung, and present the message of the hymn in a forceful way. The careful singing of this hymn even by untrained singers can be a worship experience where the beauty of the literary expression and the musical setting present the biblical truths, emphasize the theological insights, and contribute to the larger liturgical context.

"The stars declare his glory" is, in many ways, one of Dudley-Smith's finest hymns and illustrates, as does all fine hymnody, the vital interaction of the historical, biographical, sociocultural, biblical, theological, liturgical, literary, musical, and practical facets. As stated above, a more thorough understanding of the multiple and interrelated facets of such hymns calls for a comprehensive and integrated hermeneutics.

Notes

1. See *Harvard Dictionary of Music*, 2nd ed., revised and enlarged (Cambridge MA: The Belknap Press of Harvard University Press, 1969) s.v. "Hermeneutics."

2. Cleanth Brooks and Robert Penn Warren, *Understanding Poetry*, 4th ed. (New York: Holt, Rinehart and Winston, 1976) 268.

3. There are obvious exceptions to this in works such as Raymond F. Glover, gen. ed., *The Hymnal 1982 Companion*, vols. 1–5 (New York: Church Hymnal Corporation, 1994) and Carlton Young, ed., *Companion to The United Methodist Hymnal* (Nashville: Abingdon Press, 1993). Also, interpretations of hymns in some works give more comprehensive attention such as those of J. R. Watson in his *An Annotated Anthology of Hymns* and *Awake My Soul: Reflections on Thirty Hymns*. Also see his *The English Hymn: A Critical and Historical*

Study, where his interpretations often deal with biblical, theological, liturgical, literary, and historical aspects but do not treat musical aspect. Some interpretations that appear in *The Hymn: The Journal of The Hymn Society in the United States and Canada*, such as Vincent A. Lenti's interpretation of "Of the Father's Love Begotten" in *The Hymn* 60/3 (Summer 2009): 7–15, give attention to multiple aspects of hymns. None of these deal with all the dimensions discussed in this study or with the vital interrelatedness of the facets.

4. J. R. Watson, "Hymns and Literature: Form and Interpretation," *Hymn Society of Great Britain & Ireland Bulletin* 17/5 (January 2004): 132.

5. Alexander Pope, "Essay on Criticism," http://poetry.eserver.org/essay-on-criticism.html.

6. J. R. Watson, *The English Hymn: A Critical and Historical Study* (Oxford: Oxford University Press, 1999) 16.

7. Allan Bloom, "Our Ignorance," pt. 2 of *The Closing of the American Mind* (New York: Simon and Schuster, 1987) 239.

8. Many of the accepted principles of biblical hermeneutics and literary criticism apply to the hermeneutics of hymnody. Some of the following is based on Bernard Ramm, *Protestant Biblical Interpretation*, rev. ed. (Boston: W. A. Wilde Company, 1956) and on I. A Richards, "Principles of Literary Criticism," *Encyclopædia Britannica*, 2010, http://www.britannica.com/EBchecked/topic/476911/Principles-of-Literary-Criticism. See also Louis Berkhof, *Principles of Biblical Interpretation* (Grand Rapids MI: Baker Pub Group, 1950); and I. A. Richards and C. K. Ogden, *The Meaning of Meaning: A Study of the Influence of Language upon Thought and of the Science of Symbolism* (1923), *Principles of Literary Criticism* (1924), and *Practical Criticism* (1929).

9. Some of the major principles of biblical hermeneutics are discussed in chapter 2.

10. C. S. Lewis, "Edmund Spenser (1552–99)," 1954, *Studies in Medieval and Renaissance Literature*, ed. Walter Hooper (Cambridge: Cambridge University Press, 1966) para. 35, p. 143.

11. Roger Bacon, in *The Oxford Dictionary of Scientific Quotations*, ed. W. F. Bynum and Roy Porter (Oxford University Press, 2006), Oxford Reference Online, http://www.oxfordreference.com/views/ENTRY.html?subview=Main&entry=t218.e72.

12. Friedrich Schiller, *Schillers Werke*, Nationalausgabe, Norbert Oellers; Julius Petersen; Lieselotte Blumenthal; Benno von Wiese; Siegfried Seidel; Stiftung Weimarer Klassik, Schiller-Nationalmuseum (Weimar: Hermann Bohlaus Nachfolger, 2000) 17/362. The translation is by the author.

13. Richard Wagner's concept of a "Gesamtkunstwerk" in which he attempted to fuse the arts of music, poetry, drama, and the visual arts was part of this concern for the unity of the arts.

14. Curt Sachs, *The Commonwealth of Art* (New York: W. W. Norton & Company, Inc., 1946) 17.

15. Leonard Bernstein, "The Unanswered Question" 1, Musical Phonology (1973 at Harvard) Norton Lectures, no. 1 of 6, http://avaxhome.ws/music/classical/Leonard_Bernstein_The_Unanswered_Question_Musical_Phonology.html.

16. John Boslough, *Stephen Hawking's Universe* (New York: Avon Books, 1985) 77.

17. Robert B. Laughlin, *A Different Universe: Reinventing Physics from the Bottom Down* (New York: Basic Books, 2005) 208. Emergence, as used here, is the process of using basic constituent parts to form complex patterns. Most of the laws of physics themselves seem to have emerged during the course of time, and some authorities consider that emergence may be the most fundamental principle in the universe, giving rise to questions about what might be the most fundamental law of physics from which all others emerged.

18. Edward O. Wilson, *Consilience: The Unity of Knowledge* (New York: Alfred A. Knopf, 1998) 267.

19. Ibid., 11–12.

20. Ibid., 8.

21. Ibid., 27.

22. Ibid., 5.

23. Ibid., 12.

24. J. R. Watson's *The English Hymn* is a masterful study of the literary dimension in historical order and touches frequently on the biblical, liturgical, theological, and at times with the biographical, but is not concerned with the musical dimensions. Austin C. Lovelace's *The Anatomy of Hymnody* (New York: Abingdon Press, 1965) provides an excellent introduction to meter, rhyme, and poetic devices but does not deal with the biblical, theological, liturgical, musical, or historical dimensions. There are also works such as William Jensen Reynolds, *A Survey of Christian Hymnody*, 5th ed. rev. and enl. by David W. Music and Milburn Price (Carol Stream: Hope Publishing Company, 2011), and Harry Eskew and Hugh T. McElrath, *Sing with Understanding: An Introduction to Christian Hymnody*, 2nd ed. (Nashville, Tennessee: Broadman Press, 1995), both of which provide excellent introductions to the dimensions, especially the historical, and to the broader spectrum. However, as surveys, they are not concerned with the dimensions in great depth or with the ways in which the dimensions are vitally interrelated.

25. Gustave Reese, *Music in the Renaissance*, rev. ed. (New York: W. W. Norton & Company, Inc., 1959) xiii.

26. In this book, knowledgeable writers from the biblical, theological, liturgical, literary, musical, practical, and biographical/historical/sociocultural disciplines as well as other fields of study have been brought into our conversation. Given the multiple disciplines involved, it has been considered wise to refer to specialists in the various fields. Because they may not always be well known by persons in other disciplines, they have been identified. It is hoped that the perceptive reader will find these references and quotations to be refreshing reminders of the interrelatedness of the disciplines involved in hymnology and so much of life. Intersections are often interesting and important places in one's journey.

27. Frank Baker, *Charles Wesley's Verse: An Introduction*, 2nd ed. (London: Epworth Press, 1964, 1968) 22.

28. Harold Bloom, *Genius: A Mosaic of One Hundred Exemplary Creative Minds* (New York: Warner Books, 2002) xii.

29. Much might be said about the temporal dimensions of spatial art and of the spatial dimensions of temporal art, both of which can have interesting ramifications for church music. This must wait until another time.

30. Seamus Heaney, *Beowulf: A New Verse Translation* (New York: Farrar, Straus and Giroux, 2000) xxvi–xxvii.

31. William Wordsworth, "Expostulation and Reply and The Tables Turned," quoted in *The Norton Anthology of English Literature* (New York: W. W. Norton & Company, Inc., 1968) 1262.

32. J. R. R. Tolkien, *The Monsters and the Critics* (London: Harper Collins, 1997) 120.

33. Robert Louis Stevenson, "The Art of Writing," in *Contemporary Review* (April 1885).

34. Ibid.

35. One is perhaps reminded of Paul Horgan's Pulitzer Prize-winning, almost 1,000-page story of the *Great River: The Rio Grande in North American History* (Hanover, New England: University Press of New England and Wesleyan Press, 1984), which is anything but "disenchanting," and of John Graves's *Goodbye to a River* (Houston, Texas: Gulf Publishing Company, 1960).

36. Roger Scruton, *An Intelligent Person's Guide to Philosophy* (New York: Penguin Books, 1996) 12.

37. Elton Trueblood, *Philosophy of Religion* (New York: Harper & Brothers, 1957) 122–27.

38. Edward O. Wilson, *Consilience: The Unity of Knowledge* (New York: Alfred A. Knopf, 1998) 65.

39. Ibid., 210.

40. This was the approach taken by the poets, translators, critics, and editors John Ciardi and Miller Williams in their study, *How Does a Poem Mean?* 2nd ed. (Boston: Houghton Mifflin Company, 1975). It was also addressed in Cleanth Brooks and Robert Penn Warren's *Understanding Poetry*, 4th ed. (New York: Holt, Rinehart and Winston, 1976).

41. Edmund L. Epstein, *Language and Style* (London: Methuen, 1978) 1.

42. George Steiner, *Real Presences* (Chicago: University of Chicago Press, 1989) 3.

43. Frank Baker, *Charles Wesley's Verse: An Introduction*, 2nd ed. (London: Epworth Press, 1964, 1988) 64.

44. Numerous references are made throughout this work to Timothy Dudley-Smith, who is regarded as one of the finest hymnwriters of our generation and whose writings (hymn texts and prose) relate significantly to each dimension of hymnody and to their interrelatedness. His hymn texts and prose writings are taken mainly from his *A House of Praise: Collected Hymns 1961–2001*. Numerous references are also made to Charles Wesley and his hymns. These two writers provide historical and contemporary examples of many of the aspects of hymnody discussed here.

45. Timothy Dudley-Smith, *A House of Praise: Collected Hymns 1961–2001* (Carol Stream, IL: Hope Publishing Company, 2003) 136, all rights reserved, used by permission. Hereafter referred to as *A House of Praise*.

46. Timothy Dudley-Smith, *John Stott: A Global Ministry: A Biography of the Later Years*, Vol. 2 (Downers Grove IL: InterVarsity Press, 2001) 137.

47. Adrian Hastings, *A History of English Christianity 1920–1990* (London: SCM, 1991) 597. Dudley-Smith notes, "His book is the source of much of the information quoted in these paragraphs."

48. Lord Longford, *Pornography: The Longford Report* (London: Coronet, 1979) 597.

49. Adrian Hastings, *A History of English Christianity 1920–1990* (London: SCM, 1991) 602.

50. Ibid., 599.

51. Cited by Timothy Chester, *Awakening to a World of Need: The Recovery of Evangelical Social Concern* (Leicester: IVP, 1993) 17.

52. David Bebbington, "Evangelicalism in Its Setting: The British and American Movements since 1940," in Mark A. Noll, David W. Bebbington, and George A. Rawlyk, eds., *Evangelicalism: Comparative Studies of Popular Protestantism in North America, the British Isles, and Beyond, 1700–1990* (New York: Oxford University Press, 1994) 377.

53. Timothy Dudley-Smith, *John Stott*, 137–38.

54. *A House of Praise*, 369.

55. Carlton Young, *My Great Redeemer's Praise: An Introduction to Christian Hymns* (Akron OH: OSL Publications 1995) 70–76.

56. *A House of Praise*, 369.

57. Ibid., 421.

58. *Hymn Society Bulletin* (Hymn Society of Great Britain and Ireland) 11/11 (July 1987): 233–37.

59. Space does not allow exploring here the whole range of the influence of Scripture on Dudley-Smith's hymns. Some of his hymns contain quotations of distinctive words, phrases, clauses, or even sentences of a version of Scripture. Some hymns are metrical versions of Scripture. Others versify biblical passages. Some paraphrase passages. Others have clear allusions to biblical concepts or events. Some are simply "based on" Scripture. The few that are relatively free of biblical wording or of clear allusions to specific biblical ideas or events are still entirely consistent with biblical teaching. His collections regularly include scriptural indexes.

60. Derek Kidner, *Psalms 1–72* (Leicester: InterVarsity Press 1973) 97. Dudley-Smith's concern for biblical accuracy and theological soundness is evidenced in part by his having asked the biblical scholar and author Derek Kidner to examine his hymns in early drafts and to offer suggestions about the biblical usage, theology, grammar, and style. Dudley-Smith has referred to Kidner as "my unfailing friend and constructive critic."

61. John Stott, "I Believe in the Church of England," *Hope for the Church of England?* ed. Gavin Reid (Eastbourne: Kingsway, 1986) 17, as quoted in Timothy Dudley-Smith, ed., *Authentic Christianity: From the writings of John Stott* (Downers Grove IL: InterVarsity Press, 1995) 309.

62. There is in Dudley-Smith's hymns a phenomenal spectrum of Christian doctrines that may well serve as an admirable companion to theological study.

63. *A House of Praise*, 369.

64. Ibid., 368.

65. Ibid., 362.

66. Ibid., 369.

67. The spiritual maturity of the reader/singer in relation to the hymn and the experience of worship is part of the "polyphony" of hymnody and is discussed in the section "Spiritual Commitment" in chapter 8. Much of the loss of vitality in public worship may be due, in part, to an absence of private worship that could be enriched by the reading of Scripture and hymns.

68. *A House of Praise*, 369.

69. Such works as I. A. Richards, *The Philosophy of Rhetoric* (New York: Oxford University Press, 1936, 1964) and Laurence Perrine, *Literature: Structure, Sound, and Sense*, 4th ed. (New York: Harcourt Brace Jovanovich, Inc., 1983) discuss the effects in both prose and poetry that the sounds of words, even parts of words, have on feelings, moods, and thoughts beyond their grammatical or lexical meanings. This has interesting implications for the musical settings of texts and is discussed in chapter 5.

70. A similar use of sibilants is found in Wesley's "O for a thousand tongues," where fifteen sibilants occur in the same context of calm and peace in the four short lines: "Jesus, the name that calms my fears, / That bids my sorrows cease; / 'Tis music in the sinner's ears; / 'Tis life and health and peace."

71. *A House of Praise*, 369.

72. Erik Routley, *Hymns and Human Life* (Grand Rapids MI: Murray, 1967) 299.

73. These aspects are discussed in chapter 8.

CHAPTER 2

The Bible

Christian hymnody has drawn deeply from the biblical well for both content and form. What is said in hymns and how it is said are bathed in biblical ideas and imagery. We are reminded again that Jesus said, "For I did not speak of my own accord, but the Father who sent me commanded me what to say and how to say it" (ὅτι ἐγὼ ἐξ ἐμαυτοῦ οὐκ ἐλάλησα, ἀλλ ὁ πέμψας με πατὴρ αὐτός μοι ἐντολὴν σέσωκεν τί εἴπω καὶ τί λαλήσω).[1] Our Lord's message was conveyed, in part, in the medium of spoken words that captured the minds and hearts of the first hearers and has captured minds and hearts of people for more than twenty centuries.

Our Lord taught using the imagery of everyday language and breathed into the words meanings that for centuries have imbedded themselves in the memory and understanding of his followers. In the Sermon on the Mount, recorded in Matthew 5, 6, and 7, Jesus refers to some thirty-seven everyday images that served as vivid pictures for his hearers.[2] Most of these images have found their way into hymns and often carry with them their biblical meanings. Archbishop Michael Ramsey gave wise advise to ordinands at Durham: "Be ready for new experiments, but do not, by sophisticated attempts to be contemporary at all costs, blunt the force which lies in the universal imagery of the Bible: bread, water, light, darkness, wind, fire, hunger, thirst, eat, drink, walk."[3] Our Lord's words and the meanings of his message have been translated into the languages of the earth, and many have found their way in various forms into hymns sung by men and women across the world for two thousand years. His words, the words about him, and his message that fill our hymns demand the most careful hermeneutics.

God's word abounds in poetic passages not only in the beloved collection of Psalms with its vast array of themes and images but also in the songs

of Moses and Miriam, the song of Deborah, passages in the prophets, the
song of the Angels, the canticles of Zechariah, Simeon, and Mary, and our
Lord's singing a psalm together with his disciples at that last supper.

Michael O'Connor observes that "Images of Jesus Christ singing are
virtually unknown in Christian art and hymnody"[4] and aims in his essay
"to spotlight the image of Jesus as a singing person. From this, we may then
derive a sense of the intrinsic goodness of singing and the fittingness of our
practice of singing prayers to God—in our worship here on earth and in
the praise offered in heaven."[5] O'Connor emphasizes the role of music in
the culture of Jesus's time—the home life, the synagogue, and the temple—
and reminds us that "The New Testament often uses the verb 'to say' in
contexts where we might assume something more stylized than plain speech,
something more akin to singing"[6] (e.g., Luke 1:46, 67; 2:13, 28; 19:38;
Matt 21:9; Rev 4:8; 5:12-14). O'Connor makes a challenging conclusion:

> The contemplation of the singing of Jesus raises questions in Christology,
> eschatology, and Trinitarian theology. It also offers a chance to consider
> the Christological and eschatological character of music in worship: our
> liturgical song is not created by us, but given us by our high priest. He
> translated heaven's song into a truly earthly song at his incarnation, in
> order that he might make such an earthly song, together with a host of
> earthly singers, part of the worship of heaven. The singing of Jesus offers
> a rich link between the way we pray and the life we hope for, putting the
> music we use to a considerable challenge, and inspiring us in the way we
> use it.[7]

The singing of Paul and Silas in the Philippian prison is also a reminder
"of the intrinsic goodness of singing and the fittingness of our practice of
singing prayers to God." It seems unlikely that in prison Paul and Silas broke
forth into song for the first time. It is more likely that it was their custom
to sing in various contexts. The hymn fragments in Paul's letters to the early
churches are rich in wordings that apparently reflect the liturgical and hymnic speech of the day. In addition to the hymn fragments, Paul admonishes
the early Christians to "Let the word of Christ richly dwell within you, with
all wisdom teaching and admonishing one another with psalms and hymns
and spiritual songs, singing with thankfulness in your hearts to God" (Col
3:16) and to "be filled with the Spirit, speaking to one another in psalms
and hymns and spiritual songs, singing and making melody with your heart
to the Lord" (Eph 5:18-19). Paul makes an affirmation about his own

singing of psalms, hymns, and spiritual songs: "I will sing with the spirit and I will sing with the mind also" (1 Cor 14:15). The singing in heaven of a new song by the four living creatures and the twenty-four elders in Revelation 5:8-10, the new song of the 144,000 in Revelation 14:3, and the song of Moses and the song of the Lamb in Revelation 15:3 provide a dramatic, awesome picture of the role of music in eternity. The biblical attention to singing should challenge us to sing with the spirit and with the mind, and this calls for some skills of interpretation of both hymns and of Scripture.

Principles of Biblical Hermeneutics

Because Christian hymns abound in biblical words, phrases, and concepts, and because their use of Scripture must be consistent with the broader scriptural teaching, there is an awesome responsibility on those who write hymns, translate hymns, compile hymnals, choose hymns, and sing hymns to understand and honor the original biblical words and meanings. Hymns must flow from and contribute to a correct understanding and application of Scripture.

Understanding the biblical message of hymns requires first of all a sound interpretation of Scripture. While there are varying formulations of the doctrine of Scripture, Christians generally recognize the Bible as the word of God and accept its authority and relevance. Biblical scholars and others most concerned with understanding Scripture generally observe some accepted principles of interpretation. Those most concerned with a fuller understanding of Christian hymnody must consider how well every statement, and certainly any biblical reference in a hymn, honors accepted basic principles of biblical interpretation.

The *linguistic/literary principle of biblical hermeneutics* emphasizes the priority of original languages, of word structures, of the variety and nature of the types of literature (such as history, poetry, and the Gospels), and of literary figures (such as simile, metaphor, hyperbole, and parable). Writers and interpreters of hymns must at least rely on the best possible translations of Scripture. For example, concepts such as the "Kingdom of Heaven" or "Kingdom of God" mean, biblically, much more than simply a kingdom that is in heaven and require an understanding of the linguistic and literary types of expression found in Scripture. This particular concept is generally considered to refer to the rule of God, to the realm in which this Lordship is realized, and what God's creation can rightfully expect on the basis of his Lordship. The biblical language and literary form of the concept are honored in Charles Wesley's "Rejoice, the Lord is King!" when he speaks of our Lord reigning now as King and ruling over earth and heaven, of His kingdom that cannot fail, of His coming again to judge and rule His kingdom, and of His eternal home and kingdom.[8]

Poetic passages of the Bible present special problems for the translator and similar challenges for the hymn writer when casting biblical concepts into poetic language. In whatever forms Scriptures appear in hymns (quotation, metrical version, paraphrase, echo, allusion), those who write, choose, and sing hymns must consider how well the hymn honors the biblical language and literary form. Those who translate hymns that were originally written in other languages and were based on biblical poetic expressions assume a complex responsibility. The Italians have a perceptive observation in the phrase "*traduttore traditore*" (to translate is to betray). This is especially true in matters of poetry as Sir John Denham eloquently noted in his preface to *The Destruction of Troy* (1636): "Poetry is of so subtle a spirit, that in pouring out of one language into another, it will all evaporate."[9] Some translators have honored the linguistic form and the literary style of the original, capturing in beautiful English language the biblical imagery found in early Greek, Latin, and German hymns and leaving us vast hymnic treasures such as Gerard Moultrie's "Let all mortal flesh keep silence," John Mason Neale and Henry Williams Baker's "Of the Father's love begotten," and Frederic Henry Hedge's "A mighty fortress is our God."

The literal, figurative, allegorical principle of biblical hermeneutics must be honored in any use of Scripture in hymns. The Scriptures are rich in imagery, some of which finds poetic expression in hymnody, and this requires biblical knowledge, literary understanding, and the ability to discern whether a passage should be interpreted literally, figuratively, or allegorically.[10] The word "Jerusalem" has both literal and figurative meanings in Scripture and in hymns. Bernard of Cluny's twelfth-century hymn "Jerusalem the golden," translated by John Mason Neale, is virtually an allegorical vision of heaven, weaving figurative language ("milk and honey," "halls of Zion," "Prince," "pastures," "the throne of David," "robes of white," "country," "home") with phrases that are both figurative and literal ("radiancy of glory") and remaining true to the biblical language of the "the new Jerusalem" of Revelation (Rev 3:12; 21:2; and 21:10).[11]

Because the poetry of hymnody seeks to communicate thoughts and feelings of the faith and to inspire the mind to soar above the limits of discursive prose, it is imperative that any hermeneutics of hymnody pay special attention to the matter of biblical and hymnic imagery. It is to be expected that when content is of great significance, form receives great attention, and it is not surprising that a vast number of the figures of speech used in the Bible are also found in hymns. Both require careful interpretation.

The influence of Scripture on the hymns of Charles Wesley is profound, and this may account for the continuing widespread use of his hymns and their impact on singers. J. R. Watson describes what may be a model for a hymn writer's use of Scripture when he speaks of "Charles Wesley and His Art" as showing "the extraordinary range and pervasive use of the Bible . . . inspiration from almost every part of the New Testament and from many corners of the Old . . . . dense with allusion and image [of the Bible]." He continues, "what is interesting is not just the debts themselves but the ways in which they are used."[12] B. L. Manning says of Charles Wesley, "He knew that the use of a proper name with associations may start or clinch a train of thought more effectively than a flood of colourless words will start or clinch it. To you and to me, with our beggarly knowledge of Holy Scripture, this magic is less potent than it was to Wesley."[13]

Wesley's most loved hymns abound in biblical imagery. In addition to more obvious allusions, one is reminded of perhaps less familiar biblical figures as "Sun of Righteousness" and "healing in his wings"[14] from Malachi 4:2; and of indirect references such as "the panoply of God"[15] alluding to Ephesians 6:11, where Wesley's use of the word "panoply" is precisely the word used in this passage of the Greek New Testament, πανοπλια.

William Williams's hymn "Guide me, O thou great Jehovah" as it now appears in most hymnals is a fine example of biblical content and imagery.[16] J. R. Watson regards this hymn as "the greatest of all Exodic hymns" and "one of the greatest of evangelical hymns mainly because of its understatement."[17] Watson is referring to the understatement of topology in which the attentive reader/singer must (or is allowed to) make the connections between Williams's images and the biblical story of the exodus. The hymn uses the imagery of the pivotal event in Old Testament history and theology, the event that Christianity parallels to the death and resurrection of Jesus. The basic message of the hymn is God's miraculous deliverance from our slavery to sin and God's providential guidance in our wilderness wanderings toward the promised land. Israel's deliverance from Egyptian bondage is commemorated at Passover, and Jesus's institution of the ordinance of the Lord's Supper at the time of the Passover is to Christians a vivid reminder that Jesus is the Passover Lamb and that, in commemorating the Lord's Supper, we are celebrating our redemption and deliverance from sin. The hymn borrows the biblical imagery of "Jehovah," "pilgrim," "barren land," "bread," "fountain," "fire and cloudy pillar," "the verge of Jordan," and "Canaan's side." There are hints of the antithetical parallelism in the Hebrew poetry of the Psalms as found in "Great Jehovah" vs. "me . . . pilgrim" and "I am weak" vs. "Thou art mighty."

The historical principle of biblical hermeneutics requires that the use of Scriptures in hymns show sensitivity to the meaning and application that the Scripture had to the original hearers or readers. While it may be argued that the original hearers understood the meaning and application of Messianic prophecy quite differently than the hearers who live this side of the fulfillment of the prophecy, it may also be argued that many of the original hearers misunderstood the meaning and application. Isaac Watts, in his preface to his 1719 The Psalms of David Imitated in the Language of the New Testament and Applied to the Christian State and Worship, defends his "imitation" and "Christianizing" of the Psalms:[18] "Where the original runs in the form of prophecy concerning Christ and his salvation, I have given an historical turn to the sense; there is no necessity that we should always sing in the obscure and doubtful style of prediction, when the things foretold are brought into open light by a full accomplishment."

The contextual principle in biblical interpretation requires consideration of the context of an idea in a verse, in a chapter, in the whole book, in the author's other writings, in the writings of other biblical authors, and in the teachings of the Bible as a whole. Both hymn writer and hymn interpreter must consider the contextual principle of interpretation when reference is made directly or indirectly to a biblical passage. Just as in a biblical context, one's understanding of what and how a hymn means may be enhanced by a larger consideration of a concept not only in the verse, the stanza, the hymn, and the other hymns of a writer, but even of the idea in the larger body of hymnody and of Scripture. William Cowper's "Sometimes a light surprises" brims with biblical quotes and allusions that honor their biblical contexts and speak of God's providential care: "healing in his wings" (Mal 4:2); "gives the lilies clothing" (Luke 12:27); "he who feeds the ravens" (Luke 12:24); and the beautiful last stanza that paraphrases Habakkuk 3:17-18. In the context of William Cowper's own life and his struggles with extreme depression, the hymn may also be seen as almost autobiographical.

The practical/functional principle of biblical hermeneutics gives attention to the application of the meaning of a passage of Scripture and how it affects one's beliefs and actions. While hymn singing occurs primarily in the context of worship, the actual singing of hymns and certainly the messages of hymns have significant implications for the everyday living out of the Christian faith and ministering to the physical, social, emotional, and mental needs of others.[19] The Bible and hymns must be interpreted with consideration to the practical application of what is said explicitly and implicitly. The maledictions of the imprecatory Psalms confront the reader of Scripture and the writer of hymns with problems related to most all of the hermeneutical principles, but the clear, larger emphasis of Christian teaching is on the practical application of loving God and our neighbors.[20]

In much the same way that a sound hermeneutics of Scripture is necessary, so is a sound hermeneutics of hymnody, and there is wisdom in applying the principles of biblical interpretation to the interpretation of hymns.

Methods of Scriptural Usage in Hymnody

Christian hymnody has its roots in Scripture and manifests a wide variety of influences of the Bible. Some hymns contain quotations of distinctive words, phrases, clauses, or even sentences of a version of Scripture.[21] Some hymns are metrical versions of Scripture. Others versify biblical passages. Some paraphrase passages. Others have clear allusions to biblical concepts or events. Some are simply "based on" Scripture. Others, though relatively free of biblical wording or of any clear allusions to specific biblical ideas or events, may still be entirely consistent with biblical teaching. Some of the most respected hymn writers of our time have been careful to document the biblical bases of their hymns.[22]

Many hymnals devote entire sections to "Holy Scripture," "The Bible," or "Scripture" and/or list such topics in a topical index. Entire hymns address the subject of the Scriptures, such as Percy Dearmer's "Book of books, our people's strength," and numerous hymns devote a stanza to "the sacred book," such as Charles Wesley's "Come, Holy Ghost, our hearts inspire." Most hymnals now provide scriptural indexes to the hymns, giving attention to hymns that not only incorporate biblical ideas but also express gratitude and praise for the word of God. Some hymnals give the scriptural references on the hymn page. The hymnal *Rejoice*, edited by the hymnologist Erik Routley, is subtitled *A hymn companion to the Scriptures*, and the topical index lists twenty-nine "Biblical Characters" by name, and for these it lists seventy-five hymns all in addition to the hundreds of hymns under "Jesus Christ" and in addition to a four-page "Index of Scriptural allusions."

Quotations of distinctive biblical words or phrases are found in numerous hymns and from a variety of versions of the Scriptures. Both the names of people and the names of biblical places may carry powerful associations with significant events in biblical history. A single, distinctive proper name such as "Gethsemane," "Calvary," "Bethel," or "Ebenezer" can convey powerful associations. An example of how the quotation of a single, distinctive biblical word is used in hymnody can be seen in Robert Robinson's beloved eighteenth-century hymn "Come, thou fount of every blessing." The word "Ebenezer" draws on the powerful biblical imagery of Samuel's using the Hebrew word "Ebenezer" to commemorate how "the LORD thundered with a great thunder on that day against the Philistines and confused them, so that they were routed before Israel" and how Samuel "took a stone and set it between Mizpah and Shen, and named it Ebenezer, saying, 'Thus far the LORD has helped us'" (1 Sam 7:12). Some hymnals, with a worthy motive of more immediate understanding, have made unfortunate editings that have deprived hymns of their powerful biblical imagery. The word "Ebenezer" is, in some hymnals, changed to read "highest treasure" losing both Robinson's allusion and the biblical meaning in a concession to a contemporary lack of biblical knowledge. Where there are biblical references and theological meanings that may well be beyond the immediate understanding of many congregants, it may be better, in some cases, to address these in footnotes, in sermons, in explanations in the order of worship, or in the educational organizations of the church. The rich biblical imagery in hymns should not be abandoned, nor should some introduction to biblical language be neglected.

Mosaics of biblical quotes may sometimes be found in the hymns of writers who have a special command of Scripture, and in the hands of better writers these are not casual strings of references but are careful juxtapositions of related biblical concepts consistent with revealed truth.[23] A number of Dudley-Smith's hymns are scriptural mosaics made up sometimes of quotes or near quotes and sometimes of allusions. Dudley-Smith notes of "The darkness turns to dawn":

> In manuscript form, it carried one or more Bible references in the margin beside almost every line:
>
> verse 1: line 1, Isaiah 9.2; line 2, Luke 1.78; lines 3 and 4, Isaiah 9.6
> verse 2: line 1, Luke 1.32; line 2, Proverbs 8.22; line 3, Isaiah 7.14;
> line 4, Luke 19.10
> verse 3: lines 1 and 2, John 1.11; line 3, Hebrews 1.3; line 4, Isaiah 7.14

verse 4: lines 1 and 2, 2 Corinthians 8.9; line 3, Philippians 2.7; line 4,
John 1.4

verse 5: lines 1 and 2, Philippians 2.7; lines 3 and 4, 1 Peter 2.24

verse 6: lines 1 and 2, Philippians 2.8; lines 3 and 4, Hebrews 1.3

verse 7: line 1, Romans 5.5; line 2, 1 John 4.10; line 3, Luke 2.11; line 4,
Luke 1.33[24]

Metrical versions, casting the biblical text into meter but following closely the biblical use of words, word order, and sequence of thought were made first of the Psalms, such as Willliam Kethe's metrical version of Psalm 100, "All people that on earth do dwell."

All people that on earth do dwell,
Sing to the Lord with cheerful voice.
Him serve with fear, His praise forth tell;
Come ye before Him and rejoice.

The Lord, ye know, is God indeed;
Without our aid He did us make;
We are His folk, He doth us feed,
And for His sheep He doth us take.

O enter then His gates with praise;
Approach with joy His courts unto;
Praise, laud, and bless His Name always,
For it is seemly so to do.

For why? the Lord our God is good;
His mercy is for ever sure;
His truth at all times firmly stood,
And shall from age to age endure.

Erik Routley opined that Dudley-Smith's 1970 "Not to us be glory given" (based on Psalm 115) "is a model of how a modern metrical psalm should look."[25]

Not to us be glory given
    but to him who reigns above:
Glory to the God of heaven
    for his faithfulness and love!
What though unbelieving voices

hear no word and see no sign,
still in God my heart rejoices,
    working out his will divine.

Not what human fingers fashion,
    gold and silver, deaf and blind,
dead to knowledge and compassion,
    having neither heart nor mind,
lifeless gods, yet some adore them,
    nerveless hands and feet of clay;
all become, who bow before them,
    lost indeed and dead as they.

Not in them is hope of blessing,
    hope is in the living Lord:
high and low, his Name confessing,
    find in him their shield and sword.
Hope of all whose hearts revere him,
    God of Israel, still the same!
God of Aaron! Those who fear him,
    he remembers them by name.

Not the dead, but we the living
    praise the Lord with all our powers;
of his goodness freely giving,
    his is heaven; earth is ours.
Not to us be glory given
    but to him who reigns above:
Glory to the God of heaven
    for his faithfulness and love![26]

A *paraphrase* is freer than a metrical version in its use of biblical words, word order, and sequence of thought. This can be seen in comparing Isaac Watts's paraphrase of Psalm 100, "Before Jehovah's awful throne," with William Kethe's metrical version of the Psalm, "All people that on earth do dwell" (see above). Watts's text was printed first in his *Psalms of David Imitated in the Language of the New Testament and Applied to the Christian State and Worship* (London, 1791), a title that tells us much about his approach to Psalms. Given shifts in word meanings, the text has been altered over time. John Wesley made alterations, and some editors have substituted the wording, "Before Jehovah's awesome throne," "Before the Lord Jehovah's throne," and "Before the Lord's eternal throne."

> Before the Lord's eternal throne,
> ye nations, bow with sacred joy;
> know that the Lord is God alone;
> he can create and he destroy.
>
> His sovereign power without our aid
> formed us of clay and gave us breath;
> and when like wandering sheep we strayed,
> he saved us from the power of death.
>
> We are his people, we his care,
> our souls, and all our mortal frame;
> what lasting honors shall we rear,
> almighty Maker, to thy Name?
>
> We'll crowd thy gates with thankful songs,
> high as the heavens our voices raise;
> and earth, with her ten thousand tongues,
> shall fill your courts with sounding praise.
>
> Wide as the world is thy command,
> vast as eternity thy love;
> firm as a rock thy truth shall stand,
> when rolling years have ceased to move.[27]

Historically, this move from the stricter metrical versions of the Psalms to freer paraphrases and then to paraphrases of other passages of the Scripture led to freely composed hymns that were still rooted in Scripture.

Allusion, while indirect in its scriptural reference, may clearly present biblical events to the singer with fresh and powerful insights into God's word. Writers who are knowledgeable of Scripture and conscious of the evocative power of words and phrases often allude to specific people, places, items, and events of Scripture. Dudley-Smith notes that in his hymn, "He comes to us as one unknown," there is "the merest allusion to 1 Chronicles 14:15, when a 'sound of going in the tops of the mulberry trees' is a sign or signal from the Lord himself"; the NEB translation is a "rustling sound in the treetops." The theological theme of his hymn is "our perception of God's approach to the soul, and the 'sense of the divine' which is part of human experience."[28] The third stanza reads,

> He comes to us in sound of seas,
> the ocean's fume and foam;
> yet small and still upon the breeze,
> a wind that stirs the tops of trees,
> a voice to call us home.[29]

One may also find here an allusion to the experience of Elijah and the "still small voice" in 1 Kings 19:12 (KJV).

Charles Wesley's hymn, "Come, O thou traveler unknown," based on Jacob's experience at the stream Jabbok as recorded in Genesis 32, appears in many hymnals and would probably require considerable explanation for many worshipers. It draws upon a specific biblical event, but in the four or so stanzas as it appears in most hymnals (rather than the original fourteen six-line stanzas), there is no explicit mention of the persons involved. The hymn calls to mind the meaning of the powerful drama and finally describes the unknown traveler as "Love," identifying the motive of the Old Testament experience rather than the person and giving the hymn a personal, Christian meaning that in no way conflicts with the larger biblical account.[30]

It is crucial that Christian hymns be consistent with biblical teaching, important that we who sing hymns have sufficient discernment to determine whether or not a hymn is consistent with biblical teaching, and necessary that we who sing hymns continually grow in biblical understanding in the hope that we might more worthily approach the heights and depths of both the Bible and hymns.

⟪═◆═⟫

The Biblical "Voice" in a "Polyphonic" Hermeneutics

The principal voice, the "*cantus firmus*," in the polyphony of Christian hymnody is the biblical voice. It is interesting that the trained theologian and skillful musician, Dietrich Bonhoeffer, in writing to Eberhard Bethge, used this metaphor of the *cantus firmus* to speak of the polyphony of life:

> have a good, clear cantus firmus; that is the only way to a full and perfect sound, when the counterpoint has a firm support and can't come adrift

or get out of tune, while remaining a distinct whole in its own right. Only a polyphony of this kind can give life a wholeness and at the same time assure us that nothing calamitous can happen as long as the cantus firmus is kept going.[31]

Hymns must be consistent with Scripture to have validity as Christian expression. While writings in the field of hymnology have focused largely on the historical and biographical, providing the context out of which a hymn is born and contributing significantly to understanding the hymn, more must be said about the other dimensions and especially the biblical dimension of hymns. Hymns that have a clear grounding in Scripture and employ the rich biblical imagery carry with them, even if subliminally, a wealth of powerful thoughts and feelings. A hymn's consistency with revealed truth is determined not by subjective opinions but by sound hermeneutics involving linguistic, grammatical, literary, historical, contextual, and practical principles of biblical hermeneutics. The biblical "voice" in a "polyphonic" hermeneutics is intricately related especially with the theological, liturgical, and historical dimensions ("voices"), and any valid hermeneutics should explore that interrelatedness. This may be illustrated in an interpretation of the hymn "Of the Father's love begotten."

"Of the Father's love [soul] begotten" and "Of the Father's heart begotten" are translations of the Spanish-born, Roman Christian poet Aurelius Clemens Prudentius's (c. 348–c. 410) great hymn, "*Corde natus ex Parentis*," taken from his *Liber Cathemerinon* beginning "*Da puer plectrum.*" The hymn is a biblical, theological, poetic statement of orthodox Christian doctrine and appropriate in a variety of liturgical contexts.

To appreciate better the biblical bases of the theological statements of the poet, some understanding of the historical context is helpful. The hymn grows out of a time of state cults, Hellenistic philosophies, Judaism, mystery cults, heresies, renewed paganism, and general theological upheaval. Diocletian's bloody persecution of Christians had occurred 303–311, but in 311 Constantine had issued his edict of toleration. In 409 the Visigoths occupied the Iberian Peninsula, and in 410, about the time of Prudentius's death, Rome fell to the Goths and was sacked. Neoplatonism and Manichaeism were so popular that Prudentius's contemporary, Augustine of Hippo (354–430), was attracted by one and then the other before being converted in 385 under the preaching of Ambrose (c. 340–397) and becoming one of the shapers of the theology of the Latin-speaking portion of the Catholic Church. John Chrysostom (c. 345–407), the great preacher in the Greek

Church, also lived in these troubled times and gave eloquent expression of the faith. The Catholic Church had begun with the conviction that Christians should be united in one body and was faced in the early centuries with the problem of determining exactly the essentials of the faith of this one body while meeting the challenges of the heresies of Gnosticism, the mystery cults, Marcionites, Montanism, and, especially, the rise of Arianism. The first Ecumenical Council at Nicea in 325 (only twenty-three years before Prudentius) dealt with the Arian heresy. The Church Father, theologian, and contemporary of Prudentius, Athanasius of Alexandria (296/298–373), was one of the principal defenders of Christian Orthodoxy against Arianism.

During Prudentius's lifetime, in 367, we have the first complete list of the twenty-seven books of the New Testament. The Council of Constantinople (381), which condemned the views of Apollinaris, was also during Prudentius's lifetime. The Cappadocian Fathers, Basil the Great (330–379), Gregory of Nyssa (330–395), and Gregory of Nazianzus (329–389), who contributed to early Christian theology, especially the doctrine of the Trinity, were contemporaries of Prudentius. Monasticism was spreading in both eastern and western portions of the Roman Empire. Buildings were being erected for public worship. Books for public and private devotion had been coming into existence. A professional and hierarchical clergy was evolving. Early on, Christian worship had centered in the Lord's Supper/ Eucharist using the psalms of Judaism. Soon, Christian writers began composing their own hymns. Liturgies were developing. The fourth-century Te Deum and the hymns of Ambrose were being written. Hilary, Bishop of Poitiers (c. 310–366), seems to have been the first to bring the Greek models of hymnody to the West and to use them in presenting Trinitarian doctrines against the Arian heresy. Ambrose, Bishop of Milan, about the same time, adopted antiphonal singing in the Western church in complement to the direct and responsorial psalm singing and metrical hymnody.

In this turbulent and formative historical context when the church was wrestling with the relation of Jesus to God and the place of Jesus in God's plan for the salvation of humanity, Prudentius wrote his biblical, theological, poetic statement of orthodox Christian doctrine about the nature of Christ. The hymn's startling spectrum of biblically based theology is reflected in the translation by John Mason Neale (1818–1866), which was edited and extended by Henry Williams Baker (1821–1877), and in the translation by Roby Furley Davis (1866–1937), which he made for the 1906 *English Hymnal.* The Trinity referred to in Prudentius's Latin hymn is ignored by Davis in his translation of the ninth stanza. The "Father" and "the Holy

Ghost" are mentioned in different stanzas, but the "trinity" referred to in his translation is "Earth and sky and boundless ocean, / Universe of three in one," which Prudentius refers to as "*trina*."

The hymn abounds in allusions to Scripture and is a profound Trinitarian and Christological expression that opens with what is nearly a quote of John 3:16, which is considered by many to be an encapsulation of the gospel. The first three stanzas of the Neale/Baker translation are in the third person speaking of Christ. Stanza 1 speaks of the eternal nature of Christ (Rev 1:8; 21:6; 22:13) and his being the source of all things (John 1:1-2). Stanza 2 continues the thought of stanza 1 and Christ's role in all of creation (John 1:3, 10). Stanza 3 sings of Christ's incarnation (John 1:14 and Phil 2:5-8) and his death to redeem humankind (1 John 2:2; 4:10). The fourth stanza tells of the conception and birth of the Saviour (Luke 2) and the world's redeemer (Matt 1:20; Luke 1:30-35; 2:7; Acts 5:30-31). The fifth stanza calls the heights of heaven, angel host, powers and dominions on earth, and every tongue to join in extolling our God and King (Phil 2:9-10; Rev 5:11-13). Stanza 6 exclaims that this Christ, the one promised by the Old Testament prophets, is now with us, and it calls creation to praise its Lord (Acts 3:18-21). The seventh stanza is the first to address Christ directly, the righteous King and judge of all sinners (Deut 32:41-43; Ps 94:1; Isa 34:8; Luke 21:22; Rom 12:19; Heb 10:30). The eighth, a sequel to the fifth, is a call for old men, young men, and boys to sing in chorus to be answered (in ages that parallel the male voices) by matrons, virgins, little maidens with their guileless song and music of the heart. The final stanza, added by Neale, is a great hymn of praise to the Trinity in the New Testament language of Philippians 2:9-11; Revelation 1:6; and 5:11-13. The "evermore" ("*Saeculorum saeculis*") chimes eighteen times throughout the hymn, affirming the eternal existence of Christ before the worlds began and for evermore. In the Christian view, this is not simply a *chronos* measuring of the quantity of time but also a *kairos* measured by the great *kairoi* or quality of time including the preexisting Christ, the creation, the prophecies, the incarnation, the redemption, the final judgment, and evermore. This hymn is a powerful and biblically consistent expression of a breadth of Christian theology.

The hymn generally focuses on the creation, the incarnation of Christ, and the praise of the triune God. The redeeming act of Christ is proclaimed in the lines, "That the race of Adam's children / Doomed by law to endless woe, may not henceforth die and perish / In the dreadful gulf below," but one might wish, simply in the interest of a more comprehensive exposition of the life and work of Christ in one hymn, for more explicit references to

Christ's resurrection and even second coming. Prudentius's thinking about the doctrine of the incarnation and about the doctrine of the Trinity on which he focuses more in his apologetic poem, "Apotheosis," show the impact of the second- and third-century theologian, Tertullian, who indeed powerfully influenced all of Christian thinking.

As a profound statement on the incarnation, it is considered to be one of the great Christmas hymns. Routley, writing about the hymn, refers to "the richness of one of the season's profoundest and greatest hymns."[32] Actually, the breadth of thought makes the hymn appropriate for a vast number of other liturgical and non-liturgical uses.

Though there is a logical progression through the stanzas, each stanza can stand alone as a profound statement itself, especially as a response to Scripture reading or devotional thoughts. Nine stanzas are admittedly long for a hymn by today's standards, but the stanzas might be sung or read at different points in the liturgy, by different individuals and groups, or even at different times in the church year. While the whole hymn is about and to Christ, the individual nature of each stanza suggests possible different vocal media for and musical interpretation of the stanzas, not simply for variety but also for the possibility of highlighting the distinctive ideas of the hymn.

Latin text by Prudentius (348–c. 410)[33]	Translation by Roby Furley Davis, for *The English Hymnal* (1906)[34]	Translation by J. M. Neale, extended by Henry W. Baker (1851/1861)[35]
Corde natus ex parentis	Of the Father's heart begotten,	Of the Father's love begotten,
Ante mundi exordium	Ere the world from chaos rose,	Ere the worlds began to be,
A et O cognominatus,	He is Alpha, from that Fountain	He is Alpha and Omega,
ipse fons et clausula	All that is and has been flows;	He the source, the ending He,
Omnium quae sunt, fuerunt,	He is Omega, of all things,	Of the things that are, that have been,
quaeque post futura sunt.	Yet to come the distant Close,	And that future years shall see,
Saeculorum saeculis.	Evermore and evermore.	Evermore and evermore!
Ipse iussit et creata,	By His word was all created	At His Word the worlds were framèd;
dixit ipse et facta sunt,	He commanded and 'twas done;	He commanded; it was done:

Terra, caelum, fossa ponti,	Earth and sky and boundless ocean,	Heaven and earth and depths of ocean
trina rerum machina,	Universe of three in one,	In their threefold order one;
Quaeque in his vigent sub alto	All that sees the moon's soft radiance,	All that grows beneath the shining
solis et lunae globo.	All that breathes beneath the sun,	Of the moon and burning sun,
Saeculorum saeculis.	Evermore and evermore.	Evermore and evermore!
Corporis formam caduci,	He assumed this mortal body,	He is found in human fashion,
membra morti obnoxia	Frail and feeble, doomed to die,	Death and sorrow here to know,
Induit, ne gens periret	That the race from dust created,	That the race of Adam's children
primoplasti ex germine,	Might not perish utterly,	Doomed by law to endless woe,
Merserat quem lex profundo	Which the dreadful Law had sentenced	May not henceforth die and perish
noxialis tartaro.	In the depths of hell to lie,	In the dreadful gulf below,
Saeculorum saeculis.	Evermore and evermore.	Evermore and evermore!
O beatus ortus ille,	O how blest that wondrous birthday,	O that birth forever blessèd,
virgo cum puerpera	When the Maid the curse retrieved,	When the virgin, full of grace,
Edidit nostram salutem,	Brought to birth mankind's salvation	By the Holy Ghost conceiving,
feta Sancto Spiritu,	By the Holy Ghost conceived,	Bare the Saviour of our race;
Et puer redemptor orbis	And the Babe, the world's Redeemer	And the Babe, the world's Redeemer,
os sacratum protulit.	In her loving arms received,	First revealed His sacred face,
Saeculorum saeculis.	Evermore and evermore.	evermore and evermore!
Psallat altitudo caeli,	Sing, ye heights of heaven, his praises;	O ye heights of heaven adore Him;
psallite omnes angeli,	Angels and Archangels, sing!	Angel hosts, His praises sing;
Quidquid est virtutis usquam	Wheresoe'er ye be, ye faithful,	Powers, dominions, bow before Him,

psallat in laudem Dei,	Let your joyous anthems ring,	and extol our God and King!
Nulla linguarum silescat,	Every tongue his name confessing,	Let no tongue on earth be silent,
vox et omnis consonet.	Countless voices answering,	Every voice in concert sing,
Saeculorum saeculis.	Evermore and evermore.	Evermore and evermore!
Ecce, quem vates vetustis	This is he, whom seer and sibyl	This is He Whom seers in old time
concinebant saeculis,	Sang in ages long gone by;	Chanted of with one accord;
Quem prophetarum fideles	This is he of old revealed	Whom the voices of the prophets
paginae spoponderant,	In the page of prophecy;	Promised in their faithful word;
Emicat promissus olim;	Lo! he comes the promised Saviour;	Now He shines, the long expected,
cuncta conlaudent eum.	Let the world his praises cry!	Let creation praise its Lord,
Saeculorum saeculis.	Evermore and evermore.	Evermore and evermore!
Macte iudex mortuorum,	Hail! thou Judge of souls departed;	Righteous judge of souls departed,
macte rex viventium,	Hail! of all the living King!	Righteous King of them that live,
Dexter in Parentis arce	On the Father's right hand throned,	On the Father's throne exalted
qui cluis virtutibus,	Through his courts thy praises ring,	None in might with Thee may strive;
Omnium venturus inde	Till at last for all offences	Who at last in vengeance coming
iustus ultor criminum.	Righteous judgement thou shalt bring,	Sinners from Thy face shalt drive,
Saeculorum saeculis.	Evermore and evermore.	Evermore and evermore!
Te senes et te iuventus,	Now let old and young uniting	Thee let old men, thee let young men,
parvulorum te chorus,	Chant to thee harmonious lays	Thee let boys in chorus sing;
Turba matrum, virginumque,	Maid and matron hymn thy glory,	Matrons, virgins, little maidens,
simplices puellulae,	Infant lips their anthem raise,	With glad voices answering:

Voce concordes pudicis	Boys and girls together singing	Let their guileless songs re-echo,
perstrepant concentibus.	With pure heart their song of praise,	And the heart its music bring,
Saeculorum saeculis.	Evermore and evermore.	Evermore and evermore!
Tibi, Christe, sit cum Patre	Let the storm and summer sunshine,	Christ, to Thee with God the Father,
hagioque Pneumate	Gliding stream and sounding shore,	And, O Holy Ghost, to Thee,
Hymnus, decus, laus perennis,	Sea and forest, frost and zephyr,	Hymn and chant with high thanksgiving,
gratiarum actio,	Day and night their Lord alone;	And unwearied praises be:
Honor, virtus, victoria,	Let creation join to laud thee	Honour, glory, and dominion,
regnum aeternaliter.	Through the ages evermore,	And eternal victory,
Saeculorum saeculis.	Evermore and evermore.	Evermore and evermore!

Both the Neale/Baker and the later Davis translations exploit poetic language to underscore the biblical and theological concepts. Like the Latin, both translations are in trochaic meter with its directness of thought, excitement, and decisiveness and their 8.7.8.7.8.7.7 hymnic meter honors the 8's and 7's of Prudentius. Both employ a stately cross rhyme. Both translations make use of figures of speech. Davis's use of the word "heart" (nearer Prudentius's "corde") is more metaphorical in its implicit comparison to "love," even metonymic with its substitution of the word for "love," which is closely associated with it, or even more specifically as a synecdoche as a type of metaphor with "heart" being used for the whole nature of God. The biblical "alpha" and "omega" are familiar metaphors for the first and last. In the third stanza, Davis makes a beautiful use of a double alliteration in "Frail and feeble, doomed to die" to undergird the weakness and destiny of humankind and the bodily form that Christ stooped to assume. The chiming epimone, "evermore and evermore," is effectively used in both translations.

On a larger poetic scale, the first six stanzas make extensive use of antonomasia, epithets or other indirect description, rather than addressing Christ directly or referring to him by name. Christ is addressed in the seventh stanza, but not until the final stanza is Christ called by name. These nine stanzas of the hymn may, in one macro aspect of form, be thought of as something of an arch form with the "central" fifth stanza being the apex of the arch with its call to the "heights of heaven," "angel hosts," "powers," "dominions," "no tongue on earth be[ing] silent," and with "every voice" praising God the Son. The inner pillars of the fourth and six stanzas speak of Christ's conception and birth and of the prophecy of that birth. The pillars of the third and seventh stanzas refer to Christ's redemption of humankind and to his being its enthroned, exalted, righteous judge and King. The pillars of the second and eighth stanzas speak of the creation of heaven, earth, and depths of ocean and of the praise by the crown of God's creation, "old men," "young men," "boys," "matrons," "virgins," "little maidens." The outer first and ninth pillars speak of the eternal Son, born of love and of the Trinity. While no claim is made that this structure was in anyone's master plan, such might well have been at least a subconscious manifestation of Prudentius's not insignificant poetic aesthetic, which some, like *The Oxford Dictionary of the Christian Church*, say had a "profound influence upon medieval poetry."[36] This concept may well affect the choices of media, volume, and even tempo in the singing of this entire hymn and be, for sensitive interpreters, one guide to performance.

The thirteenth-century DIVINUM MYSTERIUM tune with its original text[37] was a trope to the *Sanctus* of the Mass. The 1854 appearance of the tune in Neale and Helmore's *The Hymnal Noted* (London) was probably taken from the 1582 *Piae Cantiones*. It is a beautiful vehicle for the text, and the deceptive simplicity of the melody allows for subtle changes to accommodate what is in some printings a first stanza (using the first stanza of Prudentius) affirming the eternal love of of God manifested in the creative and redeeming work of Christ; the second (the third stanza of Prudentius) calling for all creation to bow and extol our God and King; and the third (the final stanza of Prudentius) exclaiming praise, thanksgiving, honor, glory, dominion, and eternal victory to the Trinity.

In the text and in the music, carefully sung, there is both a mood of awesome meditation and a mood of exultant joy. Six of the seven musical phrases begin with an ascending, almost sequential, line—a "musical rhetoric," a "musical anaphora." As in poetry and prose, this idea is used to iterate for emphasis. This melodic idea gives unity, sets off the textual phrases, and, occurring at four different pitch levels, gives variety. The penultimate phrase inverts the motion. Inversion of pitches is a common device in music and not unrelated to antistrophe in rhetoric. This penultimate phrase of the text in each stanza carries some significant continuance of thought as well as leading to the ultimate phrase, which musically returns to the ascending figure with the epimone, "evermore and evermore!" and then settles to the final of the Ionian mode.

A comprehensive and integrated hermeneutics of hymnody requires that any discussion of the text/tune relationship consider the vital role of the actual singing.[38] The text and tune can be sung in a logogenic, Gregorian chant style or in a metric and harmonized form. The different moods of the text may be underscored by different media (solo, women's voices, or men's voices, in a direct, responsorial, or antiphonal manner, or, as occurs in certain types of organum in the medieval period, with an organ or vocal "pedal point" or drone on the dominant and tonic in the lower voices). Alice Parker suggests an interesting possible performance of this hymn and tune using the seven musical phrases in various combinations of voices in unison, antiphonally, and with pedal points for singing each of the stanzas that have come to be used traditionally.[39]

Figure 2. Words: "Of the Father's love begotten," Aurelius Clemens Prudentius (348–c. 410), trans. John Mason Neale (1818–1866). Music: DIVINUM MYSTERIUM, 13th-century Latin plainsong, arr. Charles Winfred Douglas, Church Hymnal Corp. All rights reserved. Used by permission.

Notes

1. John 12:49, NIV, and Kurt Aland, Matthew Black, Carlo M. Martini, Bruce M. Metzger, and Allen Wikgren, eds., *The Greek New Testament*, 3rd ed. (New York: United Bible Societies, 1978).

2. Christ refers to the sun, rain, bread, moth, rust, eye, body, lamp, food, clothing, birds, barns, sowing, reaping, lilies, grass, dogs, swine, loaf, stone, fish, snake, gate, way, sheep, tree, wolves, fruit, grapes, bushes, figs, thistles, rain, floods, wind, sand, and rock.

3. Michael De-la-Noy, *Michael Ramsey: A Portrait* (London: Collins, 1990) 127.

4. "And did not Jesus sing a psalm that night" from Fred Pratt Green's, "When in our music God is glorified."

5. Michael O'Connor, "The Singing of Jesus," in Jeremy S. Begbie and Steven R. Guthrie, eds., *Resonant Witness: Conversations between Music and Theology* (Grand Rapids MI: William B. Eerdmans Publishing Company, 2011) 434–35.

6. Ibid., 436.

7. Ibid., 453.

8. Montgomery's "Hail to the Lord's Anointed!" is another example of the many texts that honor the larger meaning of the "Kingdom of Heaven."

9. See also Marcus Wells, "Translating Hymns," *Hymn Society of Great Britain & Ireland Bulletin* 17/6 (April 2004): 154–62.

10. E. W. Bullinger, *Figures of Speech Used in the Bible: Explained and Illustrated* (Grand Rapids MI: Baker Book House, 1898, reprinted 1968). Bullinger systematically presents 217 figures of speech used in the Bible, identifying the etymology, giving specific Scripture passages, and citing nearly eight thousand Biblical references.

11. The figurative language of hymnody is treated in more depth in chapter 5, "Poetry."

12. J. R. Watson, *The English Hymn: A Critical and Historical Study* (Oxford: Clarendon Press, 1997) 230.

13. B. L. Manning, *The Hymns of Wesley and Watts* (London: The Epworth Press, 1942) 60.

14. "Hark! The herald angels sing"

15. "Soldiers of Christ, arise"

16. The hymn is a translation from Welsh, and there have been several reworkings.

17. J. R. Watson, *The English Hymn: A Critical and Historical Study* (Oxford: Oxford University Press, 1999) 275–76.

18. One of Watts's most popular hymns, "Jesus shall reign," an "imitation" or "Christianizing" of Psalm 72, is in this collection.

19. More is said of this in chapter 4, where the term "liturgy" is taken in its etymological, historical, biblical, and theological meanings to include every aspect of Christian ministry—worship, discipleship, proclamation, and social service.

20. The practical application of hymns is discussed further in the chapter 4, "Liturgy" and chapter 8, "Practice."

21. Such works as Donald A. Spencer, *Hymn and Scripture Selection Guide: A Cross Reference of Scripture and Hymns with over 12,000 References for 380 Hymns and Gospel Songs* (Valley Forge: Judson Press, 1977) are helpful in finding scriptural references in hymn texts. A number of denominational hymnals include separate scriptural indexes to the hymns.

22. For example, Thomas Troeger's *Borrowed Light: Hymn Texts, Prayers, and Poems* gives general or specific Scriptures for all but 4 of the 134 hymns in his collection. A biblical reference can be cited for virtually every one of the 285 hymns in Timothy Dudley-Smith's collection, *A House of Praise*. Fred Pratt Green's *The Hymns and Ballads of Fred Pratt Green*, and Jaroslav J. Vajda's *Now the Joyful Celebrations* include indexes of Scripture texts.

23. Routley discusses the scriptural mosaic of Charles Wesley's "Love divine, all loves excelling" in *Hymns Today and Tomorrow* (New York: Abingdon Press, 1964) 45–46.

24. *A House of Praise*, 312.

25. Erik Routley, "A Collection of Hymns by Timothy Dudley-Smith," *The Hymn* 33/4 (October 1982): 262.

26. *A House of Praise*, 165.

27. *Hymnbook 1982: The Hymns together with Accompaniments from The Hymnal 1982* (New York: Church Hymnal Corporation, 1985), no. 391. Hereafter referred to as *Hymnbook 1982*.

28. *A House of Praise*, 437.

29. Ibid., 237.

30. "Come, O thou traveler unknown" is discussed in chapter 5.

31. Dietrich Bonhoeffer, *Letters and Papers from Prison*, enl. ed., Eberhard Bethge, trans. Reginald Fuller et al. (New York: Macmillan, 1972) 303.

32. Erik Routley, *Hymns Today and Tomorrow* (New York: Abingdon Press, 1964) 74.

33. "*Corde natus ex parentis*," http://en.wikipedia.org/wiki/Of_the_Father%27s _Heart_Begotten.

34. "Of the Father's Heart Begotten," *The English Hymnal* (London: Oxford University Press, 1906) no. 613.

35. "Of the Father's Love Begotten," *Cyber Hymnal*, http://www.hymntime.com/tch/ htm/o/f/t/ofthefat.htm.

36. F. L. Cross and E. A. Livingston, eds., *The Oxford Dictionary of the Christian Church* (Oxford: Oxford University Press, 1977) s.v. "Prudentius."

37. *The Hymnal 1982 Companion* notes, "Both the words and music of this trope appear in European manuscripts dating from as early as the tenth century, but Frost notes that 'in the earlier MSS. [DIVINUM MYSTERIUM] is a subsequent addition, and it belongs probably to the end of the thirteenth century'" (Maurice Frost, ed., *Historical Companion to Hymns Ancient and Modern* [London, 1962] 444).

38. Attention is given to this dimension in chapter 8, "Practice."

39. Alice Parker, *Creative Hymn-Singing* (Chapel Hill: Hinshaw Music, Inc., 1976) 10–11.

CHAPTER 3

Theology

The themes of Christian hymnody, the profound issues of human existence, are theological—dealing with the God-human relationship through Jesus Christ. Christian theology typically seeks, using primarily the Scriptures, to provide a coherent statement of the doctrines of the faith in ways that contribute to the culture's understanding and application of those beliefs and often with the intent of cultivating or affirming a commitment to and continuing growth in those beliefs. A hermeneutics of hymnody is based largely on a biblical hermeneutics—how a person, group, or denomination interprets the Scriptures that shape its theology. The emphasis in this study is not simply that the major doctrines of the Christian faith, however interpreted by a denomination, have found expression in hymns but also that the expression of these doctrines is bound up with the interrelated biblical, liturgical, literary, musical, practical, and historical dimensions of hymns.

The doctrines of Christian theology and in hymnody grow out of Scripture and usually center on the basic subjects of the Trinity, God, Jesus Christ, the Holy Spirit, creation, revelation, the Scriptures, man, sin, salvation, redemption, the church, and eschatology. Some aspects of these doctrines are complex, some elusive, and some seemingly paradoxical. Some people are oblivious to aspects of the doctrines and others simply avoid them. Through hymns, these basic doctrines and their many subtle aspects are often powerfully impressed on the minds and hearts of people not only because of their profound importance to human existence but also through the beauty of language, rhyme, rhythm, melody, repetition, and the singer's active physical, mental, emotional, and social involvement with other people in expressing a text. These make no small contribution to the impression of a doctrine on the minds and hearts of individuals.

The most common methods employed in the study of Christian theology are (1) biblical theology, in which exposition of doctrine is based on the exegesis of all relevant biblical texts on the doctrines; (2) historical theology, in which exposition of doctrine is based primarily on the formulation of the doctrines in post-biblical history; and (3) systematic theology, in which the exegesis is an orderly exposition that may be based on biblical and historical theology, and on non-biblical sources that relate to the doctrines. Each method or combination of methods is also usually concerned with seeking contemporary expression of the doctrines in different contexts, cultures, and traditions. Regardless of method, the subjects of Christian theology are the doctrines of the Christian church.

Christian hymnody, at its finest, is an artistic (literary and musical) expression of a breadth and depth of Christian theology treating the nature and work of God: his transcendence and immanence; his sovereignty and love; his attributes of omnipotence, omniscience, and omnipresence; and his acts of creation, revelation, redemption, and providential care of humanity. Hymnody reflects the work of historical, biblical, and systematic theology and is a great repository of statements on the teachings of the Christian church. Hymnody has often addressed these great teachings in powerful and memorable ways that have not only expressed the doctrines of the church but, in many cases, also shaped the theology of people through the centuries.[1] Again, it has often been said, "Let me write the hymns of the church and I care not who writes the theology."

While Christian believers may interpret the Scriptures differently and express their theology in different ways, there is a core of common beliefs and a core of hymnody with which believers of the many traditions basically agree. Each denomination, indeed each congregation by its selection and use of hymns, may emphasize different doctrines, have different biblical interpretations and expressions of theology, and have different literary and musical expressions of those interpretations. Regardless, most denominational hymnals are either organized by the basic doctrines of the Christian faith or, through a topical index, provide resources for understanding and expressing the great Christian doctrines.

Biblical and Religious Language and Hymnody

Theology, thinking coherently about the basic beliefs of the Christian faith and seeking to express them clearly and convincingly, immediately confronts one with the question of biblical and religious language. John Newport emphasizes the "validity and meaning of biblical language."

> The question of the meaning of religious and biblical language is an ultimate question because it is closely related to the question of authority. . . . for the evangelical, authority means biblical authority—the total truthfulness of the Scripture—for thought and life (2 Tim. 3:15-17). However, biblical authority cannot proceed very far without considering the validity and meaning of biblical language.[2]

R. W. Hepburn notes that religious language "crucially involves metaphor, symbol, analogy, parable, paradox" and "is, typically, language avowing the inexpressible, unconceptualizable nature of its object, or the indescribability of mystical experiences which nevertheless it strives to express!"[3] John Keble, professor of poetry at Oxford and well-known hymn writer, speaks in his lectures *Praelectiones Academicae*, "*De poeticae vi medica*" (and delivered in Latin) of "a hidden tie of kindship"[4] between poetry and religion when he notes, "Poetry lends Religion her wealth of symbols and simile: Religion restores these again to poetry, clothed with so splendid a radiance that they appear to be no longer merely symbols, but to partake (I might almost say) of the nature of sacrament."[5]

In the writing and choosing of hymns, one must be aware of the cultural[6] context of the people for whom hymns are written or chosen—how well they understand biblical/religious language, how their understanding and appreciation might be improved. A significant observation regarding form, language, content, and culture is made in the editors' explanation of their principles of translation for *Die Bibel: Die Gute Nachricht in heutigem Deutsch*:

> There are certainly cases in which the form of the text presents an essential element of the passage, of the contents. This is especially true with the picturesque language of the Bible and the poetic passages of the Old Testament. Here it is essential not only to reproduce the contents but also to find an appropriate equivalent for the form—the corresponding picture, the appropriate rhythm. Where the translation reproduces texts in verse form, it does not necessarily imitate the metric form of the original. Rather, it makes use of corresponding forms from our own cultural context, because our reaction to linguistic forms is conditioned precisely by this culture. Given our culture, translating the prophetic books into verse forms has been largely abandoned even though in the original most of the

prophetic statements are cast in meter. In ancient Israeli culture, poetic form gave statements an increased emphasis, while in our feeling about language it lends the character of subjectivity or even fabrication and that would precisely contradict the prophetic message.[7]

Precisely because our reaction to linguistic forms is conditioned by our culture, it is important that hymn writers, hymnal editors, and worship leaders have an understanding of the appropriate language, form, and content of hymns and of the larger and immediate cultural contexts of the users. The singers of hymns should, at least indirectly, benefit from this understanding.

Hymnic poetry often conveys the great Christian doctrines not so much in theoretical, abstract, or speculative ways as in biblical images and concrete pictures. Alan Richardson asserts, "it is obvious that all our language about God must be analogical."[8] The poetry of hymnody, seeking to communicate thoughts and feelings of the faith and to inspire the mind to soar above the limits of discursive prose, comes to its limits in expressing certain aspects of the faith and often resorts to special forms of language and especially to biblical language.

The biblical writers often resorted to the language of "negation" to express the inexpressible. In describing the nature and work of God, there are such phrases as "how unsearchable are his judgments, and unfathomable his ways!" (Rom 11:33), "Thanks be unto God for his unspeakable gift" (2 Cor 9:15), "Now unto the King eternal, immortal, invisible" (1 Tim 1:17), and "as seeing him who is unseen" (Heb 11:27). In speaking of humanity there are negative terms such as "unbelieving," "unclean," "unholy," "unfaithful," and "unjust." To express the inexpressible, hymns are often rich in the descriptive negatives of "unwearied," "unknown," "unutterable," "unbounded," "unquenched," "undimmed," "unceasing," "endless," "ceaseless," and "loveless." Alan Richardson asks, "If God can be described only by negatives [*via negationis*] (e.g. incorporeal, infinite, impassible, invisible, indescribable, etc.), can we be said to have any knowledge of God at all?"[9] In response to the criticism about *via negationis* and in an attempt to speak something positive about God, "there was developed *via eminentiae* by which it could be asserted that every characteristic of finite being, because it was being and to that extent real and possessing some degree of perfection, must bear some correspondence to infinite being . . . must contain in a supremely *eminent* way the qualities or degrees of being (or perfection) manifested in every finite being."[10]

Because God, faith, heaven, and the like are not perceived through the five senses, there are special challenges in the language we use to speak about Christianity. Richardson reminds us "that the dogma that nothing can be known to be true which is incapable of empirical verification is itself incapable of empirical verification."[11] Because our understanding of God's invisible attributes is often gained through his visible creation, our expression of those attributes is often made with reference to his visible creation. The apostle Paul affirms, "For since the creation of the world his invisible attributes, his eternal power and divine nature, have been clearly seen, being understood through what has been made, so that they are without excuse" (Rom 1:20).

Twentieth-century philosophy, particularly existentialism and linguistic analysis, has raised the problem of meaning in religious language. We must concede the mind's inability to conceive what God has pledged in his word unless God in his grace makes it known. Richardson calls attention to Barth's assertion of the *analogia fidei* or *analogia gratiae*, which emphasizes that "God of his sheer, uncoerced grace gives to men faith by which the truth of revelation is perceived. . . . God confers upon human language the capacity to speak meaningfully about him, but this speaking will always be a speaking from faith to faith, . . . never human achievement but always a divine gift."[12]

Amos Wilder, New Testament professor at Harvard, referred to "the stultifying axiom that genuine truth or insight or wisdom must be limited to that which can be stated in discursive prose, in denotative language stripped as far as possible of all connotative suggestion, in 'clear ideas,' in short, in statement of description of a scientific character."[13] The poetic language of hymnody, with all its "vows of renunciation,"[14] is often the powerful bearer of "genuine truth or insight or wisdom."

There is a phenomenal ability of poetry and music to make clear, to give the meaning, to facilitate understanding, to communicate thoughts and feelings of faith, and to inspire the mind to soar far above the limits of discursive prose. Having recognized the inability of discursive prose to communicate fully the wholeness of the Christian faith, many Christians have found in the poetic language of hymnody an aid in their attempts both to comprehend and to express the inexpressible dimensions of religious experiences. In biblical times and throughout history, Christians have sought to move beyond the limits of discursive prose and denotative language into the connotative language, suggestion, beauty, memorableness, and force of hymnic poetry to express some of the profoundest theological truths of the Christian faith. The analogical, metaphorical, symbolic language of the art form of poetry has been called upon to help reveal truths about the spiritual situation. Paul Tillich notes, "Art indicates what the character of a spiritual situation is; it does this more immediately and directly than do science and philosophy for it is less burdened by objective considerations."[15]

Any discussion of religious language and hymnody must address the increasing attention in recent decades to the use of inclusive language in hymnody. This has been concerned primarily with gender, though contemporary Christian hymnody manifests concerns for inclusivity of language about those in situations of social injustice, poverty, hunger, and numerous forms of oppression. It may well be argued that the "maleness" in the language and in the visible leadership of Christianity does not adequately reflect the full nature of God, the fellowship of the church, or the powerful (though often less visible) role and leadership of women. While most recognized hymn writers have been men, women hymn writers have made and increasingly make powerful contributions to hymnody: Sarah Flower Adams, Cecil F. Alexander, Margaret Clarkson, Fanny Crosby, Carol Doran, Sylvia Dunstan, Charlotte Elliot, Francis Ridley Havergal, Annie S. Hawks, Karen Lafferty, Mary A. Lathbury, Elizabeth Prentiss, Betty Pulkingham, Anne Steele, Susan Toolan, and Anna L. Waring to name only a few.

In *Duty and Delight: Routley Remembered*,[16] a conversation among Fred Pratt Green, Fred Kaan, Brian Wren, and Robin A. Leaver touches on the variety of approaches to the issue of inclusive language. It did not go unnoticed by the participants that the discussion was among four men, but they were men sensitive to the issue and represented a large number of contemporary writers who show a similar sensitivity in their writing. Some have even rewritten portions of their hymns to use more inclusive language. Brian Wren has been open to feminine language for God, Fred Kahn perhaps more moderate in his approach, and Fred Pratt Green probably more conservative. Green affirmed, "I do think that the use of 'mankind' and 'man' is extremely misleading in hymnody," but also said, "to go too far in this direction is going to destroy something that belongs to the tradition of the church from the beginning. It is likely to create difficulties for a great number of people and will tend rather to weaken Christianity in the end than to strengthen it. I feel this quite strongly. What must logically follow, surely, is the rewriting of the Bible as well as of hymns?"

The issue is not only language about the people of God; it's also about the language for God himself. Less attention has been given to the Bible's use of feminine language when speaking of the nature of God. In her article, "Feminine Images for God: What Does the Bible Say?"[17] Margo G. Houts identifies numerous passages in which the Bible uses feminine language when speaking of God.[18] The images in these passages may appear with increasing frequency in future hymnody. There is a real need for more inclusive language in contemporary hymnody, language that reflects a better balance of the nature of God, the fellowship of the church, and the increasing role and visibility of women in Christianity.

Religious Language as Determinants of Theology

Fine hymns in their varied uses of religious language are not only *expressions* of our theology but are often *determinants* of it, especially for many who never study theology systematically or in any significant depth, and yet week by week have it presented in clear, powerful, memorable ways through carefully worded texts and skillfully composed music. The power of hymns to determine theology can also be frightening. It is all too easy by clever words and appealing music to insinuate a misguided or heretical theology. S. Paul Schilling, Professor of Systematic Theology Emeritus at Boston University School of Theology, has wisely reminded us that

> Not all of the discords in church music are struck audibly by singers and accompanists. Many are produced by theological concepts out of harmony with Christian truth, by religious ideas contradictory to the actual experiences and beliefs of the worshipers, by unexamined clichés, or by words that lack any clear meaning whatever.[19]

Even some fine hymns include lines that can be misleading. The fourth stanza of Elizabeth Clephane's hymn "Beneath the cross of Jesus" reads in some hymnals as "Two wonders I confess, —the wonder of redeeming love, And my own worthlessness." Most modern hymnals observe the more biblical theology of ". . . And my unworthiness." Some hymnals print the wording in Joachim Neander's "Praise to the Lord, the Almighty" to include "Ponder anew what the Almighty can do, if with His love He befriend thee" while others read "who with his love doth befriend thee." Frederick Faber's "There's a wideness in God's mercy" includes, in many hymnals, the stanza that reads "If our love were but more simple, / We should take Him at His word; / And our lives would all be sunshine / In the sweetness of our Lord," which can be misleading especially to the young.[20]

While most traditions generally agree with a common body of Christian theology, there are numerous facets of theology that are viewed quite differently in the traditions, and hymns reflect this. Some hymns may be interpreted in such a way as to satisfy somewhat different perspectives, and this may not necessarily be a weakness given that some Scriptures have that same possibility. The point remains that the theology of each hymn is a matter of primary importance and must be carefully expressed by the writer, carefully examined by the publisher, carefully taught by the teachers, carefully chosen by the worship leaders, and carefully sung by the congregation.

The responsibility of worship leaders is to offer breadth, depth, and, primarily, accuracy of theology. While a hymn chosen for private meditation may contain words, phrases, or even stanzas with which the reader may have some reservations, such hymns might not be as acceptable to publishers of denominational hymnals or chosen by those who select hymns for worship. There is certainly no justification for selecting a hymn for public worship simply because of its appealing music or clever turn of phrase if the theology is questionable. Those who write and choose hymns for congregational use are faced with an unusual challenge of dealing with the subtleties of theology, the mysterious relationship between the essential truths of Christianity and religious language, and the challenge of providing the congregation with the basic teachings of the church in hymns that can be sung with the spirit and with the mind.

Theology and Hymns

The basic doctrines of the church may be presented to a congregation in hymns in the context of the liturgy.[21] There are hymns that express or interpret a single Christian doctrine, and there are hymns that convey a surprising sweep of the life of Christ and of Christian teaching such as "O Love, how deep, how broad, how high," often attributed to Thomas à Kempis (1380–1471).[22]

The Apostles' Creed comes close to being a comprehensive, concise, and generally accepted expression of the essential truths of Christianity. Timothy Dudley-Smith's "We believe in God the Father" is the only metrical version of a creed that the General Synod approved for use as an Authorized Affirmation of Faith in the public worship of the Church of England. The hymn can be sung affirmatively to a number of standard hymn tunes such as ABBOT'S LEIGH.

We believe in God the Father,
    God Almighty, by whose plan

earth and heaven sprang to being,
 all created things began.
We believe in Christ the Saviour,
 Son of God in human frame,
virgin-born, the child of Mary
 upon whom the Spirit came.

Christ, who on the cross forsaken,
 like a lamb to slaughter led,
suffered under Pontius Pilate,
 he descended to the dead.
We believe in Jesus risen,
 heaven's king to rule and reign,
to the Father's side ascended
 till as judge he comes again.

We believe in God the Spirit;
 in one church, below, above:
saints of God in one communion,
 one in holiness and love.
So by faith, our sins forgiven,
 Christ our Saviour, Lord and Friend,
we shall rise with him in glory
 to the life that knows no end.[23]

Hymns can be found for every major Christian doctrine and for most, if not all, of the various aspects of those doctrines. Martin E. Marty concludes his article, "The Phenomenology of Hymnody," by saying "One can pick almost any basic Christian theme and find it in hymns."[24] The table of contents and the topical index in many of the finer hymnals indicate the broad spectrum of Christian doctrines and aspects of the Christian life that are addressed in hymns. Our concern at this point is simply to illustrate how the biblical and theological dimensions may be understood in their interrelatedness with the liturgical, literary, musical, practical, and historical dimensions and how these relationships may be used to make some objective evaluation of hymns.

Samuel Crossman's (1624–1684) "My song is love unknown" deals with a central theme of the Christian faith—our response to our Savior's suffering and redeeming love for humankind. The hymn was prefaced with Galatians 6:14,[25] "But may it never be that I would boast, except in the cross of our Lord Jesus Christ, through which the world has been crucified to me, and

I to the world," and is rich with biblical references and allusions regarding the atoning death of Christ on the cross.

The opening stanza speaks of the Savior's divine love in dying to redeem the lost. The Savior's love is that "greater love . . . that a man lay down his life for his friends" (John 15:13) and an "unknown" love in both the sense of "never seen before" and in that he "came unto his own, and his own received him not" (John 1:11).

The poetic form of the biblical/theological content lends significant beauty, force, and memorability to the understanding and expression of the doctrine of Christ's dying love to redeem the lost. Five times in the first stanza the word "love," a central concept of Christianity, is turned to show various facets of its meaning—our love, Christ's love, love that is shown to the loveless, that the loveless might be lovely. In this one stanza, poetic figures of mesodiplosis, antanaclasis, and alliteration serve the biblical theology. For the propitiation or forgiveness for our sin, Christ, in love, freely took frail flesh and died on the cross; this is an allusion to Philippians 2:5-8, an idea that continues through the second stanza with an allusion to Christ's own statements of his purpose in coming to earth in Luke 19:10; John 10:10; and Matthew 20:28. In the second stanza, Crossman, through the use of epizeuxis, "O my Friend, my Friend indeed," underlines an intimate relationship with Christ, alluding again to John 15:13, "Greater love has no one than this, that one lay down his life for his friends."

The third stanza alludes to both the "Hosannas" (Matt 21:9) at the triumphal entry on Palm Sunday and the "Crucify" (Mark 15:13-14) of Good Friday, both leading to the atoning death of Christ. This ambivalence of humanity continues in the fourth stanza where there is rejection of what Christ affirmed as an evidence of his Messiahship in healing the blind and the lame (Matt 11:5).

The fifth stanza continues the taunts of the crowd in calling for the release of Barabbas and the crucifixion of the "Prince of Life" (Matt 27:17-21; Acts 3:14-15) and, in contrast, hints of the Lamb of God opening not his mouth (Isa 53:7), but steadfastly facing suffering and death for his foes that they might have life more abundantly (John 10:10).

The sixth stanza refers to the Lord's exchange of the glories of heaven for the poverty of earth (Matt 8:20) and the burial of the crucified Lord in a borrowed tomb (Matt 27:59-61), exchanging heaven for the grave so that the lost might exchange the grave for heaven. The final stanza, like the first, is a song of praise for the incomparable love of Christ shown in his redeeming death.

The hymn is a profound and beautiful poetic expression of the great biblical, theological truth of the atonement. The expression is grounded firmly in clear references and allusions to Scripture, making it a model for that vital interrelation of the biblical and theological dimensions in great hymns. The liturgical uses of the hymn are obvious; the literary "techniques" perhaps less so (and this is testimony to Crossman's art), but a comprehensive and integrated hermeneutics of hymnody is sensitive to how anaphora, antanaclasis, mesodiplosis, alliteration, synecdoche, echphonesis, omission, irony, anadiplosis, and chiasmus combine in this hymn to give wings of beauty and flow to the biblical and theological concepts. The twentieth-century musical setting of John Ireland (1879–1962), LOVE UNKNOWN, properly sung, bears well the biblical, theological, and literary mood and meaning of this seventeenth-century text. The two-beat beginning gives emphasis to the important first words of the stanzas. There is a pleasing economy and balance in the rising and then falling figures. The cadence on the dominant in the fourth phrase is immediately answered by a lowered leading tone (subtonic, doubled in the soprano and bass) followed by a melodic sequence emphasizing key concepts in all seven stanzas where Crossman shifted to the four-beat rhythm. The melody and bass move interestingly in contrary motion except for the pleasing parallel 10ths in the second phrase, complementing the meaning of the texts.

My song is love unknown,
    My Savior's love to me,
Love to the loveless shown,
    That they might lovely be.
        O who am I,
That for my sake
        My Lord should take
Frail flesh and die?

He came from His blest throne
    Salvation to bestow;
But men made strange, and none
    The longed for Christ would know.
        But O! my Friend,
My Friend indeed,
        Who at my need
His life did spend.

Sometimes they strew His way,
  And His sweet praises sing;
Resounding all the day
  Hosannas to their King:
    Then "Crucify!"
Is all their breath,
And for His death
They thirst and cry.

Why, what hath my Lord done?
  What makes this rage and spite?
He made the lame to run,
  He gave the blind their sight,
    Sweet injuries!
Yet they at these
    Themselves displease,
And 'gainst Him rise.

They rise and needs will have
  My dear Lord made away;
A murderer they saved,
  The Prince of life they slay,
    Yet cheerful He
To suffering goes,
    That He His foes
From thence might free.

In life, no house, no home
My Lord on earth might have;
In death no friendly tomb
  But what a stranger gave.
    What may I say?
Heav'n was His home;
    But mine the tomb
Wherein He lay.

Here might I stay and sing,
  No story so divine;
Never was love, dear King!
  Never was grief like Thine.
    This is my Friend,
In Whose sweet praise

I all my days
Could gladly spend.

There is a profound breadth and depth of Christian theology expressed in the wealth of texts and tunes of great hymns across the centuries. Following are a few illustrations of how some of the theological concepts are expressed in the interrelated dimensions of a few hymns.

The Nature, Decrees, and Works of God

The doctrine of the Trinity figures significantly in hymnody. Often, entire hymns, such as "Come, thou almighty King" and "Eternal Father, strong to save" have a Trinitarian structure wherein the first stanza speaks of or is addressed to the Father, the second to the Son, the third to the Holy Spirit, and the fourth to the Trinity. Many hymns contain a single stanza that speaks of the Trinity as in what is often the fourth and final stanza of "Of the Father's love begotten,"—a prayer to the Trinity. Other hymns speak of or address one member of the Trinity as in Montgomery's, "O Spirit of the living God."

A primary theme in hymnody is the nature of God especially as the one who deserves our praise. The nature of God is expressed in a simple beauty of the early seventeenth-century hymn writer George Herbert's metrical version of Psalm 23, "The God of love my Shepherd is." This is no ponderous discourse on the nature of God but like the psalm, a personal and loving response to his eternal nature, to his presence and providential care, and to his forgiveness when we stray.

As in Psalm 23, first person personal pronouns abound, and the personal pronouns refering to God change at the mention of death from third person to second person, conveying both the transcendence and immanence of God. "The Lord" of the psalm is "The God of love" in the first line, and "thy sweet and wondrous love" in the final stanza emphasizes the nature of God as expressed in 1 John 4:8 and 16. There is a simple beauty in the little word "then" in stanza two where it suggests, more than a mere enumerating of events, a personal, caring sequence in God's providential care, and the metaphor of the shepherd is propelled through the stanza by the rhetorical device of zeugma where the verb "leads" serves the nouns in two prepositional phrases. In the final lines, the "forever" of the psalm, Herbert weaves God's "sweet and wondrous love" and the singer's praise into the charming couplet, "and as it never shall remove / So neither shall my praise." Cast in the most common of hymnic meters, there is a wealth of tunes that lend themselves to a variety of congregational expression of this text based on what may be the most beloved of the Psalms.

> The God of love my Shepherd is,
> And He that doth me feed;
> While He is mine and I am His,
> What can I want or need?
>
> He leads me to the tender grass,
> Where I both feed and rest;
> Then to the streams that gently pass:
> In both I have the best.
>
> Or if I stray, He doth convert,
> And bring my mind in frame,
> And all this not for my desert,
> But for His holy Name.
>
> Yea, in death's shady black abode
> Well may I walk, not fear;
> For Thou art with me, and Thy rod
> To guard, Thy staff to bear.
>
> Surely Thy sweet and wondrous love
> Shall measure all my days;
> And as it never shall remove
> So neither shall my praise.

Isaac Watts's eighteenth-century common-meter hymn "Our God, our help in ages past,"[26] based on Psalm 90:1-5, lauds the eternal nature and personal providence of "our God," "our help," "our hope," "our shelter," "our eternal home," "our defense"; employs the vivid imagery of "the stormy blast," "the shadow of thy throne," and "an ever-rolling stream"; uses consonant rhyme in "hope" and "help"; and draws on anaphora, alliteration, metonymy, metaphor, simile, and zeugma, weaving all into the service of his biblical theology.

The complex concepts of the omnipotence, omniscience, and omnipresence of God are celebrated in Walter Chalmers Smith's nineteenth-century hymn of praise,[27] "Immortal, invisible, God only wise," based on 1 Timothy

1:17 and alluding to Genesis 1; Psalm 90; and Daniel 7:9, 13. A cascade of negative comparatives and a concluding powerful paradox are significant features of the hymn. For the *English Hymnal*, Vaughan Williams appropriately selected the majestic tune ST DENIO (sometimes called JOANNA) for these words.

> Immortal, invisible, God only wise,
> in light inaccessible hid from our eyes,
> most blessed, most glorious, the Ancient of Days,
> almighty, victorious, thy great Name we praise.
>
> Unresting, unhasting, and silent as light,
> nor wanting, nor wasting, thou rulest in might;
> thy justice like mountains high soaring above
> thy clouds, which are fountains of goodness and love.
>
> To all life thou givest, to both great and small;
> in all life thou livest, the true life of all;
> we blossom and flourish, like leaves on the tree,
> then wither and perish; but nought changeth thee.
>
> Great Father of glory, pure Father of light,
> thine angels adore thee, all veiling their sight;
> all laud we would render: O help us to see
> 'tis only the splendor of light hideth thee.

Dudley-Smith's twentieth-century hymn also speaks of God throned in resplendent light (John 1:15; Rev 22:5) and brings God's transcendence and immanence into bold relief by a careful use of three prepositions—"beyond," "beside," and "within"—in the first three stanzas of his hymn, relating each of these to a person of the Trinity:

> God lies beyond us, throned in light resplendent,
>   Father eternal, source of all creation.
> To him in glory, timeless and transcendent,
>   High King of Ages, come with adoration.
>
> God walks beside us, born to be our neighbour,
>   died to redeem us, risen and ascended;
> love to the loveless, friend of all who labour,
>   Christ our Companion, till our days are ended.

God lives within us, breath and life instilling,
>   daily transforming ways of thought and seeing.
Spirit all-holy, all our spirits filling,
>   blow, Wind, about us! burn within our being.

God in three Persons, Trinity of splendor!
>   To God the Father, all in all sustaining,
and God the Saviour, adoration render,
>   with God the Spirit, One in glory reigning.[28]

In hymns such as these, biblical and theological concepts of the nature, decrees, and works of God are presented powerfully in concise and beautiful poetic language that lodges the ideas pleasantly and significantly in our memory and understanding.

Creation

God as the Creator is a basic Christian belief as affirmed in the Apostles' Creed, "I believe in God, the Father almighty maker of heaven and earth," and hymns often express this belief such as in "This is my Father's world," "All creatures of our God and King," and "The spacious firmament on high." Hymns frequently refer to various facets of creation: earth, sky, sun, moon, stars, morning, evening, harvest. They sometimes focus on humanity as the crown of creation and not only to God's creation of the world but also to his providential care and redemption of humanity. These hymns draw especially on Genesis 1 and 2, the Psalms, and John 1:1-3.

Watts, in "I sing the almighty power of God," as in his "Nature with open volume stands"[29] and others of his hymns, praises God the creator and here catalogues many (each having scriptural roots) of God's creations: mountains, seas, skies, sun, moon, stars, food, creatures, and then, in a joyous inability to enumerate the wonders, exclaims, "Lord, how thy wonders are displayed where'er I turn my eye." There are here allusions to the omnipotent ("almighty"), omniscient ("the wisdom that ordained"), omnipresent ("the Lord is forever nigh") care of God as Watts rejoices in both the reason and revelation of creation.

Revelation and the Word of God

The theology of God's revelation is intricately intertwined with creation, Christology, pneumatology, and Scripture, indeed with the whole concept of the Word. Isaac Watts's "Nature with open volume stands" is a powerful hymnic expression of what is called God's general or universal revelation in created nature, but also in what is called God's specific revelation of his redeeming love in the person of Christ. Watts affirms that while "nature with open volume stands to spread her Maker's praise abroad," it is "in the grace that rescued man his brightest form of glory shines" and it is "Here [in the cross] his whole name appears complete." This is God's supreme revelation. Watts heads the hymn "Christ Crucify'd; The Wisdom and Power of God" which is almost a quote of 1 Corinthians 1:24. Such theology, based on Scripture and clothed in beautiful, concise, and powerful poetic language provides congregations opportunities for understanding the doctrines of the Christian faith, affirming those doctrines, and expressing them in meaningful ways.

God the Son (Christology)

Christology, the doctrine of the person and work of Christ, is at the center of the Gospels, of Christianity, and of Christian hymnody. The centrality of the person of Christ is seen clearly in hymns such as "Of the Father's Love begotten" and Charles Wesley's "Christ, whose glory fills the skies" with its opening proclamation of the absolute supremacy of the transcendent Christ, the only light, the one whose glory fills the skies, the "true light" in John 1 and in Christ's own description of himself as "the light of the world" in John 8:12. In vivid, poetic, and biblical language, Wesley contrasts life-giving light with cheerless, joyless darkness, borrowing from Malachi 4:2 the phrase "The sun of righteousness,"[30] from Zechariah's hymn in Luke 1:78 the image of the "dayspring from on high,"[31] and from 2 Peter 1:19 the image of the "day star."[32] From such affirmations of the transcendence of Christ, the verbs move to the immanence of Christ: "arise," "be near," "in my heart appear." The second stanza presents the contrast of the personal, cheerless, joyless darkness: "Till Thy mercy's beams I see; / Till they inward light impart, / Glad my eyes, and warm my heart." The final stanza is a prayer for the Christ, the light, to "pierce the gloom," to fill with the "radiancy divine," and more and more to display himself "shining to the perfect day." The historical, biblical, theological, and literary facets of this hymn are intertwined with the liturgical in Wesley's use of the King James Version of the phrase "dayspring from on high" from the Benedictus that Wesley would have said or heard each day in *the Order for Morning Prayer in the Prayer Book.*

Christ, whose glory fills the skies,
    Christ, the true, the only Light,
Sun of Righteousness, arise,
    Triumph o'er the shades of night;
Dayspring from on high, be near;
Day-star, in my heart appear.

Dark and cheerless is the morn
    Unaccompanied by Thee;
Joyless is the day's return
    Till Thy mercy's beams I see;
Till they inward light impart,
Glad my eyes, and warm my heart.

Visit then this soul of mine,
    Pierce the gloom of sin and grief;
Fill me, Radiancy divine,
    Scatter all my unbelief;
More and more Thyself display,
Shining to the perfect day.

The huge number of Christmas carols and hymns and their enormous popularity attest to how firmly they have, for centuries, fixed the incarnation of Christ into the minds and hearts of people all across the world. The hymns for the annual seasons of Advent, Christmas, and Epiphany have established themselves in our cultures. Though the theological term "incarnation" is not often encountered in hymns, society is confronted regularly with Christ's incarnation, God's supreme revelation of himself, Christ's coming in human flesh, his teaching, preaching, healing, death, resurrection, ascension, and the promise of his coming again, all of which are the hope of our faith and are powerfully expressed in numerous familiar hymns.

Hymns such as F. Bland Tucker's "All praise to Thee, for Thou, O King Divine" speak of the humanity of Christ. The opening line and the final two stanzas affirm Christ's deity, but the remainder of the first stanza and all of stanzas 2 and 3 are a hymn of praise, drawn from Philippians 2:5-11, Christ's *kenosis* or self-emptying, taking upon himself the form of a servant, humbling himself, "becoming obedient to the point of death, even death on a cross." The *kenosis* of Christ is also beautifully expressed in Wesley's "And can it be" in the line, "Emptied Himself of all but love."

All of the major events in the life of Jesus have been celebrated in hymns—his baptism, temptation, teachings, healings, miracles, transfiguration, triumphal entry, betrayal, arrest, trial, crucifixion, burial, resurrection, post-resurrection appearances, ascension, and his coming again. In these central doctrines of the Christian faith, the Bible and theology converge in the poetry of hymns in ways that convey theology powerfully and memorably.

God the Holy Spirit—Pneumatology

Hymns frequently refer to Jesus's last supper with his disciples and the following discourses where he spoke at length about the promised Holy Spirit and his work (John 14:16-30; 16:5-15). The day of Pentecost and the Holy Spirit's filling God's people in a new and powerful way have given rise to a wealth of hymns for that season of the liturgical year. Numerous hymns have drawn from the traditional lists of the "gifts of the Holy Spirit" in the New Testament (Rom 12; two lists in 1 Cor 12; and Eph 4) and from the list of nine aspects of the fruit of the Spirit (Gal 5:22-23) that give insight into the work of Christ that is to be continued in the church through the Holy Spirit.

"Like the murmur of the dove's song" by Carl P. Daw, Jr., is a refreshing hymn on the Holy Spirit using the images of Pentecost as recorded in Acts 2 and with allusion to Matthew 3:16, where, immediately after the baptism of Jesus, "the heavens were opened, and he saw the Spirit of God descending as a dove and lighting on Him." The dove has become a traditional symbol of the Holy Spirit. The first stanza with its fourfold similes is a prayer that the Holy Spirit come "like the murmur of the dove and like the challenge of her flight," and it continues with the Pentecostal images of wind and flame, "like the vigor of the wind's rush, like the new flame's eager might." The second stanza is a prayer for the church using the images of the body (1 Cor 12), Christ's figure of the vine and branches in John 15, and of the gift and sign in Hebrews 2:4. Here four anaphoric prepositional phrases using the word "to" introduce each phrase before the epimone, "come, Holy Spirit, come." The third stanza is a prayer using four anaphoric prepositional phrases introduced by the word "with," praying that the Holy Spirit come "with the healing of division, with the ceaseless voice of prayer, with the power to love and witness, and with peace beyond compare" (Phil 4:7). Daw has shared that the opening line comes from the Belgian Catholic priest Louis Evely's book, *A Religion for Our Time*, and the observation that "the image of the dove was chosen . . . because of the moan. The dove murmurs all the time." This may have also suggested Daw's line "with the ceaseless voice of prayer." The overall form is a beautiful balance.[33]

Peter Cutts's tune BRIDEGROOM,[34] for which Daw wrote this text, is vastly different from his SHILLINGFORD, written for Brian Wren's "Jesus on the mountain peak" in a dissonant, non-diatonic, yet tonal style and also from his WILDE GREEN with its diatonic melody but dissonant accompaniment. BRIDEGROOM begins with a "lush" dominant 11th chord and uses a more romantic, chromatic harmony with secondary dominants to the dominant and the subdominant and an augmented sixth chord. The repeat of the 8 7 meter of the text is essentially a sequence of the first 8 7 lines, but ascends to the melodic climax for which Daw has given the words "like the new flame's eager might" in the first stanza, "to her midst as gift and sign" in the second, and "with the peace beyond compare" in the third. The concluding phrase in the contrasting 6 meter for the epimone "come, Holy Spirit, come" is introduced with a rhythmic shift of a hemiola, slowing down the pace, and the only dotted quarter and an eighth note rhythm and the only neumatic setting in the hymn on the word "Spirit" in each stanza. It has been suggested that the first musical phrase of each stanza could be sung by one group, the second phrase by a different group, and the final phrase by all.

> Like the murmur of the dove's song,
>   like the challenge of her flight,
> like the vigor of the wind's rush,
>   like the new flame's eager might:
>   Come, Holy Spirit, come.
>
> To the members of Christ's body,
>   to the branches of the Vine,
> to the church in faith assembled,
>   to her midst as gift and sign:
>   Come, Holy Spirit, come.
>
> With the healing of division,
>   with the ceaseless voice of prayer,
> with the power to love and witness,
>   with the peace beyond compare:
>   Come, Holy Spirit, come.

Ecclesiology—The Doctrine of the Church

Ecclesiology has, historically, figured significantly in hymnody, and the renewed theological interest in the doctrine of the church in the last decades has given rise to a new wave of these hymns by some of the finest of contemporary hymn writers. Hymnals often devote entire sections to the topic and the ministries of the church. Many of those hymns draw upon the biblical imagery of the kingdom, of Zion, Jerusalem, the Body of Christ, and the Bride of Christ. Hymns on the church, ranging from the seventh century to our own time, include John Mason Neale's translations, "Christ is made the sure foundation" and "Blessed city, heavenly Salem," of the seventh-century Latin hymns; the paraphrase of Psalm 84, "How lovely is thy dwelling place, O Lord of hosts," that appeared in *The Psalms of David in Meter*, 1650; John Newton's "Glorious things of thee are spoken"; Timothy Dwight's "I love thy kingdom, Lord"; Samuel Stone's "The church's one foundation";[35] Charles Wesley's "Let saints on earth in concert sing"; Harry Emerson Fosdick's "God of Grace and God of Glory"; Fred Pratt Green's "When the Church of Jesus shuts its outer door"; Brian Wren's "We are your people"; and Timothy Dudley-Smith's "Here within this house of prayer."

Anthropology—The Doctrine of Humanity

Christian hymnody deals often with the basic biblical, theological doctrine of the God-human relationship through Jesus Christ. A wide range of the dimensions of this relationship (creation in the image of God [imago dei], the fallen nature of humanity, sin [harmartiology], Christ's redemption of sinful humanity and doctrines related to it [soteriology], propitiation, grace, salvation, justification, sanctification, glorification, ministry, fellowship, and eternal life) finds expression in hymns. The doctrine of humanity created in the image of God (Genesis 1:26-27), "made a little lower than the heavenly beings [God]," "crowned with glory and majesty" (Psalm 8:5), is given less emphasis. Any emphasis should certainly not be to the neglect of the greater emphasis on the majesty of God, but there is every reason to celebrate the gift of our being created in the image of God and the stewardship we have been given of his creation. While most hymns based on Psalm 8 emphasize only the majesty of God, Dudley-Smith's "How great our God's majestic name" holds the two concepts in balance and honors the wording of Psalm 8. His third stanza reads,

And what of us? Creation's crown,
    Upheld in God's eternal mind;
On whom he looks in mercy down
    For tender love of humankind.[36]

Hymns frequently do address the multifaceted topic of Christian stewardship—of time, abilities, money, and, increasingly, the earth and ecology. An example of the topic of humanity's stewardship and the intersection of the multiple dimensions of hymnody may be seen in Dudley-Smith's "The God who set the stars in space." The hymn was written on the invitation of Professor R. J. Berry, a former President of the English Ecological Society and Professor of Genetics at University College London. Berry had sought UK signatories for a 1994 call for environmental stewardship, "An Evangelical Declaration on the Care of Creation" issued by a group of evangelical Christian leaders in America. In 1997/8, Berry prepared for the publication of a "Critical and Appreciative Commentary" on the declaration and asked Dudley-Smith to contribute a hymn on the subject for a symposium titled "The Care of Creation." Dudley-Smith notes that his text "contains a number of direct echoes from the wording of the *Declaration* and moves towards a prayer that God will fulfill his purpose in Christ to bring reconciliation and wholeness to the entire created order (Col 1.19-20). The final reference is to Heb 1.10-12 describing how the earth and the heavens 'shall wax old as doth a garment. And as a vesture shalt thou fold them up and they shall be changed. . .' And in that day, which Paul calls 'the end' when Christ delivers up the kingdom to God the Father, we read in 1 Cor 15.28 that 'God shall be all in all.'"[37]

The God who set the stars in space
    and gave the planets birth
created for our dwelling place
    a green and fruitful earth;
a world with wealth and beauty crowned
    of sky and sea and land,
where life should flourish and abound
    beneath its Maker's hand.

A world of order and delight
    God gave for us to tend,
to hold as precious in his sight,
    to nurture and defend;

but yet on ocean, earth and air
   the marks of sin are seen,
with all that God created fair
   polluted and unclean.

O God, by whose redeeming grace
   the lost may be restored,
who stooped to save our fallen race
   in Christ, creation's Lord,
through him whose cross is life and peace
   to cleanse a heart defiled
may human greed and conflict cease
   and all be reconciled.

Renew the wastes of earth again,
   redeem, restore, repair;
with us, your children, still maintain
   your covenant of care.
May we, who move from dust to dust
   and on your grace depend,
No longer, Lord, betray our trust
   but prove creation's friend.

Our God, who set the stars in space
   and gave the planets birth,
look down from heaven, your dwelling place,
   and heal the wounds of earth;
till pain, decay and bondage done,
   when death itself has died,
creation's songs shall rise as one
   and God be glorified![38]

The text abounds in biblically based theological concepts not only of ecology but also of creation, fallen humanity, sin, the crucifixion, redemption, reconciliation, grace, death, and the end of time and alludes to the covenant (referenced from Gen 6:18 to Rev 11:19), to dust to dust (Gen 3:19), and to Colossians 1:19-20; Hebrews 1:10-12; and 1 Corinthians 15:28. The message is conveyed through literary devices of anaphora, alliteration, and oxymoron; through the consistent, but natural and non-obtrusive ababcdcd rhyme scheme; and through the majestic iambic meter. Sung to Ralph Vaughan Williams's KINGSFOLD, the hymn is a powerful Christian expression of a theological concept that is finding new emphasis in our day.

Eschatology

There is not a uniform understanding regarding the theological concepts of eschatology, the last things, the end of human history. Some use the terms "the last days" or "the day of the Lord" to refer to everything after the first coming of Jesus, and some use the terms to refer to Christ's coming again, raising the dead, and judging the world. Many anticipate the second coming of Christ as the culmination of time and the fulfillment of all that Christ taught and promised. Hymn writers are usually more concerned with the latter and have often drawn from the imagery of the "peaceable kingdom" of Isaiah 2 and the animals mentioned in chapter 11 as in "Behold the mountain of the Lord" from *Scottish Paraphrases* of 1781, George Wallace Briggs's "Christ is the world's true Light," and Carl P. Daw's hymn "O day of peace that dimly shines."[39]

Death and Heaven

Christian hymnody has, through history, addressed death and the attendant matters of judgment, heaven, and eternal life. It has spoken of the sorrow of death in its penalty for sin and its separation from loved ones. But in Christian hymnody there is also joy in that death is not final, because "death no more has dominion" (Rom 6:9) and we shall "see Him as he is," (1 John 3:2). Bernard of Cluny's twelfth-century hymn, "Jerusalem the golden," translated by John Mason Neale, borrows the Old Testament image of the promised land as "a land flowing with milk and honey" and the image of John's vision in Revelation ("golden lampstands," "golden sash," "golden crowns," "golden bowls," "golden censer," "golden altar") to say that the very thought of heaven is almost more than humankind can bear ("beneath thy contemplation sink heart and voice oppres'd") and that we cannot fathom the "joys," the "radiancy of glory," the "bliss beyond compare." The second stanza sings of the "halls of Zion" filled with songs, angels, the ransomed people, and martyrs. The writer uses a meaningful zeugma to say "the cross is all their splendor, the Crucified their praise." In the third and fourth stanzas, he makes ecstatic use of anaphora: "There is the throne of David / and there, from sin released, / the song of them that triumph, / the shout of them that feast, . . . There God, our King and Portion" and, in climax borrowing from 1 John 3:2, he exults "the fullness of his grace / shall we behold forever and worship face to face." This hymn may serve as a triumphant funeral hymn for a believer.

The biblical, theological, and liturgical dimensions of this hymn are borne well in the tune by the Scot Alexander Ewing. The tune has appeared under at least six different names, but is often called EWING for the composer. As a member of the Aberdeen Harmonic Choir, Ewing was familiar with the fine music of madrigals and anthems. His tune is excellent for this text with its judicious and singable mixture of steps and skips, the rise of the first and second phrases, and the descent of the third and fourth and the seventh and eighth phrases. The rise of the fifth and sixth phrases and the climax on the sixth is a beautiful complement to the text of each stanza. John Mason Neale remarked, "I have so often been asked to what tune the words of Bernard may be sung, that I may here mention that of Mr. Ewing, the earliest written, the best known, and with children, the most popular, no small proof in my estimation of the goodness of church music."[40] This hymn again illustrates the intersection of the multiple dimensions so necessary for a more thorough understanding of hymnody.

The Theological "Voice" in a "Polyphonic" Hermeneutics

Throughout history, Christian believers have developed a hymnody that expresses a breadth and depth of their theology and its biblical basis. Any valid hermeneutics of hymnody must examine that breadth and depth and the interrelatedness of the biblical-theological concepts if there is to be a more thorough understanding of the theology, proper evaluation of the text, and meaningful expression through the singing of the hymn. There is no justification for the liturgical use or for the literary or musical expression of ideas that are devoid of the biblical/theological basis of hymnody.

The writers of hymns come from a variety of theological perspectives, and editors, worship leaders, and the singers themselves often interpret the hymns from their own perspectives, but it may be argued that there should be some respect for at least understanding the writer's original meaning in the hymn. A valid hermeneutics of hymns calls for a careful, objective consideration of the various dimensions of hymnody and for their interconnectedness. Certainly, no attempt has been made here to discuss all of the many aspects of Christian theology, nor has any attempt been made to discuss the diverse theological positions on the various doctrines. What has been attempted is to show that the major doctrines of the Christian faith have found significant expression in hymnody and to show the importance and connection of the biblical and theological basis of Christian hymnody.

Luther's "Vom Himmel hoch" is one example of how the theological voice interrelates with the other voices in a polyphonic hermeneutics. Martin Luther's (1483–1541) place in Christian history and his place in the history of church music and hymnody are well documented.[41] The larger historical context of his life, work, and influence in Renaissance Europe is marked by powerful changes in science, literature, philosophy, politics, architecture, music, and certainly in the Christian world, especially in the rise and development of Lutheranism; the Catholic Reformation, the "Reformed" tradition of Zwingli, Calvin, and Beza (all of whom had various impacts on congregational singing); the radical movements (Anabaptists and Mennonites with their own forms of church music); Pietism (with its impact later even on the church music of J. S. Bach); and the English Reformation (in which English psalmody and hymnody flourished).

Luther saw hymns as a medium of congregational expression of worship and as a means of expressing and propagating his theological perspectives. Four of the eight hymns in the first hymnbook of the German reformation, the *Etlich Christlich lider [Lieder], Lobgesang/vñ Psalm*, published in Wittenberg in 1524, are by Luther. Throughout his life, Luther translated some eleven hymns from Latin, revised and enlarged another four from prereformation popular hymns, made some seven Psalm versions, some six paraphrases of other portions of the Bible, and composed some eight, mainly original hymns. Of the mainly original, but partly borrowed from Latin and popular material, is "Vom Himmel hoch, da komm ich her" that appeared first in the 1535 *Geistliche Lieder*, published in Wittenberg. The hymn was titled "Ein kinderlied auff die Weinacht Christi" ("a children's song for Christmas").

Luther's affirmation that Scripture alone is authoritative for Christian faith and practice (*sola scriptura*) meant that his hymns (translations, revisions, enlargements, paraphrases, and originally composed texts) were intended to be consistent with Scripture. In addition to the Psalm versions and paraphrases, his other hymns made direct or indirect reference to specific Scriptures. "Vom Himmel hoch" makes explicit references to Luke 2:10-15 in stanzas 1, 2, 5, and 6 and implicit reference to John 1:3 in stanzas 5 and 9 and to Philippians 2:6-8 in stanzas 5, and 8–10.

During his time at Wartburg castle (May 1521–March 1522) where he was taken for his protection by Elector Frederick, Luther translated the New Testament from Greek into German. His subsequent translation of the entire Bible and his constant polishing not only affirms his commitment to Scripture but also provided the literary history of Germany with a dignity, beauty, and degree of standardization. His hymns reflect that commitment to Scriptures, to clear and forceful theological expression, to liturgical usefulness, and to literary beauty. His musical settings of texts reflect the commitment to the art of music as a vehicle for biblical, theological, liturgical, and literary integrity.

It is interesting that in "Vom Himmel hoch, da komm ich her," a children's song for Christmas, Luther presented theological concepts of the virgin birth (st. 2), Jesus as Christ, God, Lord (st. 3), Son of God (st. 6), creator (st. 5 and 9), and Savior to set us free from sins (st. 3), and, in stanzas 5 and 8–10, an allusion to the *Kenosis* (self-emptying of Christ) all supported by explicit or implicit reference to Scripture, cast in words of literary quality, intended for a specific liturgical occasion, provided with his own musical setting, and, according to history, used in a most practical and dramatic way. Any comprehensive hermeneutics of the hymn requires some attention to these interrelated dimensions.

The biblical and theological facets of Luther's hymns are bound up with the liturgical and the great place he gave to worship and to congregational participation in worship. In the autumn of 1523, considering that there was a need both to create new forms of worship and to return to the simplicity of primitive Christian worship, Luther published his *Formula missae*, which became a basis for later Lutheran liturgies. This was followed in 1526 by the appearance of his *Deutsche Messe*, which included three different places for the singing of German hymns. Many of his hymns were intended for specific times in the liturgical year, and "vom Himmel hoch" may have even been written as a little family drama for a Christmas Eve celebration.

"Vom Himmel hoch" is in four basic sections. Stanzas 1–5 are the words of the angel. Stanzas 6–7 are the response of the worshipers. Stanzas 8–13 are addressed to the Christ child. Stanzas 14 and 15 are affirmations of praise (st. 14 with a hint of the Magnificat and st. 15 a sort of "Gloria in excelsis"). The basic iambic tetrameter, long meter, couplet rhyme is retained in Winkworth's 1855 translation as well as the basic meaning of the German with some poetic license. The hymn expresses subjective emotions in the personal pronouns "my," (st. 7, 8, 13, and twice in st. 14), "us," (st. 6), and "I" (st. 8, 14). Stanza 7 makes use of personification and stanza 10 in the subjunctive mood is a nice poetic emphasis to the *Kenosis* (self-emptying) of Christ referred to in Philippians 2:8.

> Were earth a thousand times as fair,
> beset with gold and jewels rare
> it yet were far too poor to be
> a narrow cradle, Lord, for Thee.

Stanza 11 continues the idea of stanza 10 and uses paradox to speak of the "hay and straw" instead of the "velvets soft and silken stuff" appropriate for "Thou, King so rich and great."

1. Vom Himmel hoch da komm ich her,	1. "From heaven above to earth I come[43]
Ich bring' euch gute neue Maehr,	To bear good news to every home;
Der guten Maehr bring ich so viel,	Glad tidings of great joy I bring,
Davon ich sing'n und sagen will.	Whereof I now will say and sing:
2. Euch ist ein Kindlein heut' gebor'n	2. "To you this night is born a child
Von einer Jungfrau auserkor'n,	Of Mary, chosen virgin mild;
Ein Kindelein so zart und fein,	This little child, of lowly birth,
Das soll eu'r Freund und Wonne sein.	Shall be the joy of all the earth.
3. Es ist der Herr Christ unser Gott,	3. "This is the Christ, our God and Lord,
Der will euch fuehr'n aus aller Noth,	Who in all need shall aid afford;
Er will eu'r Heiland selber sein,	He will Himself your Savior be
Von allen Suenden machen rein.	From all your sins to set you free.
4. Er bringt euch alle Selighkeit,	4. "He will on you the gifts bestow
Die Gott der Vater hat bereit't,	Prepared by God for all below,
Dass ibr mit uns im Himmelreich	That in His kingdom, bright and fair,
Sollt leben nun und ewiglich.	You may with us His glory share.
5. So merket nun das Zeichen recht,	5. "These are the tokens ye shall mark:
Die Krippen, Windelein so schlecht;	The swaddling-clothes and manger dark;
Da findet ihr das Kind gelegt,	There ye shall find the Infant laid
Das alle Welt erhaelt und traegt.	By whom the heavens and earth were made."
6. Dess lasst uns Alle froehlich sein	6. Now let us all with gladsome cheer
Und mit den Hirten geh'n hinein,	Go with the shepherds and draw near

Zu seh'n was Gott uns hat bescheert,
Mit seinem lieben Sohn verehrt.

7. Merk auf, mein Herz, und sieh dort hin:
Was liegt doch in dem Krippelein?
Wess ist das schoene Kindelein?
Es ist das liebe Jesulein.

8. Bis willekomm, du edler Gast,
Den Suender nicht verschmaehet hast,
Und koemmst in Elend her zu mir,
Wie soll ich immer danken dir?

9. Ach Herr, du Schoepfer aller Ding',
Wie bist du worden so gering,
Dass du da liegst auf duerrem Gras,
Davon ein Kind und Esel ass.

10. Uud waer' die Welt vielmal so weit,
Von Edelstein und Gold bereit't,
So waer sie doch dir viel zu klein,
Zu sein ein enges Wiegelein.

11. Der Sammet und die Seiden dein,
Das ist grob Heu und Windelein,
Darauf du Koen'g so gross und reich
Herprangst, als waers dein Himmelreich.

12. Das hat also gefallen dir,
Die Wahrheit anzuzeigen mir:
Wie aller Welt Macht, Ehr und Gut
Fuer dir nichts gilt, nicht hilft noch thut.

13. Ach, mein herzliebes Jesulein,
Mach dir ein rein sanft Bettelein,
Zu ruhen in mein's Herzens Schrein,
Dass ich nimmer vergesse dein.

To see the precious gift of God,
Who hath His own dear Son bestowed.

7. Give heed, my heart, lift up thine eyes!
What is it in yon manger lies?
Who is this child, so young and fair?
The blessed Christ-child lieth there.

8. Welcome to earth, Thou noble Guest,
Through whom the sinful world is blest!
Thou com'st to share my misery;
What thanks shall I return to Thee?

9. Ah, Lord, who hast created all,
How weak art Thou, how poor and small,
That Thou dost choose Thine infant bed
Where humble cattle lately fed!

10. Were earth a thousand times as fair,
Beset with gold and jewels rare,
It yet were far too poor to be
A narrow cradle, Lord, for Thee.

11. For velvets soft and silken stuff
Thou hast but hay and straw so rough,
Whereon Thou, King, so rich and great,
As 'twere Thy heaven, art throned in state.

12. And thus, dear Lord, it pleaseth Thee
To make this truth quite plain to me,
That all the world's wealth, honor, might,
Are naught and worthless in Thy sight.

13. Ah, dearest Jesus, holy Child,
Make Thee a bed, soft, undefiled,
Within my heart, that it may be
A quiet chamber kept for Thee.

14. Davon ich allzeit froehlich sei,	14. My heart for very joy doth leap,
Zu springen, singen immer frei	My lips no more can silence keep;
Das rechte Susannine[42] schon,	I, too, must sing with joyful tongue
Mit Herzen Lust den suessen Ton.	That sweetest ancient cradle-song:
15. Lob, Ehr sei Gott im hoechsten Thron,	15. Glory to God in highest heaven,
Der uns schenkt seinen ein'gen Sohn,	Who unto us His Son hath given!
Des freuen sich der Engel Schaar	While angels sing with pious mirth
Und singen uns solch's neues Jahr.	A glad new year to all the earth.

Luther was an accomplished musician, regarding music as "the handmaiden of theology and second only to theology." As such, he composed texts and music for Christians to use in a variety of contexts. Early on, "Vom Himmel hoch" was set to the popular melody "Aus fremden Landen," but later in his life the melody was replaced by the VOM HIMMEL HOCH melody, usually ascribed to Luther. The last melodic phrase of VOM HIMMEL HOCH is only one note different from the last phrase of his earlier EIN' FESTE BURG.

The tune has found significant use in subsequent history. Felix Mendelssohn (1809–1847) used the melody for his cantata with the same name. J. S. Bach employed the melody in three different chorale settings in his *Christmas Oratorio*, which is a group of six cantatas composed in 1734 and in 1747; Bach also wrote a masterful set of five canonic variations for organ on "Vom Himmel hoch da komm' ich her" (BWV 769). The melody has been harmonized by many composers. Hans Leo Hassler's (1564–1612) harmonization, found in his 1608 part book is (with only two exceptions) diatonic harmony with one chord (almost exclusively in root position) to each note of the melody, and, unlike the later Bach settings, the only non-chord tone is in the melody on the penultimate beat. Such a setting gives emphasis to the melody line, which in each of its antecedent and consequent phrases gives priority to the text and its biblical/theological content.

Figure 3. Words: "From heaven above to earth I come," Martin Luther (1483–1546). Trans. Catherine Winkworth. © 1978, *Lutheran Book of Worship*. Augsburg Publishing House. Used by permission. Music: VOM HIMMEL HOCH, melody from Geistliche lieder auffs new gebessert und gemehrt, 1539. Harmony by Hans Leo Hassler (1564–1612).

Luther's concern for the expression of biblical, theological, liturgical content of his hymns and for their literary and musical quality is clearly seen in this hymn. The content of the hymn, as with much good hymnody, suggests practical applications. There are indications that the hymn may have been written for and performed in Luther's traditional family celebration involving his children on Christmas Eve. Even today it yields itself to an almost dramatic presentation. Stanzas 1–5, the message of the angel, might be sung by a soloist. Stanzas 6–7 are responses of the worshipers. Stanzas 8–13, addressed to the Christ child, might be sung by other soloists (men, women, or children) from various places in the congregation. Stanzas 14 and 15 are particularly congregational. Scripture readings (mentioned above) might precede certain verses.

Samuel Stone's "The Church's one foundation" comes from a different historical period and different theological tradition, but like Luther's, his hymn illustrates not only the interrelatedness of the biblical and theological dimensions but also something of the liturgical, literary, musical, historical, biographical, sociocultural, and practical dimensions. The doctrine of the church, ecclesiology, is expressed in the New Testament and subsequent Christian history in a variety of images as the Body of Christ, the Temple of the Presence, the Tabernacle, the People of God, The Called Out, The New Israel, the Kingdom of Christ, and, as here, the Bride of Christ. As can be seen, Stone's text is a biblically based theology.

The Church's one foundation	1 Cor 3:10-11
Is Jesus Christ her Lord,	
She is His new creation	
By water and the Word.	Eph 5:26-27
From heaven He came and sought her	
To be His holy bride;	Rev 21:2, 9
With His own blood He bought her	Acts 20:28
And for her life He died.	Phil 2:8
She is from every nation,	1 Peter 1:1-2
Yet one o'er all the earth;	Rev 5:9
Her charter of salvation,	
One Lord, one faith, one birth;	John 11:52
One holy Name she blesses,	Eph 4:4-6
Partakes one holy food,	Matt 26:26

And to one hope she presses,
With every grace endued.   2 Cor 9:8

The Church shall never perish!
Her dear Lord to defend,
To guide, sustain, and cherish,   (Stanza not in most hymnals)
Is with her to the end:
Though there be those who hate her,
And false sons in her pale,   2 Peter 2:1
Against both foe or traitor
She ever shall prevail.

Though with a scornful wonder
Men see her sore oppressed,
By schisms rent asunder,   Luke 12:37
By heresies distressed:
Yet saints their watch are keeping,
Their cry goes up, "How long?"   Rev 6:10
And soon the night of weeping   Ps 30:5
Shall be the morn of song!

'Mid toil and tribulation,   Rev 7:14
And tumult of her war,
She waits the consummation
Of peace forevermore;
Till, with the vision glorious,
Her longing eyes are blest,
And the great Church victorious
Shall be the Church at rest.

Yet she on earth hath union   (Nicene Creed)
With God the Three in One,
And mystic sweet communion   Heb 12:1
With those whose rest is won,
O happy ones and holy!
Lord, give us grace that we
Like them, the meek and lowly,
On high may dwell with Thee.

Theologically, the hymn served two purposes. First, it was one of twelve hymns Stone wrote to interpret the Apostles' Creed for his parishioners, and it was included in his *Lyre Fidelium: Twelve Hymns on the Twelve Articles of the Apostles' Creed* (Oxford and London, 1866), a book for home and the chapel. Article IX at the time referred to "The Holy Catholic Church the Communion of Saints" and stated of Christ, "He is the Head of the Body, the Church." Second, the hymn was in support of Metropolitan Bishop Robert Gray of Cape Town, South Africa, in the controversy with Bishop John William Colenso of Natal, South Africa, who beginning in 1862 published papers espousing Higher Criticism and other nontraditional theological views for this time and place. The "schisms," "heresies," "false sons," "foe," and "traitor" to which Stone refers in his hymn are controversies that had so shaken the Anglican Church that there was a call for an Anglican-wide conference to address some of them, and this led to the first Lambeth Conference in 1867. The hymn continued to speak in times of the subsequent controversies of Darwinism, Liberalism, and in the ongoing Anglo-Catholic conflict within the Anglican Church.

Liturgically, the hymn has served in several specific historical contexts and is still today one of the most popular hymns when liturgies address the subject of the church. In 1885, in response to the dean of Salisbury Cathedral's request to use "The Church's one foundation" as a processional hymn, Stone added three stanzas that were inserted between the original fifth and sixth stanzas. In 1888, during the third Lambeth Conference, in which a classic statement on the essence of the historic Christian faith was adopted, the longer version was again sung as the processional hymn in services at Canterbury Cathedral, Westminster Abbey, and St. Paul's Cathedral. The hymn was sung in 2013 during the inauguration of Justin Wilby as Archbishop in Canterbury Cathedral.

Literarily, the hymn moves in a stately 7.6.7.6 D iambic meter in cross rhyme and begins with powerful biblical images about the very nature of the church—"foundation," "new creation," "water and the Word," and "holy Bride." The feminine imagery of the church (Eph 5:27) is maintained by some twenty uses of the pronouns "her" or "she" in addition to the biblical image of the "bride" (Rev 19 and 21). The emphasis on "Jesus Christ her Lord" is achieved in the first stanza by a threefold use of mesodiplosis, the repetition of "His" in the middle of lines 3, 6, and 7: "His new creation," "His holy bride," and "His own blood." The second stanza uses anaphora and mesodiplosis to speak emphatically about the unity of the church—

"one Lord, one faith, one birth; one holy food . . . , one hope." The third stanza (usually omitted) emphasizes the imperishableness of the church defended by our Lord who will "defend . . . guide, and cherish . . . her to the end" in spite of any "false sons," "foe or traitor." The following stanzas by consistent imagery develop the concept of a living being, the bride of Christ, enduring oppression, schisms, heresies, toil, tribulation, and tumult of her war, how "men see her sore oppressed" and yet how "saints their watch are keeping" and how to "her longing eyes," "the vision glorious" becomes "the great Church victorious." In what is now generally the final stanza, reference is made to the church's union with "God the Three in One" and, in the imagery of Hebrews 12, to the "mystic sweet communion with those whose rest is won." The hymn ends with a prayer that the Church victorious, the bride of Christ, "on high may dwell with Thee."

The AURELIA tune was composed by Samuel Sebastian Wesley, the grandson of Charles Wesley, who began his musical career as a choirboy in the Chapel Royal and St. Paul's, became a noted organist at Hereford, Exeter, Leeds parish church, Winchester, and Gloucester, and beginning in 1850 taught at the Royal Academy. The tune appeared in *A Selection of Psalms and Hymns* by C. Kemble (London, 1864), and though sung first to the text "Jerusalem the Golden," it is now rather universally associated with Stone's text. The simple rhythm, singable melody, straightforward harmony, and double musical period with its climax in the third phrase support well the accents and mood of all stanzas of the text. Benjamin Britten made an interesting evaluation of AURELIA in his diary entry of 11 February 1930: "Play that most glorious of hymns, 'The Church's one foundation' (Wesley) for prayers."[44]

This hymn is rich in the multiple dimensions of fine hymnody and illustrates something of the importance of a comprehensive and integrated hermeneutics.

Notes

1. See also C. Randall Bradley, "Congregational Song as a Shaper of Theology: A Contemporary Assessment," *Review and Expository: A Consortium Baptist Theological Journal* 100/3 (Summer 2007): 351–73.

2. John P. Newport, *Life's Ultimate Questions: A Contemporary Philosophy of Religion* (Dallas/London: Word Publishing, 1989) 96.

3. R. W. Hepburn, "Religious Language," *Oxford Companion to Philosophy*, ed. Ted Honderich (Oxford: Oxford University Press, 1995).

4. John Keble, *Keble's Lectures on Poetry, 1832–1841*, trans. Edward Kershaw Francis (Oxford, 1912) i.22.

5. Ibid., ii.481.

6. "Culture" is used here to refer not only to the larger national, ethnic culture but also to the culture of a region or a city, or even to the artistic and intellectual achievements and customs within a congregation.

7. "Nachwort, Die Prinzipien dieser Übersetzung," trans. author, *Die Bibel in heutigem Deutsch* (Stuttgart: Deutsche Bibelgesellschaft, 1982) 299–300.

8. Alan Richardson, ed., *A Dictionary of Christian Theology* (Philadelphia: The Westminster Press, 1969) s.v. "Language, Religious."

9. Ibid.

10. Ibid.

11. Ibid.

12. Ibid.

13. Amos N. Wilder, *New Testament Faith for Today* (New York: Harper & Brothers, Publishers, 1955) 60. Amos Wilder also delivered lectures on early Christian rhetoric.

14. Erik Routley used this phrase to refer to the numerous restrictions that hymns must assume in order to be accessible to congregations.

15. Paul Tillich, *The Religious Situation*, trans. H. Richard Niebuhr (New York: Meridian Books, Inc., 1956 [Henry Holt & Company, Inc., 1931]) 85.

16. Robin A. Leaver and James H. Litton, eds., *Duty and Delight: Routley Remembered* (Carol Stream IL: Hope Publishing Company; Norwich: Canterbury Press, 1985) 224–28.

17. Margo G. Houts, "Feminine Images for God: What Does the Bible Say?" http://clubs.calvin.edu/chimes/970418/o1041897.htm.

18. Houts lists numerous passages that use feminine language when speaking of God and his works: a woman in labor (Isa 42:14), a mother suckling her children (Num 11:12), a mother who does not forget the child she nurses (Isa 49:14-15), a mother who comforts her children (Isa 66:12-13), a mother who births and protects Israel (Isa 46:3-4), a mother who gave birth to the Israelites (Deut 32:18), a mother who calls, teaches, holds, heals, and feeds her young (Hos 11:14). Other maternal references include Ps 131:2; Job 38:29; 1 Pet 2:2-3; God as a midwife attending a birth (Pss 22:9–10a; 71:6; Isa 66:9); God as a woman working leaven into bread (Luke 13:18-21); God as a woman seeking a lost coin (Luke 15:8-10); the hen: Matt 23:37 (par. Luke 13:34; cf. Ruth 2:12); God as Mother Bear (Hos 13:8), a fierce image associated with the profound attachment of the mother to her cubs. God's rage against those who withhold gratitude is that of a bear "robbed of her cubs."

19. S. Paul Schilling, *The Faith We Sing* (Philadelphia: The Westminster Press, 1983) 23.

20. In each of these cases, we are again confronted with the problem of fidelity to the author's intent and what may have been the understanding of the original hearers. These problems are compounded when dealing with translations.

21. Cf. Paul Westermeyer, "A Hymnal's Theological Significance," *Dialog: A Journal of Theology* 48/4 (Winter 2009): 313–19.

22. This hymn is discussed in chapter 9.

23. *A House of Praise*, 216.

24. Martin E. Marty, "The Phenomenology of Hymnody: What Is Going On When Christians Sing Hymns in Congregation?" *The Hymn* 59/3 (Summer 2008): 8–14.

25. This is the same biblical reference that is given by Isaac Watts for his "When I survey the wondrous cross" in his *Hymns and Scriptural Songs* (London, 1707).

26. John Wesley changed "Our God" to "O God" in his 1738 *Collection of Psalms and Hymns* and lessened the reiterated personal possessive pronouns that were apparently important to Watts.

27. The hymn often appears in the form adapted in the *English Hymnal* using the first three of the original six stanzas, omitting the fourth stanza, and forming a fourth stanza by combining the first two lines of stanza 5 and the first two lines of stanza 6. There was also some clarification of meter and punctuation.

28. *A House of Praise*, 77.

29. This hymn is discussed in chapter 6.

30. "But unto you that fear my name shall the Sun of righteousness arise with healing in his wings; . . ." (Mal 4:2 KJV).

31. "And thou, child, shalt be called the prophet of the Highest: for thou shalt go before the face of the Lord to prepare his ways; To give knowledge of salvation unto his people by the remission of their sins, Through the tender mercy of our God; whereby the dayspring from on high hath visited us, To give light to them that sit in darkness and in the shadow of death, . . ." (Luke 1:76-79 KJV).

32. "And this voice which came from heaven we heard, when we were with him in the holy mount. We have also a more sure word of prophecy; whereunto ye do well that ye take heed, as unto a light that shineth in a dark place, until the day dawn, and the day star arise in your hearts: . . ." (2 Pet 1:18-19 KJV).

33. More is said about Carl Daw in the discussion of his hymn, "O day of peace that dimly shines," in chapter 6.

34. Written for Emma Frances Bevan's translation of John Tauler's hymn, "As the Bridegroom to his chosen."

35. See the discussion below of Samuel Stone's "The church's one foundation."

36. *A House of Praise*, 132.

37. Ibid., 453.

38. Ibid., 267.

39. The biblical, theological, liturgical, literary, musical, and practical aspects of Daw's "O day of peace that dimly shines" are discussed in some detail in chapter 6.

40. In Percy Dearmer, *Songs of Praise Discussed* (London, 1933) 126.

41. The *Gesangbuch.org* (http://www.Gesangbuch.org) was formed for the purpose of gathering and translating German Lutheran hymnody and teaching the English-speaking church the great hymns of the Lutheran Reformation. It attempts to combine the 8,000 tunes from Zahn and the 5,000 pages of texts of Wackernagel into a single outline resource with midi-files, indexes, and English translations.

42. A cradle song or "Wiegenlied."

43. Translation by Catherine Winkworth, 1855, alt.

44. John Evans, ed., *Journeying Boy: The Diaries of the Young Benjamin Britten 1928–1938* (London: Faber and Faber, 2009) 31.

CHAPTER 4

Liturgy

The term "liturgical" is taken here in both its traditional, narrow meaning referring to the acts of worship and even more specifically to the Eucharist and in its broader, etymological, historical, and biblical meanings: "λειτουρία, ας —service, ministry; worship; offering, sacrifice"[1] referring to the broad spectrum of individual and corporate ministry or offering or work. In terms of the semantic domain in biblical Greek, Louw and Nida point out that both the noun and verb, alongside fourteen other words, carry the broad meaning "to serve, with the implication of more formal or regular service."[2] Thayer's *Greek-English Lexicon of the New Testament* gives the definition of λειτουργοῦν τω κυρίω as ". . . Christians serving Christ, whether by prayer, or by instructing others concerning the way of salvation, or in some other way: Acts xiii. 2 . . . of those who aid others with their resources, and relieve their poverty . . . Ro. xv. 27 . . ."[3] and notes that in 2 Corinthians 9:12 λειτουργίας refers to "a *gift* or *benefaction*, for the relief of the needy . . . ."[4] In Romans 13:6, Paul uses the word λειτουργοί to refer to the state's services or ministries. In Romans 15:16, Paul refers to himself as "a minister of Christ Jesus [λειτουργὸν χριστοῦ ἰησοῦ] to the Gentiles." In Romans 15:27, λειτουργῆσαι αὐτοῖς means, as Thayer defines it, to minister religious service and refers to the church ministering in material things to the poor saints in Jerusalem. In Philippians 2:25, λειτουργόν refers to Epaphroditus as being a servant or minister to Paul's needs, and Philippians 2:30 refers to Epaphroditus's completing what was deficient in the church's service (λειτουρίας). Hebrews 1:7 refers to λειτουρούς, ministers to the Lord, similar to where Acts 13:2 speaks of the church at Antioch ministering (λειτουργούντων σὲ αὐτῶν) to the Lord. Hebrews 1:14 uses λειτουργικά to speak of "ministering spirits, sent out to render service" while Hebrews 8:2 uses λειτουργός to speak of Christ as "a minister in the sanctuary and in the true tabernacle" and Hebrews 8:6 speaks of Christ and his "more excellent ministry [λειτουργίας]." In short, the word and the concept of "liturgy" etymologically, historically, biblically, and, we might affirm, theologically includes the broad spectrum of Christian ministry. Hymnody has addressed that broad spectrum of Christian ministry.

The early Christians took the words they found in the common language or dialect that were used by common people in the Roman Empire (κοινή Greek) and gave the words "the deeper and more spiritual sense with which the N. T. writings have made us familiar."[5] We would do well to perceive New Testament words as the first Christian hearers and readers perceived them and try to understand how meanings evolved in their thinking. A. T. Robertson notes that "The κοινή had all the memories of a people's life."[6] He affirms,

> The evidence that the N. T. Greek is in the vernacular κοινή is partly lexical and partly grammatical, though in the nature of the case chiefly lexical. The evidence is constantly growing. . . . We give first some examples of words, previously supposed to be purely "biblical," now shown to be merely popular Greek because of their presence in the papyri or inscriptions [λειτουργικός is one of the 39 examples] . . . . Many words which were thought to have a peculiar meaning in the LXX or the N. T. have been found in that sense in the inscriptions or papyri, . . . [Here Robertson lists more than 150 Greek words]. This seems like a very long list, but it will do more than pages of argument to convince the reader that the vocabulary of the N. T. is practically the same as that of the vernacular κοινή in the Roman Empire in the first century A.D.[7]

λειτουργία occurs several times in Robertson's illustrations of the evolution of New Testament words: "So λειτουργικός (from λειτουργία, LXX, papyri) and ὀνικός (from ὄνικός, in a contract in the Fayûm Papyri dated Feb. 8, A.D. 33)."[8] "In the N. T. λειτουργός, -ια, -εῖν, -ικός are taken over from the Attic, but they occur also in Pergamum and Magnesia."[9] "The adjective compounds used in the N. T. characteristic of the κοινή are somewhat numerous [and among his extensive list, is λειτουργικός]."[10]

We consider here then that the λειτουργία or ministry of the church and of the individual Christian may refer, in that most general sense, to the ministries of worship, discipleship, proclamation, and social concern; that the ministries of the individual Christian and of the fellowship of a Christian church can be grouped under one of these larger categories; and that hymns can be related to these four basic ministries.

The use of a hymn in any one of the broad categories of liturgy or ministry (worship, discipleship, proclamation, or service) must consider the aspects involved in a comprehensive and integrated hermeneutics, interpretation, or understanding of hymnody. How consistent is the text with biblical teaching and with the theology or doctrine of the church? How well do the literary aspects of the hymn express that biblical theology, and how appropriate is that literary expression to the sociocultural context in which it is to be used? How well does the musical setting express the literary, biblical, and theological facets, and how appropriate is it to the sociocultural context in which it is to be used? Are there insights to be gained from knowing something of the historical/biographical background of the hymn? Does something need to be done to prepare the congregation to use the hymn intelligently in this ministry? Does some special attention need to be given to the physical facilities such as lighting, air conditioning, seating, musical instruments, sound system, and the availability of hymnals and guides in this ministry? What aspects of "performance" must be considered regarding the hymn in the sequence and relationship to other hymns in such musical matters as keys, meters, tempi (within stanzas, between stanzas, and between hymns), styles, moods, dynamics, ranges, tessituras, textures, media (vocal media and instrumental accompaniments)? The liturgical use of hymns cannot be taken in isolation. It is intricately bound up with all the facets of a comprehensive and integrated hermeneutics, interpretation, or understanding of hymns.

Ministry (λειτουργία) in the Fellowship (κοινωνία) of the Church (εκκλησια)

The Christian church is a worshiping fellowship, and through "those who worship the Father in spirit and truth,"[11] God performs his ministries in the world. The ministries of worship, discipleship, proclamation, and social service are rooted in private, family, and corporate worship of God.

Worship (λειτουργέω)

There is a long and vibrant relationship between the Christian liturgy (in its narrowest and in its broadest senses) and hymns.[12] Most obvious are the Psalms, the canticles of the Gospels, and the Pauline letters that are rich in wordings that give evidence of being liturgical and even hymnic in their lyrical and exalted style. "Psalms and hymns and spiritual songs"[13] have been a part of Christian church from its earliest days. It is reasonable to assume that when the Gospels speak of Christ and his disciples "singing a hymn"[14] at the Last Supper, this was not the first time Jesus and his disciples sang together any more than Paul and Silas's singing in prison was their first time.[15] Their "singing hymns of praise to God" in the Philippian prison would suggest that singing was a usual activity for them and likely not confined to worship. New Testament scholars frequently refer to ". . . the impression that singing/chanting songs in honour of Jesus was not an occasional but a characteristic feature of early Christian worship."[16] Hymns continue to be the logical expressions of God's people in every aspect of their fellowship and their liturgy of public ministries of worship, discipleship, proclamation, and social service.

The twentieth century saw a powerful liturgical revival in Catholicism and Protestantism. *The Oxford History of Christian Worship* describes the Second Vatican Council (1962–1965) and the publication of the Constitution on the Sacred Liturgy (1963) as the ". . . instant catalyst in sparking unprecedented liturgical experimentation and revision throughout Anglicanism and in most major Protestant churches."[17] Hymnody continues to be crucial to this ongoing revival, exploration, experimentation, and revision in worship.

The culmination of all worship will be when "at the name of Jesus every knee will bow, of those who are in heaven and on earth and under the earth, and that every tongue will confess that Jesus Christ is Lord, to the glory of God the Father" (Phil 2:10-11)—when humanity will join the "heavenly hosts in ceaseless worship." In his hymn based on Revelation 1, 4, and 5 with allusions to Isaiah 6, Dudley-Smith lavishes descriptive adjectives ("Heavenly hosts," "ceaseless worship," "everlasting days"), piles strong nouns in groups of four and eight ("praise and honour, power and glory," "wealth and wisdom, power and glory, honour, might, dominion, praise"), emphasizes through repeated words and sounds, and heaps numerous superlatives ("ceaseless," "reigns alone," "all his hands have fashioned," "all creation," "all redemption," "all his creatures") to hint at this apotheosis of worship.

> Heavenly hosts in ceaseless worship
>   "Holy, holy, holy" cry;
> "he who is, who was and will be,

God Almighty, Lord most high."
Praise and honour, power and glory,
    be to him who reigns alone!
We, with all his hands have fashioned,
    fall before the Father's throne.

All creation, all redemption,
    join to sing the Saviour's worth;
Lamb of God, whose blood has bought us,
    kings and priests, to reign on earth.
Wealth and wisdom, power and glory,
    honour, might, dominion, praise,
now be his from all his creatures
    and to everlasting days![18]

Here the biblical, theological, liturgical, and literary voices are in a great polyphony. It must be remembered (and will be returned to later) that this liturgical dimension of hymnody is not only a matter of eternity, nor only a matter of the saints gathered weekly in public worship, but is also a matter of hymns in daily family and private worship.

It may be argued biblically, theologically, and historically that worship is the primary ministry of the individual Christian and of the fellowship of Christians and that worship is the ministry from which all other ministries evolve. "Liturgy," referring primarily to the church's worship and often more specifically to the fixed forms of the Eucharistic rites of the church and corporate Christian worship, springs from a variety of theological understandings and finds expression in a vast range of styles and forms, a continuum ranging from the most spontaneous, free, unstructured, and unstylized worship to the most authorized, orderly, structured, and stylized worship. Yet the most basic elements of worship are shared in many of the Christian "liturgies" in spite of a long and intertwined evolution, and there are reasons to believe that the best of these common elements come essentially from the biblical bases of true worship and from the work of the Holy Spirit in the church.

The influences on Christian worship and music in worship are diverse. Roots are found in ancient Jewish worship as early Christians borrowed much of the shape, materials, and even in biblical words from which come our "Amen," "Alleluia," "Hosanna" used in introits, graduals, versicles; and in the text of the *Sanctus*. There are Greek roots in the modes of medieval music that still occur today, and some consider that ceremonies and the use of lights show Greek influence. Elements of the Divine Liturgy of the Eastern Church and the ancient Mass of the Roman Church are present in many of the liturgies of today, and influences of the reformers—Zwingli, Calvin, and Luther—are seen in some liturgies, but the New Testament Scriptures and the institution of the Lord's Supper are the most salient features of Christian worship and permeate most liturgies.

What is basic and common to true worship in any style or form is humanity's genuine response to God's revelation of himself, and this response commonly has, in varying degrees, included awe and adoration and thanksgiving, confession, affirmation, and commitment. One of the classic biblical passages on worship, Isaiah 6, provides what has come to be for many liturgies a model in content, form, and sequence. It is an awesome and dramatic dialogue of revelation and response in which the basic elements of the dialogue are, in sequence, revelation and adoration, conviction and confession, forgiveness and gratitude, proclamation and affirmation, call and commitment, and commission and service.

While worship may, with some consistency, involve those elements of content, form, and sequence, the elements may vary greatly in length and emphasis depending on the nature of the service. Frequently, a great counterpoint of these elements may emerge in the individual worshiper or the whole community and do so over a period of time. In the attempt for a more complete expression of worship, various liturgical forms have evolved and there is always the danger that form will overtake content and meaning. Evelyn Underhill is careful to note, "it is here [when worship is embodied in some form] that we encounter the greatest of the dangers that accompany its long history; the danger that form will smother spirit, ritual action take the place of spontaneous prayer, the outward and visible sign obscure the inward grace."[19]

Roger Scruton makes significant observations about liturgy and music in *The Aesthetics of Music*. He speaks of an obvious four-fold pattern that is discernible in many kinds of religious observance—(1) "fall" or separation, (2) sacrifice "which is the primary ingredient in the process of atonement," (3) ritual "which transforms the offering from a 'natural' object into something 'supernatural' and holy," and (4) "the sacrifice becomes a sacrament." He then affirms that this pattern

> provides the central experience in our own tradition, and is the theme, whether revealed or hidden, of much Western art. It enables us to understand not only the proximity of religious and aesthetic experience, but the

role of each in defining and sustaining a common culture. . . .

We do not participate in religious rites merely so as to contemplate their meaning in the detached way that we would contemplate a play or a painting. We are genuine participants, who are engaged for the sake of our salvation and with a view to the truth. Nevertheless, there are interesting similarities with the aesthetic experience. Although the purpose of an act of worship lies beyond the moment—in the form of a promised salvation, a revelation, or a restoration of the soul's natural harmony—it is not entirely separable from the experience. God is defined in the act of worship far more precisely than he is defined by any theology, and this is why the forms of ceremony are so important.[20]

Scruton considers the similarities between religious rite and the aesthetic experience to include not only the participants' inseparableness from the experience but also the inexhaustible and endlessly renewable nature of both the religious rite and the aesthetic experience. Additionally, the similarities include the participants opening the mind to meaning not only as individuals but also as members of a culture. Furthermore, "In the religious experience too [as in the aesthetic experience] there is an implied but partly absent community: for the religious rite implicates not the living only, but the dead and the unborn."[21]

Music has the demonstrated power to cause our thoughts and feelings to soar above the limits of our usual modes of thinking and feeling, and where is this more natural and needed than in the experience of worship? Music cannot only enhance each element of a liturgy but can contribute profoundly to both the unity and dynamic progression of a total worship experience. Fred Pratt Green spoke appropriately of "the church in liturgy and song" and "How often, making music, we have found a new dimension in the world of sound, as worship moved us to a more profound Alleluia!" and how "in our music God is glorified."[22]

The combining of religious rite and aesthetic experience (especially the singing of the people of God) has been a hallmark of Judeo-Christian worship. The Psalms have been at the very heart of that tradition. From Ephesians 5:18-19 and Colossians 3:16, we know that the earliest Christians were admonished to speak to one another in "psalms, and hymns and spiritual songs, singing and making melody with your heart to the Lord always giving thanks for all things in the name of our Lord Jesus Christ to God, even the Father . . . ." The corporate expression of worship through music has continued in every Christian community from the earliest days until today. Christian hymnody has spoken to and for people in every element common to Christian worship: revelation, adoration, conviction, confession, forgiveness, gratitude, proclamation, affirmation, call, commitment, commission, and service.

The roles of hymns in worship are vital and varied.[23] Hymns may be used in educational contexts long before the act of worship, as preparation for worship immediately prior to a service, as integral elements in every part of the worship experience, or in times of reflection and meditation following the worship service. Hymns are vital to private and family devotions and through this make a profound contribution to the understanding of public worship and enrich the experience of portions of the liturgy. Hymns in educational contexts instruct persons about the nature and forms of worship. Hymns frequently quote portions of the liturgy and strengthen the understanding even of those portions that are not traditionally celebrated through congregational singing. How well these roles of hymns are realized is dependent on the interrelated dimensions of hymnody that are emphasized in this book: whether the hymns are biblically based, theologically sound from the perspective of the worshiping congregation, and truly in keeping with the spirit of each facet of the liturgy; whether the hymns and tunes are of literary and musical value that honor God's creative gifts, and are carefully and prayerfully chosen and sung; whether proper logistical preparations have been made for the service; and whether there are historical, biographical, cultural, or social matters that could contribute to the hymns' being chosen and sung with maximum effectiveness.

The roles of hymns in corporate worship are best understood in the context and flow of the common elements found in classical biblical texts on worship (e.g., Isaiah 6) and in the great worship traditions. In both the more authoritative, orderly, structured, and stylized worship seen in some Christian churches with the weekly celebrations of the Eucharist and in the freer, less structured Christian churches, there are often common elements of content and even form.

The following discussion of hymns in worship deals with broad categories and does not follow strictly the content or sequence of any one liturgical tradition. The purpose here is to show that the breadth and depth of liturgical concepts and traditions find profound expression in numerous hymns that have biblical roots and theological insight communicated with literary and musical beauty and power, and are often born out of significant Christian experiences that speak to our own time and culture.

While texts of some liturgies are considered fixed or "sacred texts," the intent and purpose of each part of most liturgies may be honored by the singing of carefully chosen hymn texts and tunes. Some of the more "fixed" traditions of worship have made a distinction between liturgical music and religious music and have permitted hymns to be sung at the beginning (Introit) and end of Mass, at the Offertory, at Communion, for the Gradual and Alleluia, places in the liturgy where there was movement—entrance, procession, recession, movement between the readings. The following attempts to emphasize that in the whole spectrum of worship—in the varied types, styles, and contexts from the simplest, most informal to the more complex and formal that have evolved over the centuries in many traditions in many parts of the world—hymns have played and can continue to play vital roles. Again, this is true in private and family devotions, in corporate worship and in educational contexts about the concepts of worship, in times of preparation prior to services, in actual worship services, and in times of reflection following worship.

Revelation and Adoration

From the human perspective, worship begins with the recognition and acknowledgment of God's revelation of himself and is expressed in feelings, thoughts, and acts of awe, reverence, and adoration. Even liturgies that "begin" with confession have to assume that both the need of confession and possibility of forgiveness are predicated on the recognition of the awesome presence of the revealed and forgiving God. Corporate Christian worship exists in Christ's promise that "where two or three are gathered together in my name, there am I in the midst of them" (Matt 18:20). While God is ever present with us and reveals himself in many ways, he is uniquely present with those who gather to worship him in spirit and truth. Gathering in Christ's name and sensing and acknowledging the unique presence and revelation of God in Christ is a first facet of the worship experience. Evelyn Underhill notes that one "is bound to take worship seriously, and ever more seriously with the deepening of his own spiritual sense."[24] It is an awesome thought that in our earthly worship we are uniquely in the presence of the "one God, the Father Almighty, maker of heaven and earth, and of all things visible and invisible"[25] and that we celebrate "with Angels and Archangels, and with the all the company of heaven."[26]

There is a natural and traditional sequence in the worshiper's response to God's revelation of himself. His presence with us invokes first awe and adoration. The true worshiper recognizes the unique and "awful" presence of God, and this recognition brings forth adoration of both the awesome God and the fact that he would reveal himself to us. It may well be argued that awe, in the fullest sense the recognition of the "awful" presence of God, is too often lacking in much of worship and, if it is, one may ask, "What is the nature of adoration and all else that follows?" Simply following tradition and ceremony hardly constitute worship. For the true worshiper, awe gives way almost simultaneously to adoration. Evelyn Underhill quotes F. von Hügel, who assumes the worshiper's recognition of God's awesome presence: "The first or central act of religion is adoration, sense of God, His otherness though nearness, His distinctness from all finite beings, though not separateness—aloofness—from them." Underhill affirms that "Such disinterested delight is the perfection of worship . . . we find at its heart the adoring response of spirit to Spirit . . . ."[27] Underhill uses the word "disinterested" in the sense of being free from personal interest, free of any selfish motive. She notes that worship and prayer are vitally interrelated and often overlap; however, "worship is essentially disinterested—it 'means only God'—but prayer is only in some of its aspects disinterested."[28] Hymns have played and continue to play a vital role in helping worshipers become uniquely aware of God's awesome presence, free themselves of any selfish motive, and give themselves in true worship which "means only God."

The fifth-century hymn "Let all mortal flesh keep silence" (Σιγησάτω πᾶσα σάρξ βροτεία καὶ στήτω μετὰ φόβου καὶ τρόμου) expresses for many the awesomeness and adoration that characterize true worship. The hymn is most understood and appreciated when interpreted from historical, biographical, biblical, theological, liturgical, literary, musical, and practical perspectives. The hymn comes from the Liturgy of St. James that is traditionally ascribed to James, the brother of Jesus. It is used by the Syrian Orthodox Church, the Armenian/Georgian churches, and the churches of Egypt and Ethiopia and is used in Jerusalem on the Sunday after Christmas. More specifically, it is taken from the "Prayer of the Cherubic Hymn" used at the presentation of the bread and wine at the Offertory. It is sung during every Divine Liturgy of the year except on Holy Thursday, when it is replaced by the troparion, "At your mystical supper," and by the celebration of Prote Anastasis on Holy Saturday. It follows the Gospel reading and is interrupted by the Great Entrance. In many modern liturgies, the hymn is used in services devoted to Christmas, the Second Coming, and often as a Communion hymn. The modern version of the text was translated and paraphrased by Gerard Moultrie (1829–1885), a public schoolmaster and

Anglican hymn writer educated at Rugby, Exeter, and Oxford. Following ordination, he served in various locations as chaplain, curate, vicar, and warden. His translations continue to appear in major hymnals of denominations across the English-speaking world.

Biblically, the hymn draws from the Old Testament (Hab 2:20) and alludes to Philippians 2:5-8; Matthew 26:26-28; and Revelation 5:11-14. Theologically, the hymn is Christocentric, marked by awe and with complete attention to the coming of the incarnate Christ who will conquer the powers of hell as the hosts of heaven, rank on rank, the six-winged seraph, and the cherubim, who in awe, with veiled faces at his presence, praise him ceaselessly.

The grandeur of the text is carried in a majestic 8.7 8.7 8.7 trochaic meter and a stately cross rhyme. There is a dynamic counterpoint of the past ("As of old on earth He stood"), an awesome present ("Christ our God to earth descendeth"), and future ("he will give to all the faithful") and a dynamic counterpoint of heaven ("host of heaven," "realm of endless day," "seraph and cherubim") and earth ("mortal flesh," "earthly," "born of Mary," "on earth he stood," "human vesture," and "in the body and the blood"). There is a beauty of language borrowed from Scriptures in the paradoxical phrase "King of kings, yet born of Mary" underlining the divine and human nature of Christ and in what may seem to us hyperbolic phrases "sleepless eye" and "with ceaseless voice they cry."

The hymn tune was originally an ancient chant used for the Offertory of the Liturgy of St. James, but today the French melody PICARDY from *Chansons populaires des Provinces de France* (1860) is widely used. The simple, chant-like nature of the melody is retained in Ralph Vaughan Williams's setting. The repeat of the A section is largely reharmonized, cadencing not on the dominant of the key as in the first statement, but in the relative major. The B section, which emphasizes the final two lines of text that climax each stanza, is made of a repeated melody reharmonized, cadencing first on the dominant of the relative major and then on the tonic. Vaughan Williams gives this simple French carol an unusual musical interest and beautifully complements the text.

As a call to worship, this text and tune can express that natural awe and adoration that is the beginning of worship. The meaning and mood of the text may be expressed by a soloist beginning softly in chant style and with the following stanzas sung by the choir and then adding the congregation singing with ever-increasing intensity as organ stops or instruments are added.

Let all mortal flesh keep silence,
and with fear and trembling stand;
ponder nothing earthly minded,
for with blessing in his hand
Christ our God to earth descendeth,
our full homage to demand.

King of kings, yet born of Mary,
as of old on earth he stood,
Lord of lords in human vesture,
in the Body and the Blood
he will give to all the faithful
his own self for heavenly food.

Rank on rank the host of heaven
spreads its vanguard on the way,
as the Light of Light descendeth
from the realms of endless day,
that the powers of hell may vanish
as the darkness clears away.

At his feet the six-winged seraph;
cherubim with sleepless eye,
veil their faces to the Presence,
as with ceaseless voice they cry,
"Alleluia, alleluia!
Alleluia, Lord Most High!"

Entering into true worship and the remembrance of our Lord's atoning death is never a casual experience. A modern expression of awe is found in Jarsolav J. Vajda's mystical communion hymn "Now the silence" and its setting by Carl Schalk's NOW, which draw a line between the usualness of life and the distinctiveness of the experience of worship. Vajda notes, "Suddenly [on the morning of March 12, 1968] the hymn began to form in my mind as a list of awesome and exciting things one should expect in worship, culminating in a Eucharist and benediction."[29] Vajda notes that "The reverse order of the Doxology/Benediction not only expressed the order in which I pictured the Trinity coming to us in worship, but also the order in which the Incarnation took place: the visitation of the Virgin Mary by the Holy Spirit, then the Son's epiphany as the incarnate Word, followed by the universal blessing that is bestowed upon all in whom this same process occurs."[30]

The hymn, which has a biblical basis in Habakkuk 2:20, is one of the most unusual hymn texts of our time, and its twenty-one-fold anaphoric "now" chimes the distinctiveness of the experience of worship. The text is carefully grouped into six sections unfolding the worship experience. The "list of awesome and exciting things one should expect in worship, culminating in a Eucharist and benediction" is presented without a main finite verb, without rhyme, without punctuation, and, the author notes, "without worn clichés, depending entirely on rhythm and repetition to make it singable."[31]

> Now the silence
> Now the peace
> Now the empty hands uplifted
>
> Now the kneeling
> Now the plea
> Now the Father's arms in welcome
>
> Now the hearing
> Now the power
> Now the vessel brimmed for pouring
>
> Now the body
> Now the blood
> Now the joyful celebration
>
> Now the wedding
> Now the songs
> Now the heart forgiven leaping
>
> Now the Spirit's visitation
> Now the Son's epiphany
> Now the Father's blessing
>
> Now Now Now[32]

The opening portions of the different liturgies that focus on the worshiper's response of awe and adoration to God's revelation of himself may take a variety of forms: the Opening or Entrance Rite, an organ prelude, a procession, an opening acclamation, the Lord's Prayer, The Ten Commandments, the Kyrie, the Trisagion, or the Gloria in Excelsis. Each of these has found some expression in hymnody.

One of the great hymns of awe and adoration is Ray Palmer's translation of "Jesus, thou joy of loving hearts," which Erik Routley regarded to be "one of the best known and finest of American hymns."[33] John Julian opined,

> Most of Dr. Palmer's hymns have passed into congregational use, and have won great acceptance. The best of them by their combinations of thought, poetry, and devotion, are superior to almost all others of American origin. . . . His hymns written for that important collection [*Sabbath Hymn-Book*, 1858] rank amongst the best that America has produced. This is especially true of the first four . . . from the Latin ["Jesus, thou joy of loving hearts" is the first of these.][34]

Palmer was an 1830 graduate of Yale University, pastor of Congregational Churches in Maine and New York, and later Corresponding Secretary to the American Congregational Union, New York. The hymn is a translation and paraphrase of "Iesu dulcedo cordium," part of "Iesu dulcis memoria," which, based on the earliest extant manuscripts, has been considered to be of English origin possibly of the twelfth century.[35]

The hymn is a fervent prayer to Jesus and has references to John 6:35-40. In the fifth stanza one is reminded of Luke 24:29. The text is sometimes altered and begins "O Jesus, joy of loving hearts" and omits Palmer's second stanza. The text appears in this form in *The Hymnal 1982* and also appears with "a traditional Latin tune in a form found in the *Liber Usualis*, where it is matched with the Latin text from which this translation is derived."[36] In Routley's *Rejoice in the Lord*, the five stanzas of "Jesus, thou joy of loving hearts" are associated with the tune NÜRNBERG arranged by John Wilson from an original tune by J. S. Bach in Schemelli's *Gesangbuch*.

Conviction and Confession

The dialogue of worship moves logically (as in the Isaiah 6 model) from revelation and adoration to conviction and confession and, again, hymns are vital to these aspects. As Evelyn Underhill observes, worship swings between the poles of "Glory be to Thee" and "have mercy upon me!"[37] Isaiah 6 affirms that God's revelation of himself causes not only awe and adoration but also conviction, recognition of our own sinfulness before God, and the need for confession—"Woe is me, for I am ruined! Because I am a man of unclean lips, and I live among a people of unclean lips; for my eyes have seen the King, the Lord of hosts" (Isa 6:5).

"God be merciful to me," adapted in Routley's *Rejoice in the Lord*[88] from *The Psalter* (1912), is based on Psalm 51, considered to be David's great confession of his double sin of adultery and murder. The hymn follows closely the ideas, the form, and the wording of English translations of the psalm. The biblical text and hymns related to it play significant roles in the church's theology of sin and confession (personal and corporate sin against God), the need for confession, and the assurance of forgiveness.

While biblical texts such as Psalm 51 and hymns related to them also figure prominently in many liturgies, there is abundant evidence that confession often plays a less significant role in many non-liturgical traditions. The use of hymns such as "O God of earth and altar," "Out of the depths to thee I raise the voice of lamentation," "Lord Jesus, think on me," "Ah, holy Jesus," and "Jesus, name all names above" could help address that deficiency. In "God be merciful to me," the entreaty throbs in twenty-four personal pronouns in the three stanzas, in the immediate repetitions of words (expizeuxis), in repetition in the middle of successive lines (mesodiplosis), repetition at the beginning of successive lines (anaphora), and repetition of the same sound in successive words (alliteration) and with the trochaic meter and couplet rhyme.

> God be merciful to me;
> on thy grace I rest my plea.
> plenteous in compassion thou,
> blot out my transgressions now;
> My transgressions I confess;
> grief and guilt my soul oppress;
> I have sinned against thy grace,
> and provoked thee to thy face.
>
> Wash me, wash me pure within,
> O cleanse me from my sin;
> I confess thy judgments just;
> Speechless, I thy mercy trust
> Thou alone my Savior art,
> Teach thy wisdom to my heart;
> Make me pure, thy grace bestow
> Make me thus thy mercy know.
>
> Gracious God, my heart renew,
> Make my spirit right and true;

From my sins O hide thy face,
Blot them out in boundless grace.
Cast me not away from thee:
Let thy Spirit dwell in me;
Thy salvation's joy impart;
Steadfast make my willing heart.

Joseph Parry's harmonization of ABERYSTWYTH is a fine vehicle for the text melodically, harmonically, and formally. The transition to the relative major key in the fifth phrase and the climax in the sixth phrase provide a worthy complement to the text.

In some traditions, prayers of the people follow the Scripture reading, the sermon, and the creed and take the form of a litany with biddings to which the people respond with "Kyrie eleison" or the English form, "Christ have mercy." Directions for the intercessions often allow for adaptations suitable to the occasions and sometimes conclude with a collection that expresses some special need in the life of the local congregation. Many intercessory prayer hymns serve this portion of the liturgy.

Forgiveness (Absolution) and Gratitude

Conviction leads to confession of sins and confession of sins leads to absolution, which leads to gratitude. "If we confess our sins, He is faithful and righteous to forgive us our sins and to cleanse us from all unrighteousness" (1 John 1:9). The forgiveness of sin is recorded in such passages as Isaiah 6, "Then one of the seraphim flew to me with a burning coal in his hand, which he had taken from the altar with tongs. He touched my mouth with it and said, 'Behold, this has touched your lips; and your iniquity is taken away and your sin is forgiven.'" The normal response of gratitude for forgiveness finds expression in numerous hymns such as the versification of Psalm 32, "How blest are they whose trespass hath freely been forgiv'n," from *The Psalter*, 1912, and in stanzas such as those in "Jesus, name all names above," John Mason Neale's translation of Theoctistus of the Studium's ninth-century hymn, referring to the prodigal, Mary Magdalene, and the penitent thief on the cross and with the words "pardon," "lost condition," "contrition," and a twice-repeated "Woe" as in Isaiah's great confession in Isaiah 6.

Brian Wren's "I come with joy, a child of God," a contemporary expression of gratitude for forgiveness and joy in worship was, he says, originally written for the congregation at Hockley to sum up a series of sermons on the meaning of the communion. The hymn tries to use simple words to suggest important theological themes. It begins with the individual ("I come") and moves gradually into the corporate . . . stanza 4 relates Christ's "real presence" to the communal nature of the occasion.[39]

The text is much in keeping with Psalm 122:1, "I was glad when they said to me, 'Let us go to the house of the LORD,'" but here gladness becomes joy of Christ's forgiveness, love, freedom, and of Communion. Wren made some interesting revisions of his text. The words were copyrighted in 1971, and in the 1983 *Faith Looking Forward*, the opening couplet reads "I come with joy to meet my Lord, forgiven, loved, and free," but in the 1995 *Faith Renewed* it reads, "I come with joy, a child of God, forgiven, loved, and free." It is significant that the joy of forgiveness is retained. Wren's revisions also incorporated inclusive language. While the change of "That love that made us makes us one" to "The love that made us makes us one" is certainly smoother (as is the omission of the repeated last line), it is not as theologically significant as the change in the fourth stanza that he earlier noted "relates Christ's 'real presence.'" "His presence, always near," now reads "The spirit of the risen Christ, unseen, but ever near . . . ." The change from "we'll go our different ways, / and as his people in the world, / we'll live and speak his praise" to "by all that God has done, / we'll go with joy, to give the world, / the love that makes us one" is a stronger emphasis on what God has done, on the unity of the children of God, and on their ministry in the world. The revision also nicely turns the beginning "I come with joy" into "We'll go with joy," emphasizing again the corporate nature and the going to minister.

There is a joyous lilt to the rhythm and effective uses of alliteration to propel the text through its meanings. The charming American folk melody, adapted and harmonized by Annabel Morris Buchanan, nicely complements the "simple words" of which Brian Wren spoke and provides the joyous lilt. The tune has made its way through nineteenth-century shape-notes hymnals and into major hymnals of our day with its present name, LAND OF REST. Here is another example of a biblical theologian/pastor using literary skills to explain the liturgy, and his carefully edited words are set to music that conveys well the mood and meaning of the text.

I come with joy to meet my Lord,	I come with joy, a child of God,
forgiven, loved, and free,	forgiven, loved, and free,
in awe and wonder to recall	the life of Jesus to recall,
his life laid down for me,	in love laid down for me.
his life laid down for me.	
I come with Christians far and near	I come with Christians far and near
to find, as all are fed,	to find, as all are fed,
the new community of love	the new community of love
in Christ's communion bread,	in Christ's communion bread.
in Christ's communion bread.	
As Christ breaks bread and bids us share,	As Christ breaks bread and bids us share,
each proud division ends.	each proud division ends.
That love that made us makes us one,	The love that made us makes us one,
and strangers now are friends,	and strangers now are friends.
and strangers now are friends.	
And thus with joy we meet our Lord.	The spirit of the risen Christ,
His presence, always near.	unseen, but ever near,
is in such friendship better known;	is in such friendship better known:
we see and praise him here,	alive and among us here.
we see and praise him here.	
Together met, together bound,	Together met, together bound,
we'll go our different ways,	by all that God has done,
and as his people in the world	we'll go with joy, to give the world,
we'll live and speak his praise,	the love that makes us one.[41]
we'll live and speak his praise.[40]	

Proclamation and Affirmation

The proclamation or affirmation of the word of God has, through all of Christian history, remained central to worship. This emphasis on the word of God may range from the reading of Scripture and a sermon to a more elaborate sequence of events in "The liturgy of the Word," including the collect of the day, the Old Testament Lesson, the Epistle, the gradual, the Holy Gospel, the sermon, and often the personal and corporate affirmation or proclamation of one's faith in Christ, a statement of beliefs, or the affirmation of a creed. In addition to the spoken word, anthems, graduals, antiphons, sequences, and hymns hold a prominent place in the proclamation of God's word. The reading of Scripture is a significant area of commonality between the "liturgical" and "non-liturgical" services. The word of God is the basis of Christian belief, and the reading of Scripture in worship should be central to the worship experience and form the basis not only for the sermon but for the selection of hymns as well.

The brief prayers of the collects are characterized by a certain rhythm and symmetry and a rather rigid structure of (1) address or invocation, (2) petition, and (3) conclusion and have a significant place in the long history of the liturgy. In certain seasons and on special days, the collect of the day expresses the emphasis of the season or day and sometimes presages the lections to be read. These qualities of terseness, rhythm, symmetry of form, and biblical richness make the collects a fertile field for hymn writers. Dudley-Smith speaks of the collects being inspirations for numerous lines of his hymns.[42]

The Old Testament has always been central to the people of God. The reading of the Old Testament in the synagogue services and the reading of the Old Testament along with Christian writings played a significant part in worship in the early Christian communities. The development of lectionaries provided systematic patterns for the readings of Scripture, and some lectionaries provide for the reading of a large part of the Old Testament and almost all of the New Testament over a three-year period. The Old Testament lesson is the first reading at a Eucharist, and many of these readings have a significant relationship to the Gospel of the day. The role of the Psalms in Christian hymnody has been and continues to be profoundly important. The scriptural indexes to hymnals give ample evidence of the important place that the Old Testament continues to hold in hymnody. Hymnal indexes to scriptural references or allusions list hundreds of Old Testament passages that are reflected in hymns across the centuries.

In some traditions, the second reading is from the Pauline Epistles. In some traditions, the general Epistles and Revelation are read in the Easter season. Portions of almost all of the Pauline Epistles have been inspirations for hymns. This seems appropriate since fragments of early Christian hymns are found in several of the Pauline Epistles.

Since the early days of the church, psalms have been sung between readings from the Old Testament and the Epistles. This practice has continued in some traditions. Often, the psalm appointed for the gradual is related to the preceding Old Testament lesson. These sung psalm texts became known as graduals because the singer stood on one of the steps (gradus) rather than ascending to the top of the ambo, which was reserved for the Gospel. Marion J. Hatchett notes, "On some occasions a hymn which is a metrical version of an appointed psalm . . . would be an appropriate substitute for the responsorial or direct singing or reading of the gradual."[43] Numerous metrical versions of the psalms could find great use as gradual hymns, as could New Testament passages. Dudley-Smith says his "Faith and truth and life bestowing,"[44] based on the parable of the sower in Matthew 13:3-9 with references to Romans 10:17 and John 15:16, is intended as a hymn "to sing before the Scriptures are read or taught: a short hymn before the sermon, or perhaps a Gradual hymn."[45]

With the suppression of the Old Testament lesson, which was widespread by the fifth century, the gradual was shortened in some traditions to a single verse and immediately followed by the Alleluia or the tract that is sung before the Gospel, in the place of the alleluia on days during certain seasons. The gradual (Psalm) was normally sung responsively. First the cantor, or later the choir, sang the antiphon, which would be repeated by the people after each psalm verse or groups of verses. The antiphonal or responsorial singing done in ancient Israel's singing of some of the psalms and in early Christianity in the antiphon may be employed in the singing of a number of hymns that are appropriate at this point in worship.

Historically, there came to be at this point in the liturgy (except during Lent) the use of Alleluias, psalms that contained Alleluia or to which an Alleluia could be added, and later metrical psalmody or hymnody was included in anticipation of the reading of the Gospel. This early liturgical expression of rejoicing comes from the songs of the saints in glory (Rev 19:1, 3, 4, 6) and is found in many hymns.

The reading from the Gospels is the foundation of the Christian lectionary and the climactic reading in the liturgy. A hymn may precede the reading as part of the Gospel procession to the pulpit or to the midst of the congregation where, with the people standing, the Gospel is read by a priest or deacon. Historically, the book and the reading of the Gospel symbolized the presence of Christ in the liturgy of the word similar to the way the Eucharistic prayer and elements symbolized the presence of Christ in the liturgy of the table. In some traditions, the Gospel of John is read during Lent and Easter and some other occasions in a three-year cycle. The Synoptic Gospels are read, with the exception of certain special days or seasons, throughout the remainder of the church year. Hymnal indexes to scriptural references or allusions are replete with New Testament passages that are reflected in hymns across the centuries.

The sermon is most often an exposition of one or more of the lections just read. Given the vast number of hymns based on and alluding to biblical passages, hymn texts are a rich reservoir relating to the sermon. Many hymns are metrical versions or paraphrases of Scripture, and some are themselves sermonic expositions of Scriptures. There is much to commend the practice of encouraging worshipers to read, as a family, the Scriptures and the hymns that will be read and sung the following Sunday.

The affirmation of faith is a significant part of many worship traditions and in many traditions follows the sermon. John H. Leith remarks, "The church liturgy has been one of the primary occasions that called for the development of creeds; for worship is incomplete without an affirmation of faith in hymns, prayer, and sermon."[46] The Nicene Creed is the most universal of the creeds, and Dale Moody notes that "a careful reading of the final form reveals how much even the most non-creedal Christians owe to this historic formulation of Christian faith."[47] Both the Nicene and Apostles' Creed draw upon the Trinitarian statements in Matthew 28:19-20 and were intended to be baptismal confessions in the face of threats of heresy. Moody emphasizes that "their influence on the development of Christian theology has been enormous."[48]

Both creeds have had their theological detractors. As Marion J. Hatchett notes, "Some continental reformers, rejecting the [Nicene] Creed because it contained nonscriptural phrases, substituted the Apostles' Creed," and "At the time when the American Proposed Book was being prepared there was considerable opposition to its being included in the Eucharist, largely because of the 'unscriptural phrases' it was said to contain."[49] The phrase "He descended into hell" from the Apostles' Creed has been problematic for many, and Dale Moody notes, "Even Anglican theology, which is often more empirical and traditional has found it necessary to wrestle with this problem."[50] Several hymns have been based on the creed or portions of the creed. Dudley-Smith's metrical version of the Apostles' Creed, "We believe in God the Father," is the only metrical version of a creed approved by the General Synod for use as an Authorized Affirmation of Faith in the public worship of the Church of England.[51] It is his single most consciously "comprehensive" theological hymn. He states his purpose in writing this hymn: "There are, of course, a number of hymns affirming basic Christian doctrines . . . but few are close enough to a traditional and universal creed for particular liturgical use."[52] The hymn is based on the version of the Apostles'

Creed used in the *Alternative Services Book*, 1989, of the Church of England, following that of the International Consultation on English Texts.

The Peace is an exchange by ministers and people and often includes such phrases as "the peace of the Lord be always with you," and it may serve in some respects as an introduction to the liturgy of the table. The biblical concept of peace figures frequently in hymns, and many could be used in this portion of a worship service.

Our remembrance of our Lord's atoning death, whether called "Holy Communion," "The Eucharist," or "The Lord's Supper," is at the heart of worship for many traditions. Evelyn Underhill states what is true for much of Christendom:

> . . . the whole liturgic life of Christendom is built on a double foundation: the Bible and the Eucharist. The uttered Word and the living Presence, the holy doctrine and the holy food, the message of salvation and the sacrifice of praise, are the gathering points of devotion wherever Christian worship retains and expresses its real character, as a loving and grateful response of the creature to the self-revelation and self-giving of God.[53]

While there are in the great traditions of Christendom differing theologies about the observance, differing methods of observance, and differing terms to identify the observance, there is much that is common. The observance is biblical, based on the accounts of Christ's institution of the Last Supper as recorded in the Synoptic Gospels (Matt 26:26 ff; Mark 14:22 ff; Luke 22:1 ff). It is in keeping with the practice of the early church as recorded by Paul in 1 Corinthians 11:23 ff. It is in obedience to Christ's command to "do this in remembrance of me" (Luke 22:19). It is specifically in remembrance of Christ's atoning death. Most traditions include the words of institution and other Scripture, prayers, and, as was done at Christ's Last Supper with his disciples, a hymn.

Fred Pratt Green's "An upper room" begins with our Lord's preparation for his last supper with the disciples "he loved until the end" and then speaks of his disciples who still gather in celebration of the "lasting gift Jesus gave his own to share his bread, his loving cup." The third stanza draws on John 13:1-17 with the disciple's firsthand account of Christ's washing the disciples' feet. In this stanza, Pratt Green brings together in a simple, yet beautiful statement the interrelated biblical, theological, liturgical (in both the narrow and broad senses of the word), and literary dimensions. The musical dimension is beautifully present with the text's being sung to FOLK-SONG, the English traditional melody as harmonized by John Wilson.

> An upper room did our Lord prepare
> for those he loved until the end:
> and his disciples still gather there,
> to celebrate their Risen Friend.
>
> A lasting gift Jesus gave his own,
> to share his bread, his loving cup.
> Whatever burdens may bow us down,
> he by his Cross shall lift us up.
>
> And after Supper he washed their feet,
> for service, too, is sacrament.
> In him our joy shall be made complete
> sent out to serve, as he was sent.
>
> No end there is! We depart in peace.
> He loves beyond our uttermost:
> in every room in our Father's house
> he will be there, as Lord and host.[54]

Timothy Dudley-Smith's earlier hymn with the same idea, "An upper room with evening lamps ashine," begins also with the "then" of the Last Supper and moves to the "now" of the Holy Communion. In the two following stanzas, he draws on the biblical accounts and carefully borrows key biblical words to offer a theological statement using literary devices of hypotyposis, alliteration, and oxymoron and moves from that first "upper room with evening lamps ashine" to "take for ourselves the pledges of his love, foretaste and token of that feast in heaven." The ELLERS tune is a good vehicle for the text.

George Wallace Briggs's (1875–1959) Communion hymn, "Come, risen Lord, and deign to be our guest," begins not with the Thursday evening of the Lord's Supper with his disciples, but speaks of our supper with the Lord by a comparison with the two disciples in Emmaus (Luke 24:13-35) on the Sunday evening of the resurrection. The text then speaks of our communion with Christ, "as in that upper room they met." Briggs recounts an interesting theological exchange regarding our Lord's institution of the ordinance:

> I originally concluded verse one with: "In thine own sacrament of bread
> and wine." Dr. Percy Dearmer, who edited *Songs of Praise*, had come to
> his own views about the institution of the Sacraments, and he was not
> prepared—at that state of his life, for his doctrinal pilgrimage was a
> strangely chequered one—to say that Christ ordered the continuance of
> the Sacrament. He therefore begged leave to alter "In thine own sacra-
> ment" to "In this our sacrament." I reluctantly consented—and have ever
> since regretted it. As Professor F. C. Burkitt said, whether our Lord did or
> did not directly order the continuance of the Sacrament, it was undoubt-
> edly His sacrament, or the Church would never have continued it.[55]

In keeping with Luke's account of the Emmaus supper, Briggs speaks of
Christ as guest, but then as host, and in the original text the three-fold statement of "thine" emphasizes "the feast is thine; thyself at thine own board
make manifest in thine own Sacrament of Bread and Wine."

The final two stanzas, with a nine-fold statement of "one," emphasizes
the oneness of believers in Christ. The careful repetitions (anaphora,
mesodiplosis, and mesarchia) are not simply rhetorical devices, but are ways
of emphasizing theological concepts.

The ROSEDALE[56] tune is a fine expression of the text, especially with
the climax coming on the dominant of the relative minor that is resolved
deceptively and with the fine descant countermelody written for the climactic third stanza. Leo Sowerby wrote the tune for the celebration of the
dedication of the Gloria in Excelsis Tower at Washington Cathedral on May
7, 1964. His musical stature is attested to by his having received a Pulitzer
Prize for music and, in his time, being frequently referred to as the "Dean
of American church music."

The liturgy of Holy Communion often begins with the bringing from
the congregation the oblations, with the offerings of money, and sometimes
with at least the symbolic bringing of the bread and wine for Communion.
This sometimes includes an offertory anthem or presentation hymn. At this
point in the late Middle Ages, especially in the eastern orthodox tradition,
a "rite of prothesis" developed in which the preparation of the gifts and the
transfer took on a ritual significance, and hymns and prayers were a part of
this "Great Entrance." Remnants of this procession and the singing of
hymns have persisted in some traditions. The receiving, the procession, and
the presenting of oblations are today accompanied in many traditions not
only by the congregational singing of hymns or psalms but also by the choral
singing of anthems or motets. Many hymns speak to the concepts of "Offertory," "Dedication and renewal," "Stewardship," and "Thanksgiving."

As part of the Great Thanksgiving in some liturgies, the various Eucharistic prayers of Holy Communion are central and are often referred to in the singular—"Eucharistic Prayer." In some ancient liturgies, it was the sections from the *Sursum corda* through the people's amen that were referred to as the "Eucharistia" or thanksgiving. The Eucharistic prayer(s) have inspired many hymn writers. If there are proper Prefaces (the day of and six days after Christmas, Easter, and Ascension Day, and the day of the Feast of Trinity), the prayers follow the *Sursum corda*. The "*Sursum corda*" admonition, or "Lift up your hearts," is a frequent phrase in hymnody.

The canon corresponds to the anaphora of the Eastern Church (Greek word for "lifting up" or "offering" from Heb 7:27) that extends from the *Sursum corda* to the dismissal. In some traditions, the canon is said silently while the *Sanctus* is being sung by the choir and does not include the Communion and the following devotions. The profound meanings in the words that normally lead to the "*Sanctus*" are more than the human mind can fully comprehend—"Therefore with Angels and Archangels, and with all the company of heaven, we laud and magnify thy glorious name: evermore praising thee, and saying: Holy, Holy, Holy, Lord God of hosts, heaven and earth are full of thy glory: Glory be to thee, O Lord most High. Amen." The thrice holy occurs in many hymns. The solemn, consecratory Eucharistic prayer has remained unchanged from at least the sixth century. It begins with the versicles and responses before the Preface and ends with the "Amen" of the people before the Pater Noster. The Anamnesis, Greek for "recollection," is done in commemoration or in memory such as this first prayer following the Consecration of the Mass.

William Bright's "And now, O Father, mindful of the love" is a paraphrase from the oblation or offering of the bread and wine from the Canon of the Mass in the Roman rite. Bright (1824–1901), a church historian, was born at Doncaster, West Riding of Yorkshire, England, and was educated at Rugby School and University College, Oxford. He was elected a Fellow at the college in 1847 and later became a tutor. He served as tutor at Trinity College, Glenalmond for a time, but returned to Oxford where he became Regius Professor of Ecclesiastical History and Canon of Christ Church. He wrote extensively in the areas of church history, theology, devotional literature, and poetry, including translations and original hymns. "And now, O Father, mindful of the love" is a liturgical, biblical, and theological expression of the ideas in the oblation,[57] and there is a fine literary expression of the theological[58] concept of propitiation, the atoning and reconciling death of Christ, in the second stanza (Rom 3:25; 1 John 2:2; 1 John 4:10). William

Henry Monk's UNDE ET MEMORES was written for Bright's text and is discussed in chapter 6.

The elevation, or raising of the bread and of the wine after each element is consecrated, occurs at this point in some celebrations of the Lord's Supper. This showing of the elements to the people is an act of reverence; the words "*Ecce Agnus Dei. Ecce qui tollit peccata mundi* (Behold the Lamb of God. Behold him who takes away the sins of the world)" are taken from the saying of John the Baptist in John 1:29, and that text may be sung at this point. Where this portion of the liturgy may be accompanied by organ, choral, or congregational music, Matthew Bridges's hymn, "Behold, the Lamb of God" sung to Samuel Sebastian Wesley's WIGAN, is an appropriate textual and musical expression.

The Lord's Prayer is said at this point in the Roman rite, but comes after the Fraction in the non-Byzantine Eastern and non-Roman Western rites. Timothy Rees's "God of love and truth and beauty," sung to Herbert Murrill's tune CAROLYN,[59] or James Montgomery's "Our Heav'nly Father, hear" sung to the ST. MICHAEL tune, could give congregational expression at this point in a liturgy.

The breaking of the bread (the Fraction) for distribution at the Eucharist is in imitation of Jesus's action (Luke 22:19) at the Last Supper and, for many, symbolizes Christ's death. In some traditions, an anthem or hymn may be sung during and after the initial breaking of the bread, and numerous hymns could be used here. Some traditions include the *Pascha nostrum* ("Christ our Passover") said or sung by the celebrant, said as a versicle and response, or sung by the people, a cantor, or a choir.

The Prayer of Humble Access that begins "We do not presume to come to this thy Table, O merciful Lord, trusting in our own righteousness, but in thy manifold and great mercies. We are not worthy so much as to gather up the crumbs under thy Table" is based on Matthew 8:8 and Mark 7:28. It is an appropriate prayer given the awesome warning of Paul in 1 Corinthians 11:27–29. Bright's "And now, O Lord, mindful of love" is truly a hymn of humble access.

At the showing of the sacrament in some traditions and immediately before the administration of Communion, the *Sancta sanctis* phrase, "The gifts of God for the People of God" (or "Holy things to the holy people"), may be said, and sometimes the people respond with, "One is holy, one is Lord, Jesus Christ, to the glory of God the Father" or the "*Benedictus qui venit*" ("Blessed is he that cometh in the name of the Lord," from Mark 11:9) as a welcome to the coming forth of the sacrament for Communion.

In some contexts, hymns as diverse as James Montgomery's "Hail to the Lord's Anointed" or Theodulph of Orlean's "All glory, laud, and honor" might be appropriate here.

The words of administration, "The body of Christ" and "The blood of Christ," are spoken, and many traditions permit the singing of "hymns, psalms, or anthems" during the ministration of Communion. Historically, some of the most popular Communion psalms have been Psalm 34, with verse 8 as the antiphon, and Psalm 145, with verse 16 as the antiphon (sometimes antiphons were not from the psalm but from another passage of Scripture with connotations to Communion) and the great Hallel (Psalms 113–118). Hymns based on these psalms and hymns for "Holy Communion" or "Passiontide" could be sung at this point.

Another provision for sung texts in some traditions is a hymn, anthem, or motet to cover the ablutions or removal of the Sacrament and here again a number of Communion or Passiontide texts may be appropriate.

Call and Commitment

In Isaiah 6, that great picture of worship, the proclamation of God's word is followed by God's call, "Whom shall I send, and who will go for us?" and Isaiah's response of "Here am I. Send me!" Hymnals abound with texts related to call, commitment, and consecration.

It is written that Daniel March said his hymn "Hark the voice of Jesus calling [originally "crying"]" was written in 1868 "in great haste" to follow a sermon on Isaiah 6:8 he was to preach in Philadelphia. The hymn also has echoes of John 4:35-36 and Isaiah 21:11-12. Frances Ridley Havergal wrote, out of her own commitment, more than once on the matters of call, commitment, and consecration. In 1867 she wrote "Master speak!" related to Samuel's experience recorded in 1 Samuel 3. In 1872 she wrote "Lord, speak to me, that I may speak," again showing her commitment to God's call, and this was even before she experienced on Advent Sunday in 1873 what she called "full surrender" and "the blessedness of true consecration." Soon after that experience, she wrote yet another hymn of consecration, "Take my life, and let it be consecrated, Lord, to thee." Fred Pratt Green's "How clear is our vocation, Lord" is a more contemporary (1981) expression and addresses the dangers of "worldly pressures" that can be hindrances to our committing ourselves to the call of Christ, and yet we are reminded, "We mark your saints, how they became in hindrances more sure, / whose joyful virtues put to shame the casual way we wear your name . . . ." The frequent plural

pronouns emphasize that this is a corporate expression of the need and challenges of commitment. This text is sometimes appropriately set to the
REPTON tune by Charles Hubert Hastings Parry, who is often regarded as
one of the most influential British musicians of his generation.

Commission and Service

In the broader etymological, historical, and biblical meaning of liturgy, the
liturgy of worship leads to the liturgy of service. In Isaiah 6, God's response
to Isaiah's commitment is "Go, and tell this people . . . ." Timothy Dudley-
Smith's hymn, "An upper room with evening lamps ashine," speaks to the
concept that the conclusion of the service of worship is the beginning of the
life of service. Dudley-Smith notes that the final stanza "begins with a conscious echo of the closing prayer of the Service of Holy Communion in the
Alternative Service Book 1980 of the Church of England which was super-
seded by *Common Worship* in 2000."[60]

> So send us out, to love and serve and praise,
>   filled with his Spirit, as the Master said:
> love, joy and peace the wine of all our days,
>   Christ and his life our true and living bread.[61]

One of the biblical or traditional blessings often precedes the dismissal.
Similar to the procession at the beginning of the service, a recession and
hymn at the end may by its movement back to or through the congregation
lend order, dignity, distinctiveness, and outcome to the experience of worship and symbolize the movement of God's people into the world to act out
what they have just celebrated, to do the work of God.

Matthew 26:30 and Mark 14:26 indicate that a "hymn" (Psalm) was
sung by our Lord and his disciples after the Last Supper: "And after singing
a hymn, they went out to the Mount of Olives." Through history, a post-
Communion hymn has, in many traditions, been sung at the end of the
Eucharist and before the post-Communion prayer or formal conclusion after
Communion. A hymn was sung after Communion in some German church
orders, and in the Reformed church one or more of the Hallel psalms were
sung at this point. Parts of the great Hallel (Psalms 113–118) are thought
to be the hymn sung by Jesus and his disciples at the institution of the Lord's
Supper. Hymns based on portions of Psalms 113–118 such as Benjamin
Schmolck's "Open now thy gates of beauty"; Watts's paraphrase of Psalm

117, "From all that dwell below the skies"; or Charles Wesley's "Come, let us with our Lord arise," referring to Psalm 118:24, could be appropriate here as would the final two stanzas of Fred Pratt Green's "When in our music God is glorified," beginning "And did not Jesus sing a psalm that night / when utmost evil strove against the light? / And may God give us faith to win the fight, Alleluia!"

A formal dismissal of the people has ancient roots. The Apostolic Constitutions and other early Eastern liturgies had a simple "Depart in peace." The Roman rite has its "*Ite missa est,*" while Gallican churches used the "*Benedicamus.*" In medieval times a response of "*Deo gratias*" was spoken in acknowledgment of having heard what was said. In joyous times, such as Easter, alleluias were added, and in times of penitence, a festive dismissal was replaced with "Let us bless the Lord." An understanding of the various meanings of these dismissals might be aided by instruction through the study of such benediction hymns as John B. Geyer's "The Lord in mercy bless us now," based on the benediction in Numbers 6:24;[62] Fred Kaan's "Lord, as we rise to leave this shell of worship"; or John Ellerton's "Savior, Again to thy dear name we raise."

A postlude may conclude the service, and this is often based on one of the hymns sung in the service or at least in the spirit of the service. The Isaiah 6 model of worship ends with God's commissioning of Isaiah, and his response as recorded in the remainder of his book is one of service. Humanity's acceptance of God's call to service involves the whole range of ministries including not only worship but also discipleship, proclamation, and social service that are discussed later in this chapter.

Again, it has been the emphasis here to show that whether a worship service is of the simplest, most informal type or of more complex and formal types that have evolved over the centuries in many traditions in many parts of the world, hymns play vital roles in every aspect of the worship: in the service itself, in educational contexts dealing with worship and the hymns in preparation for the service, or in times of meditation following the service.

The Divine Office. In addition to the weekly services of the Lord's Day, and the annual cycle of the Christian Year, many Christians observe daily worship services. Evelyn Underhill speaks with high regard of the Divine Office as

. . . corporate Christian worship . . . its classic form: the Divine Office, or non-eucharistic liturgical sequence of praise. . . . the ordained form within which the whole Church performs from hour to hour, by night and by day, that unceasing praise of God which is the chief purpose of her existence.[63]

Hymns have been based on numerous liturgical portions of the offices as well as the Mass, and many of these liturgical portions are based directly on Scripture, are bound up intricately with the theology of the traditions, and have a literary beauty that has been carried into hymns worthy of musical settings. In some traditions, the traditional eight "Hour Services" of the earlier church were amalgamated into Morning Prayer and Evening Prayer, though in the nineteenth century there was a revival of the hours and compline was used in theological colleges and on retreats.[64] Morning and Evening Prayer of the Anglican community have the same basic principles and structure and are intended to provide for the continuous and orderly reading of the Bible and the reciting of the psalms. The basic structure of Morning prayer is (1) Introduction, (2) the Lord's Prayer and versicles, (3) the *Venite*, (4) Psalms, (5) two lessons, each with its own canticle, (6) Apostles' Creed, (7) the Lord's Prayer and suffrages, (8) three collects, and (9) concluding prayers. Forms of the *Jubilate Deo* (Psalm 100), *Benedicite* (the Song of the Three Holy Children from the Greek addition to Daniel 3 as found in the Old Testament Apocrypha), and *Te Deum*, A Prayer of St. Chrysostom, are sometimes sung. Evening Prayer in some traditions is based on the same principles and form as Morning Prayer, and a number of hymns relate to this service. Numerous hymns have been based on various sections of the offices. The *Magnificat* is one of the most familiar canticles for Evening Prayer, and Dudley-Smith's "Tell out, my soul, the greatness of the Lord" is a fine hymnic expression of the canticle.

Christian Year. In many faiths, the central acts of worship move in a meaningful annual cycle. As William Maxwell expresses it, "worship has a circumference as well as a centre, and piety early sanctified days, weeks, and year by a cycle of daily prayer and praise."[65] Hymns have been written for every aspect of the Christian year, though those related to Advent, Christmas, Epiphany, Lent, and Holy Week are perhaps the most familiar.

One example of a hymn for one feast of the church year may serve to illustrate what is a vast body of hymns for every day and season. The transfiguration (Matt 17:1-9; Mark 9:2-10; Luke 9:28-36; 2 Pet 1:16-18), an event that affirms the basic theological concept of Christ as the Son of God and seems to have been a turning point in the disciples' understanding of the nature of Christ and his ministry, has been a major feast in the Eastern church since the fourth century and in the West since the ninth century. It has had a varied history in the different traditions celebrated variously on the last Sunday in the Epiphany season, the seventh Sunday after Trinity, the eighth Sunday after Pentecost, or the second Sunday of Lent. Hymns for the Transfiguration range from the stanza of the anonymous tenth-century Latin hymn in Laurence Housman's translation, "O light of light, love given birth," to Bland Tucker's twentieth-century stanza added to Christopher Wordsworth's nineteenth-century "Songs of thankfulness and praise" and to Brian Wren's "Jesus on the mountain peak."

Brian Wren notes of his hymn on the Transfiguration, "It makes little attempt to probe the imagery or historical 'placing' of the transfiguration story, but retains some validity, perhaps, in its atmosphere of worship and adoration."[66] Though this was, as Wren notes, the second hymn he wrote,[67] there is a mature quality to the literary expression of this biblical/theological concept and pivotal event in the life of Christ. The opening couplet is a dramatic picture of when "Jesus on the mountain peak stands alone in glory blazing." The account is from the perspective of the three apostles, especially Peter, who in awe and adoration exclaims, "let us, if we dare to speak, with the saints and angels praise him. Alleluia!" There is, perhaps, a poetic ambiguity in the "us" of the first stanza that allows the reader/singer to participate in the drama. The second stanza continues the awe in trembling and sees Christ in the presence of Moses and Elijah, and through them "All the Prophets and Law shout through them their joyful greeting. Alleluia!" The third stanza speaks of "the cloud of glory" and of God's "proclaiming in its thunder Jesus as his Son," and the stanza challenges, "Nations, cry aloud in wonder—Alleluia!" The final stanza reaffirms, "This is God's beloved Son," and that "Law and Prophets sing before him" (with allusions to Hebrews); then it affirms Christ as "first and last and only One" (with allusions to Revelation) and ends with an all-encompassing "All creation shall adore him—Alleluia!" This final thought of the hymn was changed from "Let creation now adore him!" to the climactic affirmation "All creation shall adore him," echoing Philippians 2:10-11. The "Alleluia" that concludes each stanza is integral to the stanzas, not an appendage. The trochaic, 78.78 meter with the four-fold Alleluias sets the mood of adoration, and the cross rhyme scheme, ab ab, is natural and well spaced to the developing thoughts. The drama is alive with characters—preeminently Christ, the three apostles, Moses and Elijah and all the Prophets, all the nations, and all creation.

At least three very different tunes have been used for Wren's text. Wren remarks that "Peter Cutts' tune [SHILLINGFORD], written soon after the words, and under the influence of Hindemith, catches this aspect [the 'atmosphere of worship and adoration'] unforgettably."[68] The German composer Paul Hindemith (1895–1963) was known for his complex, contrapuntal, neoclassical style, and his influence on Cutts can be seen in the dissonant, non-diatonic but tonal style of SHILLINGFORD.[69] In *English Praise*,[70] the earlier text is set to the twelfth-century melody, CHRIST IST ERSTANDEN, harmonized chiefly by G. R. Woodward (1848–1934) with three jubilant, neumatic "alleluyas," each beginning on a different beat of the measure, giving a powerful, cascading effect. The tune MOWSLEY[71] by the Reverend Canon Cyril Taylor was composed for the also jubilant Easter text, "Jesus lives!" but is a fine expression of Wren's text. Taylor (1907–1991) made significant contributions to English church music serving as Precentor of Bristol and Salisbury Cathedrals and as Assistant to BBC's Director of Religious Broadcasting, where he was involved in the *BBC Hymn Book*. He contributed to this book some twenty tunes, the most famous being ABBOT'S LEIGH, which John Wilson describes as "in Britain the most popular new tune of its generation."[72] The strong, repeated first beat of Taylor's MOWSLEY and the ascending major sixth set the dramatic "atmosphere of worship and adoration." Already in the third measure, the G major tune moves toward the dominant only to transition then into A minor, rush into E minor, and climax on a C major chord before settling into the tonic. The melody for the third line of each stanza begins as a sequence of the beginning melody and is a powerful complement to the development of the textual ideas. Yet another melodic sequence (measures 6 and 7), combined with the tonal shifts, provides strong emphasis to the important final line of each stanza. The textual and musical climax in the antepenultimate measure occurs on the words "angels praise him," "joyful greeting," "aloud in wonder!" and "now adore him." Yet another though abbreviated sequence rushes this time onto the fourth beat in the eighth measure, beginning the melodic sequence before the musical/textual phrase has ended and anticipating the "Alleluia."

An analysis of the text and tune, as always, suggests ways the hymn may be sung. The hymn is written from the perspective of Peter (2 Pet 1:16-18), and the first three stanzas may well be sung as a solo and the final stanza by the congregation.

Figure 4. Words: "Jesus on the mountain peak," Brian Wren (b. 1936). © 1977 Hope Publishing Company. Carol Stream IL 60188. All Rights Reserved. Used by permission. Music: MOWSLEY, Cyril Vincent Taylor (1907–1991). © 1985 Hope Publishing Company. Carol Stream IL 60188. All Rights Reserved. Used by permission.

Private and Family Worship. There are indications that private and family worship have, in recent years, suffered a serious decline to the detriment of the Christian life in general and especially to public worship, which might be considered to be either the natural outgrowth of private and family worship or as the very motivation of private and family worship. The reading (and singing) of hymns in private and family worship is of profound significance in itself and as a major preparation for meaningful public worship.

Church leaders would do well to encourage families to observe some regular worship in the home and to include the reading or singing of hymns, some of which will be part of the following Sunday's public worship. Reading hymns aloud (rather than singing) often brings insights into the meaning of hymns that may later be reinforced in singing.

Special Occasions. Numerous hymns that are suitable for such occasions as baptisms, confirmations, weddings, and funerals and are easily found through the topical indexes of hymnals. Reading, as well as singing, may be unusually meaningful in such occasions. The multiple dimensions of these hymns may well be studied before use if their full meaning and value are to be experienced.

Daily Work. The daily work of the Christian provides inumerable opportunities for calling forth hymns that express thoughts and feelings relative to everyday events and provide guidance for the daily tasks. The six stanzas of Charles Wesley's "Forth in Thy name, O Lord, I go my daily labor to pursue" address matters of daily life and work. David Wright begins and ends his historical survey of "What do hymns say about work" with Charles Wesley's 1739 hymn, "Son of the carpenter":

Son of the Carpenter, receive
    This humble work of mine:
Worth to my meanest labour give,
    By joining it to thine.[73]

In the third stanza of his "God lies beyond us, throned in light resplendent," Timothy Dudley-Smith reminds us that

God lives within us, breath and life instilling,
    daily transforming ways of thought and seeing.
Spirit all-holy, all our spirits filling,
    blow, Wind, about us! burn within our being.[74]

For the sensitive Christian, Christ is "daily transforming ways of thought and seeing." Recalling a hymn may sometimes be the avenue by which the transformation occurs.

Worship is the motivating act for all the other ministries of the individual Christian and for the Christian church. The act of worship as given in the Isaiah 6 model concludes with God's call and mankind's commitment, then God's commissioning and mankind's response in the other ministries. Christ's final words at the conclusion of his earthly ministry were words of commission to go, to make disciples, to baptize, and to teach. Many hymn texts approach these ministries with breadth and depth. There is a theology of "liturgy" in its biblical, etymological meaning that calls for the living out of the Christian faith in the ministries of discipleship, proclamation, and social concern.

Discipleship (μαθητωύω, διδάσκω)

Each ministry of the individual Christian and of the Christian church can, in some way, be grouped under one of the larger categories of worship, discipleship, proclamation, and social concern, and hymns relate significantly to each of these ministries. Christians who truly worship Christ are also Christians deeply committed to maturing spiritually and to helping others mature spiritually. Μαθητεύω (be a disciple, make a disciple of), Μαθητής, οῦ (disciple, pupil, follower), and Διδάσκω (teach) are the New Testament words that most specifically refer to the ministry of discipleship and teaching. In our day, this involves Bible study, prayer, meditation (solitude, simplicity, submission), learning, following Christ, growing in spiritual maturity, and discipling others. Hymns can relate significantly to every aspect of discipleship.

It is the responsibility of the individual Christian to follow Christ, to experience Christ, to grow in Christ, to seek to have the mind of Christ, and it is the responsibility of the church to provide avenues for this following, experiencing, growing, and seeking. John Newport notes that "The task of Christian educators . . . is . . . to induct Christians into the faith community, to give them the skills, insights, words, stories, and rituals they need to live this faith in a world that neither knows nor follows the One who is truth."[75] Christian disciples must understand the historical context in which they live and should seize on hymns that contribute beautiful, forceful, memorable avenues for giving skills, insights, words, stories, and rituals needed for Christians to live this faith in such a world.

Gilbert Chesterton's "O God of earth and altar" is a powerful hymn that speaks to the human condition in which the church and individual Christians have to minister. Chesterton speaks to political corruption, pride, terror, aimlessness, greed, scorn, gullibility, and disrespect of God that characterize society, and he prays that God will lift up a living nation. With almost no biblical wording or clear allusion to Scripture, the hymn rings with the message of the Old Testament prophets: Isaiah's warning of God's judgment on Judah's disobedience to God, Amos's warning of judgment on the rich leaders of Israel, and Micah's warning to the rich of Judah and Israel; and with the message of the New Testament and Jesus' warnings to the rich and to the hypocritical religious leaders. The hymn addresses the theological concepts of humanity's sinful nature and God's judgment and is a prayer of confession and entreaty. Chesterton cast the biblically consistent theology and its suitability for public worship in powerful literary language using a series of ten strong verbs and ten powerful groupings of vivid images, some thrown into bold contrast, some presented through alliteration. Erik Routley considered the hymn to be "a noble piece of literature."[76] The *Hymnal 1982 Companion* sets the historical context out of which the hymn was written:

> At the beginning of the twentieth century, England was a nation experiencing the end of the long reign of Queen Victoria, the beginning of the Edwardian era, and the Second Boer War. It was a time of national self-confidence and pride, of materialism and moral laxity. In response to this, the critic and writer G. K. Chesterton penned a strong and poignant plea to God for social and political justice.[77]

Chesterton, journalist, essayist, novelist, and poet, left the Church of England for Roman Catholicism, remained a defender of orthodoxy, and wrote about the literary-religious life in England.

Since Percy Dearmer's first use of the text in the 1906 *English Hymnal,* it has often been sung to the English melody KING'S LYNN. The Aeolian mode (pure minor) melody is in an A B B' A form. In Ralph Vaughan Williams's adaptation and harmonization, the harmony of the B section ends in the relative major, and though only three notes of the B' section melody are different from its first statement, Vaughan Williams changed the harmony and cadenced on the dominant of the pure minor. The harmony at the beginning of the return of A is briefly in the key of the dominant major before being an exact repeat of the melody and harmony of the opening of the hymn. The words and meaning are, by the rhythm, melody, and harmony, given prominence in every stanza.

Chesterton's hymn is a powerful indictment of our own age and a prayer for God to lead us into Christian discipleship. Hymnals abound with hymns that address most every aspect of Christian discipleship as well as provide materials for teaching almost every major doctrine of the Christian faith.

Proclamation (Evangelism, Missions) (κήπυγμα)

A fellowship of Christians who worship Christ "in spirit and in truth" will be a fellowship committed to evangelism—sharing the good news of Christ. Most hymnals have a section or at least hymns devoted to proclamation, evangelism, or the church's mission. In her hymn, "O Zion haste, thy mission high fulfilling," Mary Ann Thomson addresses the church, the new Zion (Heb 12:22; Rev 21:2), and its mission of evangelism: "to tell to all the world that God is light, that he who made all nations is not willing one soul should perish, lost in shades of night"; to "publish glad tiding of redemption of Jesus, redemption and release"; and to "proclaim to every people, tongue, and nation . . . how he stooped to save his lost creation, and died on earth that we might live above." Mary Ann (Faulkner) Thomson (1834–1923) grew up in England, in the home of an Anglican priest, came to America as the wife of the librarian of the Philadelphia Free Library, and joined the Episcopal Church. Of her more than forty hymns, only this one seems to have survived, but several stanzas, in varying order, have found great popularity in hymnals in England and America.

James Walch's tune, TIDINGS, usually associated with this text, was written in 1875 or 1876. The *Hymnal 1982 Companion* notes, "It is to be remembered that Sankey and Moody toured England in 1872, and about two years later the English publishers Morgan & Scott issued *Sacred Songs and Solos* by Sankey, which well may have influenced Walch, who served as a musician in nonconformist churches."[78]

Fanny Crosby's "To God be the glory, great things he hath done" shares several features with Mary Ann Thomson's text. Each was written in the same time frame, is pointedly evangelistic, has an added chorus (saving the term "refrain" for a repeated line that is integral to the stanza), and is more objective than the usual subjective gospel song. It is sometimes the tune and added chorus that moves a hymn (or gospel hymn) to the nature of a gospel song (as happens with some of the texts of Isaac Watts). Fanny Crosby's text has allusions to Psalm 29:2; 67:3, 5 (itself a refrain or chorus); 126:3; 150:1; and John 3:16. While "O Zion haste, thy mission high fulfilling" is a call for the church to proclaim the gospel message, "To God be the glory, great things he hath done" is a call to "every believer" and "the vilest offender."

John Newton's "Amazing Grace" and Charles Wesley's "And can it be" are believers' personal testimonies to Christ's saving grace. Charles Wesley's testimony, "And can it be," is probably less well known than Newton's "Amazing Grace," but it is a powerful proclamation of the gospel and a fine example of the intersection of Bible, theology, literary expression, historical and biographical (here autobiographical) background, and sociocultural context. Wesley writes in his journal about his conversion experience on Whitsunday, May 21, 1738. During an illness, he was visited by his brother and some friends who "sang an hymn to the Holy Ghost. My comfort and hope were hereby increased. In about half-an-hour they went. I betook myself to prayer . . . ." He heard the man in whose home he was staying, and the man's sister, praying. He then read the Scripture and notes. "I now found myself at peace with God, and rejoiced in hope of loving Christ."[79]

Wesley, as did Newton, expresses his astonishment at God's grace and love in words such as "And can it be," "how can it be," "Amazing love," "mystery," "His strange design," "mercy," and in sentences such as "In vain the first-born seraph tries to sound the depth of love divine" and "'Tis mercy all, immense and free; for, O my God, it found out me!" In six broad eight-syllable lines per stanza and a cross rhyme that accelerates to couplet rhyme at the end of stanzas, Wesley uses vivid language where "imprisoned," "bound," "night," "dungeon," and "chains" change into "flames with light," "chains fell off," "free," "rose, went forth," and "clothed in righteousness."

The hymn rests on solid biblical theology. He speaks of Christ's self-emptying of himself for the redemption of humanity—the *kenosis* spoken of in Philippians 2:5-11 and the assurance that faith is met with grace and there is now therefore no condemnation (Rom 8:1). J. R. Watson has called attention to Wesley's use of "gain," "interest," and "possession" and notes, "These images are associated with the biblical narratives concerning stewardship and land-owning, and to that extent they are to be expected as part of Charles Wesley's intricate use of the Bible."[80]

> And can it be, that I should gain
> an interest in the Saviour's blood?
> Died He for me, who caused His pain
> for me, who Him to death pursued?
> Amazing love! how can it be
> that Thou, my God, shouldst die for me?
>
> 'Tis mystery all! The Immortal dies:
> who can explore His strange design?
> In vain the first-born seraph tries
> to sound the depths of love divine.
> 'Tis mercy all! let earth adore,
> let angel minds inquire no more.

He left His Father's throne above,
so free, so infinite His grace,
emptied Himself of all but love,
and bled for Adam's helpless race:
'Tis mercy all, immense and free;
for, O my God, it found out me!

Long my imprisoned spirit lay
fast bound in sin and nature's night;
Thine eye diffused a quickening ray,
I woke, the dungeon flamed with light;
My chains fell off, my heart was free,
I rose, went forth and followed Thee.

No condemnation now I dread;
Jesus, and all in Him, is mine!
Alive in Him, my living Head,
and clothed in righteousness divine,
bold I approach the eternal throne,
and claim the crown, through Christ my own.

Ministry to the Temporal Needs of People (Social Service) (διακονία)

λειτουργία includes every aspect of Christian ministry including social service. In Hebrews 1:14, the writer speaks of the "ministry" (λειτουργικὰ) of "service" (διακονίαν), "οὐχὶ πάντες εἰσὶν λειτουργικὰ πεύματα εἰζ διακονίαν ἀποστελλόμενα διὰ τοὺς μέλλότας κληπονομεῖν σωτηρίαν" ("Are they not all ministering spirits, sent out to render service for the sake of those who will inherit salvation?").

Thayer's Greek-English Lexicon of the New Testament notes that in 2 Corinthians 9:12 λειτουργίας refers to "a gift or benefaction, for the relief of the needy."[81] Hymns may not only awaken Christians to this ministry to the temporal needs of people—to their physical, social, emotional, or mental needs—but may also be a part of the church's moving out of the more narrow definitions of "liturgy" and becoming directly involved in these societal/non-liturgical contexts of ministering to the temporal needs of people.

The increasing recognition and application of the possibilities of music in physical, mental, and emotional therapy have opened new avenues of ministry for hymns. The social/emotional roles of hymn singing in retirement centers with their awakening of special memories and of memory in general is another evidence of growing "non-liturgical" values of hymns. These values may be viewed as extensions of the most basic purposes of hymns and not scornfully dismissed as simply peripheral at best.

Lionel Adey deals with this "secularization," observing,

> The cutting loose of hymns from their liturgical moorings to become independent expression of mass emotion or sources of musical entertainment shares with many similar processes the ill-sounding name "secularization."
> . . .
> This transference of religious emotion and ritual was but one form of a secularization that has continued in increasing measure for two centuries or more. Many who have described its various facets in relation to the arts, literature, and learning in the West, and the majority of social or economic historians, think secularization a great benefit. . . .
> [Adey's reflections] . . . are intended to interest any open-minded student not only of religion but of related disciplines: literature, psychology, history, or sociology. The past and future direction of Christianity in English-speaking countries and the effects upon the individual or collective psyche of Christian folk poems ceaselessly reiterated, especially in childhood, are matters too important to be confined to in-groups or fenced into a corner labeled "theology."[82]

Adey also calls attention to the list of fifty-two "national anthems" that Erik Routley refers to in his 1952 *Hymns and Human Life*.[83] It may be that hymns in these societal/non-liturgical contexts may, for some people outside the church, be powerful reminders of a meaningful but abandoned relationship and even be powerful calls for a return to the fold. In this context, these hymns may indeed be "liturgical" in the etymological sense of "service, ministry, offering."

There are in hymns numerous references to serving one's neighbor in "physical, social and spiritual dimensions." Lionel Adey speaks of "the social strain" and the reference to "the hungry fed, the humble lifted high" in one of Dudley-Smith's most familiar texts.

> The lapse of time between the "Magnificat" and hymn texts on the relief of poverty and suffering supports the contention by John Hick and his fellow essayists[84] that the "Myth of God Incarnate" deflected attention from the implementation of Christ's ethical teaching. In Dudley-Smith's inspiring paraphrase of the "Magnificat" the refrain line "Tell out, my

soul, the greatness of the Lord" and the keynote of praise overlay the social strain, which is confined to "Proud hearts and stubborn wills are put to flight, the hungry fed, the humble lifted high."[85]

J. R. Watson regards Dudley-Smith's hymn, "Lord, for the years your love has kept and guided," as

one of the most effective modern hymns that approaches the problems of a modern secular society, preoccupied with the pursuit of pleasure and the glorification of wealth: this one sums up the problems ('oppressed by pleasure' is particularly neat) followed by a prayer for the commonwealth and nation. This is not, I think the 'Commonwealth', the loose union of states following the dispersal of the British Empire, but the 'commonwealth', what used to be called 'the common weal', the ideal society to which each person contributes a necessary part. The verse is a reminder, not only of our tendency to secularism and materialism, but also of our responsibility to one another.[86]

Charles William Humphreys's hymn, "Strengthen for service, Lord, the hands that holy things have taken," is a metrical version of John Mason Neale's prose translation from the Indian *Liturgy of Malabar*, which in turn was a translation of a Syriac prayer that goes back to the fourth-century Syrian theologian, poet, and hymn writer, Ephrem of Edessa (c. AD 307–373). The text, altered by Percy Dearmer, reads,

Strengthen for service, Lord, the hands
    that holy things have taken;
let ears that now have heard thy songs
    to clamor never waken.

Lord, may the tongues which "Holy" sang
    keep free from all deceiving;
the eyes which saw thy love be bright
    thy blessèd hope perceiving.

The feet that tread Thy holy courts
    from light do Thou not banish;
the bodies by thy body fed
    with thy new life replenish.[87]

Dearmer's alteration (with Humphreys's permission) to an 87.87 meter was done to fit ACH GOTT UND HERR, a melody in the 1682 *Neu-Leipziger-Gesangbuch* adapted and harmonized by J. S. Bach. David McKinley Williams provided for this text a simple, logogenic, singable, largely diatonic melody and harmony, in shifting meters and in a balanced form that complements the text and climaxes in the final phrase. The tune name is, appropriately, MALABAR. Williams (1887–1978), a Welsh-born American church musician, organist, composer, and teacher, studied in Paris with some of the most recognized French organists of the time. He became organist and choirmaster of St. Bartholomew's Church in New York and was head of the organ department of the Juilliard School of Music and member of the faculty of the School of Church Music at the Union Theological Seminary. He served as a member of the Joint Commission on Church Music and the Joint Commission on the Revision of the Hymnal that produced *The Hymnal 1940*.

Fred Pratt Green, in his hymn "An upper room did our Lord prepare," reminds us that "service, too, is sacrament."

> And after Supper he washed their feet,
>   for service, too, is sacrament.
> In him our joy shall be made complete
>   sent out to serve, as he was sent.[88]

Over the years, hymns have addressed a wide spectrum of social, emotional, mental, and physical needs, and called attention to the biblical and theological bases for Christians to give themselves to ministry to persons with these needs.

Again, "liturgical" is taken here in its broader etymological, historical, and biblical meaning to refer to service, ministry, and the whole spectrum of individual and corporate ministry or offering or work and grows naturally out of true worship. It is significant that Evelyn Underhill closes her classic work on worship by emphasizing that

> the selfless spirit of worship pours itself out in that sacrificial effort which seeks to transform the material order, and especially the human scene—cleansing, healing, saving, reconciling, and making of it a fit vehicle of the divine indwelling Life—giving, in fact, concrete and social expression to the Eucharistic ideal. Nor without such concrete and costly expression, carried to its utmost limits, can Christian adoration be complete.[89]

While hymnody relates most obviously to the ministry of worship, it also, as we have seen, plays a significant role in advocating and supporting the ministries of discipleship, proclamation, and social service. Fine hymns speak to every aspect of "liturgy," identifying the biblical bases, illuminating the theological implications, and expressing it all in worthy literary language admonishing involvement. As Underhill reminded us, Christian adoration cannot be complete "without such concrete and costly expression, carried to its utmost limits . . . ."[90]

The Liturgical "Voice" in a "Polyphonic" Hermeneutics

The "liturgical" voice of hymnody, in its narrower traditional meaning of public worship and in its broader meaning (λειτουργία) of service, ministry, worship, offering, and sacrifice moves in careful polyphony with the biblical and theological "voices." Christian liturgy is biblical and theological. Though many distinctive details have accrued over the centuries, the great liturgies of the western church share many basic aspects, and even many of the more non-liturgical and free churches share the most basic elements of adoration of God, confession of sins, affirmation of the gospel, and dedication of one's self. Through the centuries, hymns have given profound expression to virtually every aspect of public worship that has come to be a part of most of the "liturgies" of the Christian faith.

Worship in the Christian church—biblically, theologically, and historically—has, in many traditions, centered on the Liturgy of the Word and the Liturgy of the Upper Room (Scripture and sacrament). The Last Supper of our Lord has continued to be done in remembrance of him, and hymns have played a major role in that rite. The third book of Isaac Watts's *Hymns and Spiritual Songs* (1709) is headed, "Prepared for the Holy Ordinance of the Lord's Supper." In that collection, in that book, and in the hymn, "Nature with open volume stands," Watts focuses on the biblical and theological concepts of the redeeming grace of God as manifest in the atoning death of Christ on the cross, which gives the hymn a variety of general and specific liturgical uses.

Nature with open Volume stands
To spread her Maker's Praise abroad

And every Labor of His Hands
Shows something worthy of a God.

But in the Grace that rescu'd Man
His brightest Form of Glory shines;
Here, on the Cross, 'tis fairest drawn
In precious Blood and crimson Lines.

Here His whole Name appears compleat;
Nor Wit can guess, nor Reason prove
Which of the Letters best is writ,
The Power, the Wisdom, or the Love.

Here I behold his inmost Heart
Where Grace and Vengeance strangely joyn,
Piercing His Son with sharpest smart
To make the purchas'd Pleasures mine.

O the sweet Wonders of that Cross
Where God the Savior lov'd and dy'd!
Her noblest Life my Spirit draws
From His dear Wounds and bleeding Side.

I would forever speak his Name
In Sounds to mortal Ears unknown,
With Angels join to praise the Lamb,
And worship at his Father's Throne.[91]

The larger and diverse historical/cultural context in which Watts poetically expressed his theology was filled with some of the great figures of
history and may contribute to understanding his emphasis that it is "in the
Grace that rescu'd Man / His brightest Form of Glory shines" and his
emphasis on the cross: "Here, on the Cross, 'tis fairest drawn / In precious
Blood and crimson Lines," "Here His whole Name appears compleat," and
"Here I behold his inmost Heart." It was a time marked by the rise of the
party politics between what came to be know as the Tory (who favored royal
privilege and the Anglican church) and, on the other hand, the Whig (who
favored Parliamentary supremacy and toleration of the Protestant dissenters)
parties. Watts was Noncomformist and dissenting and lived under the reign
of eight different English sovereigns, beginning with Charles II and the
restoration and ending during the reign of George III and the impending

Industrial Revolution. A year before the birth of Watts, Benjamin Keach's congregation of the Particular Baptist Church in Southwark had allowed the singing of hymns at the close of the Lord's Supper. Tate and Brady with their *A New Version of the Psalms of David, fitted to the tunes used in Churches* (1696), compiled in Watts's time, made freer, more literary paraphrases of the psalms than those of the still popular Sternhold and Hopkins Psalter. Some of the hymnists contemporary with Watts were Baxter, Crossman, Ken, Doddridge, and Wesley. On the continent were Neander, Schmolck, and Zinzendorf. In literature, it was the time of Bunyan, Dryden, Pepys, Defoe, Swift, Addison, Pope, Fielding, and Goldsmith. Watts's contemporaries in science were Boyle, Newton, Leibniz, and Halley. In philosophy were Spinoza and Locke. In painting there were Vermeer, Canaletto, and Hogarth. The outstanding English architect of the time was Christopher Wren. In English music there was Purcell and on the continent Lully, Rameu, Domenico Scarlatti, Stradivari, Buxtehude, Pachelbel, Handel, and Bach.

With all this in Watts's world, he was not confined to the realm of hymnody or removed from the kinds of thinking that characterized his time. He was exposed to the languages of Latin, Greek, French, and Hebrew. He authored *The Knowledge of the Heavens and the Earth Made Easy; or the First Principles of Astronomy and Geography Explained with the Use of Globes, Maps, etc.*, and his *Logic, or, The Right Use of Reason in the Inquiry after Truth: With a Variety of Rules to Guard against Error in the Affairs of Religion and Human Life, as Well as in the Sciences* was used in the universities. But, given all that was flourishing around him and all in which he was involved, Watts considered that God's "brightest form of glory shines" in the cross of Christ and in God's "grace that rescued man."

The opening stanza of Watts's hymn affirms poetically Paul's declaration that the divine nature of God can be seen in all of created nature, "since the creation of the world His invisible attributes, His eternal power and divine nature, have been clearly seen, being understood through what has been made, so that they are without excuse" (Rom 1:20). Watts goes on to affirm John's testimony, "And the Word became flesh, and dwelt among us, and we saw His glory, glory as of the only begotten from the Father, full of grace and truth" (John 1:14), and even further to affirm that the glory and grace of God shine brightest in the cross and blood of Christ: "In Him we have redemption through His blood, the forgiveness of our trespasses, according to the riches of His grace" (Eph 1:7). The title page to Watts's *Hymns and Spiritual Songs* (1709) quotes Revelation 5:9, "And they sung a new Song, saying, Thou are worthy, &c. For thou wast slain and hast redeemed us, &c." and the final stanza is an acclamation of praise—eternal, beyond human speech, with angels around the throne of God, alluding to Revelation 5:11-14.

Erik Routley, speaking of the "intimacies as well as the grandeurs of the Christian doctrine of our redemption," calls this hymn "the greatest of all hymns on the atonement written since the reformation . . . the greatest of all is one that is hardly known outside one or two branches of English Dissent."[92] Routley makes perceptive and essentially positive observations about the fourth stanza and an essentially negative observation about the way congregations sing:

> . . . the palling image of the Father punishing the Son. It is almost repellent. . . . Probably we are right not to ask congregations to sing it in the unpremeditated state in which congregations nowadays come to their hymn singing. . . . it does not matter if to Watts it was a commonplace sentiment. As it stands, for today, it is a dangerous one. The danger is of a special and valuable sort.[93]

Watts's theology of the cross and of its supremacy over "the whole realm of nature" is expressed in two hymns of Book 3: this hymn (no. 10) and "When I survey the wondrous cross" (no. 7).

Were the whole Realm of Nature mine,
That were a Present far to [sic] small;
Love so amazing, so divine
Demands my Soul, my Life, my All.[94]

In the six stately, iambic, long meter, cross-rhymed stanzas of "Nature with open volume stands," Watts jubilantly affirms the motivation and means of Christian worship. In a beautiful metaphor comparing nature to a book (stanza 1), Watts contrasts the grace of God on the cross to all the glories of nature and pronounces that it is here in the cross that God's brightest glories shine. He continues the metaphor of the book in stanza 2 and speaks of grace being drawn in lines of precious blood—crimson lines. In the third stanza he affirms that God's whole being appears complete in the grace shown in the redeeming death of Christ and continues the book metaphor by saying that neither wit nor reason can guess which of the "letters" (power, wisdom, or love) is written best. The three final stanzas are now in the first rather than the third person, and the worshiper sees both the grace and vengeance of God manifested in the piercing of His own son and in the purchasing of redemption for humanity. In three anaphoric uses of "here," he focuses even more on the cross of Christ, and the third of these (stanza 4, omitted in some hymnals) is that first use of the first person and speaks of his (Watts's and the worshiper's) spirit (feminine) drawing its noblest breath from Christ's redeeming death.

The text is often sung to the ELTHAM tune, a melody in N. Gawthorn's 1730 *Harmonia Perfecta* and harmonized in 1872 by S. S. Wesley. In *English Praise: A Supplement to the English Hymnal*, the text is set to NÜRNBERG, a hymn tune by J. S. Bach adapted by John Wilson. In practice, the first stanza may well be sung by a soloist and then, contrasting grace to nature, the choir might sing stanzas 2 and 3. Stanzas 4–6 should be a profoundly personal expression of the congregation, especially in the great acclamation of praise in the final stanza. A sensitive organist will undergird this singing with appropriate registrations, tempi, and volumes.

Routley's comment (above) about "the unpremeditated state in which congregations nowadays come to their hymn singing" is a powerful indictment of congregations, but perhaps more so of those who are responsible for educating, planning, and leading congregational singing. Congregations, with some help, are often much more capable of meaningful singing than they are shown how to do, called on to do, or even allowed to do. The "unpremeditated state" may describe some worship planners who fail to do comprehensive interpretations of hymns as described in this work and who fail to help congregations come to some understanding of the breadth and depth of the dimensions of hymnody. This does not require extensive training of the congregations and is likely done best in "premeditated" planning, providing the context for meaningful singing, and modeling the best of hymn singing.

This hymn shows again the multiple and interrelated dimensions that characterize fine hymnody. In the final analysis, the true liturgical "voice" in the polyphony of hymnody is largely dependent on the ministers' and individual Christian's sensitivity to and interpretation of the biblical and theological meanings of hymns and their applications to specific liturgical contexts. For those sensitive to the deeper natures and relationships of the biblical, theological, liturgical, literary, and musical facets in the singing of a hymn, the "polyphony" of hymnody can be a rich spiritual experience.

Notes

1. Kurt Aland, Matthew Black, Carlo M. Martini, Bruce M. Metzger, and Allen Wikgren, eds., *The Greek New Testament*, 3rd ed. (New York: United Bible Societies, 1978) 107 of "A Concise Greek-English Dictionary of the New Testament."

2. See domain 35.B in Johannes P. Louw and Eugene A. Nida, eds., *Greek-English Lexicon of the New Testament Based on Semantic Domains*, 2 vols. (New York: United Bible Societies, 1988) 1:460–62.

3. Joseph H. Thayer, *Thayer's Greek-English Lexicon of the New Testament* (New York: Baker Book House, 1977 reprint) 375.

4. Ibid., 375–76.

5. G. Milligan, *The Greek Papyri with Special Reference to their Value for N. T. Study* (n. p., 1912) xxx, as quoted in A. T. Robertson, *A Grammar of the Greek New Testament in the Light of Historical Research* (Nashville: Broadman Press, 1934) 81–82.

6. Ibid., 83–84.

7. Ibid., 80–81.

8. Ibid., 158.

9. Ibid., 193.

10. Ibid., 168–69.

11. John 4:23.

12. One introduction to the use of hymns to illustrate aspects of liturgy is found in David H. Tripp, "Illustrating Liturgical History with Selected Hymns: An Invitation to a Conversation," *The Hymn* 51/1 (January 2000): 6–11.

13. Colossians 3:16 and Ephesians 5:19.

14. Matthew 26:30 and Mark 14:26.

15. Acts 16:25.

16. Larry W. Hurtado, *At the Origins of Christian Worship: The Context and Character of Earliest Christian Devotion* (Grand Rapids MI/Cambridge UK: William B. Eerdmans Publishing Company, 1999) 87.

17. Geoffrey Wainwright and Karen B. Westerfield Tucker, eds., *The Oxford History of Christian Worship* (Oxford: Oxford University Press, 2006) 526.

18. *A House of Praise*, 200.

19. Evelyn Underhill, *Worship* (New York: Harper Torchbooks/The Cloister Library, Harper & Brothers, 1957) 14.

20. Roger Scruton, *The Aesthetics of Music* (Oxford: Clarendon Press, 1997) 459–60.

21. Ibid., 461.

22. From Fred Pratt Green's hymn, "When in our music, God is glorified," in *The Hymns and Ballads of Fred Pratt Green* (Carol Stream IL: Hope Publishing Company, 1982) 51.

23. See also Robin Knowles Wallace, "Hymns as a Resource for the Language of Worship," *The Hymn* 58/3 (Summer 2007): 33–37.

24. Underhill, *Worship*, 5.

25. *Book of Common Prayer and Administration of the Sacraments and other Rites and Ceremonies of the Church Together with the Psalter or Psalms of David according to the Use of the Church of England* (Cambridge: Cambridge University Press, 1968) 240; *Book of Common Prayer and Administration of the Sacraments and other Rites and Ceremonies of the Church Together with the Psalter or Psalms of David according to the Use of the Episcopal Church* (New York: Oxford University Press, 1990) 327.

26. Ibid., 334.

27. F. von Hügel, *Selected Letters* (J. M. Dent & sons ltd., 1928) 261 as quoted in Underhill, *Worship*, 5.

28. Underhill, *Worship*, 9.

29. In Marilyn Kay Stulken, *Hymnal Companion to the Lutheran Book of Worship* (Philadelphia: Fortress Press, 1981) 286.

30. Jaroslav J. Vajda, *Now the Joyful Celebration* (St. Louis: MorningStar Music Publishers, 1987) 158.

31. Carl Schalk's tune for the text is discussed in chapter 6. Vajda wrote a second text to be sung to Schalk's NOW, "Then the glory," based on 1 Cor 2:9 and 2 Cor 4:13-18 and suitable for the end of Communion. Vajda says of the text, "Subsequent to the writing of 'Now the silence' I wrote this 'sequel' to the hymn that summarizes the elements of a worship service" (*Now the Joyful Celebration*, 162).

32. Vajda, *Now the Joyful Celebration*, 27. © 1969 by Hope Publishing Company, Carol Stream, IL 60188. All rights reserved. Used by permission.

33. Erik Routley, *A Panorama of Christian Hymnody* (Collegeville MN: The Liturgical Press, 1972) 71. Routley, in his 1985 Rejoice in the Lord, and others considered "Jesu dulcedo cordiium" to be an "anonymous Latin poem, c. 1200."

34. John Julian, ed., A *Dictionary of Hymnology* (New York: Dover Publications, 1907) ii, 877.

35. See F. J. E. Raby, "The Poem 'Dulcis Iesu Memoria,'" *Bulletin of the Hymn Society* 33 (October 1945): 1–6; and Maurice Frost, ed., *Historical Companion to Hymns Ancient & Modern* (London: William Clowes & Sons, Limited, 1962) 249.

36. Raymond Glover, gen. ed., *The Hymnal 1982 Companion* (New York: The Church Hymnal Corporation, 1994) 1191.

37. See Underhill, *Worship*, 78.

38. Erik Routley, ed., *Rejoice in the Lord: A Hymn Companion to the Scriptures* (Grand Rapids MI: Wm. B. Eerdmans Publishing Company, 1985) no. 104.

39. Brian Wren, *Faith Looking Forward* (Carol Springs IL: Hope Publishing Company, 1983) notes to number 25.

40. Wren, *Faith Looking Forward*, no. 25. © 1983 Hope Publishing Co. Used by permission.

41. Wren, *Faith Renewed* (Carol Stream IL: Hope Publishing Company, 1995) no. 12. © 1983 Hope Publishing Co. Used by permission.

42. *A House of Praise*, 121, 125, 239, 280, 361, 363, 438, 461.

43. Marion J. Hatchett, *Commentary on the American Prayer Book* (San Francisco: HarperSanFrancisco, 1995) 328.

44. *A House of Praise*, 120.

45. Ibid., 360.

46. John H. Leith, ed., *Creeds of the Churches: A Reader in Christian Doctrine from the Bible to the Present* (Chicago: Aldine Publishing Company, 1963) 5.

47. Dale Moody, *The Word of Truth: A Summary of Christian Doctrine Based on Biblical Revelation* (Grand Rapids MI: William B. Eerdmans Publishing Company, 1981) 7.

48. Ibid., 8.

49. Marion J. Hatchett, *Commentary on the American Prayer Book* (San Francisco: HarperSanFrancisco, An Imprint of HarperCollins Publishers, 1995) 334.

50. Moody, *Word of Truth*, 386.

51. The hymn appears in *Common Worship, 2000* on page 146 and appears above in chapter 3.

52. *A House of Praise*, 216.

53. Underhill, *Worship*, 120.

54. Green, *Hymns and Ballads of Fred Pratt Green*, 44–45. © 1974 by Hope Publishing Company, Carol Stream IL 60188. All rights reserved. Used by permission.

55. The Joint Commission on the Revision of the Hymnal of the Protestant Episcopal Church in the United States of America, *The Hymnal 1940 Companion*, 3rd rev. ed. (New York: The Church Pension Fund, 1951) 146.

56. *Hymnbook 1982*, no. 305.

57. The text and translation is "*Unde et memores, Domine, nos servi tui, sed et plebs tua sancta, eiusdem Christi, Filii tui, Domini nostri, tam beatae passionis, necnon et ab inferis resurrectionis, sed et in caelos gloriosae ascensionis: offerimus praeclarae maiestati tuae de tuis donis ac datis hostiam puram, hostiam sanctam, hostiam immaculatam, Panem sanctum vitae aeternae et Calicem salutis perpetuae*" (Therefore, Lord, we your servants, and also your holy people, mindful of the so blessed passion of the same Christ, your Son, our Lord, and of his resurrection from the world beneath and his glorious ascension to heaven, offer to your exalted majesty, from what you have bestowed and given, a pure victim, a holy victim, a stainless victim, the holy Bread of eternal life and the Chalice of perpetual salvation).

58. However, in reference to another stanza, *The Hymnal 1982 Companion* observes that opinions differ about the hymn on the basis of "the theological implications of the concluding phrase of st. 2" (in Raymond F. Glover, gen. ed., *The Hymnal 1982 Companion* [New York: Church Hymnal Corporation] IIIa, 630).

59. Murrill's tune is discussed in chapter 6.

60. *A House of Praise*, 339.

61. Ibid.

62. The respected theologian John B. Geyer was among those who met in Dunblane, Scotland, and produced the influential *Dunblane Praises* (1962) and *Dunblane Praises II* (1964).

63. Underhill, *Worship*, 114.

64. The series of eight "Hour Services" observed throughout the day in the Western Church came to be (1) Nocturnes, also called Mattins, which began at midnight; (2) Lauds, which immediately followed Nocturnes; (3) Prime upon rising; (4) Terce at 9 a.m.; (5) Sext at noon; (6) None at 3 p.m.; (7) Vespers in the evening; and (8) Compline before retiring.

65. William D. Maxwell, *An Outline of Christian Worship: Its Developments and Forms* (London: Oxford University Press, 1936) 163.

66. Brian Wren, *Faith Looking Forward* (Carol Stream IL: Hope Publishing Company, 1983) no. 17.

67. Ibid. Wren's "first hymn written for public singing" was "Lord Christ, the Father's mighty Son," also written in 1962 (*Faith Looking Forward* [Carol Stream IL: Hope Publishing Company, 1983] no. 23.

68. Wren, *Faith Looking Forward*, no. 17.

69. *Hymnbook 1982*, no. 130.

70. *English Praise: A Supplement to the English Hymnal*, Full Music Edition (London: Oxford University Press, 1975, 1977) no. 52.

71. Named for the village in Leicestershire where Taylor's father was rector and where the composer grew up.

72. John Wilson, "Looking at Hymn Tunes: the Objective Factors," in Carlton R. Young, Robin A. Leaver, and James H. Litton, eds., *Duty and Delight: Routley Remembered* (Carol Stream IL: Hope Publishing Company, 1985) 144.

73. See David R. Wright. "What Do Hymns Say about Daily Work," *Hymn Society of Great Britain & Ireland Bulletin Occasional Paper*, 3rd series, no. 2.

74. *A House of Praise*, 77.

75. John Newport, *Life's Ultimate Questions: A Contemporary Philosophy of Religion* (Dallas: Word Publishing, 1989) 515.

76. Erik Routley, *Hymns Today and Tomorrow* (New York: Abingdon Press, 1964) 92.

77. Raymond Glover, gen. ed., *The Hymnal 1982 Companion* (New York: The Church Hymnal Corporation, 1994) 1090. At almost the exact same time, Frank Mason North in America wrote "Where cross the crowded ways of life," shot full of biblical allusions and dealing with the similar pitiful conditions of society and calling for God's intervention.

78. Raymond Glover, gen. ed., *The Hymnal 1982 Companion* (New York: The Church Hymnal Corporation, 1994) 1005.

79. Charles Wesley, http://wesley.nnu.edu/john-wesley/john-wesley-evangelist/john-wesley-evangelist-chapter_5.

80. J. R. Watson, *The English Hymn: A Critical and Historical Study* (Oxford: Oxford University Press, 1999) 255.

81. In Philippians 2:25, λειτουργὸν refers to Epaphroditus as being a servant or minister to Paul's needs, and Philippians 2:30 refers to Epaphroditus's completing what was deficient in the church's service (λειτουργίας) (Joseph H. Thayer, *Thayer's Greek-English Lexicon of the New Testament* [New York: Baker Book House, 1977] 375–76).

82. Lionel Adey, *Hymns and the Christian "Myth"* (Vancouver: University of British Columbia Press, 1986) x–xi.

83. Erik Routley, *Hymns and Human Life* (London: John Murray, 1952) 288.

84. John Hick, ed., *100 Hymns for Today*, nos. 89, 86, "The Myth of God Incarnate" (London: SCM Press 1977) esp. 8, 173–76 (Hick); 53–54, 57–59 (Michael Goulder); 140–41 (Don Cupitt).

85. Lionel Adey, *Class and Idol in the English Hymn* (Vancouver: University of British Columbia Press, 1988) 250.

86. J. R. Watson, *Awake My Soul: Reflections on Thirty Hymns* (London: SPCK, 2005) 151–52.

87. *Hymnbook 1982*, 312.

88. Green, *Hymns and Ballads of Fred Pratt Green*, 45.

89. Underhill, *Worship*, 341–42.

90. Ibid., 342.

91. Isaac Watts, *Hymns and Spiritual Songs* (London: Printed by J. H. for John Lawrence at the Angel in the Polutrey, 1709) as printed in Selma L. Bishop, *Isaac Watts Hymns and Spiritual Songs 1707–1748: A Study in Early Eighteenth Century Language Changes* (London: The Faith Press, 1962) 357.

92. Erik Routley, *Hymns Today and Tomorrow* (New York: Abingdon Press, 1964) 68.

93. Ibid., 162–63.

94. Watts, *Hymns and Spiritual Songs*, as printed in Bishop, *Hymns and Spiritual Songs 1707–1748*, 353.

CHAPTER 5

Poetry

The Importance of Hymnic Poetry as Expressions of the Christian Faith

Hymns are an imaginative, creative type of poetic language that shapes diction, syntax, sound, tone, voice, meter, rhyme, rhetorical figures, rhythm, form, and the interrelations of these to communicate thoughts and feelings of the faith. Hymns inspire the mind to soar above the limits of discursive prose. The beauty, power, and memorableness of hymnody can contribute significantly to expressing to and for Christians the breadth and depths of thoughts and feelings that are so much a part of the Christian faith.

Christian hymnody is capable of constantly unfolding new layers of meaning as those who sing and read them grow in experience and insight. This is true even though hymnody works within severe limitations of being relatively short, set to strophic hymn tunes, and written for people who for the most part are not biblical scholars, theologians, or highly skilled in literature or music. Such thoughts and feelings are best cast by persons who have shared those thoughts and feelings or have experienced them even more deeply than others and who have the gift and skill to express thoughts and feelings in imaginative, powerful, and memorable ways.

Poetic Language in Scripture and Christian History

Throughout history, God's people have turned again and again to the distinctive nature of poetic language[1] in the highest and lowest moments of life. In Old Testament times, this is seen most obviously in the Psalms and passages in the Prophets. In the New Testament this is seen in the Canticles, in the Epistles, in references to psalms, hymns, and spiritual songs, in Revelation, and in the numerous passages that many scholars consider to be poetry or even hymn fragments.

It is highly significant that both content and form were important to Jesus, who spoke his message in memorable parables and with turns of phrases that have for centuries locked the message into our memory and understanding.[2] It must be emphasized again that the final statement of Jesus's public ministry as recorded in John 12:49 is "the Father Himself who sent Me has given Me a commandment as to what to say and what to speak" (NASB) or "the Father who sent me commanded what to say and how to say it" (NIV).

Christian history abounds with forms of poetry and music that have been called into the service of the church. From the beginning of Christianity with its "psalms and hymns and spiritual songs" (Eph 5:19), every age and every culture has developed a "hymnody" to express the breadth and depth of thoughts and feelings regarding the Christian faith and ministry. Theologians through history have been intrigued with religious language and recognized the inability of either everyday or "scientific" language to communicate adequately the wholeness of the Christian faith. Again, Amos Wilder, the New Testament scholar, poet, minister, and literary critic, has referred to "the stultifying axiom that genuine truth or insight or wisdom must be limited to that which can be stated in discursive prose, in denotative language stripped as far as possible of all connotative suggestion, in 'clear ideas,' in short, in statement or description of a scientific character."[3] Paul Tillich makes a related statement:

> Art indicates what the character of a spiritual situation is; it does this more immediately and directly than do science and philosophy for it is less burdened by objective considerations. Its symbols have something of a revelatory character while scientific conceptualization must suppress the symbolical in favor of objective adequacy. Science is of greater importance in the rise of a spiritual situation but art is the more important for its apprehension.[4]

William Wordsworth spoke of poetry as "the spontaneous overflow of powerful feelings: it takes its origin from emotion recollected in tranquility,"[5] and this concept was shared by a number of subsequent poets. T. S. Eliot, in his essay, "A Dialogue on Dramatic Poetry," observes that "in intense emotions, and in its approach to the permanent and the universal, the human soul tends to express itself in verse."[6] Through Christian history, one significant form of verse in which the human soul tends to express its intense emotions and tends to approach the permanent and the universal is some type of hymnody.

Distinctives of Poetic Language and Its Potential as Religious Language

Sir Philip Sidney (1554–1586) in his "The Defense of Poesy," which some regard as the beginning of literary criticism in England, spoke eloquently, even extravagantly, of poetic language,[7] "the planet-like music of poetry,"[8] and its use in the Holy Scripture and by Jesus Christ:

> . . . the poet, with that same hand of delight, doth draw the mind more effectually than any other art doth. . . . poetry is of all human learnings the most ancient and of most fatherly antiquity, as from whence other learnings have taken their beginnings; since it is so universal that no learned nation doth despise it, nor barbarous nation is without it; . . . in moral doctrine, the chief of all knowledges—he doth not only far pass the historian, but for instructing is well nigh comparable to the philosopher, and for moving leaveth him behind him; since the Holy Scripture, wherein there is no uncleanness, hath whole parts in it poetical, and that even our Saviour Christ vouchsafed to use the flowers of it; . . . the laurel crown appointed for triumphant captains doth worthily, of all other learnings, honor the poet's triumph.[9]

The legitimate need for immediate and contemporary expressions has spawned in our day a body of hymns that is relatively devoid of literary merit.[10] On the contrary, the high purpose, the noble theme, the profound message should call forth the finest expressions of literary merit. It is false to assume that artistic merit is always esoteric or erudite, false to assume that the "average" worshiper today is incapable of appreciating literature that has craftsmanship and artistic merit, and certainly false to assume that the "average" worshiper, given careful and intelligent exposure and education, is incapable of developing appreciation for such literature.

Much of the appeal and expressiveness of the poetic language of hymnody is in its allusions and associations. Allusions in hymns to events, people, places, and stories can be both satisfying and carry a flood of meanings. Certain hymns also have for many people a wealth of associations—

some that are clear and strong, and others that may be relatively vague but just as strong.

Allusion

Much of the power of carefully crafted hymns resides in their ability to inspire the mind to soar above the limits of discursive prose, to suggest meanings, to allude to Scripture and other sources, to make what Amos Wilder called "connotative suggestion."[11] The importance of allusion can be seen in T. S. Eliot's remark about the poet's being "occupied with frontiers of consciousness beyond which words fail, though meanings still exist . . . ." Eliot wrote,

> It is a commonplace to observe that the meaning of a poem may wholly escape paraphrase. It is not quite so commonplace to observe that the meaning of a poem may be something larger than its author's conscious purpose, and something remote from its origin. . . . If, as we are aware, only a part of the meaning can be conveyed by paraphrase, that is because the poet is occupied with frontiers of consciousness beyond which words fail, though meanings still exist. A poem may appear to mean very different things to different readers, and all of these meanings may be different from what the author thought he meant . . . there may be much more in a poem than the author was aware of.[12]

Diction, as used in literary criticism referring to word choice, is one of the most distinctive and significant aspects of poetic language. A wealth of meanings, thoughts, and feelings may be brought to mind in a single word. As one example, William Williams's "Guide me, O thou great Jehovah," a prayer for guidance, abounds in allusions to the exodus, the wilderness wanderings, and the entrance to Canaan. Scriptural allusions, in particular, can carry with them a special flood of meanings, and some may be "different from what the author thought he meant" or even, by the inspiration of God, "more . . . than the author was aware of."

Association

To a significant degree, the power of hymnody rests in the familiarity and powerful associations that hymnic poetry can evoke. The power of familiarity is indeed strong, and the way the mind seems to respond to it is fascinating. In hymnody, as in any form of poetry, each person brings one's own configuration of knowledge, understanding, experience, and attitude as they relate to the various dimensions. Even the nonbeliever, D. H. Lawrence, gave compelling testimony of the power of association in his affirmation: "The hymns which I learned as a child and never forgot, mean to me almost more than the finest poetry, and they have for me a more permanent value. . . ."[13]

Before turning to the more artistic matters of poetic "techniques," a word should be said about what may seem to be the mundane literary matters of format, indentation, punctuation, spelling, and capitalization. These are significant matters but are not always appreciated by laypersons or observed in the same way by all writers or editors.

Format

Visual Representation

The traditional visual presentation of poetry in rhymed verses (lines)[14] may sometimes hinder the grasp of some important aspects of a poem or hymn, even the full flow of thought. A mechanical reading of the meter and rhyme of lines or a musical setting or a reading that ignores the movement of thought beyond the poetic "lines" may hinder the meaning and auditory aspects of carefully crafted hymnic poetry. The average reader or singer may be helped little by the typical printed page to understand either the linear, temporal flow of hymnic poetry or the counterpoint of its various dimensions. The typographical conventions of poetry might mislead one to conceive of poetry as a somewhat visual, spatial art whereas it is a temporal, linear, and to a large extent oral art. Both the traditional form of printing of poetry and, even more violently, the traditional interlining of hymn texts within the staves of music are different from the traditional printed page, and all of these forms are, of course, different from the actual auditory, linear conception. In the speaking and singing of languages, there is less certainty of where one word ends and another one begins. I. A. Richards notes that "The written form gives words far more independence than they possess as units of sound in speech and we derive thence a habit of supposing that they have far more independence as regards their meanings than they usually have in either written or spoken discourse."[15] Hymns (poetry) are best read aloud with sensitivity to understand the poetic subtleties, the sounds, and the temporal/linear apects.

Meter and rhyme are largely matters of motion and rhythm moving in the dimension of time, not visual space, and there is also a multitude of counter rhythms of the very sounds of words and the poetic or rhetorical devices, many of which are built on the concept of patterns of repetition and rhythms that move beyond verses (lines). In addition, there are counter rhythms of biblical quotes and allusions, theological concepts, and liturgical aspects.

Much of the fascinating and significant dimension of motion is, and should be, subliminal, but unfortunately many are simply not perceived at all. One could be richer for perceiving better the finer aspects of the linear and contrapuntal dimensions of hymnic poetry. For the Christian, there is a responsibility for increasingly understanding the fuller meanings of our faith, and these meanings are often conveyed through the subtleties of literary forms that are best perceived by at least being sensitive to, if not always conscious and analytical of, the techniques of hymnic poetry.

We have lamented the absence of "counterpoint" in prose while writing about hymnody. We might also lament the absence of a true, visual representation that better conveys the linear, temporal aspects and multiple dimensions of hymnic/poetic texts. Such a representation may be possible with current technology and might contribute to a fuller understanding of hymnody in an educational setting, but it would be impractical and inappropriate especially in the context of corporate worship.

Indentation. When hymns are printed as poetry and not interlined in the music, indentation is usually related to the rhyme scheme. In a four-line cross rhyme (abab), the second and fourth lines are often indented.

When I survey the wondrous cross
 on which the Prince of Glory died;
my richest gain I count but loss,
 and pour contempt on all my pride.[16]

In a four-line couplet rhyme (aabb), there is typically no indentation, while in an abba rhyme scheme the middle two are often indented.

Ride on, ride on, in majesty!
Hark! all the tribes Hosanna cry;
O Savior meek, pursue Thy road
With palms and scattered garments strowed.[17]

Strong Son of God, immortal Love,
    Whom we, that have not seen thy face,
    By faith, and faith alone, embrace,
Believing where we cannot prove: . . .[18]

In an ababcc rhyme, indentation may be used for only the final couplet.

Be still, my soul: the Lord is on thy side;
bear patiently the cross of grief or pain;
leave to thy God to order and provide;
in every change, he faithful will remain.
    Be still, my soul: thy best, thy heav'nly Friend
    through thorny ways leads to a joyful end.[19]

One may see in short meter 6.6.8.6. a couplet rhyme (abab), or in an abcb rhyme the first, second, and fourth lines "indented" leaving the longer line extended to the left.

    Stand up, and bless the Lord,
    Ye people of His choice;
Stand up, and bless the Lord your God
    With heart and soul and voice.[20]

Capitalization, Punctuation, and Spelling. While much poetry capitalizes the beginning of verses or lines, contemporary practice seems to be forsaking the capital letter at the start of a new line unless it is the beginning of a sentence. Some hymn writers do prefer capitalizing pronouns that refer to the deity. The better hymn writers, like the better poets, usually use standard spelling and punctuation, and where there are alternative forms they attempt to be consistent. Punctuation may often be a better means than the meter and the rhyme layout of verses in determining the message of a hymn and how it is to be read, understood, and sung. Compare the two forms of a stanza from Samuel Crossman's hymn, "My song is love unknown."

He came from His blest throne
    Salvation to bestow:
But men made strange, and none
    the longed-for Christ would know.
        But O my Friend,

my Friend indeed,
who at my need
His life did spend!

He came from His blest throne salvation to bestow; but men made strange, and none the longed-for Christ would know. But O my Friend, my Friend indeed, who at my need, His life did spend!

Technical Aspects

We turn now to the more technical aspects of poetry that function in good hymn writing. By the skillful use of the distinctive elements of poetry, writers draw the reader into new realms of thoughts and feelings that come through a flow of language, propelling thought and feeling through sound and imagery and even through the mental or physical feel of forming the words. However, to the extent that any of the techniques or devices of poetry call attention to themselves, they distract from the quality and purpose of the hymn. We must not assume that even the finest hymn writers have formal experience with rhetoric or the technical aspects of poetry. Some, such as John and Charles Wesley, certainly had formal experience with rhetoric. John advocated its use in preaching and Charles employed it extensively in his hymn writing as discussed below. The finest do have innate gifts and a sense of the subtleties of language and are skillful enough in the employment of techniques to achieve desired effects and avoid the distraction of misuse. The better writers employ a balance of the precision of meaning with the suggestion of thoughts and feelings to help the mind of the reader/singer soar in both consciousness and in imagination, and to explore the impossible frontiers of the broad and deep experiences of devoted believers and careful thinkers.

The distinctive ways in which the finer hymn writers employ techniques define their style. John Ciardi and Miller Williams, both of whom are poets, translators, critics, and editors, in the introduction to their excellent work, *How Does a Poem Mean?* share the following story pertinent to the concept of "poet as technician":

One evening Robert Frost spoke to an audience about what he called his "technical tricks." He mentioned, among much more, his use of hendecasyllables, synechdoche, kinds of rhyme, some effective ways of using repetition, and what he called "bright ideas" in

metaphor. It was a brilliant exposition of the sort of specific man-
agement that occupies the poet as a technician of his form. He had
hardly finished when an elderly woman in the audience—clearly a
high-minded "appreciator of the beautiful," was on her feet. "Mr.
Frost," she said in some agitation, "surely when you are writing one
of your bee-oo-ti-ful poems (and her voice lingered over "bee-oot-
i-ful"), surely you are not thinking of (and here her voice spat the
words indignantly) *technical tricks!*"

She might as well have asked Pablo Casals if he cares about the
chords he plays. Frost thought for a second or two, then leaned forward into the microphone and said in a playfully gravelly tone, "I
revel in 'em!"[21]

J. R. Watson uses the phrase "relishing the words themselves" as he
records how Michael Ramsey, the former Archbishop of Canterbury, made
"an impromptu commentary of a hymn" sung before his sermon and "seized
on some of Charles Wesley's phrases in his sermon, when talking about the
Holy Spirit."

> I suggest that when Michael Ramsey was drawing attention to particular
> words and phrases, he was not just celebrating their content but relishing
> the words themselves. Much discussion of hymns has been concerned with
> their content but a more appropriate criticism would acknowledge that
> form and content are inseparable; that the images and language used actu-
> ally determine our sense of what those ideas are.[22]

This interplay of form (including the technical aspects) and content is
close to the heart of this present work. We shall discuss briefly the technical
aspects of hymnic poetry: diction, syntax, voice, tone, speed, movement,
mood, physical aspects of pronunciation, sound, meter, rhyme, rhythm and
counter rhythm, figures of thought, figures of speech, form, and the interrelations of these.

Sound and Sense: Diction, Syntax, Voice, and Tone

The relationship between sound and sense has been a consideration from
antiquity, and there have been theories about the effect of certain spoken
and musical sounds on human thoughts and feelings. Great speakers and
religious leaders have drawn upon qualities that came to be known as rhetoric and oratory and often borrowed attributes of musical language to give

forceful expression to their thoughts. The spoken poetic utterances of the prophets with their vivid and powerful imagery has captured people's thoughts ever since. The imaginative language of the sung psalms that exploited the qualities of Hebrew poetry has expressed the thought and feelings from their first utterances. Sound has been considered therapeutic, and it was the psalmist David who is referred to in 1 Samuel 16:16 when Saul's servants advised, "Let them seek a man who is a skillful player on the harp; and it shall come about when the evil spirit from God is on you, that he shall play the harp with his hand, and you will be well." In ancient Greece, orators deliberately exploited the eloquence of rhetoric and qualities of music to persuade their listeners. Ethos was, in one definition, the belief that the Greek musical modes embodied and aroused in the listeners certain ethical or moral attributes.

Through history, Christian apologetics with its defense, justification, and clarification of the faith has been concerned with both the message and the medium and has not only drawn upon the qualities of musical language but also turned to music itself to help carry the Christian message. The relations of music to language, of sound to rhetoric, are obvious. Christopher Hill identifies the uses of the term "rhetoric":

> In public speaking, the means of effective advocacy; in prose and poetry, the codification of verbal strategies that enhance the reception of a text; in music, the conscious, consistent use of patterns and formal arrangements to engender in an audience a sense of aesthetic satisfaction or psychological plausibility that clarifies or heightens the intended effect of a composition or performance.[23]

Ancient music theory was related to speculative philosophy and mathematics, and early writings on rhetoric refer to the music of language. Hill notes,

> Isocrates' [436–338 BC, Socrates' pupil] school had begun teaching style as a function of the music of language, that is, its cadence of consonants and its euphonious succession of vowels. In these approaches to style lay, eventually, rhetoric's greatest significance for music.[24]

Aristotle considered the musical properties of volume, pitch, and rhythm essential to rhetoric and capable of moving an audience emotionally. Much has been written on the mutual relationships of poetry and music referring to elements they share, to each borrowing the language of the other, to poetry's references to music,[25] and to the musical setting of poetic texts. Hill nicely summarizes the many manifestations that show "an awareness of the ineluctable musicality of human utterance that is as historically resilient as it has been theoretically elusive."[26]

Sir Philip Sidney (1554–1586), in his "The Defense of Poesy," began his tracing of philosophers, historians, and poets with the note that they "sang their natural philosophy in verses." He continued,

> the philosophers of Greece durst not a long time appear to the world but under the masks of poets. So Thales, Empedocles, and Parmenides sang their natural philosophy in verses; so did Pythagoras and Phocylides their moral counsels; so did Tyrtaeus in war matters, and Solon in matters of policy; or rather they, being poets, did exercise their delightful vein in those points of highest knowledge which before them lay hidden to the world.[27]

In the Middle Ages and Renaissance, rhetoric or oratory was powerfully at work within the church in the moving sermons of Savonarola, Martin Luther, John Calvin, and John Knox, and a highly codified rhetoric became an essential part of university education. Many Medieval and Renaissance writers also attributed ethical or affective qualities to the musical modes of their days.

In the seventeenth and early eighteenth centuries, it was widely held, possibly by analogy with the aims of rhetoric, that the aims of music were to arouse affections or passions. Many writers of this period spoke about the affective character of intervals, scales, timbres, and types of music. Many German scholars went even further in identifying certain stereotyped musical figures, intervals, scales, and musical types with certain affections. The nineteenth-century rise of Methodism saw the great evangelical preachers like John Wesley and George Whitefield and many consider that the emotional appeal of their sermons was due in part to sounds themselves. Qualities of music were seen to affect the oratorical style of many politicians as well as preachers. The reciprocal influences of rhetoric and music are seen again in the extra-musical aspects of nineteenth-century nationalism in program music, opera, and the art songs. George A. Kennedy speaks of the importance of rhetoric in literary composition: "In the second half of the twentieth century, scholars of whom Heinrich Lausberg was a distinguished example, have rediscovered rhetoric as a systematic discipline that shaped literary composition from classical antiquity to the modern period."[28]

Diction, in poetry the choice of words, is a fundamental concern of the sensitive poet, not only for their explicit meanings but also for their implications, allusions, connotations, associations, and sounds.[29] The choice of words is related to syntax, voice, and tone or mood.

Syntax, the way in which words are organized, is a principal determinant of literary style. Poetic style is often distinguished by a syntax that may invert the adjective to follow the noun, the adverb to follow the verb, a delayed verb, or the subject to follow the verb. The best hymn writers show a concern for clarity, emphasis, flow, and rhythm, and their texts do not seem stilted or contorted in some way simply to accommodate a meter or rhyme. Poetic language often draws on the beautiful and powerful figures of speech, and these play a significant role in the syntax of poetry.[30]

Voice may refer to the distinctive features of a literary work using the terms of spoken utterance and to a set of characteristics shown by the way in which the narrator, speaker, or author addresses the reader in terms of style or personality. In hymnody it may also refer to whom the words are addressed—God, fellow Christians, non-Christians, the larger world, one's self, or even to inanimate objects ("thou burning sun with golden beam, thou silver moon with softer gleam"). The speaker in Wesley's "Come, O thou Traveler unknown" uses the second person singular as he consistently addresses the "Traveler," "thee," "thyself," "thy," "thou," and finally "Love," "Pure Universal Love," which is to say "Christ." In his "Come, we that love the Lord," Watts addresses the first person plural except in the contrasting second stanza he refers to the third person plural, first of those "that never knew our God" and then to the "Children of the heavenly King." In yet another summoning hymn, Wesley addresses "thou long-expected Jesus."[31] The person or persons to whom a hymn (or Scripture[32]) is addressed says much regarding how it is to be interpreted and might be sung.

Tone or mood may refer to the writer's emotional attitude toward his subject (introspective, meditative, devotional, festive, joyous, serious, solemn, somber, satirical); to the writer's attitude toward his audience (formal, informal, colloquial, intimate, abstract, concrete, literal, or figurative); or to the color or timbre or sound of individual words. It is principally the latter use of the term "tone" that will concern us here.

In the music of opera, ballet, the art song, in program music with its extra musical dimensions, and in the music that forms the background of motion pictures, a whole repertoire of timbres has developed over the years, and when combined with certain temporal, melodic, and dynamic patterns it has come to be associated (even if subliminally) with relatively specific thoughts and feelings. To a more limited degree, similar timbral associations function in literature, certainly in poetry, even in hymnody.

The flow, motion, expectations, or inevitability of poetic language often involves distinctive, meaningful sounds, and even repetitions and patterns of sounds as is obvious in the rhythmic patterns of meter and rhyme. But beyond the inevitability, fulfillment, and satisfaction of sounds, and the rhythmic patterns of rhymed sounds, there is the ability of sounds themselves, inherently or by association, to convey powerfully both mood and meaning. The eighteenth-century poet Alexander Pope (1688–1744) says in his poem "Sound and Sense," "The sound must seem an echo to the sense . . . ."

Though the specific effects of sounds may be highly subjective, there is a surprising degree of consensus. Certain sounds in language and in music, by tradition or by association, may convey certain moods. Cambridge professor I. A. Richards discusses these aspects in some detail.[33] There has been considerable study into the effects that the very sounds of words, even parts of words, have on feelings, moods, and thoughts beyond their grammatical or lexical meanings. This approaches a musical dimension of poetry, and Sidney Lanier, the American poet and musician, gave much attention to this. C. Hugh Holman notes,

> Tone or tone color is sometimes used to designate a musical quality in language which Sidney Lanier discussed in *The Science of English Verse*, where he asserts that the sounds of words have qualities equivalent to timbre in music. "When the ear exactly coordinates a series of sounds with primary reference to their tone-color, the result is a conception of (in music, flute-tone as distinct from violin-tone, and the like; in verse, rhyme as opposed to rhyme, vowel varied with vowel, phonetic syzygy, and the like), in general . . . *tone-color*."[34]

I. A. Richards, in his chapter on "The interinanimation of Words," discusses the relationship and explains that words

> are said to share a morpheme when they have, at the same time, something in common in their meaning and something in common in their sound. The joint semantic-phonetic unit which distinguishes them is what is called a morpheme. It is the togetherness of a peculiar sound and a peculiar meaning for a number of words.[35]

Richards is careful to note that it is not the actual correspondence between sound and meaning that is the explanation, but the existence of a group of words that have a common sound and meaning. It is then, in this case, not so much the sound per se but that "these expressive or symbolic words get their feeling of being peculiarly fitting from the other words sharing the morpheme which support them in the background of the mind."[36] He even suggests that "a wider extension would include not only influences from words which in part sound alike, but from other words which in part overlap in meaning."[37] He goes so far as to say that we can "extend this notion of a word as being backed up by other words that are not uttered or thought of."[38] An even wider extension would include words that overlap in "feeling," suggesting some common emotion. This is part of the evocative and connotative force of poetry that we see in the uses of biblical words in hymns.

I. A. Richards, Laurence Perrine,[39] and others discuss the correspondence between sound and sense, and much of their study of traditional poetic literature applies to hymnody. Sounds are not invariably associated with an idea, but there is enough association between the sounds and the ideas to suggest some sort of intrinsic, though obscure relationship.[40] Many writers have noted the frequent association of the long "o" or "oo" with melancholy or sorrow in such words as "moan," "groan," "woe," "mourn," "forlorn," "toll," "doom," and "gloom."

An initial "st-" is often found in words that suggest strength as in "staunch," "stalwart," "stout," "sturdy," "stable," "steady," "stocky," "stern," "strong," "stubborn," and "steel." Wesley employs this sound and sense relationship in his "Soldiers of Christ, arise" where the word "strong" begins two almost successive lines and the word "strength" occurs five times, once separated by only one word. The word "stand" begins two successive stanzas and recurs in the final line of the first of these.

The silibant "s" alone is often a soothing sound, as in Wesley's "O for a thousand tongues," where fifteen sibilants occur in the same context of calm and peace in the four short lines: "Jesus, the name that calms my fears, / That bids my sorrows cease; / 'Tis music in the sinner's ears; / 'Tis life and health and peace." Watts achieves a similar effect in the contrasting awe of the third stanza of "When I survey the wondrous cross" in his use of "s" and "z" words "see," "his" (three times in one line), "hands," "sorrow," "such," "sorrows," "thorns," "compose," and "so" all in four lines.

The long, bright "i" sound (often combined with the "r" as in "bright" and "brightness,") is meaningful by its inherent sound and by its association with words such as "light," "bright," "brightness," "white," "shine," "sight," "life," and "arise."

Perrin notes that a medial or final "-are" sometimes occurs in words with the idea of a large light as in "flare," "glare," and "stare," and I. A. Richards notes that an initial gl- frequently occurs in word having the idea of light as in "glare," "gleam," "glint," "glisten," and "glow."[41] When Watts speaks of God the creator and "great mysterious King,"[42] he employs words such as "wondrous great and glorious bright," "dazzling light," "our soaring spirits upward rise," and "climbs above the skies," using the very sound of words to express the sense. A similar use of sound and sense exists in his "Nature with open volume stands" with the line "his brightest form of glory shines." Wesley achieves a similar effect in the opening lines of "Hail the day that sees him rise / glorious to his native skies" and places the sounds on accented rhymes.

Beyond these "phonetic intensives" there is a continuum from euphonious to cacophonous sounds. A preponderance of vowels tends to create a more melodious flow, and the long vowels are more full and resonant than the short vowels. Liquid consonants ("l," "m," "n," and "r"), the soft "v" and "f" sounds, the semivowels ("w" and "y") and the combinations such as "th" and "wh" flow more gently and pleasantly. More cacophonous sounds result from the harsher and sharper plosives ("b," "d," "g," "k," "p," and "t").

Speed, Movement, Mood, and the Physical Aspects of Pronunciation

Speed and movement obviously influence mood. Unaccented syllables go faster than accented. Therefore the anapestic and dactylic triple meters are "swifter" than the iambic and trochaic duple meters. The physical aspects of pronunciation may affect speed and mood. It has been noted that the sentence, "Watch dogs catch much meat" takes more time and effort to say than "My aunt is away," though they have the same number of syllables. Though it is quality rather than length that is distinctive in English, the tense vowels (as in "seed," "wait," and "cool") and diphthongs (as in "how" and "joy") take longer to pronounce than the lax vowels (sit, set, pull). The fricatives (f, v, s, z, sh, and the voiced version of "zh" found in "pleasure") have a duration that the stops (p, t, k, b, d, g) do not have. The liquids (l and r) and the nasals (m, n, and the consonant at the end of "sing") have duration and add length. These different sounds, especially when they come in groups, may tend to significantly influence the tempo and flow and consequently the mood and meaning. Hymns are vocalized and, when sung, the music should honor the speed, movement, mood, and even physical aspects of pronunciation. Here we encounter again the issue of how well a musical setting honors the dimensions of the poetry and how important it can be to simply read hymns aloud.

Numerous writers mention the connection between the physical act of pronunciation and the mood and meaning of words. The breath and muscular activity used in pronunciation produce various kinds of feeling, and this can be enhanced or contradicted by the music with which the words are associated. Ciardi and Miller note,

> every word has a muscular feel of its own. When the muscular play tends more or less definitely to enact the denotation of the word . . . then the word may be called *mimetic*. When the sound of a word imitates the sound of what the word denotes . . . then the word may be called *onomatopoetic*. . . . the muscles and the nervous system are involved in the process of speech and its meaning.[43]

In two of his hymns, Dudley-Smith alliterates "weight" and "woe" and slows the movement by the requirements of that pronunciation: "Dear Lord, who bore our weight of woe / and for our pardon died, . . ."[44] and "He bears between the Roman guard / the weight of all our woe . . . ."[45] "Woe" is frequently placed in a strong rhyming position in his hymns. In the previous and following example, "woe" is rhymed with "go," which in the contexts is a laborious movement burdened with consonantal sounds such as "weight of . . . woe" and "grief and loss" and "cruel cross."

Child of Mary, grief and loss,
    all the sum of human woe,
crown of thorn and cruel cross,
    mark the path you choose to go.[46]

It is probably a subliminal phenomenon, but the very formation of sounds in congregational singing often provides a physically, tactically satisfying experience to the organs of speech and to the physical and aural satisfaction of the familiar and the delight of the new. The physical, tactical experience may also contribute to the reinforcement memory. This is, of course, related to the obvious physical aspects of posture, breathing, and the uncommonly sustained speech as well as the corporate nature of the experience. Poetry, like most literary works, has certain conventions, or established practices concerning subject matter, style, technique, and structure that result from some implicit agreements or customary precedent rather than by any natural necessity. Sounds decidedly figure in these conventions or practices.

The Sounds of Poetry and the Sounds of Music

There are obvious distinctive, even enormous, challenges regarding the sounds of hymnic poetry when it is sung. The music may contradict, complement, or even enhance the sounds or pronunciation of the text. This challenge is magnified by the strophic (the same music to several stanzas) nature of hymnody. Obviously, in singing, the physical aspects of pronunciation may be exaggerated and combined with the tempo and pitch, may enhance or impede the movement and mood. While these matters of sound and sense may be subtle and even subliminal for the average reader of hymns and even more so for the singer in a congregation, it may nevertheless account for some aspects of appreciation, or enjoyment, and the perception of meaning.

Mood and meaning can be enhanced in poetry by the choice of words and the placement of important words in strategic places through meter, alliteration, assonance, consonance, rhyme, figures of speech, figures of thought, and other forms of repetition. The music should honor these approaches to the mood and meaning by appropriate meter, rhythm, tempo, pitch, timbre, dynamics, and form. In hymnody the textual and musical sounds must complement each other if they are to convey the mood, the sense, and meaning in the best possible way. If the writer becomes enamored with the technique, or if the listener or singer is distracted by it, neither the poetry, nor the music, nor the message is served.

Meter

Meter powerfully influences the moods and meanings of the text, the rhythmic flow of the hymn, the settings of the words to music, and the unifying of the congregation in the expression of the text. Much of the charm, memorableness, and force of hymnic poetry can be attributed to the regularly recurring rhythmic patterns of meter, and skillful hymn writers probe the multiple aspects of poetic and hymnic meter. The most obvious aspects of hymnic meter are the patterns and rhythms of the stresses, the number of syllables, and the number of verses or lines. These aspects are, in their best employment, bound up with the meanings and even the sounds of the words and, in hymnody, these are intricately bound up with the musical setting. In addition, there are with certain meters, especially when they are coupled with appropriate music, powerful associations in many people's minds. In the hands of a skillful writer, these multiple aspects of meter can be servants of the message, the bearers of meanings. Meter is a fundamentally important aspect of hymnody, not simply because of its aid in congregational singing but even more for the inherent and traditional suggestions of meanings that meters bear. In hymnody, there is a vital interplay of poetic, hymnic, and musical meters.

Poetic Meter

Poetic meter is basically the perceived pattern of stressed and unstressed syllables. Most English poetry and hymnody observe an accentual-syllabic meter with a regular number of syllables and stresses in the line. In addition to this type of meter, there are three other basic types that figure in hymnody: quantitative meter is a pattern of long and short syllables (this can be seen in the Greek and Latin hymns); syllabic meter is a pattern of a fixed number of syllables regardless of the number of stresses (this occurs in Romance language poetry and in Chinese and Japanese but rarely in English); and accentual meter with a regular number of stressed syllables in the line with a varying number of unstressed syllables, "sprung rhythm," as can be found in Gelineau psalmody.

Foot. The basic unit of a pattern of stressed and unstressed syllables (a group of syllables without regard to words) is called a *foot.* A foot may be duple (two syllables) or triple (three syllables). The most common feet in English hymnody are as follows:

• *iamb* (u /)—an unstressed syllable followed by a stressed syllable as in "The head that once was crowned with thorns is crowned with glory now."
• *trochee* (/ u)—a stressed syllable followed by an unstressed syllable as in "Hark! The herald angels sing."
• *dactyl* (/ u u)—a stressed syllable followed by two unstressed syllables as in "Praise to the Lord, the Almighty, the King of creation."

• *anapaest* (u u /)—two unstressed followed by a stressed syllable as in "O how happy are they / who the savior obey" and "O worship the King, all glorious above!"

The poetic meters convey, inherently and by tradition, certain moods. The iambic meter is generally stately, even noble, while the trochaic is more direct, even urgent. The triple feet, anapaestic and dactylic, are usually more exuberant, even ecstatic.

A greater nuance is provided in the four degrees of stress or accent that are traditionally acknowledged by structural linguistics: (1) primary, (2) secondary, (3) tertiary, and (4) weak. This subtly of degree is often accommodated within the standard patterns by the sensitive hymn writer and is honored in the musical settings by the more sensitive composers.

Sensitive hymn writers are not always slavish to the basic patterns of feet in a verse or line, but for emphasis or freshness may slightly modify the patterns according to the mood and meaning. These modifications are usually easier perceived in reading than in singing. Three of the more common modifications in hymnody are what have been called substitution (demotion or promotion), "imperfection," and combination. There may be a substitution of one foot for another in a line such as when the first iamb is replaced by a trochee, as Wesley does in the opening line of his basically iambic "Come, O Thou Traveller unknown," in the line "Look on Thy hands, and read it there," and in that strong "refrain," "Wrestling I will not let Thee go." Demotion is the use of a stressed syllable in what is usually an unstressed position in the meter as in Wesley's "And as a bounding hart fly home." In retaining some of the syllable's normal stress, demotion often serves to slow the rhythm of the line. Promotion is the use of an unstressed syllable in what is usually a stressed position in the meter as is subtly done in Wesley's line, "Thy new, unutterable name." In retaining some of the syllable's normal lack of stress, promotion may serve to accelerate the rhythm of the line.

Frank Baker refers to "modulations"[47] that relieve monotony and provide a fresh expressiveness. There may be an "imperfect foot" (catalexis or incomplete last foot in a verse as opposed to acatalectic or complete foot) or anacrusis (one or more extra unaccented syllables at the beginning of a verse). There may be a combined foot (choriambus) where trochee (/ u) is combined with an iamb (u /) to make a foot of four syllables (/ u u /). In the hands of a skillful poet, these metric variations, substitutions, or combinations may affect movement and lend freshness and emphasis. Good poets work by ear and feel rather than by meticulously following rules. They vary the expected regularity by inserting unaccented syllables, displacing expected accents, increasing the number of stresses, and handling the pauses, stops, and enjambments all to accelerate or retard the movement and enhance the mood of the text.[48] Not all of these metric devices are at the full disposal of hymn writers, but the better hymn writers also work by ear and feel rather than by mechanically following expectations of rhyme, stress, and movement. While these subtleties are usually lost in congregational singing, they may well be observed in reading or in solo or choral singing of hymns.

Fine hymn writers such as Wesley may consciously create subtle shifts from the rigid metrical patterns and yet remember their "vow of renunciation." Those concerned with congregational expression in worship should be aware of the implications these shifts may have for the musical setting and for the corporate body singing the text. Privately and in corporate worship, the singing or reading of hymn texts ought, as far as possible, to reflect the natural flow of the text and not any mechanical meter.

Verse (Line). Feet are combined into a *verse* or *line*, and the length of a line is determined by the number of feet in a line. The number of feet in a line is expressed in terms such as *monometer, dimeter, trimeter, tetrameter, pentameter, hexameter, heptameter, octameter.* A common length in English hymnody is four feet in a line, which is referred to as *tetrameter.* Both the pattern of feet and the number of feet or length of line are described in such expressions as "iambic tetrameter." The verse (line) itself usually has some demarcation by rhyme or printing format, but the flow of thought and grammatical structure may be carried across two or more verses by enjambment or run-on. This allows for a breadth and development of ideas, but in hymnody this requires being set to a tune that does not unduly interrupt the flow of thought.

Stanza. Verses (lines) are combined into a stanza that shares the same meter, lengths of verses, and (usually) rhyme scheme as the other stanzas. Stanzas are usually printed with a space between them. A four-verse quatrain is very common in hymnody.

The Hymn as a Whole. The stanzas combine to form the hymn in its entirety. The same metrical patterns are retained for each stanza, and the same hymn tune is usually used for all the stanzas. This strophic form of music contributes to the accessibility and singability of hymn tunes but also to the difficulty of honoring the possibility of very differing moods and meanings of the various stanzas.[49]

Hymnic Meter

In hymnody, where a major consideration is the setting of the tune to a text, hymnic meter refers to the number of syllables per verses (lines) and the number of verses per stanza. Hymnic and poetic meter are related. Most hymnals have a metrical index that allows the choosing of different tunes for the texts, tunes that may be more familiar to a certain congregation or chosen for textual or musical reasons. Some hymnic meters are so traditional, they have names such as "common meter" (CM) with 8 syllables in the first and third verses and 6 syllables in the second and fourth verses (8 6 8 6); "short meter" (SM) with 6 syllables in the first and second verses, 8 in the third verse, and 6 again in the fourth verse (6 6 8 6); and "long meter" (LM) with 8 syllables in each of the four verses (8 8 8 8). Any of these may be doubled (CMD, SMD, and LMD) to create eight-verse stanzas. These traditional meters are iambic. Less traditional meters are indicated by numbers as in 7676, 8787, etc. According to David R. Wright's study[50] based on David Perry's *Hymns and Tunes Indexed*,[51] the meters found most frequently in hymnals are in order of frequency: LM 8888; CM 8686; 8787; 7676; SM 6686; 7777; 888888; 10 10 10 10; 777777; and 878787. Of the less traditional meters, the 10's and 88's are iambic. 87's and 77's are trochaic. The 76's are most often iambic, but may be trochaic.

Some hymnals and textbooks on hymnody group the numbers to show the unit of verses that have the same rhyme and use a dot or space to show a contrast in the rhyme (e.g. 6.6.6.6.66 indicates an abcbd d rhyme scheme, while 66.6.66 6 indicates an aa b cc b rhyme scheme). Some hymnals are also careful to separate and identify the hymns that have the same hymnic meter but different poetic meter (e.g., 11.10.11.10 iambic and 11.10.11.10 dactylic). Many hymnals use a dot or a space to indicate a cross or more extended rhyme than a couplet. The absence of the dot or of the space indicates a couplet rhyme.

The meanings of individual words and phrases, as well as the message and the mood of the hymn as a whole, rest to no small degree on the interrelated aspects of meter. Skillful writers choose carefully the rhythmic patterns of meters for their suitability in bearing particular feelings and thoughts. The hymn writer, hymnal editors, and worship leaders should be concerned with the broad matters of mood and association of both text and tune and even with the subtler matters of placement of certain words in relation to a tune.

Musical Meter

Musical meter,[52] like poetic meter, is traditionally organized in successions of rhythmic patterns of stressed and unstressed pulses and, like poetic meter, is often either basically duple meter with the basic unit or beat recurring in groups of two, or triple meter with the basic unit recurring in groups of three, or quadruple meter with the basic unit recurring in groups of four. The beats themselves may be divided into twos (simple meter) or into threes (compound meter). The patterns are traditionally set up by a primary dynamic accent (an accent by volume) with additional secondary, tertiary, and weak accents. In addition to the dynamic accent, there are tonic accents, determined by pitch, and agogic accents, determined by length. The complex interaction of these types and levels of accents, together with rhythmic figures that play in and around them, create much of the subtle, artistic facets of music. When this complexity of musical meter is skillfully combined with a similar complexity of poetic and hymnic meters of texts, there are phenomenal possibilities of expression that are relished by the most sensitive, sensed by many, ignored by the masses, and probably completely unnoticed by most congregants.

Rhyme

The Nature and Functions of Rhyme

Rhyme, the discernable reiteration of sounds at certain points, infuses poetry with an array of delights, not the least of which is the delight of involvement with a distinctive type of literature that is historically associated with the compelling expression of significant thoughts and feelings. This associative quality offers a sense of community with others who share interests in the fine expression of meaningful ideas and emotions. Part of the delight is in the motion, the direction, the fulfillment of expectation. The temporal quality of rhyme has a momentum of anticipation and distinctiveness based on the patterns and frequency of the rhyme.

One traditional function of rhyme is to accentuate a rhythm and "melody" of the words. There is a rhythm to the rhyme scheme depending on the lengths of the verses and on whether the rhyme is in successive lines (couplet rhyme), in every other line (cross rhyme), within lines (internal rhyme), or in some other scheme. The very sound of the rhyme combined with the rhythm creates what may, in musical terms, be spoken of as a sort of "melody." The rhythmic pattern of the sound, the expectation, and the fulfillment of that expectation contribute to a degree of "inevitability" and the sense that *what* is said is of such significance that *how* it is said is important. The rhythm of the rhyme may propel the mind by its immediate repetition of sound or suspend the mind by some delayed repetition.

A second traditional function of rhyme is structural, which is an extension of the rhythmic pattern of the rhyme scheme. Rhyme binds verses into couplets, quatrains, stanzas, and the poem as a whole. This structural quality is based largely on the interplay of sameness and difference and functions at many levels—the rhythm of vowel sounds of syllables between verses, the pattern or scheme of rhyme within stanzas, and the repeated pattern or scheme that functions between stanzas. Rhyme can contribute to an understanding of form, and the form (consciously or unconsciously perceived) may contribute to the comprehension of meaning.

A third traditional function of rhyme relates to the sound of the rhyme and its relations to other sounds in the text. The sound, tone, or timbre of a word may, as we have seen, have a significant relation to the mood and meaning of the word and the larger message. There may even be a counterpoint of sounds and meanings, the creation of a foil of timbres. When the rhythm of rhyme coincides with the very meaning of the word, there is a special emphasis to meaning. These are artistic dimensions of poetry that may move at the subliminal levels of not only the reader or singer but even of the writer; lack of awareness of certain techniques of the craft or art, however, should not imply that the aspect is less potent. A technique functions more powerfully by calling attention to the meaning and message and not to itself. These are dimensions that one may not normally expect to find in hymnic poetry, but they can be found in some of the finer writers. Some of these subtle and even subliminal aesthetic aspects may, in some small part, account for the appreciation that some hymns enjoy and for the longevity of some of the great traditional hymns of the church as their meanings unfold in the repeated singings. This may also explain why some texts cannot bear repetition and become threadbare and trite after a few encounters.

A fourth traditional function, or at least byproduct, of rhyme is that this rhythm of sounds aids memory. This mnemonic quality is important because hymnody is so often intricately bound up with Scripture, because hymnody is often a concise statement of theology, and because hymnody, as a repository of powerful expressions of a range of thoughts and feelings of Christians across the ages, should be readily available expressions of those thoughts and feelings.

Ultimately, in fine poetry and hymnody the associative, temporal, timbral, structural, and mnemonic qualities of rhyme bring sound and sense into a powerful and delightful relationship.

Types of Rhyme

Pure Rhyme. There is a range of types of rhymes, each involving discernible reiterations of sounds that carry along the ear, mind, and physical articulation, build rhythms, create form, enhance memorability, and emphasize the meanings of the text. Some of the types are obvious, some are subtle, and some almost elusive. Essentially, the focus is on the accented vowel sounds and on the consonants preceding and following that vowel. Pure (true, full, or perfect) rhyme has a correspondence of sound (not necessarily spelling) in the accented vowels and the succeeding consonants, but a difference in the preceding consonants.

Half Rhyme. Half (slant, false, imperfect, pararhyme, near) rhyme has an *almost* corresponding sound in the accented vowels and the succeeding consonants, and different consonants preceding the vowel as in "Love" and "have." Chris Baldick notes that half rhyme

> appeared only as an occasional poetic license in English verse until the late nineteenth century, when Emily Dickinson and G. M. Hopkins made frequent use of it. The example provided by W. B. Yeats and Wilfred Owen has encouraged its increasingly widespread use in English since the early twentieth century.[53]

In his "Come, Thou long-expected Jesus," Wesley rhymes "Jesus" with "release us," "deliver" with "forever," and "Spirit" with "merit"—none of which are pure rhymes. There are also occasions of what Baldick calls "historical rhymes"[54] that were originally true rhymes, but because of changes in pronunciation have ceased to be. Watts and Wesley could rhyme "mine" or "divine" with "join."

It should be noted that the related types of rhyme—"slant," "false," "imperfect," "pararhyme," "near," "assonance," "consonance," and "dissonance"—do not indicate a weakness or lack of "purity." In "Soldiers of Christ, arise," Charles Wesley uses some fourteen imperfect rhymes in the sixteen verses. They may well provide a flow and subtlety to the meanings where pure rhyme might be too expected or provide too strong a pulse. While the music may sometimes contradict such subtleties, the more sensitive of those who are responsible for the congregational singing of hymns will find ways for honoring such subtleties, at least for their own sensitivity and musicianship.

Assonance. Assonance has a correspondence of sound in the accented vowels, but different consonants before *and* after the accented vowels as in Wesley's "O for a thousand tongues to sing" where "praise" is rhymed with "grace." *The Oxford Companion to English Literature* explains nicely, "The term is now more broadly used to cover a wide range of vowel correspondences, from the deliberate reverberation . . . to the subtle echoes and repetitions."[55]

Consonance. Consonance has different accented vowels, but the same consonants before and after the accented vowels as in "Prone to *leave* the God I *love*" in Robert Robinson's "Come, Thou fount of every blessing." It is a counterpart to assonance and, as a combination of alliteration and terminal consonance, is sometimes known as "rich consonance."

Dissonance. Dissonance is more remote, having sameness only in the consonants following the vowels. The vowels and the preceding consonants are different. In Dudley-Smith's "How faint the stable-lantern's light," the words "hearth" and "path" fall in accented places though perhaps not intended as rhyme.

Eye rhyme. Eye rhyme looks in spelling like pure rhyme, but the accented vowel is actually pronounced differently. Charles Wesley, in "Ye servants of God," rhymes "save" with "have" and John Newton, in "Amazing Grace," rhymes "come" with "home."

Identity. There are occasions when the same word occurs at the end of lines. This may be done with more concern for emphasis than for rhyme.

The range of types shows the variety and subtleties of rhyme at the disposal of sensitive, skillful writers. Robert Pinsky says, regarding the larger field of poetry, that

> This system of like sounds happens to correspond to some preference of my own ear, a personal taste: for me such rhymes as, say, "swans/stones" or "gibe/club" or "south/both" . . . often sound more beautiful and interesting than such hard rhyme combinations as "bones/stones," "rub/club," or "south/mouth." This idea of harmony seems even more clear with disyllabic or "feminine" endings: "faces/houses" is more appealing than "faces/places"; "flavor/quiver" has more interest than "flavor/savor" or "giver/quiver."[56]

Much depends on the tradition of the type of poetry and hymnody and on the ear of the writer and of the reader/singer. The average readers of hymns are probably unaware of the subtle moves away from pure rhyme unless they conflict with some preference of their own ears, and even they may be less aware in the singing than in the reading.

Again, some artistic dimensions move at a subliminal level. Conscious acceptance of sounds that are beautiful, interesting, and conveying of meaning may be evidence of the quality of craftsmanship. A technique will indeed function more powerfully by calling attention to the meaning and message than to a slavish following of a technique. One may not normally expect to find these subtler dimensions in hymnic poetry, but they can be found in some of the finer writers. Some of these subtle and even subliminal aesthetic aspects of rhyme, as in meter, may in some part account for the appreciation that some hymns enjoy and for the longevity of some of the great traditional hymns of the church when meanings and feelings continue to open to the singer/reader.

There are times when the meaning or allusion is more important than the "purer" sound, and there are times when something less obviously rhythmic than the pure rhyme may contribute to the flow of line and thought. The particularly musical dimensions of poetic texts create both opportunities and dangers since hymnic poetry is to be sung by a largely untrained (at least unrehearsed) congregation. For the sensitive composer, writing a hymn tune for a particular hymn may have real opportunities and yet offer distinct challenges, especially because the same music is used for several stanzas that may have very different moods and meanings.

Number of Syllables Rhymed

Most frequently, only one syllable is rhymed, and this is called masculine rhyme. When two syllables are rhymed, it is referred to as feminine or double rhyme. Triple rhyme refers to the rhyming of three syllables. When double or triple rhyme uses more than one word, it is sometimes called mosaic rhyme as in Dudley-Smith's "Chill of the nightfall" where he rhymes nightfall/light fall, December/remember, midnight/bid night, is ended/befriended, starlight/far light, before him/adore him, daybreak/they break.

Location of the Rhyme

Traditionally, rhyme comes at the ends of verses (lines) and is called end rhyme. If it comes at the beginning of verses, it is called head rhyme, initial rhyme, or alliteration (which may involve the initial sounds of neighboring words and not either end of lines). If it occurs within verses, it is called internal rhyme. A special type of internal rhyme ("leonine" rhyme) occurs when words at the middle and the end of certain lines rhyme. Chris Baldick notes that the term "crossed rhyme" is sometimes used to describe "the rhyming of one word in the middle of a long stanza with a word in a similar position in the next line."[57]

Rhyme Schemes

The sound pattern of the rhymed line endings yields a motion, rhythm, and a degree of inevitability and may contribute to the mood and meaning of a poem or hymn. In traditional hymnody these rhymes are usually rather simple as in couplet rhyme (aabbcc, etc.), cross rhyme (abab, abcb, etc.) or enclosed rhyme (abba).

Before leaving the crucial matter of rhyme in hymnody, another word might be said about the "rhyming" of ideas that is, of course, at the heart of Old Testament (Psalms) parallelism in its various forms.

Musically, the rhymed sounds or "rhymed" ideas may be underscored by rhythm, melody, and/or harmony of the hymn tune, and the strophic singing may help the sensitive reader/singer to grasp the ideas of these more-spaced "rhymed" ideas at least on subsequent encounters.[58]

Word Units

Some hymn writers make effective use of word groupings (dyads, triads, and even tetrads[59]), which are rhythmic, expressive, and sometimes evocative. They can be thoughtfully chosen and carefully grouped, providing motion and stimulating thought in meaningful and memorable ways. In Timothy Rees's "God of love and truth and beauty," the verse "fount of order, law, and duty" achieves in these two textual triads more than simply rhyme and rhythm.

Figures of Thought and Figures of Speech

One of the most significant and vibrant elements in hymnody is the use of figures of thought and figures of speech with their richness of comparisons, contrasts, substitutions, repetitions, descriptions, modes of address, omissions, additions, and changes in the normal usage of words yielding beauty, clarity, force, and memorableness to the meanings. It is significant that Jesus made extensive use of figures of speech (these were mostly metaphors in parables) and that the Gospel writer John calls attention to them and the need for their interpretation: "This figure of speech Jesus spoke to them, but they did not understand what those things were which He had been saying to them" (John 10:6). In John 16:25, Jesus himself says, "These things I have spoken to you in figurative language; an hour is coming when I will not longer speak to you in figurative language, but will tell you plainly of the Father." In John 16:29, the disciples refer to Christ's "not using a figure of speech." The figures of speech (metaphors and parables) that Jesus used were vivid and familiar pictures that should have been understood by the disciples, but the spiritual aspects were not always immediately grasped by them. Once understood, the figures and parables become memorable, part of the Gospels, and meaningful to Christians throughout history.

It must be emphasized again that the language of hymns, as does all religious language, "crucially involves metaphor, symbol, analogy, parable, paradox. It is, typically, language avowing the inexpressible, unconceptualizable nature of its object, or the indescribability of mystical experiences which nevertheless it strives to express!"[60] Interpreting religious language is a crucial dimension of a hermeneutics of hymnody.

Frank Baker says of Charles Wesley, one of the most important hymn writers in the history of English-language hymnody, that "most of this artistic use of words is so skilful that it is only noticed when pointed out, yet it is the secret of Charles Wesley's most characteristic effect, the compact tautness of his verse, the epigrammatic intensity, as if a powerful steel spring had been compressed into his lines, so that they were always trying to burst their restraints."[61] Baker notes that for Wesley, steeped in the rhetorical devices of the ancient classics, "the appreciation, the terminology, and the practice of rhetoric had become almost as essential an element of his approach to literature as his A B C."[62]

The finest use of the figures or any aspect of technique is its enhancement of the meaning, the effect, and the purpose of its use without calling attention to itself. For those probing the breadth and depth of hymnody, it is entirely appropriate to call attention to these artistic, rhetorical figures and how their effect ultimately enhances meaning. One often encounters the twofold classification of figures of thought (tropes) and figures of speech (rhetorical figures).

We use here the term "figures of thought and figures of speech"[63] rather than the terms "poetic devices" or "rhetorical devices," or "forms of repetition," terms that might imply more "fixed" or "mechanical" uses than are often the case in skillful writing. The skillful writer is not simply employing a device or a repetition, but is carefully choosing sounds and words and phrases at precisely chosen places so they enhance the thought and feeling that is desired. Even the idea of "choosing" may imply more craft than art for the skillful poet or hymn writer who may create more intuitively than by simply selecting the right technique or device for the right place. A misuse, overuse, or even obvious use of the figures can distract from the purpose of their use, and, as Baker so aptly describes it, "the machinery tends to creak."[64]

There are also subtleties within and interrelations among many of these figures that move beyond their obvious definitions. Alliteration, for example, in addition simply to having words with the obvious same beginning sounds, may employ similar sounds that subtly suggest the meanings and moods that are desired, and even sounds that are at more separated intervals than consecutive words, sounds that are repeated on strategic words, sounds that are internal rather than initial, sounds that create various rhythms or even counter rhythms or provide an acceleration or retarding of the movement, or sounds that combine these subtleties.

Both the Old and New Testaments in their original languages and in various translations are replete with such figures, and numerous works identify and explain the biblical uses.[65] The figures are used in Scripture and in hymnody as powerful and memorable expressions of eternal truths and must not be regarded as simply beautiful writing to please the imagination. The observant Bible-reading Christian should not find such language strange in hymnody. Much of the figurative language in hymnody is itself borrowed from the Testaments, and those who read and sing hymns would do well to be aware of the biblical origins.

From antiquity until the present, works on rhetoric have named, defined, characterized, illustrated, and classified the hundreds of figures. In their finest uses, these figures add beauty and meaning and are, probably for writers, not so much "devices" called into service as they are simply natural, beautiful, and forceful ways of thinking and speaking. Many of these figures have become a vital part of hymnic poetry.[66] Among these numerous and extensive systems of classification of the vast number of rhetorical devices and figures of speech is E. W. Bullinger's classification in *Figures of Speech Used in the Bible*, in which he systematically presents 217 figures of speech used in the Bible, identifying the etymology, giving specific Scripture passages, and citing nearly eight thousand biblical references. The Scriptures and hymns often draw upon the same figures of speech, and both require careful interpretation.[67]

Figures of Thought

Figures of thought (sometimes referred to as tropes) are those in which there is a departure from the accepted literal sense, or an extension of the meaning of words often involving comparison, contrast, description, or allusion. In her chapter on "Trope and Thought" in *A Poet's Guide to Poetry*, Mary Kinzie notes that "Poets also find it tempting to appeal to a wide audience by making allusions to large patterns of shared cultural experience."[68] For hymnwriters and readers and singers of hymns, the allusions to biblical events, places, people, or concepts often form those "large patterns of shared cultural experience."[69]

Comparison

One form of figures of thought or trope involves comparison, and the two most common types are metaphor and simile.

Metaphor. A metaphor is an implicit comparison that involves a word or phrase ordinarily meaning one thing referred to by a word or expression normally denoting another thing and implying some common quality shared by the two. Watts, in "O God, our help in ages past," uses the metaphors of "shelter from the stormy blast" and "shadow of thy throne." I. A. Richards observes that it was Aristotle, no lesser man, who said, in *The Poetics*, "The greatest thing by far is to have a command of metaphor." But he went on to say, "This alone cannot be imparted to another: it is the mark of genius, for to make good metaphors implies an eye for resemblances."[70]

Richards formulated the distinction between the "vehicle" (that which is borrowed from another context and carries the meaning) and the "tenor" (the meaning itself). He contends that it is the complex interaction between the vehicle and the tenor that lends the full meaning to a metaphor.

Hymns are rich in the metaphors and similes borrowed from Scripture and Christian tradition. Some hymns are actually mosaics of metaphors such as the metaphors in the Gospel of John—bread, door, shepherd, light, resurrection life, living vine, way, truth, life.

Simile. A simile is an explicit comparison of objects dissimilar in some aspect and uses the words "as" or "like." Watts, in "O God, our help in ages past," uses the similes of "like an evening gone," "as the watch that ends the night," "like an ever-rolling stream," and "as a dream dies at the opening day." Hymns are replete with simile, many borrowed from Scripture.

Contrast

Another group of figures of thought or trope involves contrast, and the most common types are irony, paradox, and oxymoron.

Irony. Irony is a perception of inconsistency in which an apparently straightforward statement or event is undermined by its context so as to give it a different significance—an apparent discrepancy between what is said and what is really meant. Verbal irony involves a contradiction between what is said and what is meant. Samuel Crossman, in "My song is love unknown," poses the question of our Lord's "crime" and answers ironically, "He made the lame to run, He gave the blind their sight." Irony appears in satire, which is almost absent in hymnody, but in his notes to "Christ from heaven's glory come," which sprang from comparing the rejection of Christ with those who experience rejection today, Dudley-Smith remarks that "the note, almost of satire, which emerges in this text was certainly not in my mind when I sat down to begin work on it . . . in the final verse [stanza] ironic emphases should be replaced by sincerity of prayer and purpose."[71]

Paradox. Paradox is a statement containing two opposite ideas. While earlier thinking considered paradox to be a figure of speech rather than a figure of thought, more recent thinking has "given it a higher importance as a mode of understanding by which poetry challenges our habits of thought."[72] This is often not simply a literary device, but in hymns on the incarnation the device reinforces the theological paradox of the divinity and humanity of Christ. In "Hark! the herald angels sing," Wesley speaks of "offspring of a virgin's womb" and "veiled in flesh, the Godhead see."

It is important that we not simply identify the presence of any of the figures of thought or figures of speech but that we see them in the larger context of a comprehensive and integrated hermeneutics. This may be illustrated in part by stopping to look at how Sylvia Dunstan, in her "*Christus Paradox*" ("You, Lord, are both Lamb and Shepherd"), makes an extended and effective use of paradox. This hymn illustrates again how the multiple "voices" interrelate in fine hymnody. Fourteen different paradoxes are expressed in four well-constructed stanzas, each with the fourth-line refrain, "You, the everlasting instant [itself a paradox]," and a concluding summary line to the stanza. Anaphora is used effectively thirteen times with "you" and four times with "worthy" without any sense of being belabored. The 87.87.87 meter moves in a stately cross rhyme that moves with meaning and not simply sound. The hymn is based on Isaiah 11, Isaiah 53, Philippians 2:5-11, and Colossians 1:15-20. Biblical metaphors abound, and every line of the text has a biblical basis. Biblical theology is replete with paradox, and this hymn is a fine study of that dimension of Christian theology. William McDonald says of Kierkegaard's thinking about the concept Dunstan used as the refrain in her hymn,

> He [Kierkegaard] moved from a position of "armed neutrality" with respect to church politics, to one of decisive intervention in "the instant." "The Instant" [Øieblikket—lit., "the glint of an eye"] was Kierkegaard's final frenetic publication. The Concept of Anxiety had identified "the instant" as the point of intersection of time and eternity. It is the moment of decision, the moment of transfiguring vision, the moment of contemporaneity with Christ. It was also the moment to let go of indirect communication and to speak directly. "The Instant" was the name of a broadsheet Kierkegaard published to continue his attack on the state

church. . . . It was not a direct communication about eternal truth, but a timely intervention in contemporary politics.[73]

Dunstan's text is appropriate for a wide range of liturgical uses as well as for sermons on any of the passages referred to in the hymn. The later hymnal from Dunstan's denomination, *Voices United: The Hymn and Worship Book of The United Church of Canada*, lists a wide variety of liturgical uses of this text.[74]

One setting for Dunstan's text is WESTMINSTER ABBEY,[75] derived from Henry Purcell's anthem, "O God, Thou art my God." Sir Sydney Nicholson, organist at Westminster Abbey (1919–1928) and one of Purcell's successors in that position, gave the hymn tune its name. This tune matches the mood and thought of the text, and by the fresh movement from E minor to E major in the fifth phrase beautifully highlights the paradoxical refrain, "You, the everlasting instant." A descant on the fourth stanza would undergird the climactic four-fold anaphora of "worthy." Even though Dunstan thought initially of WESTMINSTER ABBEY, she was not satisfied with the setting and her friend John Van Maanen wrote the tune CHRISTUS PARADOX.

As is often the case, historical context and biographical insight can contribute to understanding and interpreting hymns. Sylvia Dunstan (1955–1993),[76] a native Canadian, grew up with her grandparents, who had Methodist and Salvation Army backgrounds. She wrote that with her grandparents she "sang hymns, choruses, and gospel songs—these were to be the foundation of my religious understanding."[77] Her college degree was in history, and she went on to receive the M.Div. and Th.M. degrees and was ordained in the United Church of Canada. She served first as pastor and then duty chaplain of a maximum security jail while editing the United Church's worship publication, *Gathering*. She brought to her hymn writing the perspective of a "Renaissance woman," reflected in her love of Renaissance music and jazz, parish and prison, books and hymnals, liturgies and sermons, cooking and fine wines, Kierkegaard, female poets, and science fiction. Of her early texts she noted, "Congregational resistance to unfamiliar tunes led me to use the hymn book tunes as the vehicle for the texts. In the process of using hymn book tunes I learned that structure (meter, rhyme, etc.) empowered the people's singing. . . . tradition-loving classicism took place from 1981 to 1983."[78]

In *In Search of Hope and Grace*, Dunstan relates that she drafted this text "on a commuter bus after a particularly bad day at the jail" and that

You, Lord, are both Lamb and Shepherd.	John 1:36; John 10:14-16; Revelation 5:6
You, Lord, are both prince and slave.	Philippians 2:6-8
You, peace-maker and sword-bringer	Ephesians 2:14-18; Matthew 10:34
Of the way you took and gave	Luke 1:79; John 14:6
You, the everlasting instant;	Revelation 1:8; Isaiah 9:6
You, whom we both scorn and crave.	Philippians 2:8-9
Clothed in light upon the mountain,	Matthew 17:2; Mark 9:2-3; Luke 9:29
Stripped of might upon the cross,	Matthew 27:35
Shining in eternal glory;	Philippians 3:21
Beggar'd by a soldier's toss,	Matthew 27:35
You, the everlasting instant;	Revelation 1:8; Isaiah 9:6
You who are both gift and cost.	John 15:13; Luke 14:26-33
You, who walk each day beside us,	Luke 24:15
Sit in power at God's side.	Luke 22:69; Ephesians 1:20; Colossians 3:1
You, who preach a way that's narrow,	Matthew 7:13-14
Have a love that reaches wide.	John 3:16
You, the everlasting instant;	Revelation 1:8; Isaiah 9:6
You, who are our pilgrim guide.	John 16:13-14
Worthy is our earthly Jesus!	Hebrews 2:17; Hebrews 4:14-15
Worthy is our cosmic Christ!	Hebrews 3:3
Worthy your defeat and victory.	Revelation 4:11; Revelation 5:9, 12
Worthy still your peace and strife.	John 14:27; Matthew 10:34
You, the everlasting instant;	Revelation 1:8; Isaiah 9:6
You, who are our death and life.	John 12:25

the hymn "owes much to [her] longstanding relationship with Søren Kierkegaard."[79]

Oxymoron. Oxymoron, a compressed paradox, is similar to paradox and combines words that are seemingly contradictory. Watts speaks of "the wondrous cross" and twice in "Ride on! Ride on in majesty," H. H. Milman proclaims, "In lowly pomp ride on to die." Samuel Crossman, in "My song is love unknown," speaks of "sweet injuries!" In the opening stanza of "The stars declare his glory," Dudley-Smith uses an oxymoron wrapped in a most meaningful alliteration of sibilants signifying the silences of space and announces that "their soundless music sings."

Substitution

The group of figures of speech or trope that involves some form of substitution includes metonymy, antonomasia, and synecdoche.

Metonymy. The substitution of the name of one thing for the name of something else closely associated with it is called metonymy. The use of metonymy in hymns is much the same as in Scriptures. The cross and Calvary, of course, are often used in hymnody to speak of the whole redeeming work of Christ.

Antonomasia. The replacement of a proper name with an epithet or other indirect description is called antonomasia. In hymnody, antonomasia is also often borrowed from Scripture such as "Word of God," "Lamb of God," and "Son of God" for Jesus, and powerful descriptions are given for Jesus—"Christ, child of earth," "Judge of all," "King of kings," "Lord," "Son of Man," "King," and "Priest."

Synecdoche. A synecdoche is a type of metaphor, a kind of metonymy, in which the name of a part is substituted for the quality of a whole or vice versa. In the great train of biblical synecdoches, "Israel" refers to the entire people of God; "heart," "lips," "tongue," "arm," "the maker's hand," "the Saviour's head" refer to the actions or feelings associated with these parts.

Two other common figures of thought (tropes) are hyperbole and personification.

Hyperbole

Exaggeration for emphasis is called hyperbole or overstatement, as in Wesley's "O for a thousand tongues to sing my dear Redeemer's praise." There is sometimes a suggestion of hyperbole in the "negative superlatives" of "un-" and "-less," which occur often in hymnody. What may seem hyperbole may not always be exaggeration for the believer in such expressions as "endless exultation."[80]

Personification

In personification, abstract ideas or inanimate things are treated as if they were human, as in St. Frances of Assisi's "All creatures of our God and King," where he addresses, in W. H. Draper's translation, the "burning sun," the "silver moon," the "rushing wind," the "clouds that sail in heav'n above," the "rising morn," the "lights of evening," the "flowing water," the "fire so masterful and bright," and "mother earth."

Figures of Speech

In addition to the figures of thought or tropes, there are the figures of speech or rhetorical figures that involve contrast with other words, the repetition of words in various patterns, description, changing the usual direction or order, the omission of words, breaking off in mid-sentence, the addition of words, or assuming special modes of address.

Contrast

An important group of figures of speech employ contrast. Hymns frequently draw on the power of contrast that is common in the Scriptures, especially in the parallelism of Hebrew poetry as seen in the Psalms.

Antithesis. An emphasis made by sharply contrasting or opposing ideas in some balance is called antithesis. In his "My song is love unknown," Crossman draws several bold contrasts: "He came from his blest throne salvation to bestow,/ but all made strange, and none the longed-for Christ would know" and ". . . resounding all the way Hosannas to their king./ Then 'Crucify!' is all their breath."

Repetition

A major group of figures of speech employs the repetition of letters, words, phrases, and even clauses.

Alliteration. Alliteration is a commonly used form of repetition, as in Roby Furley Davis's translation of "Of the Father's Love begotten" in the phrase "Frail and feeble, doomed to die" and in Samuel Crossman's sentence, "O who am I, / That for my sake / My Lord should take / Frail flesh and die?" from "My song is love unknown." Alliteration is discussed in more detail below under the repetition of sounds.

Epizeuxis. Emphasis by immediate repetition of the same word or words is referred to as epizeuxis, as employed in William H. Draper's translation of St. Francis of Assisi's "All creatures of our God and King," "Praise, praise the Father . . ." [81] and twice in the refrain to William Dix's "What child is this?": "This, this . . ." and "haste, haste."

Anaphora. The repetition of words or phrases at the beginning of successive lines, clauses, or sentences is called anaphora, and it can provide a strong emphasis to ideas and a significant rhythm. In the eighth stanza (of the original sixteen) of "Soldiers of Christ, arise," Charles Wesley uses the word "believe" to begin three of the lines. In the twelfth stanza, he uses the word "pray" to begin four of the lines; in two of those he also ends the lines with the word (epanadiplosis), and in one of those he further uses the word in the middle of the line (mesodiplosis). He uses the word "prayer" before the line employing mesodiplosis to make five uses of a form of the word in three lines! Anaphora is usually at the beginning of successive lines, but it may occur with an intervening line or lines and still provide a strong emphasis to more expanded ideas as in Wesley's "Hark! the herald angels sing" where there is a clear anaphora in the lines "Christ, by highest heaven adored" and the successive line "Christ, the everlasting Lord," but six lines later, in some versions, in the same stanza is "Christ is born in Bethlehem." [82] In his "Soldiers of Christ, arise," a masterful study in repetition, [83] "Stand" begins successive stanzas, separated by seven verses (lines), and the word occurs in the preceding verse (anadiplosis).

Epanadiplosis. The repetition of the initial word or words at the end of the line or sentence is called epanadiplosis, and the word is given emphasis by both the repetition and by the circular completeness. Wesley's plea, "hide me, O my Savior hide," is an effective use of this figure of speech in his "Jesus, Lover of my soul." George Herbert's "King of glory, King of peace" has the line, "Seven whole days, not one in seven." It often has a certain solemnity in the breadth of its repetition.

Mesodiplosis. The repetition of words in the middle of subsequent lines, phrases, or sentences is called mesodiplosis. It is similar to internal rhyme and accelerates the rhythm. This figure is used in the second and third lines of George Herbert's "King of glory, King of peace"—"I will love thee; and that love may never cease, I will move thee." [84] In Dudley-Smith's "The stars declare his glory," based on Psalm 19, the final stanza becomes a very personal prayer, and the significant word "my" is implored in the middle of lines (mesodiplosis), at the beginning and middle of lines, and in virtual immediate repetition (epizeuxis).

> So order too this life of mine,
>   direct it all my days;
> the meditations of my heart
>   be innocence and praise,
> my Rock, and my redeeming Lord,
>   in all my words and ways.[85]

Epistrophe. The repetition of a word or phrase at the end of several successive clauses, verses, or sentences is referred to as epistrophe. George Herbert, ever rich in poetic rhetoric, uses this figure in the internal lines of "King of glory, King of peace" between the rhymed lines:

> King of glory, King of peace,
>   I will love thee;
> and that love may never cease,
>   I will move thee.
> Thou hast granted my request,
>   thou hast heard me;
> thou didst note my working breast,
>   thou hast spared me.

The same pattern of "thee" and "me" is used for the next two stanzas, all told with ten different verbs.

Anadiplosis. The repetition of a word, phrase, or concept at the end of one clause, sentence, or stanza and at the beginning of the next is called anadiplosis. It may provide a meaningful repetition and emphasis, establish a satisfying rhythm, and serve a structural function. The opening stanzas of Wesley's "O for a thousand tongues" illustrate this figure of speech at work between stanzas.

> O for a thousand tongues to sing
> my dear Redeemer's praise,
> the glories of my God and King,
> the triumphs of his grace!

My gracious Master and my God,
assist me to proclaim
and spread through all the earth abroad
the honors of thy Name.

Jesus! the Name that charms our fears
and bids our sorrows cease;
'tis music in the sinner's ears,
'tis life and health and peace.[86]

Climax

A sequence of three or more words or phrases linked by chain-like rep-etition and in ascending order of intensity is called climax. The ancient affirmation "Christ has died! Christ is risen! Christ will come again!" is part of many liturgies and forms the climax of each of the five stanzas of Fred Pratt Green's "This is the threefold truth."

Epimone

The repetition of part of a verse, a verse, or a group of verses, often at the end of each stanza, is called an epimone or refrain.[87] An epimone or refrain may appear other than at the end of each stanza. In Omer Westen-dorf's "You satisfy the hungry heart," and in some folk hymns such as "Jesu, Jesu," the refrain is sung at the beginning, between stanzas, and at the end. In Isaac Watts's "Give to our God immortal praise" and in Brian Wren's "There's a spirit in the air," there is a double refrain. There is also a biblical precedent for the double refrain in Psalm 107. Frank Baker notes,

> [Charles] Wesley's use of the refrain really demands an essay in itself. He uses it in strict moderation, knowing how easily a refrain can become forced or feeble, or the cloak for poverty of thought or craftsmanship. Wesley's are always strong phrases which readily stand up to repetition in a prominent position, though they are often movingly simple.[88]

In "Rejoice, the Lord is King!" Wesley employs an epimone based on Philippians 4:4. "Lift up your heart, lift up your voice, / Rejoice, again I say, rejoice." Frank Baker also calls attention to the anaphora in the first line, the epanadiplosis in the second line, and, with the first word of the hymn being repeated as the last word of the hymn, the extended epanadiplosis.[89]

Description

Hypotyposis. The use of a vivid description to bring a scene to mind is called hypotyposis and is seen in Watts's "When I survey the wondrous cross."

> See, from his head, his hands, his feet,
>> sorrow and love flow mingled down!
> Did e'er such love and sorrow meet,
>> or thorns compose so rich a crown?

Diaeresis. Diaeresis, in which parts or attributes of something are enumerated rather than repeated, may be employed to call attention to the many parts or attributes of a theme or to utilize the rhythm and momentum that enumeration can lend. This is part of the impact of Watts's line, "See, from his head, his hands, his feet."

Change of Word Order

Another group of figures of speech involving change is those that affect the arrangement and order of words. Some involve separate words while others involve phrases, clauses, or sentences.

Chiasmus. Chiasmus is, historically and rhetorically, a significant figure of speech in which the order of words or ideas in the first of two parallel clauses is reversed in the second clause. This figure of speech, named after the Greek letter chi (X) because of its "crossing" of terms or concepts, occurs not only in poetry but also in prose throughout history,[90] and the principle of chiasmus is found in the visual and musical arts.[91] In a larger sense, chiasmus form is sometimes a key to the central message of a writing or to the relationships between ideas. J. C. Fenton, in *Saint Matthew,*[92] speaks of the overall arrangement of the book of Matthew as chiasmus (a,b:b,a) in length and to some degree in subject matter. Among other parallelisms in this Gospel, there is the similarity between the first discourse (chapters 5–7) and the last discourse (chapters 23–25), and between the second discourse (chapter 10) and the fourth discourse (chapter 18), while the third discourse (chapter 13) forms the central point and contains the parables of the kingdom. There are chiasmus structures in the words of Jesus as recorded in

Matthew 6:24 and 7:6 (NASB).[93] Derek Kidner has spoken much of the literary devices in Old Testament Scripture, and in his commentary of Isaiah 52:13–53:12 he notes that this long and powerful fourth "Servant Song" is cast in chiasmus form by its themes and its wording. It has been noted that the first "poetic statement" in the Scriptures is chiastic, "God created man in His own image, in the image of God He created him" (Gen 1:27), and this form is honored in most versions and languages.

Chiasmus is seen in a number of Wesley's hymns such as "Jesus, Lover of my soul."

> Just, and holy is Thy name
>> I am all unrighteousness,
> False, and full of sin I am,
>> Thou art full of truth, and grace.

In "The Universal love of Christ," Wesley's lines are "Let earth and heaven agree, / Angels and men be joined . . . ."

Similar chiastic and anadiplosis-like turns of phrases, akin to the parallelism of Hebrew poetry, are found in Tate and Brady's 1696 *A New Version of the Psalms of David, Fitted to the Tunes used in Churches,* as in the stanza from "Through all the changing scenes of life" (Ps 34): "O magnifie the Lord with me, / With me exalt his Name."

It is not inappropriate to have dwelt on this figure of speech. It is, as Frank Baker has pointed out, "one of the natural out workings both of the essential paradoxes of the Christian faith and of the antithetical processes of Charles Wesley's literary art"[94] and is present in the hymns of other writers. Baker notes that Wesley's "mind was so accustomed to manipulating the intertwined formulae of logic as well as the figures of rhetoric that his sentences often quite unconsciously assumed this form of patterns within patterns. Almost always the chiasmus in grammatical arrangement is combined with an antithesis in meaning."[95] In the hymns of the finest hymn writers, there is often this same unconscious or innate grasp of language and the skill of expressing truths in powerful ways that convey meaning without calling attention to the sometimes extensive and almost ingenious technical aspects.

Hyperbation. When the normal word order in a sentence is transposed or rearranged in a major way for rhetorical or poetic effect, it is referred to as hyperbation. In Isaac Watts's "O [Our] God, our help in ages past," the main verb in the first sentence does not come until the second stanza!

Antistrophe. The term antistrophe describes the figure of repetition in which the order of words in one clause is reversed in the next as occurs in the final line of a stanza from Wesley's "Hark! The herald angels sing"— "Thine to ours, and ours to Thine."

Zeugma. Zeugma is the "yoking" of one word so that it refers to two others in the same sentence, such as a verb or preposition with two objects. In Samuel Crossman's "My Song is love unknown," the verbs "have" and "was" each serve two objects (based on Matt 8:20 and Mark 15:42-47)— the ideas of "home" and "tomb," and "life" and "death," alluding back to stanza 2 and speaking beautifully of Christ's kenosis (self-emptying) based on Philippians 2:7.

> In life no house, no home
>   my Lord on earth might have;
> In death no friendly tomb
>   but what a stranger gave.
>   What may I say?
>   Heav'n was His home;
>   but mine the tomb
>   wherein he lay.

Antanaclasis. The repetition of the same word but with a slight difference in meaning or with some change in the direction of thought is called antanaclasis. In his Communion hymn, "An upper room with evening lamps ashine," Dudley-Smith employs a meaningful and beautiful combination of antanaclasis with the different (death and ritual) meanings of "pour" and "break" and a widely spaced chiasmus, where the order of ideas in the first of two parallel clauses is reversed in the second (pour wine, break bread /broken body, blood outpoured).

> An upper room with evening lamps ashine,
> the twelve disciples, and the table spread;
> now in our turn Christ bids us pour the wine,
> and in remembrance bless and break the bread.

> We see by faith upon the cross displayed
> his body broken and his blood outpoured;
> in that dread robe of majesty arrayed
> we gaze in worship on the dying Lord.[96]

Omission

Another group of figures of speech involves the omission of some expected or usual word or words, breaking off in mid-sentence, or changing the usual order. These omissions are common to rhetoric and poetry and may accelerate the thinking, propel the meaning and emphasis into the forefront, or allow the mind to soar beyond the obvious or expected.

Ellipsis. The omission of a word or words that would normally be required for complete clarity but that can usually be understood from the context of the sentence is referred to as *ellipsis.* In the third stanza of "My song is love unknown," Samuel Crossman omits the object of the verb "strew." "Sometimes they strew his way, / and his strong praises sing, / resounding all the day / Hosannas to their King." From the context, the verb clearly refers to Matthew 21:8; Mark 11:8; Luke 19:36; John 12:13, and, taken together, the Gospels speak of "their coats and leafy branches from the palm trees." Crossman's omission is more of an addition, allowing those biblically perceptive to bring to mind what would have taken several words to explain. The economy of the thought-provoking and expressive allusions is typical of finer poetic language in hymnody.[97]

Addition

Another group of figures of speech involve the addition of words for the sake of emphasis or color.

Polysyndeton. The repeated use of conjunctions to link words is called polysyndeton. Dudley-Smith makes effective us of polysyndeton in "Praise the Lord of heaven,"[98] where the conjunction "and" occurs eight times in the second stanza and emphasizes the enumeration of things in God's creation that are called on to praise him.

Periphrasis. Periphrasis refers to something by means of a several-words description instead of naming it directly in a single word or phrase. In "All flowers of garden, hill and field," Dudley-Smith, with an interesting suggestion but without naming the tomb, describes the tomb as "Joseph's plot where olives bloom and tangled branches twine."[99] Periphrasis differs from tautology, which is needless repetition without the addition of any color or force, and from circumlocution, which is unnecessarily wordy and indirect language to avoid getting to the point.

Mode of Address

Question. Another group of figures of speech involves assuming special modes of address. There is often a certain involvement or dramatic dimension to a question. One is reminded again of the liturgical drama of the Middle Ages. The first known Easter play, the *Visitatio sepulchri,* found in the Winchester Regularis Concordia of circa 970, consists of the "*Quem quaeritis?*" ("Whom do you seek?") dialogue between the women who came to the tomb and the angel who guarded the tomb. Detailed rubrics indicate that this was sung and was the basis of liturgical drama. William Dix's "What child is this?" in the first stanza is answered in the refrain, and "Why lies he in such mean estate" is answered in the following sentence and reinforced in the refrain. Four times in his "Wilt thou forgive that sin?" John Donne asks "wilt thou forgive?" In "Who is He in yonder stall?" Benjamin Russell Hanby poses seven questions sung by a soloist and responded to by the congregation.[100]

The rhetorical question is a special mode of address in which the asking is for the sake of persuasive effects rather than a request for information and implies that the answer is too obvious. In the eight opening lines of "And can it be?" Wesley poses a series of rhetorical questions.

Apostrophe. Apostrophe addresses a dead or absent person or an abstraction or inanimate object. A good example is in the final stanza of Charles Wesley's "Eternal Beam of Light Divine," where, using the words of 1 Corinthians 15:55, the writer challenges, "O death, where is thy sting? Where now / thy boasted victory, O grave?"

Punctuation

Some classifications of figures of speech include punctuation.

Echphonesis. Echphonesis is the use of the exclamation point, and one of its most familiar uses is in Wesley's "Hark! The herald angels sing" or Doddridge's "Hark! The glad sound!"

Parenthesis and Dash. Parenthesis and dash are used for parenthetical expressions. The parenthesis and echphonesis occur with strong effect in the line "He left his Father's throne above (so free, so infinite his grace!)," from Wesley's "And can it be."

Figures of Sound

An important group of the figures of speech is those involving the repetition of sounds. Because no grouping of the figures of speech is absolutely discrete, some figures carry qualities that apply to more than one category. We must, at least, call attention to the figures that share some common aspects of sounds and the repetition of sounds.

Alliteration

The repetition of the same sounds (usually consonants or the stressed syllables) in any sequence of neighboring words (usually the same first letter or sound in a group of words) is referred to as alliteration.[101] Alliteration is one of the most common and, if used carefully, can be one of the more effective devices to give flow, motion, rhythm, expectation, or inevitability and memorability to poetic language and to help give wings to the thoughts and feelings and stimulate the mind to fresh thoughts, images, suggestions, and allusions. It often captivates the ear by distinctive repetitions and patterns of aesthetically pleasing sounds. It can even provide a physical, tactile experience to the organs of speech and may provide the satisfaction of the familiar and the delight of the new.

Alliteration was once a required element in Old English poetry and revived (or continued) in the fourteenth-century "alliterative revival." Margaret Drabble notes that "R. W. Chambers, in his essay 'On the Continuity of English Prose from Alfred to More' (1932), saw this alliterative thread as a common factor in English writing from Old English to the Renaissance."[102] It has continued to be an important device in English-language speaking and writing.

Alliteration is one way of using the sounds of words to relate words to one another, to reinforce their meanings, and to give rhythm and motion to the words and thoughts. As with all aspects of poetic language, effective alliteration moves beyond simple definition. With alliteration it is not simply the repetition of the same sounds; the very properties of the sounds and the meanings of the words of which they are a part can contribute to the true effect. There may be mental, aural, visual, and tactile aspects of the pairings. Alliteration is the repetition of sounds and not the repetition of letters. It is aural and not simply visual. This is seen in the frequent alliteration of words beginning with "k" and "c": "Kingly courts." As we might speak of half or slant rhymes, we might speak of half or slant alliterations as the "c" and "g" in "cross and grave" and the "g" and "k" in "God and King." Roby Furley Davis, in his translation of "Of the Father's Love begotten," makes powerful use of alliteration in his phrase "Frail and feeble, doomed to die," and Samuel Crossman makes a similar use of sound and meaning in the sentence, "O who am I, / That for my sake / My Lord should take / Frail flesh and die?"

Assonance

The repetition of identical or similar vowel sounds in the stressed syllable and sometimes in the following unstressed syllables of neighboring words is referred to as assonance or vowel rhyme. We have discussed assonance under rhyme, but rhetorical assonance differs from rhyme in that although the vowels or diphthongs match and the consonants differ, it does not occur at the ends of lines, but within and between lines for musical effect or for emphasis. In "Teach me, my God and King," George Herbert ends successive verses with "stone" and "gold." While not part of his rhyme scheme, it is an effective juxtaposition of sounds and meanings.

Consonance

The repetition of identical or similar consonants in neighboring words is called consonance. When combined with alliteration and terminal consonance it is sometimes referred to as "rich consonance," as in John Jacob Niles's Christmas carol "I wonder as I wander."[103]

Syzygy

Some prosodists[104] refer to syzygy as the use of consonant sounds at the end of one word and at the beginning of another that can be spoken together easily and harmoniously. The meaning comes from the Latin for "conjunction," and from the Greek σύζυγος (syzygos) meaning to join or yoke and is related to the literary terms elision (usually a vowel sound at the end of one word and the beginning of the new, as in Watts's "I sing the almighty power of God) and syncope (the omission of letters, as is common in "heav'n" and "o'er"). Syzygy affects articulation and consequently movement as in Dudley-Smith's "royal law for all creation" from his "God of old whom saints and sages" or in "more rich than any prize" from his "The stars declare his glory." Other prosodists use the term to designate two coupled feet serving as a unit.

Onomatopaeia

Onomatopaeia is where a word is an imitation of the sound of the action, as the word "blast" in Watts's "O God, our help in ages past," or where words, by their sounds, evoke a mood.

These figures of thought, speech, and sound are another aspect of the true poetry of hymns. The reader/singer of hymns does well to develop sensitivity to the beauty and force of these elements that abound not only in poetry and prose of biblical translations but also in hymnody. A more thorough appreciation of hymnody obviously requires some innate sense of poetry, and some will prefer to approach any art purely intuitively and without exploring the techniques. While the preceding analyses may be considered by some readers/singers of hymns as unnecessary and even distracting to their appreciation, it is hoped that for many it will contribute to their understanding of the craft of skillful writers and to their appreciation of how the beauty and meaning of texts undergird their noble theme. The more skill and sensitivity the reader/singer brings to the inner workings, the less inclination there will be to be distracted by them and the more inclination to be drawn to the beauty and meaning that they contribute.

Form

Form is present to some degree in most aspects of life. If not present in some recognizable way, then the mind often seeks to impose order. The most fundamental attributes of form are the balances between elements of unity or sameness and elements of variety or contrast of various aspects. In the arts, unity may be achieved by strict repetition or some relatively slight variation of some aspects, while variety or contrast may be achieved by significantly or completely altering any or all aspects. Some degree of cohesiveness and repetition is fundamental to the concept of form, and the most common or obvious cohesive or unifying threads in hymn texts include the poetic, hymnic, and musical meter, the rhyme scheme for each stanza, and a common theme running through the text. Some development of thought is usually considered necessary for a definable overall structure of a hymn. Form in hymns,[105] as in most art forms, may be considered in both its micro and macro dimensions. Repetitions, especially if patterned in some way, serve at least micro-structural functions by binding sounds, words, lines, ideas, figures of thought, and figures of speech into units that contribute to the macro form of the hymn as a whole. Form or overall structure is crucial in fine hymnody because form is frequently vitally related to the meaning.

Morphemes, Sounds, Words, Verses, Couplets, Stanzas, Hymn

At the most micro level, form may involve the repetition of one letter or sound, which begins to create a pattern and influence shape. Parts of words (or morphemes as in the case of prefixes and suffixes) may set up small patterns and shape phrases and clauses, and contribute to an overall shape. In the works of the finer hymn writer, there is a sensitivity to subtle sounds and repetitions of even morphemes and their relationships to larger aspects of structure. Alliteration may be microscopic and possibly even subliminal to many singers or readers, but the repetition of sound contributes to sameness, familiarity, motion, rhythm, and a sense of shape. Many of the figures of thought and speech contribute to form. Anaphora is structural, forming words and ideas into units. Anadiplosis, binding stanzas together by repeating the final words or verse of one stanza as the opening words or verse of the following stanza, serves a more macro dimension of form. Macrorhythms of form can also be seen in uses of the rhythms of verse lengths, rhymes, and theme or logical development.

Pause/Reversal and General/Specific Delineations of Form

In the most complete sense, one can discuss form only by considering the accumulation of all the elements of a hymn. John Ciardi and Miller Williams, in their discussion of how a poem means, note that "once the student has acquired some specific ways of identifying different kinds of diction, metaphor, rhythm, and counterrhythm, he is prepared to discuss form," and when the student can identify the poem in action with its pause and counterthrust, "He will have seen how it means."[106]

It is the nature of poetry to suggest meanings far beyond the definitions of the words. Hymns, especially in their use of biblical language, certainly suggest meanings far beyond the specific definitions or description. The "pause and reversal" and movement from specific to the general may be seen in many hymns. This is often the case in the final stanzas, especially hymns in Trinitarian form (see below).

Dudley-Smith is a master of form, and "pause and reversal" occur in several of his hymns; the collected edition often sets off the final stanzas by three spaced asterisks. Sometimes, in his notes, he calls attention to the breaks. Of "Christ from heaven's glory come," he remarks, "The asterisks between verses 4 and 5 mark, of course, a change of mood (which might well be emphasized by a pause) and in the final verse ironic emphases should be replaced by sincerity of prayer and purpose."[107] Though he remarks that the hymn "seems unlikely to find a place in ordinary congregational worship," it must be considered to be a powerful and unusual hymn. It is powerful and unusual in its form (stanza 1, a picture of Bethlehem; stanza 2, of Egypt; stanza 3, of Christ's miracles, temptation, and betrayal; stanza 4, of Christ's trial and crucifixion [Matt 21:37, John 19:7, and Pilate's words and actions from John 18:38 and Matt 27:24]; and stanza 5, a prayer). It is powerful and unusual in the contrast between the odd and even verses of each of the first four stanzas, which he suggests might be sung "perhaps with an antiphonal 'echo' taking the alternate lines." It is also powerful and unusual in its form, content, and message as a Christmas hymn.

In some hymns, this pause and reversal is not set off by asterisks. In "Soft the evening shadows," Dudley-Smith refers to the way the ending of the hymn draws "the mind on from the events of Christmas to the demands of everyday discipleship . . . . This is brought home especially by the concluding verse and the repeated refrain, not now addressed to Mary and Joseph, or to the Magi, but to ourselves."[108] Sometimes the final couplet of a stanza provides a significant twist of Scripture as in "We bring you, Lord, our prayer and praise" of which he notes, "The final couplet of stanza 3 is a sad reversal of the Messianic prophecy of Isaiah 2.4; echoing the word of judgment of Joel 3.10."[109]

Both the pause and reversal and this movement from specific to the general are also seen in "In the same night in which he was betrayed." Dudley-Smith notes of the hymn,

> As can be seen the first three verses are narrative, visually imagined. There is a break following them, since all those who hear them will know very well what happened in the courtyard, and can reflect upon it rather than be given words in which to recount the sad story. When the verse resumes

it is no longer narrative but prayer, recognizing Peter's position as our own; with the recognition leading to line 4 (a deliberate echo, for those who care to recognize it, from Tennyson's "In Memoriam") and so to line 6—the only possible conclusion.[110]

The pause and reversal and the movement from specific to general is also seen in such hymns as "Exult, O Morning Stars Aflame,"[111] which is shaped around five titles of Jesus: "the Child of Bethlehem," "the Man of Galilee," "the Lamb of Calvary," "the Christ in Majesty," and "the Prince of Peace." Each of the five stanzas ends with the phrase "for love and love alone," each of the stanzas is addressed to a different being (stanza 3 addressed more indirectly to the faithful), and again, Dudley-Smith sets off the final stanza with three asterisks to signal "a change of mood (which might well be emphasized by a pause)" as the entire world is addressed.

In "With all who in this hallowed place," we find a fascinating counterpoint of structural concepts in the overall form of the hymn—one biblical ("the Way, the Truth the Life"), one theological (God the Father, God the Son, God the Holy Spirit), and one chronological (the past, the present, the future). Dudley-Smith notes that he was

> asked for something which would reflect the dedication of the church to St John [Nevelles Cross, Durham]; and this accounts for the use of John 14.6; Christ the Way, the Truth and the Life, as a connecting link between the verses. Verse 1 looks back over the past (in the case of St John's Church, over the past century), the middle verses are concerned with the church of the present in its living experience of Christ today; and the conclusion looks ahead to a church renewed for mission in preparation for its next 100 years.[112]

This extended discussion of pause and reversal or even pause and summary or pause and application seems justified because of its importance in understanding the message of so much of hymnody and because it has, or should have, a profound impact on the manner of singing the text.

Typical Forms

The basic structures that one most often encounters in hymnody might be classified under several large headings: "Trinitarian," "Development," "Chronological (Narrative)," "Allegorical," "Dialogical," "Comparative," "Contrastive," "Symmetrical," "Climactic," "Acrostic," or "Cumulative."

Trinitarian. The Trinitarian form is common in hymnody with one stanza each about or addressed to each person of the Trinity and a fourth, climactic stanza about the Trinity and the unity of the three. "Come, Thou almighty King" and "Eternal Father, strong to save" are familiar examples of this form.

Developmental. Many hymns have an overall structure that grows from the logical development of some biblical passage, theological concept, aspect of the liturgy, or combinations of any or all of these. Psalm versifications follow the development of thought that is to be found in the psalm, and this faithfulness to the biblical flow of thought is true of many hymns. As seen in chapter 3, the major doctrines of the Christian faith find expression in hymns, and some are concise statements or logical developments of certain theological concepts. "Immortal, invisible, God only wise" is a logical development of aspects of the nature of God. James Montgomery's "Prayer is the soul's sincere desire" is a logical discourse on prayer.

Chronological (Narrative). James Montgomery's "Songs of praise the angels sang" begins with creation and moves through the birth of Christ, our Lord's resurrection and humankind's redemption, the new heaven and the new earth, and the saints' song of eternal joy. James D. Burns's narrative hymn, "Hushed was the evening hymn," is based on 1 Samuel 3:1-10 and was set to music by Arthur Sullivan. It is natural for hymn writers who are steeped in Scripture to choose the narrative form to convey truths.

Allegorical. Allegory is not common in hymns, but James Montgomery, in his famous preface to *The Christian Psalmist,* speaks of the form of Augustus G. Spannenberg's Moravian Brethren hymn and its presentation of the nature of God's salvific work. Montgomery notes, "'High on his everlasting throne,' &c though considerably abridged from the original, contains one of the most consistent allegories that can be found in verse, on the manner in which it has pleased God, by the ministry of the Gospel, to reclaim a lost world from the desolation which sin hath made."[113]

Dialogical. Some hymns are based on or imply dialogue, inquiry, or response as in Stephen of Mar Saba's (Judea) eighth-century Greek hymn "Art thou weary, art thou languid?" as translated by John M. Neale with its questions and answers. This form is seen also in John Bowring's "Watchman, tell us of the night," with its dialogue between the watchman and the trav-

eler. The concept is reflected sometimes within a stanza as in Montgomery's
hymn "Songs of praise the angels sang" with the question, "And will man
alone be dumb / Till that glorious kingdom come? No;—the Church
delights to raise / Psalms and hymns, and songs of praise."

Comparative. Comparison becomes a structural principle in some
hymns. In Percy Dearmer's "As the disciples, when Thy Son had left them,"
the odd-numbered stanzas speak of "as the disciples . . ." and the even-
numbered stanzas pray "so may we . . . ." Three stanzas of W. Chatterton
Dix's "As with gladness men of old" are also in this form.

Contrastive. Contrast can also be a structural principle in hymns such
as "Christ, whose glory fills the skies," where Charles Wesley draws a bold
contrast between the presence of Christ in the first stanza and the absence
of Christ in the second stanza. The third stanza is a prayer for the radiancy
of Christ to "pierce the gloom of sin and grief," giving the hymn a "Hegelian
dialectic" form of thesis, antithesis, synthesis.

Symmetrical. It has been noted that each of the five verses of each of the
four stanzas of George Matheson's "O Love that wilt not let me go" consistently follows a symmetrical pattern of the first line of each stanza addressing
"love," "light," "joy," and "cross"; the second line speaking of the singer's
response; the third line telling the purpose of the response; and the fourth
line identifying the results of the response. Carl Daw's "Like the murmur of
the dove's song" is in perfect symmetry with each of the four opening phrases
in each of the three stanzas beginning with the same word: "like" in the first
stanza, "to" in the second, and "with" in the third, and concluding each
stanza with the epimone, "come, Holy Spirit, come."

Climactic. The climactic form is related to the logical development, but
more dramatic. F. Bland Tucker's "All praise to thee, for thou, O King
divine," based on Philippians 2:5-12, is one example of this form.[114]

Acrostic. An acrostic[115] construction is employed in nine of the psalms,
most obviously in Psalm 119, though many translations do not call attention
to the device or make any attempt at reflecting it in translation. In modern
hymnody, the form may present more challenges to overcome than technical
creations for expression. However, there may be useful purposes for this
form in hymns. Dudley-Smith made effective acrostic English paraphrases

of the acrostic Psalm 25 in his "All my soul to God I raise," and of the acrostic Psalm 34 in "All our days we will bless the Lord," omitting the letters X, Y, and Z.[116]

Cumulative. An unusual structure is what may be called "cumulative verses or lines." Dudley-Smith explored this principle in his "O Prince of peace whose promised birth," in which a phrase is added to the final line in each of the four stanzas. It is a study in the meaningful Hebrew greeting of "Peace," and the word occurs seventeen times in the hymn. Erik Routley supplied a tune, RECTORY MEADOW, for this unusual form.

The finer hymns are carefully constructed, and the content gives rise to the form. It is a hallmark of fine hymns that they manifest a definite shape delineated by a development of thought and reinforced at multiple levels by a judicious balance of elements of unity and variety. These qualities can be seen in the hymns of fine writers who naturally, skillfully, and yet unobtrusively blend the various literary elements, letting them complement one another to produce in the simple, short form of hymns (a "lyric under a vow of renunciation") expressions that relate to the most important aspects of the Christian life.

The Poetic "Voice" in a "Polyphonic" Hermeneutics

For many hymn writers, theology is a biblical theology and liturgy is a biblical/theological liturgy. The interrelated biblical, theological, and liturgical dimensions may be thought of as the content or "what" of hymnody. The literary voice may be thought of as the form or "how" of hymnody. What J. R. Watson says of the hymns in Charles Wesley's 1780 Collection can also be said of other fine hymn writers: "the vitality of that doctrine is owing to his expression of it. And that expression owes much to his supple and skilful adaptations of biblical phrases and episodes to the human condition."[117] What Aristotle called logos, the logical content of a speech, and the lexis or rhetorical style and delivery of a speech, must be considered inseparable. Meaning and language are intricately interrelated. One's thinking is often powerfully influenced by the very ways in which ideas are conceived and expressed; and how thinking is expressed powerfully influences how thoughts (content) are received and understood by others. The literary expression in hymns can make the biblical, theological, and liturgical content clear, beautiful, powerful, and memorable. The literary expression is actually a vital part of what is being said.

A vital integration of the facets of hymnody may be seen in Wesley's "Come, O Thou Traveler unknown," titled "Wrestling Jacob."[118]

Wrestling Jacob

Come, O Thou Traveler unknown,
    Whom still I hold, but cannot see!
My company before is gone,
    And I am left alone with Thee;
With Thee all night I mean to stay,
And wrestle till the break of day.

I need not tell Thee who I am,
    My misery and sin declare;
Thyself hast called me by my name,
    Look on Thy hands, and read it there;
But who, I ask Thee, who art Thou?
Tell me Thy name, and tell me now.

In vain Thou strugglest to get free,
    I never will unloose my hold!
Art Thou the Man that died for me?
    The secret of Thy love unfold;
Wrestling, I will not let Thee go,
Till I Thy name, Thy nature know.

Wilt Thou not yet to me reveal
    Thy new, unutterable Name?
Tell me, I still beseech Thee, tell;
    To know it now resolved I am;
Wrestling, I will not let Thee go,
Till I Thy name, Thy nature know.

'Tis all in vain to hold Thy tongue
    Or touch the hollow of my thigh;
Though every sinew be unstrung,
    Out of my arms Thou shalt not fly;
Wrestling I will not let Thee go

Till I Thy name, Thy nature know.
What though my shrinking flesh complain,
 And murmur to contend so long?
I rise superior to my pain,
 When I am weak, then I am strong
And when my all of strength shall fail,
I shall with the God-man prevail.

Contented now upon my thigh
 I halt, till life's short journey end;
All helplessness, all weakness I
 On Thee alone for strength depend;
Nor have I power from Thee to move:
Thy nature, and Thy name is Love.

My strength is gone, my nature dies,
 I sink beneath Thy weighty hand,
Faint to revive, and fall to rise;
 I fall, and yet by faith I stand;
I stand and will not let Thee go
Till I Thy name, Thy nature know.

Yield to me now, for I am weak,
 But confident in self-despair;
Speak to my heart, in blessings speak,
 Be conquered by my instant prayer;
Speak, or Thou never hence shalt move,
And tell me if Thy name is Love.

'Tis Love! 'tis Love! Thou diedst for me!
 I hear Thy whisper in my heart;
The morning breaks, the shadows flee,
 Pure, universal love Thou art;
To me, to all, Thy mercies move;
Thy nature and Thy name is Love.

My prayer hath power with God; the grace
 Unspeakable I now receive;
Through faith I see Thee face to face,
 I see Thee face to face, and live!
In vain I have not wept and strove;
Thy nature and Thy name is Love.

I know Thee, Savior, who Thou art.
    Jesus, the feeble sinner's friend;
Nor wilt Thou with the night depart.
    But stay, and love me to the end,
Thy mercies never shall remove;
Thy nature and Thy name is Love.

The Sun of righteousness on me
    Hath risen with healing in His wings,
Withered my nature's strength, from Thee
    My soul its life and succor brings;
My help is all laid up above;
Thy nature and Thy name is Love.

Lame as I am, I take the prey,
    Hell, earth, and sin, with ease o'ercome;
I leap for joy, pursue my way,
    And as a bounding hart fly home,
Through all eternity to prove,
Thy nature, and Thy name is Love.

Erik Routley, with his breadth and depth of knowledge of hymnody, made the bold assertion, "I believe that here you have a hymn whose deep mysterious language will unerringly lead the singer toward a depth of faith which no other hymn can quite achieve for him."[119] The support of such an astonishing statement rests in the quality of the hymn's interrelated biblical, theological, liturgical, and literary aspects. Only a sound hermeneutics that is comprehensive and integrated will provide an appropriate interpretation of such a hymn.

Charles Wesley's literary content and style spring from the Bible. Their message and wording are saturated with the meanings and phrasings of Scripture. His hymns are poetic expressions of biblical theology, and his breadth and depth of understanding of Scripture and the many and varied ways in which that understanding is expressed are studies in themselves. Any sound hermeneutics of his hymns must not only identify the direct and indirect biblical references but must also consider how those Scriptures are bound up with his theology, their liturgical uses, and how his literary skills brought those dimensions into a beautiful and meaningful polyphony.

The entire fourteen stanzas of "Come, O Thou Traveler unknown" are based on Genesis 32:24-32, and Wesley, with some debt to Matthew Henry, weaves with poetic skill a commentary on the passage, giving a Christian interpretation of the "grace unspeakable" shown in "the Man that died for me" and in the "Saviour, who Thou art, Jesus, the feeble sinner's Friend." Wesley's literary skill brings into bold relief the very nature of the Christian faith and Christ's identifying the greatest commandment to be, "'Tis Love! 'tis Love! . . . Pure universal Love." Wesley's command of Scripture allows him to express, in the most natural way, his thoughts with allusions to biblical passages and even in biblical language. As do the Scriptures, he identifies "name" and "nature" as intricately related. In the phrase "Look on Thy hands, and read it there" in stanza 2, Wesley identifies the nature of God by an allusion to Isaiah 49:16[120] and God's expression of memorable love for Zion with the words, "Behold, I have inscribed you on the palms of My hands." There may be an allusion to John 20:27 and Christ's showing his pierced hands to Thomas, or to Luke 24:39-40 and his showing his pierced hand to the disciples. Drawing on 2 Corinthians 12:10, Wesley puts into Jacob's mouth the phrase, "When I am weak, then I am strong," and drawing from Malachi 4:2, Jacob proclaims that the "Sun of righteousness on me / Hath rose with healing in His wings." In the final stanza, he borrows the simile of "the bounding hart" from Isaiah 35:6.

As is often the case in Wesley's hymns (and in many other fine hymns), the biblical and the theological voices move in intricate polyphony. The hymn is a dramatic picture in monologue of the resolute Jacob wrestling with the messenger of God to determine his name and nature. While the emphasis is typically on the admirable tenacity of Jacob, it should be remembered that the angel is God's messenger and that it is God who in love pursues the person. The "Hound of Heaven" acts in divine love and grace. Jacob's growing perception of that nature as reflected in the final verse of the ninth stanza, "And tell me if Thy name is Love," is confirmed in the opening verse of the following stanza in a climactic epizeuxis, "'Tis love! 'tis Love!" The nature is affirmed again in the fourth line of that stanza, "Pure universal Love Thou art," and in the closing line of that stanza, "Thy nature, and Thy name is love," which becomes the closing line of the next five and final stanzas and the final line of the hymn!

In Wesley's unfolding of the story, Jacob becomes increasingly aware that the traveler unknown is the traveler known and that he is the Christ. He questions, "Art Thou the Man that died for me?" (stanza 3, verse 3). In stanza 10, Jacob becomes fully aware of the person with whom he is wrestling, and in stanza 12 is his full and explicit statement, "I know thee, Saviour, who Thou art, / Jesus, the feeble sinner's Friend." As in his "Hark!

The herald angels sing," where he borrows the metaphor from Malachi 4:2, Wesley, again with clear reference to Christ, puts into the mouth of Jacob the affirmation, "The Sun of righteousness on me / Hath rose with healing in His wings" (stanza 13).

The hymn is a dramatic picture of anyone's determined discovery of God's nature and finding God who "so loved the world that he gave his only begotten son." Routley suggests that "Wesley thinks that he [Jacob] saw straightforward to the redemption of the Crucified (see st. 2, 1. 4). This conceit he uses to enable the singer to place himself where Jacob was and avail himself of the same redemption."[121] This is an appropriate theological observation, especially in light of Jesus's own statement in John 1:50-51. In Jacob's vision in his earlier experience recorded in Genesis 28:12 ("He had a dream, and behold, a ladder was set on the earth with its top reaching to heaven; and behold, the angels of God were ascending and descending on it."), Jesus says, "Truly, truly, I say to you, you will see the heavens opened and the angels of God ascending and descending on the Son of Man."

Intricate weavings of the biblical and theological dimensions of hymns are not likely to be fully understood by the average singer, especially in the press of singing, but hymns that express a biblical theology in excellent poetry have the potential for unfolding new meanings each time they are sung, especially if church leadership encourages spiritual maturity and provides opportunities for learning.

Some lectionaries call for the reading of Genesis 32:22-31 on the seventh Sunday after Pentecost in conjunction with the Gospel reading from Matthew 14:13-21 and the feeding of the five thousand when the disciples remarked, "This place is desolate and the hour is already late" (Matt 14:15). The specified reading from Psalm 17 on that Sunday includes the Psalmist's affirmation, "You have tried my heart; You have visited me by night." This hymn has much to offer the reader/singer in a formal liturgy, in a freer tradition, or in private devotion. The hymn's biblically based theological statements about the nature of God, about the Saviour, Jesus, about humanity's weakness, and about the roles of grace and faith give the hymn both general and specific liturgical uses.

Just as the biblical, theological, and liturgical voices move in intricate polyphony in great hymnody, the literary voice often brings the other voices into bold relief. In a rather standard 8.8.8.8.88 iambic meter with two cross rhymes followed by a couplet rhyme, Wesley skillfully employs figures of speech across fourteen stanzas to highlight his meanings. Routley's first sentence in his discussion of this hymn is "Charles Wesley, of course, is the world's most versatile master of poetic device in hymnody."[122] In the first stanza, by the use of epizeuxis/anadiplosis and its immediate repetition across lines, he focuses attention on the unknown traveler, and, in stanza 10 with the climactic epizeuxis "'Tis love! 'tis Love!" he focuses on the name and nature of the *known* traveler. The refrain, "Tell me" (stanzas 2, 4, 9), and the even more persistent refrain, "wrestling, I will not let Thee go, / Till I Thy name, Thy nature know" (stanzas 3, 4, and 5), underscore the entreaty that so much characterizes the hymn. The phrase "Till I Thy name, Thy nature know" recurs a fourth time by itself in stanza 8.

The same biblical/theological/poetic counterpoint is seen in another of Wesley's hymns, "Shepherd Divine, our wants relieve," where the role of our faith (our wrestling) is clearly bound to God's interceding grace.

> Thy spirit of interceding grace
>   Give us in faith to claim;
> To wrestle till we see thy face,
>   And know thy hidden Name.[123]

The phrase, "I will not let Thee go, [unless Thou tell thy name to me]," is set off in an anadiplosis between the fourth and fifth stanzas of "Shepherd Divine, our wants relieve."

In stanzas 5, 6, and 7 of "Wrestling Jacob," Wesley calls forth a series of vivid physical images (hypotyposis) from the Genesis 32 account to show both the struggle of the wrestling and Jacob's admitted weakness. But drawing from the allusion to 2 Corinthians 12:10, Wesley points to Jacob's strength in his weakness with an acclamation by epizeuxis/anadiplosis in stanza 7 and in stanza 8 emphasizes Jacob's determination, "I fall, and yet by faith I stand; / I stand and will not let Thee go."

Again, the final lines of the hymn borrow the simile from Isaiah 35:6, presenting the great biblical, theological, literary counterpoint: "And as a bounding hart fly home, / Through all eternity to prove, / Thy nature, and Thy name is Love."

Wesley's words are carefully chosen, but occasionally the pronunciation of words has changed, resulting in less than their original pure rhyme and more significantly the changes in the meanings of words. To be sure, the word/phrase "Thy bowels move" in stanza 10, line 5 has since not only become archaic, but even inappropriate outside of a medical context. Modern versions often render the line "To me, to all, thy mercies move" or, borrowed from stanza 11, line 5, "thy mercies never shall remove."

The unusual features of this text present special challenges for composers and hymnal editors. The length of the hymn, the challenge of which stanzas to set or print, the dramatic monologue form, the distinctive nature of the final couplets (especially in the stanzas where it serves as an epimone or refrain), and the carefully reasoned argument all make obvious demands.

Numerous hymn tunes have been written for the text, many anthem settings have been made of it, and a variety of existing tunes have been associated with it. In several respects, Routley's setting, WOODBURY,[124] addresses well a number of the challenges of the text. There is a hint of an "overture" to the drama in the descending line of the two-measure introduction. Given the dramatic monologue nature of the text, there is something to commend a unison setting and the use, as here, of something other than a "traditional" hymn tune. The first two musical phrases (four lines of text, 8.8.8.8.) are nicely rounded, and the repetition in the second phrase of the first seven notes of the first phrase contribute something to the entreaty of the drama. Wesley's highly significant closing couplet (four times as a plea and, with slight modification, six times, including the final stanza, as an affirmation) is set with contrasting melody, pitch, tessitura, rhythm, and harmony, but is not fully exploited in Routley's choice of stanzas 1, 2, 9, and 10. The closing Picardy third is a fitting "punctuation" to the final stanza, which is no longer a plea but an affirmation.

In *The United Methodist Hymnal*, the text is set to a traditional Scottish melody harmonized by Carlton Young and named CANDLER for the Candler School of Theology, Emory University, were Young served as professor of church music. Young's long meter tune calls for a not inappropriate repeating of the final two lines of stanzas 1, 2, 9, and 10. The hymn tune is in an A A' B A' form with the final A accommodating the repeated lines.

Hymnals often use only stanzas 1, 2, 8, and 9 or 10, and sometimes 4, 11, 12, or 13.[125] The entire hymn could be read aloud in less than five minutes and could be a meaningful worship experience. It is not unthinkable that with proper planning and execution, different tunes might be used for selected stanzas, especially when singing numerous stanzas, nor would it be inappropriate, given the dramatic monologue it is, for some stanzas to be read by the singer with music in the background.[126] With proper preparation and accompaniment, the dramatic and involving monologue may well be sung as a solo and may be more "congregational" than a thoughtless singing by the congregation.

The hymn is closely identified with Charles Wesley's own spiritual wrestling that culminated in his conversation on Whitsunday in 1738. In

1788, John Wesley ended his obituary tribute to his brother, Charles, at the Methodist Conference with these words: "His least praise was his talent for poetry: although Dr. Watts did not scruple to say that that single poem, Wrestling Jacob, was worth all the verses he himself had written."[127] Some two weeks after his brother's death, John Wesley, while preaching at Bolton, referred to the hymn and broke down when he came to the lines, "my company before is gone, and I am left alone with thee."[128]

Routley's own experience with this hymn also bears on the historical, biographical, and sociocultural aspects of hermeneutics. Routley relates, in a personal way,

> I should like for a moment to be autobiographical here . . . . I first heard this hymn when I was thirteen, at school, sung to a peculiarly arresting homemade tune (since printed, by the way, as No. 496 in *Congregational Praise*, where it is called "Cotswold") [*Rejoice*, no. 512]. I can seldom remember being so profoundly moved by a hymn at the first time of singing. Partly it was the tune, but partly also—my memory has never lost hold of this—it was the word "traveller" in the opening line. I am now pretty sure that Wesley used the word: "traveller" as a neutral apposition for this mysterious angel of Peniel. But to a youngster of the earlier twentieth century "traveller" at once spelled romance. . . . Images can attach themselves to words after the words have been put down by their authors. If they do and they are good, it is entirely to the benefit of the hymn. Thus attracted, as I remember, I was never put off by the obscurity of the rest of the hymn. I was, on the contrary, intrigued. I wondered who was addressing whom, and what on earth about. It was a great day when—years later, of course—I found that it was all there in Genesis 32. But in the meantime there was something in the wrestling and struggling that came through the hymn that suggested all the time that it is a representation of a young man's discovery of Christ. Jacob in Genesis 32 was middle-aged and a substantial citizen, but he discovered that night something which left him weaker, yet immeasurable stronger.[129]

Here, in Wesley's hymn, we find again the multiple and interrelated voices that create the great polyphony that characterizes the finest of Christian hymnody and requires a sound, comprehensive, and integrated hermeneutics for a more complete interpretation.

Notes

1. See chapter 3 for a discussion of biblical and religious language.

2. See C. Clifton Black, *The Rhetoric of the Gospel* (St. Louis MO: Chalice Press, 2001) and E. W. Bullinger, *Figures of Speech Used in the Bible: Explained and Illustrated* (Grand Rapids MI: Baker Book House, 1898; repr., 1968).

3. Amos N. Wilder, *New Testament Faith for Today* (New York: Harper & Brothers, Publishers, 1955) 60.

4. Paul Tillich, *The Religious Situation,* trans. H. Richard Niebuhr (New York: Meridian Books, Inc., 1956; Henry Holt & Company, Inc., 1931) 85.

5. William Wordsworth, *Lyrical Ballads with Pastoral and Other Poems in Two Volumes* (London: Longman, Hurst, Rees, and Orme, 1805) preface, L, p. 50, <http://www.bartleby.com/39/36.html>.

6. Thomas Stearns Eliot, "A Dialogue on Dramatic Poetry," *Selected Essays* (new ed., New York: Harcourt, Brace and Company, 1950) 34.

7. "Biblical and Religious Language" in chapter 3 and "The Musical Dimension of Hymnody," chapter 6, provide further discussion of language, musical aesthetics, and textual relationships.

8. Sir Phillip Sidney, "The Defense of Poesy," in Charles W. Eliot, ed., *English Essays from Sir Philip Sidney to Macalay. The Harvard Classics* (New York, P. F. Collier & Son, 1910) xxvii, 55.

9. Ibid., xxvii, 27–28, 32–33.

10. Not only in public worship but also in private devotion, much is to be gained from the writings of those who have the gift of expressing to us and for us thoughts and feelings that are beyond our limitations.

11. Wilder, *New Testament Faith for Today,* 60.

12. T. S. Eliot, *On Poetry and Poets* (London: Faber, 1957) 30.

13. D. H. Lawrence, *The Evening News* (London), 13 October 1928, included in Anthony Beal, ed., *Selected Literary Criticism: D. H. Lawrence* (Oxford: Heineman, 1956) 6f.

14. The term "verse" (sometimes called "line") typically refers to a single line. The term "stanza" refers to the group of lines with the same number and lengths of verses (lines), meter, and rhyme scheme forming a section and separated by spaces from the other sections. The terms "verse" and "stanza" are used in this work with these meanings.

15. I. A. Richards, *The Philosophy of Rhetoric* (New York: Oxford University Press, 1936, 1964) 47–48.

16. Isaac Watts, "When I survey the wondrous cross."

17. Henry Hart Milman (1791–1868), "Ride on, Ride on in majesty."

18. Alfred, Lord Tennyson (1809–1892), "Strong Son of God," *The English Hymnal with Tunes* (London: Oxford University Press, 1933) 483.

19. Katharina von Schlegel (1752), trans. Jane Borthwick (1855), "Be still my soul," Erik Routley, ed., *Rejoice in the Lord: A Hymn Companion to the Scriptures* (Grand Rapids MI: Wm. B. Eerdmans Publishing Company, 1985) 154.

20. James Montgomery, "Stand up, and bless the Lord."

21. John Ciardi and Miller Williams, *How Does a Poem Mean?* 2nd ed. (Boston: Houghton Mifflin Company, 1975) xix–xx.

22. J. R. Watson, "Hymns and Literature: Form and Interpretation," *Hymn Society of Great Britain & Ireland Bulletin* 17/5 (January 2004): 129–31.

23. Christopher C. Hill, s.v. "Rhetoric," in Don Michael Randel, ed., *The New Harvard Dictionary of Music* (Cambridge MA: The Belknap Press of Harvard University Press, 1986).

24. Ibid.

25. An important and interesting work in this respect is John Hollander, *The Untuning of the Sky: Ideas of Music in English Poetry, 1500–1700* (New York: W. W. Norton & Company, Inc. 1961, 1970).

26. Hill, s.v. "Rhetoric," in Randel, ed., *New Harvard Dictionary of Music*.

27. Sir Phillip Sidney, "The Defense of Poesy," in Charles W. Eliot, ed., *English Essays from Sir Philip Sidney to Macaulay*, The Harvard Classics (New York, P. F. Collier & Son, 1910) xxvii, 9.

28. George A. Kennedy, foreword to Heinrich Lausberg, *Handbook of Literary Rhetoric: A Foundation for Literary Study* (Leiden, Boston, Köln: Brill, 1998) xix.

29. A discussion of sound must deal not only with words but also with morphemes, the smallest unit of grammatical meaning. Morphology is the branch of linguistics that analyzes the structure of words.

30. The figures of thought and speech are discussed later in this chapter.

31. See "Come, Thou long-expected Jesus."

32. The addressees in Psalms are of major importance in understanding the meaning of the psalmist, possibly in understanding how the psalms may have been performed, and ideally how they may be performed or even read today.

33. I. A. Richards, *The Philosophy of Rhetoric* (New York: Oxford University Press, 1936, 1964).

34. C. Hugh Holman, *A Handbook to Literature*, 4th ed. (Indianapolis: Bobbs-Merrill Company, Inc., Publishers, 1983) 444. Holman defines this "syzygy": "In classical prosody, a term used to designate two coupled feet serving as a unit. As used by Sidney Lanier and later prosodists, it refers to the use of consonant sounds at the end of one word and at the beginning of another that can be spoken together easily and harmoniously. Both Poe and Lanier were greatly concerned with *syzygy*" (439). This meaning of syzygy is from the Latin for "conjunction" and from the Greek σύζυγος (*syzygos*), meaning to join or yoke, and is related to the literary terms elision and syncope. It affects both sound and pronunciation as in Dudley-Smith's "royal law for all creation" from "God of old whom saints and sages" or in his "more rich than any prize" from "The stars declare his glory."

35. Richards, *Philosophy of Rhetoric*, 59.

36. Ibid., 62. As there are semantic domains in language, one might also think of timbral domains.

37. Ibid., 63.

38. Ibid.

39. Laurence Perrine, *Literature: Structure, Sound, and Sense*, 4th ed. (New York: Harcourt Brace Jovanovich, Inc. 1983) 709.

40. Ibid., 701–702.

41. In this context, the long "o" sounds take on a mood different from other contexts.

42. "How wondrous great, how glorious bright."

43. Ciardi and Williams, *How Does a Poem Mean?* 103.

44. "Dear Lord, who for our pardon died" (*A House of Praise*, 54).

45. "A purple robe, a crown of thorn" (*A House of Praise*, 51).

46. "Child of Mary, newly born," (*A House of Praise*, 11).

47. Frank Baker, *Representative Verse of Charles Wesley* (Nashville: Abingdon Press, 1962) xlvii–xlviii.

48. See Ciardi and Williams, *How Does a Poem Mean?* 303; and Chris Baldick, *The Oxford Dictionary of Literary Terms* (Oxford: Oxford University Press, 1990) s.v. "Demotion," "Promotion," and "Substitution."

49. A more detailed discussion of the strophic form and of musical meter is given in chapter 6.

50. David R. Wright, "The many mysteries of meter," *Hymn Society of Great Britain & Ireland*, bulletin 232, vol. 16, no. 11 (June 2002): 266–69. Wright notes, "with metre there are two groups of experts: musicians, with their Italian words, and literature experts who love words of Greek origin. Both regard metre and rhythm as 'theirs'. Both educate their 'chosen few' to know a lot about metre; to use complicated words, and to rejoice in subtleties—and leave 95 percent of the population out of their half-secret world."

51. David W. Perry, *Hymns and Tunes Indexed by First Lines, Tune Names, and Metres* (Croydon: The Hymn Society of Great Britain & Ireland and The Royal School of Church Music, 1980).

52. See chapter 6 for a more thorough discussion of the musical dimension of hymnody.

53. Baldick, *Concise Oxford Dictionary of Literary Terms*, s.v. "Half-rhyme."

54. Ibid.

55. Margaret Drabble, ed., *The Oxford Companion to English Literature*, 5th ed. (New York: Oxford University, 1985) 46. s.v. "Assonance."

56. Robert Pinsky, *The Inferno of Dante: A New Verse Translation* (New York: Farrar, Straus & Giroux, 1994) "Translator's Notes."

57. Baldick, *Concise Oxford Dictionary of Literary Terms*, s.v. "Crossed rhyme."

58. This is discussed more fully in chapter 6.

59. These terms are used in music theory and seem appropriate here because the meaningful groupings are sometimes timbral and have melodic implications.

60. R. W. Hepburn, "Religious Language," *Oxford Companion to Philosophy*, ed. Ted Honderich (Oxford: Oxford University Press, 1995).

61. Frank Baker, *Charles Wesley's Verse: An Introduction*, 2nd ed. (London: Epworth Press, 1964, 1988) 35.

62. Ibid., 36.

63. The definitions used here are drawn largely from Baldick, *Concise Oxford Dictionary of Literary Terms*, s.v. "Figure." Not all the figures are discussed in that work, and there are other classifications and varying definitions of the terms.

64. Baker, *Charles Wesley's Verse*, 64.

65. Louis Berkhof, *Principles of Biblical Interpretation* (Grand Rapids MI: Baker Pub Group, 1950); E. W. Bullinger, *Figures of Speech Used in the Bible: Explained and Illustrated* (Grand Rapids MI: Baker Book House, 1898, repr., 1968); Thomas Hartwell Horne, *An Introduction to the Critical Study and Knowledge of the Holy Scripture* (London, for T. Cadell by A. & R. Spottiswoode, 1828) 1:359–72; and Merrill F. Unger, *Principles of Expository Preaching* (Grand Rapids MI: Zondervan Publishing House, 1955).

66. An important work in the larger field of rhetoric is Heinrich Lausberg's, *Handbook of Literary Rhetoric: A Foundation for Literary Study*, trans. Matthew T. Bliss, Annemiek Jansen, and David E. Orton, ed. David E. Orton and Dean Anderson (Boston: Brill, 1998). John Holme's 1755 *Art of Rhetoric* listed more than two hundred and fifty rhetorical terms.

67. E. W. Bullinger, *Figures of Speech Used in the Bible: Explained and Illustrated* (Grand Rapids MI: Baker Book House, 1898, repr., 1968) is a monumental work, both in size (more than 1,100 pages) and in its contribution to the understanding of this aspect of biblical language. While some of Bullinger's theological positions may rightly be questioned by many, his contributions are significant. A hypertext outline of the work may be found at http://rhetoric.byu.edu/figures/groupings/by%20author/bullinger.htm.

68. Mary Kinzie, *A Poet's Guide to Poetry* (Chicago: The University of Chicago Press, 1999) 164.

69. The biblical dimension of hymnody is discussed in chapter 2.

70. Richards, *Philosophy of Rhetoric*, 89.

71. *A House of Praise*, 297.

72. Baldick, *Concise Oxford Dictionary of Literary Terms*, 360.

73. William McDonald, "Søren Kierkegaard (1813–1855)," *Internet Encyclopedia of Philosophy: A Peer-reviewed Academic Resource*, http://www.iep.utm.edu/kierkega/.

74. Life in Christ: Christ Incarnate—Public Ministry; The Christian Year: Reign of Christ; Christian Year: Transfiguration; Christian Year: Christ the King/Reign of Christ; Jesus Christ: Lamb of God; Jesus Christ: Shepherd; Epiphany Last/Transfiguration: Year A; Lent 2: Year A; Proper 11: Year B; Lent 5: Year C; Easter 7: Year C; Reign of Christ: Year C.

75. According to Joan Halmo, "Hymn Interpretation," "You, Lord, Are Both Lamb and Shepherd," *The Hymn* 53/2 (April 2002): 46, in a conversation with Alan Barthel, Dunstan "thought initially of WESTMINSTER ABBEY."

76. Some of this information on Sylvia Dunstan is based on Paul Westermeyer, *Tongues of Fire: Profiles in 20th-Century Hymn Writing* (St. Louis: Concordia Publishing House, 1995) 53–62.

77. Sylvia Dunstan, *In Search of Hope and Grace: 40 Hymns and Gospel Songs* (Chicago: GIA, 1991) preface.

78. Ibid.

79. Ibid., 44.

80. *A House of Praise*, 79.

81. Routley, ed., *Rejoice in the Lord*, 4.

82. *Hymnbook 1982*, 87.

83. See Timothy Dudley-Smith's insightful discussion of "Soldiers of Christ, arise" in *The Canterbury Dictionary of Hymnology*. © 2013, Canterbury Press. All rights reserved. http://www.hymnology.co.uk/s/soldiers-of-christ,-arise.

84. *Hymnbook 1982*, 382.

85. *A House of Praise*, 136.

86. *Hymnbook 1982*, 493.

87. An epimone or refrain is different from a "chorus" that has no grammatical or syntactical connection to the previous text, as often happens in gospel songs.

88. Frank Baker, *Charley Wesley's Verse: An Introduction*, 2nd ed. (London: Epworth Press, 1988) 47.

89. Ibid., 48.

90. See John W. Welch, ed., *Chiasmus in Antiquity: Structures, Analyses, Exegesis* (Hildesheim: Gerstenberg Verlag, 1981), a 353-page book on the single linguistic and literary phenomenon of chiasmus. See especially chapters by Yehuda T. Raddy, "Chiasmus in Hebrew Biblical Narrative"; by Wilfred G. E. Watson, "Chiastic Patterns in Biblical Hebrew Poetry"; and by John W. Welch, "Chiasmus in the New Testament." See also Nils Lund, *Chiasmus in the New Testament: A Study in the Form and Function of Chiastic Structures* (Peabody MA: Hendrickson Publishers, 1992).

91. One of its most obvious manifestations in musical form is arch form or *Bogenform* (ABCBA), used by such church composers such as Schütz, Buxtehude, and Bach.

92. J. C. Fenton, *Saint Matthew* (Hopkinton MA: Penguin Press, 1963).

93. "No one can serve two masters; for either he will hate the one and love the other, or he will be devoted to one and despise the other" (Matt 6:24). "Do not give what is holy to dogs, and do not throw your pearls before swine, or they will trample them under their feet, and turn and tear you to pieces" (Matt 7:6). We have spoken of some of the biblical uses of this device in chapter 2, "The Biblical Dimension of Hymnody."

94. Baker, *Charles Wesley's Verse*, 57.

95. Ibid.

96. *A House of Praise*, 86.

97. Ibid., 176.

98. Ibid., 274.

99. *A House of Praise*, 119.

100. Routley, ed., *Rejoice in the Lord*, 354.

101. See "head or initial rhyme" above.

102. Margaret Drabble, ed., *The Oxford Companion to English Literature*, 5th ed. (New York: Oxford University, 1985) 19, s.v. "Alliterative Prose."

103. John Jacob Niles, *Songs of the Hill Folk*, set 14 of Schirmer's Folk Song Series: Twelve Ballads from Kentucky, Virginia and North Carolina (New York: G. Schirmer, 1934).

104. E.g., Sidney Lanier in his *The Science of English Verse*.

105. Form in hymn tunes is discussed in chapter 6.

106. Ciardi and Williams, *How Does a Poem Mean?* 2nd ed. (Boston: Houghton Mifflin Company, 1975) xxii.

107. *A House of Praise*, 298.

108. Ibid., 311.

109. Ibid., 460.

110. Ibid., 319.

111. Ibid., 20.

112. Ibid., 352.

113. James Montgomery, *The Christian Psalmist* (Glasgow, 1825) vi.

114. In the *Hymnbook 1982*, no. 477, the final, climactic stanza is supplied with a descant.

115. More specifically, abecedarian. Technically, in an acrostic poem or hymn the first letter, syllable, or word of each verse or stanza spells out a word or message. In a more specific and simpler acrostic, as in hymns, the letters of the alphabet in order are used to begin each verse or stanza and may be referred to as being abecedarian.

116. It may be of interest to some readers that Charles Haddon Spurgeon in his commentary on Psalm 34 in his *The Treasury of David* expressed his opinion that there are "useful purposes" in indicating or even in reproducing the acrostic (abecedarian) form of the psalms that were written in the form. "The Alphabetical Psalms, the psalmi abcedarii, as the Latin fathers called them, are nine in number; and I cannot help thinking it is a pity that, except in the single instance of the hundred and nineteenth, no hint of their existence should have been suffered to appear in our authorised version. I will not take it upon me to affirm, with Ewald, that no version is faithful in which the acrostic is suppressed; but I do think that the existence of such a remarkable style of composition ought to be indicated in one way or another, and that some useful purposes are served by its being actually reproduced in the translation."

117. J. R. Watson, *The English Hymn: A Critical and Historical Study* (Oxford: Oxford University Press, 1999) 233.

118. The text printed here seems to be the more usual form seen today and is the form referred to in Dudley-Smith's article on the hymn in *The Canterbury Dictionary of Hymnology*. The text printed here differs from that in *A Flame of Love: A Personal Choice of Charles Wesley's Verse*, in which Dudley-Smith states, "The text I have followed throughout is that of Dr. G. Osborn in his monumental *The Poetical Works of John and Charles Wesley* (thirteen volumes, Wesleyan Methodist Conference Office, London 1868–72). His edition includes the last corrections of the authors and modernizes a certain amount of spelling, capitalization and the use of italics" (Timothy Dudley-Smith, *A Flame of Love: A Personal Choice of Charles Wesley's Verse* [London: Triangle SPCK, 1987] xiv).

119. Erik Routley, *Hymns Today and Tomorrow* (New York: Abingdon Press, 1964) 44.

120. Timothy Dwight alluded to the same Scripture in his "I love Thy kingdom, Lord" and coupled it with allusions to metaphors used in several Old Testament passages (Deut 32:10; Ps 17:8; Prov 7:2): "I love Thy church, O God! / Her walls before Thee stand, / dear as the apple of Thine eye, / and graven on Thy hand."

121. Erik Routley, *Hymns Today and Tomorrow* (New York: Abingdon Press, 1964) 44.

122. Ibid., 42.

123. *Songs of Praise*, enlarged edition (London: Oxford University Press, 1976) no. 118.

124. See Routley's setting, WOODBURY, in Routley, ed., *Rejoice in the Lord*, 46.

125. *The United Methodist Hymnal* also prints all fourteen stanzas (no. 387).

126. There may occasionally be justification for such a use of "melodrama" (in the technical definition of instrumental accompaniment to spoken text). Beethoven used it powerfully in the melodramatic monologue of *Fidelio* during the grave-digging scene of that opera.

127. Minutes of Conference, 1788.

128. Contributed by Dr. Frank Baker to *The United Methodist Hymnal* (Nashville: The United Methodist Publishing House, 1989) no. 386.

129. Erik Routley, *Hymns Today and Tomorrow* (New York: Abingdon Press, 1964) 44.

CHAPTER 6

Music

Humanity has sought, within its limitations, the highest expression of its thoughts and feelings. When thoughts and feelings exceed the boundaries of language, people often turn to music. Some of the most profound thoughts and deepest religious feelings of humankind in all of history and in every culture have found their way into musical utterance, often in some form of cantillation, chant, metrical psalmody, chorales, or hymns.

The Scriptures and church history affirm again and again the vital importance of God's people singing together, and both have provided great texts that the church has, in various forms, sung for thousands of years. The book of Psalms, itself a "hymnal," abounds in admonitions to "sing to the LORD" (Pss 33:2; 95:1-2; 147:7; etc.). Our Lord and his apostles sang a hymn (psalm) after their last supper together. Paul and Silas were singing hymns even in prison (Acts 16:25), and Paul admonished the early church to "be filled with the Spirit, speaking to one another in psalms and hymns and spiritual songs, singing and making melody with your heart to the Lord" (Eph 5:18–19). Augustine, the early fifth-century Bishop of Hippo, spoke of the moving experience of hearing "sweet singing in church." The Reformation abounded in psalmody, hymnody, and chorales. The great Wesley revival in England and the evangelistic movements in America were carried on the wings of song. In our own day, the famous German Theologian, Karl Barth, has resoundingly proclaimed the singing of the Christian community as "one of the indispensable basic forms of the ministry of the community."

> What we can and must say quite confidently is that the community which does not sing is not the community. And where it cannot sing in living speech, or only archaically in repetition of the modes and texts of the past; where it does not really sing but sighs and mumbles spasmodically, shame-

facedly and with an ill grace, it can be at best only a troubled community which is not sure of its cause and of whose ministry and witness there can be no great expectation. In these circumstances it has every reason to pray that this gift which is obviously lacking or enjoyed only in sparing measure will be granted afresh and more generously lest all the other members suffer. The praise of God which finds its concrete culmination in the singing of the community is one of the indispensable basic forms of the ministry of the community.[1]

What is attempted in this chapter is an introduction to the basic aspects of the vital musical dimension of hymnody in hopes that, in the interpretation of hymns, the fullest possible significance of the music may be realized in its relation to the other dimensions of hymnody.

The tunes discussed in this work are taken from the thirteenth century through the twenty-first century and come from Roman areas, France, Mexico, Taiwan, and Africa, including Latin plainsong, German chorale tunes, psalm and hymn tunes from England and the United States,[2] and tunes from contemporary worship songs.

Hymn Tunes, Rhetoric, and Aesthetics

Musical aesthetics, the study of the relationship of music to the human senses and intellect, is part of that branch of philosophy called axiology, which concerns the theory of value. Aesthetics is traditionally defined as the philosophy or study of the beautiful, but the ultimate goal of such a study is to establish the criteria for determining beauty while the definition of "beauty" may even accommodate what some would consider the opposite of beauty.[3] As mentioned earlier, Alfred North Whitehead defined beauty as

> the internal conformation of the various items of experience with each other, for the production of maximum effectiveness. Beauty thus concerns the interrelations of the various components of Reality, and also the interrelations of the various components of Appearance, and also, the relations of Appearance to Reality.[4]

From a Christian perspective, God is the origin of beauty.[5] The "various items of experience" are his creation, any "internal conformation" that humanity can create of the various items of experience is a gift of God, and the "maximum effectiveness" will be in keeping with his purpose. "The various items of experience" that we shall discuss here are the traditional properties of music and how they conform within a hymn tune for the production of maximum effectiveness. An understanding of these properties is crucial to understanding the role of music and how hymn tunes may relate to hymn texts.

Music helps us experience and express feelings in ways that language cannot. C. S. Lewis, in *Perelandra*, the second book of his space trilogy, records the conversation between the narrator and Ransom, who has just returned from a voyage to the planet Venus. In the process of trying to find out about the trip, the inquirer says,

> "Of course, I realize it's all rather vague for you to put into words," when he [Ransom] took me up rather sharply, for such a patient man, by saying, "On the contrary, it is words that are vague. The reason why the thing can't be expressed is that it is too definite for language."[6]

This is precisely one of the fundamental reasons for church music. The religious experience is, in many ways, too profound and "too definite for language." Philosopher Susanne K. Langer affirms that

> *music articulates forms which language cannot set forth.* The classifications which language makes automatically preclude many relations, and many of those resting-points of thought which we call "terms." It is just because music has *not* the same terminology and pattern, that it lends itself to the revelation of non-scientific concepts. To render "the most ordinary feelings, such as love, loyalty or anger, unambiguously and distinctly," would be merely to duplicate what verbal appellations do well enough. . . .
>
> Because the forms of human feeling are much more congruent with musical forms than with the forms of language, music can *reveal* the nature of feelings with a detail and truth that language cannot approach.[7]

It is to the literary and musical facets of hymnody that the term "art" is most obviously applicable. These facets must, in themselves, virtually apart from the content and meaning of the text, possess artistic qualities. They are part of how the message is conveyed, but they are also part of the message itself. Music, in itself, quite apart from texts, conveys powerful thoughts and feelings that are understood and felt often with an amazing consensus across much of the world. To be sure, there are subjective interpretations, and these too have their own strong impact on individuals.

The literary dimension of hymnody can hardly be separated from the content and nature of the text, and it may often be difficult, but not impossible, to appreciate the artistic quality of the literary aspects apart from the content of the text. One might concede some artistic qualities of a text and still not agree with or may even oppose what is advocated in the text. Conversely, one may agree with what is advocated in the text and still acknowledge that its statement has little artistic merit. The fact remains that the literary quality cannot easily be separated from the text and is often difficult to separate from the meaning of the text.

On the other hand, the separation of the music from the text is possible. Admittedly, in some cases of hymnody this may be difficult because certain hymn tunes have such powerful associations with certain texts, or at the least with certain concepts or emotions, that many listeners find it difficult to separate fully the traditional musical medium from the textual content and its literary form. The unusual musical merit itself of certain hymn tunes has caused some of the great musicians to utilize them in their compositions, though sometimes the textual and emotional associations may be part of their reason for borrowing the tunes. For example, it seems obvious that both the artistic merit and the textual and emotional associations caused Mendelssohn to incorporate EIN' FESTE BURG into his fifth symphony, the "Reformation Symphony," and Benjamin Britten made highly symbolic use of SOUTHWELL ("Lord Jesus, think on me"), MELITA ("Eternal Father, strong to save"), and TALLIS' CANON (used to sing "The Spacious firmament") in his opera, *Noye's Fludde*. Numerous other outstanding melodies of Christian hymnody have indeed made their way into the great art music of western civilization. Buxtehude, Bach, Beethoven, Wagner, Debussy, Stravinsky, Ives, Copland, and scores of others have drawn on chorale and hymn tunes. Many hymn tunes intended primarily to be sung by a congregation in public worship, despite their constraints, have significant musical qualities that have appealed to some of the world's great musicians.

Our purpose here is to discuss the hymn tune on its musical merits, but also on its merits in relation to the literary form, the biblical and theological content, and the liturgical application of hymn texts. There is an incredible burden on the short, "simple," strophic, oft-repeated hymn tune in its composition, in its selection, and in its "performance" to have artistic integrity in itself, to honor the subtleties of fine literature, to bear the biblical and theological message, and to be singable by relatively untrained and unrehearsed singers. These are truly unusual constraints, structures, and strictures, especially considering that the hymn tune is designed for the expression of thoughts and feelings relating to the most crucial aspects of human existence—humanity's relationship with God!

To truly understand and appreciate music and to have some discernment about it, one should listen thoughtfully and intelligently to a range of music, being aware of the multitude of aspects of the art and of the intricate interrelations of those aspects. The definition of beauty given by Alfred North Whitehead, "the internal conformation of the various items of experience with each other, for the production of maximum effectiveness,"[8] assumes some discernment about what are "the various items of experience" that must be considered, how their "internal conformation" is achieved, and what is "maximum effectiveness."

In music, "the various items of experience" are those most fundamental elements of rhythm, timbre (tone color), melody, harmony, texture, dynamics, and form, each of which has entire books written about them. Beyond the vast dimensions of each of these are the vital, intricate interrelations of any or all of them—what Whitehead calls "the internal conformation of the various items." There is a virtually infinite number of internal conformations of these various elements "for the production of maximum effectiveness" and an infinite number of experiences in which these conformations may occur. The quality of these aspects and their interrelations determine whether a hymn tune has artistic merit in itself and then whether it contradicts, distracts, accommodates, complements, or even enhances a specific text.

Again, for a simple, strophic hymn tune to have musical merit and to enhance, complement, or even accommodate a great hymn text is incredibly challenging. Beyond its own musical merit, the music must convey the basic mood or moods of the text; give the proper accents of the words; and show attention to the nature and meaning of certain key words. It must carry the thoughts of the text without distraction or interruption, must do this in music that is accessible to the understanding, memory, vocal range, and tessitura of persons often not musically trained or rehearsed, and must be capable of doing all this with music that is the same for each of the stanzas, though each stanza may have meanings and moods quite different from the others. It is clearly, in the fullest sense, an almost impossible task in which many concessions must be made.

When there is "the internal conformation of the various items of experience with each other for the production of maximum effectiveness," music articulates "forms which language cannot set forth." The music of hymnody and the texts of hymnody must each have artistic merit in their own rights, and there must be an artistic integrity in the combining of words and music. The great chorales of J. S. Bach not only carried the texts but were also, and have continued to be, musical expressions of the highest order.[9] In every period of history there have been hymn tunes that had and continue to have artistic integrity, that convey the great hymn texts, and that help express the profound thoughts and feelings of the Christian faith that move beyond the words.

Some people speak casually of a good wedding between text and tune and are often speaking of obvious and general matters such as meter, accent, and mood. With the best of hymnody, there is an inherent musicality of the spoken texts, and with the best of hymn tunes there are, at times, rhetorical aspects of the music. Given these characteristics, the best wedding of text and tune involves many and often subtle aspects of textual and musical relationships.

The music and poetry of hymnody share with rhetoric a common purpose of effective, enhanced (persuasive) communication (including some of the basic common elements discussed in chapter 5). While each demands its own distinctive properties of expression and skills of interpretation, they share, in their own distinctive language and in broad ways, some basic principles. Because rhetoric, poetry, and music are temporal arts, moving in time, they share, among other properties, elements of direction, repetition, and modification. Whereas spoken poetry and rhetoric are generally monophonic, music may also be homophonic or polyphonic and has at its disposal extended properties of pitch, duration, intensity, and timbre that extend its possibilities of direction, repetition, and modification for the purpose of forceful communication. These possibilities may be relatively simple, even obvious, but may also involve artistic sophistication and, for their fullest appreciation, require some esoteric understanding. It may contribute something to the understanding and interpretation of the music of hymnody to view it, partly, from a poetic or rhetorical perspective. This is appropriate since the music of hymnody is a primary vehicle for expressing the poetry that often involves many principles of rhetoric. Understanding and appreciation may be enhanced by perceiving, if not fully understanding, some musical subtleties of pitch, duration, intensity, and timbre. This chapter attempts, in part, to contribute to an increased sensitivity to the role of music in hymnody.

Christopher C. Hill speaks of "the ineluctable musicality of human utterance that is as historically resilient as it has been theoretically elusive."[10]

Hill speaks also of the vital relationship between musical aesthetics and rhetoric:[11]

> So pervasive are the concepts of rhetoric in present aesthetic vocabulary that it is hardly possible to imagine critical discussion without them. . . . Rhetoric provided music theory with both the authority of antiquity and the very font of the critical vocabulary that had previously served music's sister arts.[12]

The names of many traditional rhetorical devices have been applied to comparable, characteristic musical passages. Musicologists have written about the relationship between music and rhetoric. George J. Buelow speaks of the evolution of the "complex and systematic transformation of rhetorical concepts into musical equivalents,"[13] and Blake Wilson notes that music historians rediscovered in the twentieth century the importance of rhetoric as the basis of aesthetic and theoretical concepts in earlier music: "An entire discipline that had once been the common property of every educated man has had to be rediscovered and reconstructed during the intervening decades, and only now is it beginning to be understood how much Western art music has depended on rhetorical concepts."[14]

Even in hymnody, there are occasions of some transformation of rhetorical concepts into musical equivalents. The same principles and patterns of repetition of sounds that occur in the rhetoric of speech are possible in the rhetoric of music—such as alliteration, anaphora, epizeuxis, mesarchia, mesodiplosis, epistrophe, epanadiplosis, anadiplosis, epiploce, and climax.[15] The "rhetorical" sounds may be rhythmic, melodic, harmonic, tonal (timbre), formal, or combinations of these. While it would obviously be expecting too much to think that the musical rhetoric would coincide with literary rhetoric at all, much less in a strophic form, some of the rhetorical patterns might well be effectively employed in a well-written hymn tune and contribute to conveying a text.

A hymn text that employs anadiplosis (the repetition of a word, phrase, or concept at the end of one stanza and at the beginning of the next) might be provided with a hymn tune in which a rhythmic, melodic, or harmonic figure (or any combination these) that ends the hymn tune is similar enough to its beginning to enhance that structural principle of the text. In the motto masses of the fifteenth and sixteenth centuries, a musical idea recurs at the *beginning* of each major section of the mass and is, in a sense, an example of musical anaphora on a large scale. There are recurring rhythmic, melodic, and harmonic patterns that occur especially at the points of cadence, which in the broadest sense may be conceived in their recurrence as musical rhyme and identifiable with textual rhyme. Even the rather sophisticated rhetorical device of chiasmus has been identified in music ranging from simple phrasal structures A B C B A to the form of large, multi-movement compositions[16] as seen in the works of such church composers as Schütz, Buxtehude, and Bach.[17] This chiastic principle abounds in many types of art and literature.[18] It is obvious that these subtleties may function at subliminal levels, but so do many aspects of music and texts. Hearers and singers rarely identify or are even conscious of how the most basic elements of rhythm, melody, harmony, and timbre powerfully affect them.

Even when the "simpler" music of hymnody does not consciously or extensively include elements that have been defined traditionally as musical rhetorical devices, the finest musicians involved in hymnody seek in their composition, in their selection of tunes for texts, and in their singing to express the text in meaningful and convincing ways and to facilitate the utterance of thoughts and feelings beyond the limits of our ordinary utterances. Fine composers themselves may well capture some of these aspects unconsciously and innately, and most members of the congregation will perceive them only subliminally, but the lack of awareness of a technique and a heightened sensitivity to the text may be precisely when a technique is most effective.

The fascinating affinity between rhetoric and art, language and music, was the topic of Leonard Bernstein's Norton Lectures delivered at Harvard University in 1973. In 1971, Bernstein had been invited to be the Charles Eliot Norton Professor of Poetry at Harvard University, a position held earlier by such notable musicians as Igor Stravinsky and Aaron Copland, and by such notable poets as e. e. cummings and W. H. Auden. The great conductor and composer spoke of his fascination since childhood with words, poetry, and language ("the notion of a worldwide, inborn musical grammar has haunted me") and, in 1969, of coming into contact with Chomsky's *Language and Mind* and the academic discipline of linguistics. This contact strengthened his notion that there was a worldwide, inborn musical grammar similar to Chomsky's idea that there was an inborn set of "rules" for creating and responding to language. Bernstein spoke in his lectures of linguistics, aesthetic philosophy, acoustics, and music history as well as musical phonology, syntax, and grammar!

Roger Scruton acknowledges, "Maybe you could say that we have tacit knowledge of grammar, as Chomsky does. But in that sense we have tacit knowledge too of music. This knowledge is expressed not in theories but in acts of recognition."[19] But Scruton also states emphatically that "linguistic theories of musical structure will never really capture what we understand, when we understand sound as music."[20] Yet linguistic theories may contribute something to our understanding of aspects of music, especially music that is so bound up with language as is hymnody. Bernstein's biographer, Humphrey Burton, opines, "the Norton Lectures have proved to be among the most valuable and stimulating contributions he [Bernstein] ever made to musical education: In the brief history of television they stand on a par with Kenneth Clark's essays on civilization."[21] The relations between rhetoric, poetry, and music are profound.

The affinity among rhetoric, art, and theology is ancient and intrinsic, and it is in the poetry and music of hymnody that much of Christianity has its closest affinity to art. Many share Paul Tillich's view that art is implicitly religious, or has "ultimate concern," because it is the means by which we wrestle with the full and deep reality of our situation in the world. Samuel H. Miller, of the Harvard Divinity School faculty, remarks,

> Art and religion at their best, seek to get at the fundamental reality of life by stripping it of its superficial aspects. . . . They both work in images, by the endless and patient exercise of the imagination, delving beneath the surface of the customary and taken-for-granted, encountering the immediate and original mysteries of beauty and holiness.[22]

Amos Wilder has noted the need for an art/theology dialogue:

> If the artist often calls theology and piety back to an "essential integrity," one can say that art as a whole, the aesthetic order, is always an indispensable corrective and nourishment to faith. Recurrently threatened by docetism and irrelevance, the Christian faith is in need of recurrent baptism in the secular, in the human, to renew itself. It has to be continually reimmersed in the vitalities of nature to be saved from a spurious and phantom Christ. Art mediates the order of creation to us.[23]

The most artistic forms of church music have been, arguably, the oratorios, cantatas, and organ chorales of J. S. Bach, and these are, in varying ways, musical/textual art forms. Bach is recognized as one of the greatest composers ever to have lived, and most of his life was devoted to those art forms and to the chorales, the hymns of his day, that were at the heart of the art forms. While most hymn tunes do not have the artistic merit of the chorales of J. S. Bach, there is often real musical value and there is no doubt that to many of the millions of people who sing hymns each week across the world, much of the charm is in the music, much of the memorableness of the texts is because of the tunes, much of the fond association and joy is through the actual singing, and much of the understanding of the text comes from the musical setting.

In hymnody, we are dealing with texts and music that have significant restrictions. The music of hymnody, like the text of hymnody, is "under a vow of renunciation." Much of the value of the artistic dimensions of the literature and music of hymnody comes from the very constraints the works honor and from the discipline the works require if they are to be experienced in the fullest way possible by congregations. In our own day, people often recognize the increasing need for the constraints and discipline that art can provide. It is interesting that those who know the constraints and disciplines of scientific study often have a high appreciation of the qualities of art. Douglas R. Hofstadter, Professor of Cognitive Science at Indiana University, also teaching in the departments of Comparative Literature, Computer Science, Psychology, and Philosophy, and the author of the Pulitzer Prize-winning work *Gödel, Escher, Bach: an Eternal Golden Braid: A Metaphorical Fugue on Minds and Machines in the Spirit of Lewis Carroll,* is an avid music lover and pianist. In his later book, *Le Ton beau de Marot: In Praise of the Music of Language,* of which he opines, "this is probably the best book I will ever write,"[24] he quotes a tiny poem sent to him by James E. Falen, professor of Russian at the University of Tennessee:

> Every task involves constraint,
> Solve the thing without complaint;
> There are magic links and chains
> Forged to loose our rigid brains.
> Structures, strictures, though they bind,
> Strangely liberate the mind.[25]

Hofstadter notes, "The closing rhyme could be taken as the theme song of this book." Of his earlier work, *Gödel, Escher, Bach: an Eternal Golden Braid,* Hofstadter writes, "The work was in my view, a work of art, one of whose prime characteristics was its esthetic aspect."[26] The work, as its subtitle tells us, is "a metaphorical fugue," and musicians are intrigued with this scientist's frequent references to music: canons, two-part inventions, three-part inventions, ricercars, the sonata, prelude, fugue, ground, and English, French, and German suites—and musicians delight in the numerous musical puns such as "a Musico-Logical Offering," "contracrostipunctus," "Little Harmonic Labyrinth," "Intervallic Augmentation," "Chromatic Fantasy, and Feud," "Crab Canon," "Mu Offering," "Air on G's string," "Toy of Man's Designing," and the ending with "a 'translation' into words of the most complex piece in the Musical Offering: the Six-part Ricercar."[27]

Many people in our society today, not only highly trained scientists but also people who worship, people who sing hymns each week, recognize the need for the constraints, structures, strictures, and discipline found in art that can "liberate the mind" and delight the spirit. Few works of literature or music have more constraints, structures, and strictures and yet deal with such profound issues of human existence as do hymns and hymn tunes. The challenge is that the concise textual and musical expressions, the familiarity, and the repetitions do not lead to a thoughtless rote experience, but that they be bound strongly to the message and meaning of texts and that they open possibilities of freshness, new insights, and new experiences. Only music of merit can meet these challenges and open these possibilities.

There are for each of us certain hymn tunes that are strongly associated with texts, events, places, people, liturgical functions, or even with general, abstract thoughts and feelings in our own experiences. Powerful associations are often assigned to those tunes, and certain tunes are not easily taken from their traditional place or time. Tunes associated with Christmas or Easter texts are not easily accepted for other texts even with similar moods, messages, and meanings. Associations can also be part of corporate experiences as well as individual experiences, and associations may be particularly strong when they are shared with another individual, a small group, or even a congregation in meaningful contexts. On the other hand, there is the possibility of a tune's being used for a new text and bringing with it some positive association from the earlier text, place, or time, resulting, in the best of circumstances, in something of a counterpoint of moods and meanings. Whether from thoughtful musical insights, from some unconscious feelings, or from some combination of these, familiarity and associations with the rhythm, melody, harmony, form, and timbre of a hymn tune can be a powerful force in conveying the message and meaning of the texts of hymnody.

Aspects of the Musical Dimension of Hymn Tunes

Discussions of hymn tunes too often focus simply on matters of meter (number of verses [lines], number of accents to the verse) or on the provenance and history without probing more deeply into the matters of melody, rhythm, timbre, harmony, and form, or into the subtler matters of how a tune relates to the words. Hymn tunes are composed for the congregational singing of texts, and a discussion of the musical dimension of hymn tunes must ultimately consider the text/tune relationship and how the hymn might best be sung.

The relationship between text and music has been a major issue in the whole history of vocal music, considering particularly how music relates to the phonetic, syntactic, and semantic features of the text. At times music was thought of in rhetorical terms, when certain aspects of music had relatively specific, recognized, and accepted relationships with certain emotions and even words and meanings. The qualities of certain feelings or thought have been, in various ways through history, related to certain musical aspects. In Greek antiquity, music was considered to have an ethical or moral character, an ethos, and each of the modes was considered to embody certain attributes (passion, lasciviousness, manliness, strength, etc.) and capable of arousing those attributes in the listeners. Rhythm and instruments also played a role in this ethos. Madrigalism in the late Renaissance sought to illustrate in somewhat literal ways some aspect of the text. In the seventeenth and early eighteenth centuries, *Figurenlehre* (the doctrine of musical figures) and *Affektenlehre* (the doctrine of affects) considered the aim of music to be to express the affections, and, thinking of music in rhetorical terms, many composers and theorists related certain musical figures, intervals, scales, musical types, etc. with specific affections such as love, hate, joy, fear, anger, etc. In the program music of the Romantic era, as well as in the late Renaissance and Baroque eras, word painting played a role in vocal music. In film music of our own day, certain emotions and other aspects have often come to be associated with combinations of rhythm, tempo, pitch, volume, and timbre. Hymn tunes do not often move at these levels of association, but they flourished in the contexts of all these periods with significant phonetic, syntactical, or semantic relationships between text and music. Bach, in his cantatas and chorales, was sensitive to individual words and how they should be set. John Wilson even refers to John Wesley's more suitable association of the melodic direction of a tune with the mood and meaning of a text:

"Certain English books have surprisingly matched its [SAVANNAH's] downward scales with triumphant Easter lines like 'Love's redeeming work is done' and 'Lives again our glorious King.' John Wesley . . . used it more suitably for a penitential text."[28]

With any concern for a more comprehensive and integrated interpretation of hymns, it is startling how relatively little attention has been given to some of the subtler matters of text/tune relations. Routley, in his study, *The Music of Christian Hymnody* (an abridgement of his Oxford thesis),[29] gives surprisingly little attention to texts. Nor in the preface, the prologue, or the conclusion does he give any rationale for not probing more into the vital relationship between tunes and texts. Routley mentions some 1,100 tunes in the 175 pages. Of his 208 musical examples, only 25 have texts printed with them and only 28 of the tunes are supplied with harmony, showing that his concern was with the melody, rhythm, form, and history.

J. R. Watson explains a similar separation of text and music in his critical and historical study of the texts of the English hymn, but he states,

> I am convinced that the tunes are important, but I am not qualified to write about them; the best examination of them is (in my view) John Wilson's essay [[30]] . . . . For the purposes of the present book, Wilson's article renders further discussion unnecessary, in that it says all that I would have wanted to say (and more) . . . .[31]

However, while John Wilson is careful in his article to emphasize the influence of a hymn's meter on the tune, he devotes little time to the subtleties of the text/music relationship, but speaks in broad terms of the relationship of form between text and tune and provides the texts to only five of his twenty-seven musical examples. He concentrates on melody, rhythm, harmony, and form and states, "To keep the discussion general we shall ignore the special influence of favourite words, important as this can sometimes be."[32] Wilson does make an important reference to Caryl Micklem's "most appealing hymn-and-tune. . . . Notice . . . the close matching of melody and text, and the elegant economy of the harmony,"[33] and Wilson for this hymn does print both text and tune. It is important to note that Micklem wrote both the text and the tune. As we have seen, tunes composed for a specific text and texts written for a particular tune often show a closer and more sensitive relationship. In both cases, it is possible for the author or composer to make textual and musical adjustments that result in a closer matching of melody and text (even across stanzas).

To be sure, Routley, Watson, and Wilson were focusing in masterful ways on their subject at hand, but there is a need in the discussion of hymn tunes for attention to matters beyond meter, general mood, the basic matters of melody, rhythm, harmony and form, provenance and history, and for careful attention to be given to the text/tune relationship.

Given the importance of Routley's study, *The Music of Christian Hymnody*, and in the interest of a better understanding of the musical dimension of hymnody, we must return to his study, consider some of his key statements about hymn tunes, and look carefully at some of the surprisingly few statements he does make about tune/text relationships. In the prologue, after identifying the interaction of the "disciplines" of melody, harmony, rhythm, and metre, Routley admits, ". . . we might add a fifth; the discipline imposed on the tune by the sense of the words to which it is set. This we shall find to be an intricate subject, and we shall find also that the application of this discipline is entirely inconsistent in history; at times it is carefully applied, at other times it is ignored."[34]

It is of great importance to note that in the few times he does address the relationship, his statements about what he considers to be sensitive, even subtle settings of words are in reference to tunes by composers of the first rank, certainly not what he calls the "hack-work" writing of "common," generic tunes by lesser composers. Routley praises Thomas Tallis's (c. 1505–1585) text setting: "Only a song-writer, sensitive to words, could so faithfully interpret the internal rhymes of the verses as Tallis does in his SIXTH tune and in his THIRD."[35] Routley speaks of Orlando Gibbons's (1583–1623) tunes and regards SONG 47 as "one of the most skilful of them all," but then offers the interesting statement that it "has as yet not found a hymn to carry it."[36] More commonly the search is for a tune to fit a text. Gibbon's contemporary, Heinrich Schütz (1585–1672), always sensitive to the text, often used technical figures that at the time made musical analogies to poetry or oratory or rhetoric. Routley speaks of Schütz's PSALM 84 as "a piece of pure word-painting, a melody which makes no sense without supporting harmony, a beautiful choral setting of 'My soul longeth, yea fainteth . . . .'"[37] Schütz's settings of texts in his 1628 *Psalmen Davids* were sensitive, dramatic, and powerful motets for choir, and, though Schütz did not intend them for congregational use, they were adapted as hymn tunes and may seem to be overwritten. Routley notes that in eighteenth-century England we find "the music taking charge completely at the expense of any kind of literary sense." With specific reference to Handel, who composed three tunes for hymns of Charles Wesley, Routley notes "the complete ascendancy of music over verbal rhythm . . . [and observes] the music develops autonomous forms, and the words fit in where they can . . . . The music may distort the rhythm of the words, but it always illuminates their general sense."[38]

In his discussion of John Bacchus Dykes (1823–1876), Routley notes, "His sensitiveness to words produces, time and again, a really arresting first line," and says that Gustav Holst (1874–1934) "lets the words mould the tune into a new and intriguing rhythmical shape."[39] These are significant references to the text/tune relationship, but it remains surprising that Routley's major study of hymn tunes, devotes such little attention to their vital relationship to the texts.

Hymn tunes without texts and purely instrumental music in and outside the church are, obviously, of profound importance in the history of music. Even when the words are not sung or seen, the music often brings to mind moods, meanings, and the words. Mendelssohn's *Lieder ohne Worte* ("Songs without words") is a magnificent collection and reflects a profound philosophy shared by many composers. The fact remains that hymn tunes are written primarily for the singing of texts, and it is safe to say that much of the appreciation of hymn tunes comes from their association with a specific text. When asked to identify a hymn tune, most people will quote part of the text. A hymn tune may certainly be applied to more than one text, but upon close examination it will often be found that a tune may not serve two texts equally well. How well any tune fulfills its basic function cannot be explained by a study only of the music or even of the text/tune relationship by simply speaking of the "wedding" in terms of general mood, number of verses, and accents of the text.

One assumes that Routley, in his discussion of the adaptation of instrumental music for vocal music in general and hymns in particular, may be speaking somewhat ironically when he notes that "the instrumental movement is designed for concert performance, not for the hack-work of the hymn tune."[40] A short, "simple," strophic hymn tune intended for congregational singing hardly has the luxury of extended musical development or subtleties that are present in longer, artistic compositions, and it may be "hack-work" in the sense of serving a larger cause but not in the sense of run-of-the-mill, common, mediocre, or unimaginative drudge work. When a text has some prevailing basic mood, emphasizes certain keywords, or makes significant use of a poetic device, it not unreasonable to expect a composer, editor, or the person who selects hymn tunes for congregational singing to make some effort to provide a tune that in its melody, rhythm, harmony, or form honors at least something not only of that prevailing basic mood but also, to the extent possible, of keywords or even poetic devices—or at least provide a tune that does not contradict them. The phrase "to the extent possible" is important because hymn tunes are admittedly short, strophic forms intended for congregational singing, but there can be creative approaches to hymn tunes as some of Routley's statements show.

Some of the better hymn-tune composers who write for specific texts are sensitive to matters beyond the obvious general mood and accent. This does not suggest that the average singer of hymns is conscious of such subtleties or even should be. Attention may be given easiest to the distinctive form of the text, and this may be seen clearest in tunes written for less common meters. The tunes in the most frequently used meters have too often been considered simply as a body of generic tunes that may be drawn on for a vast number of texts in those meters. Sensitive writers of hymn texts sometimes employ less frequently used meters to express more expanded concepts or subtler aspects of thinking, and sensitive composers of hymn tunes find here fertile ground for musical expression. The less common 6.6.6.6.4.44.4 meter used, for example, by Samuel Crossman for "My song is love unknown" is in each stanza a carefully crafted sequence of thoughts that calls for a tune, such as John Ireland's LOVE UNKNOWN, which in rhythm, melody, harmony, and form honors the sequence of thoughts, key words, and shades of meaning. Routley notes, "The greatness of this melody . . . is in the felicitous way in which it brings out the sense of the words, not only of the first verse, but also throughout the hymn."[41]

Herbert Brokering's "Earth and all stars" with its Psalm-like summons to some thirty-six aspects of created nature, human relations, professions, and musical instruments, all in a probably unique meter, has been set by David N. Johnson (EARTH AND ALL STARS) to delineate each summons in joyfully singable melodic turns with fresh rhythmic ideas and with expressive melismas on "Lord" and "marvelous." John Henry Hopkins composed the tune GRAND ISLE specifically for Lesbia Scott's "I sing a song of the saints of God," and here again the distinctive form of this irregular meter calls for careful attention to the text/tune relationship as is seen most obviously in the climactic melodic sequences that identify six specific "people" and the seven specific "places." Gustav Holst composed a sensitive setting of Christina Rossetti's very irregular meter, "In the bleak midwinter," CRANHAM, a beautifully simple composition in which the mood is nicely painted and the imagery and subtle poetic devices of simile, contrast, and anaphora are honored.

Conversely, in some cases, hymn writers have written texts for a specific tune and some have shown a similar sensitivity for the text/tune relationship well beyond meter and general mood. We have seen how Dudley-Smith wrote his text, "From life's bright dawn to eventide," for the tune PROSPECT, and we noted his care for placing the word "heaven" in the same place in all three verses to meet the demands of the melody. Carl P. Daw wrote "O Day of Peace that Dimly Shines" to be sung to C. H. H. Parry's JERUSALEM, using the tune to undergird the fervent entreaty for peace and putting the words "grace" and "peace" on the climactic high note.

The long and fascinating history of the music of hymnody has been traced in a variety of works.[42] A broader understanding of the musical dimension is sometimes gained from knowing the larger historical context out of which the music was borne—the larger society, the personal life of the composer, the circumstances of the composition, the composer's intent, and even the subsequent history of the composition.[43] What is attempted here is not a history but an inquiry into the essential properties of the music, how these aspects interact, and how they relate to texts.

The music for hymn texts is traditionally called a "hymn tune" and refers to the total music and not only to the "tune" or melody. The hymn tune usually bears an identifying name, traditionally written in all capital letters, e.g., NICAEA. The names may be given by the composer or someone else and are often based on such things as places, people, events, or some aspect of an associated text. Some hymn tune names are meaningful, some interesting, and some simply identifying.[44] The practice is quite ancient, and many scholars consider that some of the superscriptions in Psalms may refer to the music to which a particular psalm was sung.[45]

Ideally, every aspect of the hymn tune should, in addition to achieving its own musical integrity, combine with the other aspects to accommodate the basic meaning and mood of the text and, in some cases, even certain phrases or words. There is inherently, or at least traditionally, some basic mood in each of the poetic meters, and the better hymn writers carefully choose the musical meters and other musical properties to reflect the moods of the specific text they are setting. Sensitive composers or those who choose the tunes for the texts will honor the moods of those metric choices of the authors and see that the temporal, melodic, harmonic, and tonal (timbre) aspects of hymn tunes combine to create a mood of the music to enhance the text. The roles of these aspects should be observed in the singing.

The "internal confirmation" of the various musical elements contributes to tunes having basic moods. The hymnologist Alan Luff speaks of a "sturdy" hymn tune. Erik Routley, in *The Music of Christian Hymnody*, speaks of tunes that are of "sheer contemplative beauty," "cheerful friendliness," "youthful but not bumptious vigour," "lusty strength," "old-world courtesy," "grave dignity," being "modest, but penetrating."[46] Percy Dearmer described PICARDY in his *Songs of Praise Discussed* (Oxford 1933) as "'dignified and ceremonious', and well matches the mood of the words."[47] While such descriptions are admittedly general and, in part, subjective, there will often be considerable agreement among musicians about the basic ideas of such descriptions, and the thoughtful associations of texts with certain tunes will often affirm those descriptions.

Understanding hymn tunes requires some knowledge of the fundamental properties of music—volume, timbre, the temporal elements of rhythm and tempo, the pitch elements of melody amd harmony, texture, form, the interrelationships of these elements, and their relationships to the text. No attempt is made here to burden the reader unduly with detailed explanations of the vast technical terms and various approaches that musicians use to describe their art. Even so, some of the technical aspects must be introduced. It is helpful, at least, to be aware of the many facets that constitute the beauty of music, the fascinating interrelationships of these facets, and the contributions they make to the expression of the biblical, theological, and liturgical contents of hymnic literature.

We must look more deeply into each major aspect of the musical dimension and see how they interact to create a hymn tune of artistic merit and how they relate to the text. This is again at the risk of the disenchantment of showing the springs and mechanism of an art,[48] but with the hope of showing the enchanting counterpoint of the facets of hymnody.

The Temporal Aspects: Meter and Rhythm

Music is a temporal art, and in the sequence of time our first perceptions of sound are volume and timbre. The perception of tempo may occur next and often precedes our comprehension of fully developed rhythmic or melodic ideas. Melody and harmony may be perceived somewhat simultaneously. Form, as a result of the whole, is perhaps one of the last of the aspects that we fully perceive. As a temporal art, the complex interaction of these basic aspects of volume, timbre, tempo, rhythm, melody, harmony, and form constantly evolves and is in continual interplay even in a short hymn tune. To discuss fully this complex interaction would again require that unattainable contrapuntal prose that would allow us to present the simultaneity and fascinating interaction of these aspects. Hymnal editors do not usually indicate timbre, volume, or tempo on the printed music.[49] These are usually matters of choice in the "performance" and are discussed in chapter 8. A logical sequence for discussing the basic musical aspects would be the temporal aspects of meter and rhythm, then melody, timbre, harmony, form, and finally the interrelations of the aspects.

Meter, whether poetic or musical, concerns the recurring pulses or beats, their grouping by accents, and their division. Various patterns are set up that may have their own feeling, and the patterns may be continued or altered. Within the meter there may be a multitude of rhythms set up in poetry by the subtle stresses of words and in music by a variety of articulations of sounds.

Musical meter concerns the basic grouping and division of beats and accents found in each measure of a composition and is usually indicated by the time signature. In hymn tunes, the recurring pulses are usually grouped into patterns of twos, threes, or fours (duple, triple, or quadruple meter), and the pulses are usually divided into twos or threes (simple or compound meter), resulting in combinations such as simple duple, compound duple, simple triple, etc. Most hymnals notate the basic pulse by a quarter note in simple time or a dotted quarter in compound time, but some hymnals such as *The English Hymnal* indicated that "both minims [half notes] and crotchets [quarter notes] have been employed, the former for the slower and more solemn hymns and the latter for those of a brighter nature."[50]

The syllabic stresses of the text patterns may be musically accommodated by any or all of three basic forms of accent in music: dynamic, agogic, and tonic. A dynamic accent is made when a note or chord is of a different volume, often louder than the other tones in its context. The dynamic accent of the text, which in the text is a matter of correct pronunciation, is usually undergirded by the natural emphases inherent in the various musical meters with their primary and secondary accents. An agogic accent is achieved by the change in length, often a longer duration. A tonic accent is achieved by the change in pitch, often higher. William Henry Monk makes effective use of all three accents in his UNDE ET MEMORES (see figure 10).

The most basic temporal concerns for the hymn tune composer are that the music supports the proper number of syllables per line, the proper number of verses per stanza, and the proper accentuation of the text in the grouping and division of the perceived pattern of stressed and unstressed syllables that characterizes poetic meter. Most hymn tunes have a relatively simple and regular metric and rhythmic structure and depend principally on the melody to create freshness and variety. Some settings do have metric variety, such as the psalm tunes of England and Scotland in their earlier (sixteenth-century) forms with interesting metrical and rhythmical shifts (see WINDSOR, figure 5). Metric and rhythmic freshness often characterize folk melodies as is seen in the Sussex tune, MONK'S GATE, as adapted and harmonized by Ralph Vaughan Williams.

Some hymn tunes have, in the melody, the same basic rhythmic pattern repeated almost throughout, as does the familiar ST ANNE. Some hymn tunes are non-metric with a logogenic or word-born rhythm as in Gregorian chant, such as DIVINUM MYSTERIUM in its more original form. (See Figure 2.)

Curt Sachs, in his classic work, *Rhythm and Tempo: A Study in Music History*, speaks eloquently of the profound and permeating importance of rhythm:

> Rooted deep in physiological grounds as a function of our bodies, rhythm permeates melody, form, and harmony; it becomes the driving and shaping force, indeed, the very breath of music, and reaches up in the loftiest realm of aesthetic experience where description is doomed to fail because no language provides the vocabulary for adequate wording.[51]

Harold Powers describes rhythm as covering "all aspects of musical movement as ordered in time" and denoting "a patterned configuration of attacks that may or may not be constrained overall by a meter or associated with a particular tempo." He also notes that "it is necessary only that there be more than one attack, that the attacks not be too far apart, and that the musical convention in play accept the succession of attacks as mutually connected and not independent of each other."[52] These concepts are broad enough to address the divergent rhythmic ideas of the speech-like cantillation of Jewish Psalmody, the various forms of early and medieval Christian chant, the liturgical hymnody of the Renaissance including Reformation chorales, metrical Psalmody, and the hymn tunes of the last four centuries.

The interrelations of the temporal aspects are part of the melody, harmony, and form and bear on the meanings and moods of the text. Honoring the meanings and moods of the text can be challenging in that there are often different meanings and moods from one stanza to the next, and the music must at least allow for that variation. Singers should be helped to sense, to some degree, those musical aspects to express the differing moods in the stanzas.[53]

Rhythm functions not only at a micro level but also in macro time-organizing patterns. Curt Sachs notes that

> . . . the notion of rhythm has been expanded to encompass the whole "form" or structure of a piece. The basic idea of such expansion is this: In dealing with rhythm, we find a generating, time-organizing pattern in two phases, say long and short, or strong and weak, or heavy and light, or dark and clear, or whatever the contrast may be. . . . [In the repetition of patterns we have] a process that can theoretically be continued ad infinitum. Hence the old idea that rhythm and "form" are more or less two names for the same thing.[54]

Patterns of meter may help define the form of the tune especially when reinforced by melodic and harmonic ideas. On the relatively fixed "trellis" of meter, the "vine" of rhythm can, with considerable flexibility, create interesting figures and patterns to carry or enhance the syllables, accents, and mood(s) of the text, and even help shape the form. While the congregational purpose of hymn tunes precludes subtleties of rhythm and extremes of tempo, and while the text dictates many aspects of rhythms, hymn tunes can show an interesting variety of "musical movement as ordered in time."[55]

An important facet of rhythm is the composite rhythms that result from the combination of voice lines. Some tunes are homorhythmic, in which a musical texture has the same or very similar rhythm in all voices, sometimes called chordal style, familiar style, or note-against-note style. Rhythmic independence may occur when moving notes such as passing tones make for a quicker composite rhythm and contribute to the overall motion as happens in Bach's harmonization of JESU, MEINE FREUDE. The melody's basically quarter-note rhythm becomes, in its composite rhythm, predominantly an eighth-note movement. The important, and often neglected, aspect of harmonic rhythm will be considered under the discussion of harmony.

Cyril Vincent Taylor's hymn tune, ABBOT'S LEIGH, is an example of how the aspects of music cannot be fully understood in isolation, but must be examined in relation to the other aspects. John Wilson describes ABBOT'S LEIGH as "in Britain the most popular new tune of its generation [1940s]."[56] The tune is an appropriate setting of an exultant, trochaic, 87 87 D text such as John Newton's "Glorious things of thee are spoken." The thirty-two-bar ABBOT'S LEIGH melody is composed of five basic rhythmic figures. In addition to the musical meter (with qualitative, strong or weak pulses by dynamic accents), which stresses the proper syllables of the text, three of the five figures provide also a quantitative (long and short—agogic accent) emphasis to proper syllables. While it can be enlightening and interesting to discuss only the rhythm, it must be acknowledged again that ultimately, a musical work must be taken as a whole. If we look ahead in our discussion, the melodic contour of this tune (high and low—tonic accent) also stresses the proper syllables of the text, as does the harmonic rhythm. The three types of accents then are, nicely and rather consistently, complementary to the text, and there are interesting and singable metric, rhythmic, melodic, and harmonic ideas.

H. Walford Davies's 1917 hymn tune, VISION, though an unusual 15.15.15.7 meter, is rather metrically consistent and rhythmically predictable until the final phrase where there is a dramatic rhythmic shift by doubling the length of the melody line while the accompaniment continues its steady march to the end. This augmentation of rhythm supports nicely the phrase, "may the living God be praised!" that closes each stanza of Fred Pratt Green's "It is God who holds the nations."

Diversity can be seen in the three rhythmically different tunes that have been suggested for Dudley-Smith's text, "Holy Child." David Peacock's FAIRMILE[57] has a different rhythm in every measure except one and employs syncopation in the final measures of each of the two musical phrases. Michael Baughen's equally romantic and rhythmically diverse common meter HOLY CHILD arranged by Noël Tredinnick is a double length tune accommodating two stanzas of text for each singing. Ralph Vaughan Williams's THE CALL is a lilting triple-meter (long-short) lullaby with a melisma that, appropriate to both rhythmic interest and the meaning of each stanza, lengthens words near the ends of each of the seven stanzas—"Christmas," "frankincense," "promises," "sin," "silent," "Lord," and "Christmas."

The important temporal aspect of tempo and its modifications of ritard, accelerando, rubato, and rests as well as such matters as staccato, tenuto, and fermata are rarely indicated in hymnody and are matters of practice and tradition. These are mentioned in chapter 8.

Melody

Though a hymn tune is much more than the "tune" or melody, it is melody that is usually the most distinctive musical aspect and the one with which singers are most familiar. The melody, which is the succession of tones (pitches, rhythms, and timbres), must complement the text, be simple enough to be sung, interesting, and easy enough to be memorized. It should have a direction or certain inevitableness and yet enough freshness to avoid being overly predictable. Melodies often combine phrases into periods involving a statement or antecedent phrase followed by a counterstatement or consequent phrase arriving at some cadence. The rhythm and length of the melodic line may be determined by the hymnic meter, but freedom may be expressed in the relations of phrases (their antecedent and consequent natures), the use of melodic figures, motifs, and sequences, and whether there will be one (syllabic) or several (neumatic) or many (melismatic) notes to a syllable. Most often, the hymn tune will have one note for each syllable of the text (a "syllabic" setting) as when Bunyan's/Dearmer's "He who would valiant be" is sung to ST. DUNSTAN'S. Occasionally there are two or three notes for a syllable ("neumatic") as when Bunyan's/Dearmer's "He who would valiant be" is sung to MONK'S GATE. Less frequently, there may be several notes for one syllable ("melismatic") as in George Herbert's "Come, my Way, my Truth, my Life" when sung to Ralph Vaughan Williams's THE CALL. On rare occasions in hymnody, there is one note for more than one syllable ("multisyllabic") as occurs when there is an elision of vowels as in the opening line of Watts's "I sing the almighty power of God" when sung to the FOREST GREEN tune.

The qualities of inevitability, freshness, memorability, and singability in melody apply to the rhythm and to matters of pitch such as the direction or the rise and fall of the line and whether the movement is by step (conjunct) or skip (disjunct). There is usually some prudent variety in these matters of motion, some climax, and some drive to points of rest or cadence. Because a hymn tune is to be sung by a congregation, the melody will also honor the vocal range (high and low) and the tessitura (the prevailing pitch level) limits of congregations. Hymn tunes are relatively short and should have qualities that allow congregations to comprehend and retain the melody with some ease, both to facilitate good singing and to provide time for the mind to focus on the text.

Good melodic writing that is particularly fresh and singable can be found in some of the traditional, folk, and folk-like melodies. As we have seen, the joyous old American hymn tune LAND OF REST fits well with common meter texts such as Wesley's "O for a thousand tongues" or Brian Wren's "I come with joy." The tune with its balance of steps and skips, its convincing rise and fall of phrases, its compound meter, its flowing rhythms, its reasonable range and tessitura contribute to the tune's singableness, and the phrasing nicely honors the enjambments between the first and second and between the third and fourth lines of Wren's text.

Ideally, a hymn tune should be written for a specific hymn text attempting to have musical value in itself, but also to complement as fully as possible the text through its rhythm, melody, harmony, and form. Given the number of hymn texts, this would obviously yield an impossible number of tunes for unskilled singers to learn. Writers of hymn texts often write in "standard" poetic and hymnic meters for each of which there are a number of tunes. Sometimes a hymn writer writes a text with a specific tune in mind that may enhance the possibility that the music will convey the basic mood or moods of the text, give the proper accents of the words, honor the nature and meaning of certain key words, and carry the thoughts of the text without distraction or interruption.

Dudley-Smith's "From life's bright dawn to eventide,"[58] was written for the tune PROSPECT[59] William Walker's American tune book, *Southern Harmony* of 1835 (see Figure 19), which is pentatonic, missing the 4th and 7th degrees of the scale. While the rhythm is rather monotonous in the division of the third beat of almost every measure, it is nicely relieved by the inverted dotted rhythm (generally known as a "Scotch snap" because of its frequent use in Scottish folk tunes) that occurs in the tenth full measure providing a tonic (pitch), agogic (length), and dynamic (volume, because of its pitch) accent. In his "Within a crib"[60] (his only use of the 888 7 meter), the same is done with three "alliterated" key words, "crib," "cross," and "crown," occurring at the same place in each stanza and allowing the music to reinforce the word each time.

Most hymn tune melodies have some tonal center (key) or point of gravitation, and the relationships of the other tones to this center may take many shapes—usually some modal or tonal configuration depending on where the whole and half-steps fall. A rich variety of keys and modes has been used to express the wide array of moods and meanings of texts. The modality, distinctive melodic line, and free, word-born (logogenic) rhythms of medieval chant often yield an unusual musical beauty and textual emphasis.

While a melody must have musical integrity, its basic task is to accommodate, maybe complement, sometimes enhance the text and never distract from and certainly not contradict the text. The challenges of the relations of multiple melodic elements to the text are compounded by the strophic form of hymns. The basic moods of stanzas may be very different, or even if the moods are the same or similar, the important words may not come in precisely the same place in each stanza. Some of these challenges of strophic form may be addressed by a careful choice of media (voices and accompaniment and organ registration), a sensitive singing in different dynamics (soft or loud) and different tempi (slow or fast), or a different harmonization.

Counterpoint

A fascinating aspect of melody is the combination of melodies or counterpoint. The voice leading of the individual lines of Bach's chorales frequently creates "counter melodies" of interest in themselves, provides needed rhythmic independence and interest, and often, through non-chord tones, generates meaningful tensions and releases. These can all be seen in Bach's harmonization and adaptation of JESU, MEINE FREUDE, used as a setting for Johann Franck's "Jesus, priceless treasure" (translated by Catherine Winkworth) in the unusual 66.5.66.5.7.86 meter.

Counterpoint can be seen clearly in tunes that can be sung canonically and in the use of descants. Some hymnals provide tunes that can be sung in canon (where the melody stated in one part is soon imitated strictly and entirely by one or more voices) or in round (a perpetual canon, i.e., the tune and its imitation can be repeated indefinitely).[61] In some cases, the concentration on the text and melody that is required to maintain the independence of a line in this type of singing might, rather than distracting from the text, result in a deeper attention to and understanding. Such a singing of the text may sometimes be thought of as a somewhat "instrumental" interpretation. One of the most famous of all canons is the sixteenth-century composer Thomas Tallis's long meter tune called TALLIS CANON or THE EIGHTH TUNE, which, like Billings's WHEN JESUS WEPT, can be used for a large number of long-meter texts.

A descant, a more ornamental melody above the melody of the hymn tune, can often provide not simply an interesting counterpoint but also a complement or climax. Many hymnals print descants, and creative worship leaders can write or find additional descants for voices or instruments.[62] Craig Sellar Lang's descant for LOBE DEN HERREN provides a fine ornament to the main melody and an interesting rhythmic shift (hemiola, a shift from a triple meter to a duple meter) in the seventh and eighth measures from the end. When used for Dudley-Smith's "Thanks be to God for his saints of each past generation," this descant provides, in that rhythmic shift, a tonic, agogic, and dynamic accent to an important word in each of the four verses—"Jesus," "rose," "Christ," and "Jesus." A popular style melody and an "Instrumental or vocalized descant" are seen in T. Brian Coleman's OASIS for "As water to the thirsty."[63] GENERAL SEMINARY is an example of a fine two-voice contrapuntal setting of George Herbert's "King of glory, King of peace."[64]

Timbre

Timbre is the distinctive quality or "color" of an instrument or voice that distinguishes it from other instruments or voices. Timbre and volume are our first perceptions upon hearing a sound, and neither is usually indicated in hymnals. The organ registration and the choice of media (solo, choral, congregational, male or female voices, instruments, etc.) are usually left to the organist or minister of music. Given the varieties of voices and instruments, there is an enormous number of combinations of tone colors that can powerfully enhance the moods and meanings of texts. Timbre (especially when subtly combined with tempo and volume) can be a significant means of distinguishing and contrasting the variety of moods and meanings that occur between stanzas of many hymns and avoid the thoughtless singing of strophic settings.

Volume (Dynamics)

Volume (dynamics) is rarely indicated in hymnals and depends on the size and reverberation of the room, the number of singers, and the meaning and mood of the text. It can be effectively conveyed to the congregation by the organist and choir and can contribute significantly to the interpretation of the text.[65]

Harmony

Harmony is the relationship among simultaneously sounded tones and the ways they are organized in time. Though most congregational singing is in unison, harmony is a crucial element of the choral or instrumental support. Joseph Swain contends that "the harmonic element is arguably the most sophisticated aspect of the Western musical tradition."[66] In most of hymnody, the simultaneously sounded tones are chords formed by the superimposition of the intervals found in the first few partials of that natural acoustical phenomenon called the overtone series. The simultaneously sounded tones may be arranged in many different configurations—different tones of the chord in the bass and in the soprano; different tones repeated or doubled; tones spaced in varieties of ways; and tones included that "do not belong," creating non-chord tones or dissonances (tensions), and resolutions (releases).

The relationships are not simply among the simultaneously sounded tones but also among the progressions in a successive series of such chords that usually function according to some accepted principles of the time. The progressions function to some degree on certain principles of physics and on expectations from tradition. This is often most obvious or predictable at the points of rest or the cadences. The center or point of gravitation (key), mentioned in reference to melody, is further strengthened by the addition of harmony, and there is the possibility of changing that center or point of gravitation temporarily as in a transition or more permanently as in a modulation.

The tune YORK[67] is a simple yet rhythmically interesting, vigorous melody with hints of modal harmony, and an A B A C form. In *The English Hymnal*, an "Alternative Version" of YORK is printed with the melody in the tenor, as has been done through history and is sometimes referred to as fauxbourdon, and with the note that "this version may be used, in connection with the other, for stanza 2, the people singing the melody as usual." Choral enhancements make for an interesting musical contrast to set off certain stanzas of text not only harmonically but also through tone color. Here harmony and timbre (as well as volume and tempo) can redeem a weakness of strophic hymnody. YORK tune is a fine setting for a number of common-meter texts.

Harmonic Vocabulary

The harmonic vocabulary of hymn tunes may range from relatively limited (a few different chords) to the rich and varied palette that is found in Bach's harmonizations of the hymn tunes (chorales) of his days. Individual chords are most commonly constructed of superimposed thirds: the root, third, and fifth of the chord, forming (depending on the half-steps involved) major, minor, diminished, or augmented triads and, with an added third, forming seventh chords, and with yet an additional third forming ninth chords, and so on. Each chord has a different sound depending on its inversion (which of the tones of the chord is in the bass) and the other configuration of tones. In the typical four-part writing of hymn tunes, one of the tones of a triad is doubled, creating yet another distinctive sonority, and the distance between the soprano and tenor may create a further distinctive sonority. If that distance is an octave or more it is called open position, and if less than an octave it is called close position. An effective use of open position to contrast with the prevalent close position occurs in the third phrase of William Henry Monk's UNDE ET MEMORES[68] (see figure 10), the tune written for William Bright's "And now, O Father, mindful of the love." It is in this third phrase, with its slight shift of thought in each stanza, that this open position undergirds and propels the tune into a transition to the dominant in the fourth phrase, and the climax of the fifth phrase before settling in the final phrase again into the close position.

Harmonic Progression

In language, the meaning and effectiveness of vocabulary depends much on context and syntax. In music the effectiveness of harmonic vocabulary often depends on the tonal context and the harmonic syntax or progression—how the functions and relationships of simultaneously sounded tones (chords) are organized in time, in succession. The common progressions in many hymn tunes are based on the principles of eighteenth-century harmony, and "less common" progressions are sometimes described by such terms as regression or elision. At cadences or resting points, chord progressions are often quite defined and, depending on the progressions, described as authentic, plagal, half, Phrygian, or deceptive, and these can be "perfect" or "imperfect" depending on what tones are in the bass and the soprano, and referred to as feminine or masculine depending on whether they occur on weak or strong beats in a measure. Progressions may provide anticipation, fulfillment, or denial. How the various tones or voices move in relation to one another (similar, contrary, oblique motion) contributes both to the interest of the individual voice lines and to the composite fabric of the progressions.

Non-chord Tones and Altered Chords

As the simultaneously sounded tones (chords) progress, the harmony may be further enriched by non-chord tones, those that are foreign to the chord, creating dissonances that may call for resolution. Depending on how those tones are approached and left, they too create distinctive sonorities and have been given specific names such as passing tone, auxiliary tone, appoggiatura, escape tone, suspension, retardation, and pedal point.

What was said in the discussion of melody about the tonal center or point of gravitation and the relationships the other tones of the melody have to this center is now greatly expanded and enhanced with the addition of harmony. Chords may function entirely within the tonal center (diatonic harmony) as in AZMON, or there may be chords that draw from tones outside the tonal center (chromatic harmony), sometimes called altered chords as seen in John Bacchus Dykes's MELITA. Some have classified the chromatically altered chords by such terms as "borrowed" (from a minor key), secondary dominant or secondary leading tone triads and seventh chords, augmented triads, Neapolitan sixths, and augmented sixth chords. The augmented sixth chords are further subdivided into Italian, French, and German and the enharmonic German augmented sixth chords still further divided into "first" and "second" German. Such classifications are based on the degree of the scale (diatonic or altered) the chord is built on, how the chord is spelled, and how it functions in the harmonic scheme (approached and resolved). The altered chords can provide rich and varied sonorities in relation to the tonal center and may generate fascinating harmonic progressions that may lead to a temporary (transition) or more permanent (modulation) shift of tonal center. John Wilson observes, "it is rather curious that rich chords (such as those known to musicians as the 'diminished seventh' and the 'augmented sixth'), frequently used by Beethoven and later masters, are branded as sentimental when used in hymn-tunes."[69] The use of such chords by the masters is not confined to their larger works but is also found in short vocal forms such as the Lied, and may lend musical interest and text enhancement in hymn tunes. Peter Cutts employs two full diminished seventh chords and one half diminished seventh chord in his tune WYLDE GREEN, and an augment sixth chord in his tune BRIDEGROOM.

Harmonic Rhythm

An important aspect of harmony is the matter of harmonic rhythm, the rate at which chords change. The composer/theorist Walter Piston defined harmonic rhythm as "the rhythmic pattern provided by the changes of harmony. The pattern of the harmonic rhythm of a given piece of music, found by noting the root changes as they occur, reveals important and distinctive features affecting the style and texture."[70] Joseph Swain devoted an entire book to the subject that he described as "one of the great resources of the Western musical tradition."[71] Another contemporary composer/theorist, Roger Sessions, says, "Possibly no single factor has so much importance in the achievement of good harmonic writing as rhythm."[72] The mounting concepts in each verse of John Mason Neale's translation of the fifteenth-century Latin hymn, "Light's abode, celestial Salem," are nicely supported by the accelerated harmonic rhythm in the Welch tune, RHUDDLAN.[73] While the opening two verses of text and the next two verses are sung to the same melody, the slow harmonic rhythm of the first two verses (two to six beats for each chord) is quickened in the next two verses by a slight reharmonization of the next section (one to two beats per chord). In the final phrases, a further acceleration of harmonic rhythm complements the "accelerated" ideas of the text. The fifth phrase includes a melodic sequence, and the only dotted eighth-sixteenth rhythm falls on important words in each stanza.

These brief comments about harmony only hint at the many facets of this important aspect of the music of hymnody, but perhaps remind musicians responsible for congregational singing that it can be a significant aspect of interpretation. Harmony can make a profound contribution through the many different sounds it can take in support of a melody. While the congregation may repeat a simple melody for the several stanzas of a text, instrumentalists and the choir may weave an enormous array of harmonies, colors, and textures around that melody to create musical interest and to enhance the expression of the text. This is what Bach did in his composition, harmonization, and improvisation of the hymn tunes (chorales) of his day and what the better composers and worship leaders of today strive to do.

Form

The most fundamental attributes of musical form, as we have seen in textual form, are the balances between elements of unity or sameness and elements of variety or contrast. Unity may be achieved by strict repetition or some slight variation of such aspects as meter, tempo, rhythm, melody, harmony, tonality, dynamics, texture, or timbre. Variety or contrast may be achieved by significantly altering or by completely changing any or all of these aspects.

The choice of the overall form of a hymn tune is not only a matter of musical aesthetics but also a matter of textual support. The form of a text includes the number of syllables in each verse, the number of verses in a stanza, the relationships between the verses—whether the following verse of text repeats the idea, continues the thought (enjambments), completes an earlier thought, or adds something new, and the relationship between stanzas. The hymn tune should have an aesthetically satisfying musical form and a form that complements the structural aspects, mood(s), and meaning(s) of the text. At a more subtle or micro level, the tune may complement certain words, the patterns and sounds of the rhyme scheme, or certain rhetorical devices.

There is basically a phrase of music for each verse of text in a stanza, and the meter of the text indicates the number of verses and the number of syllables per line, which, in a general way, indicates approximately the number of notes per phrase and, in a general way, dictates something of the form. At a larger level, most hymns have four to six stanzas and most stanzas contain four, six, or eight verses or lines of text. The strophic settings of hymns (the same music to each stanza) can be varied by changes in harmony, by timbre or media (choral, congregational, solo, instrumental), and by modifications of tempo and volume.

Hymn tunes are almost always relatively short (often some eight to sixteen measures and lasting as little as twenty seconds and most often less than one minute), usually simple in form, frequently in some three or four basic sections (musical phrases), and most often with one or more of these sections repeated. The most common forms of hymn tunes are (1) a repeated first section, followed by a section of new musical material (A A B); (2) the first section followed by the intervention of some new musical material before returning to the first section (A B A); (3) a combination of these where the repetition of the first section is followed by the intervention of some new material and then the return of the first section (A A B A).[74] If a hymn tune does not repeat sections, it is said to be through-composed (A B C D) and will achieve its unity through rhythm, tempo, some melodic repetition, or key. Other forms may occur in hymn tunes, and there are internal aspects of repetition and variations of shorter rhythmic and/or melodic figures or motifs, sometimes repeated at a different pitch level (a sequence). In the better weddings of tune to text, the musical form (sameness and contrast) contributes to those qualities in the text.

Biblical parallelism that is sometimes captured in hymn texts (not only in psalmody) can also be complemented by "musical parallelism." Richard F. French notes that historically "the musical importance of the Psalter is directly related to the structure [parallelism] of the Psalms and their content."[75] F. F. Bruce, in his "The poetry of the Old Testament,"[76] identifies the most common forms of biblical parallelism as (1) identical or synonymous, (2) antithetical, (3) "emblematic" or comparative, and (4) introverted or chiastic. Musical form may complement an identical or synonymous textual parallelism by a "repetition" of the musical ideas (AA); complement an antithetical textual parallelism by presenting a new musical idea (AB); complement a comparative textual parallelism by some slight variation of the first idea (A A'); complement some developmental "parallelism" by variations of subsequent ideas (A A' A" A'"); and complement introverted or chiastic textual parallelism by repeating the second musical idea then returning to the first musical idea (A B B A) or by a A B C B A musical pattern. The repetition and variation may come from entire sections, from musical phrases, or even from distinctive rhythmic, melodic, or harmonic figures or motifs within phrases. In strophic form, the obvious challenges come with the subsequent stanzas of text being sung to the same music. Again, the more subtle musical suggestions of repetition, variation, or contrast may come from tempi, dynamics, or media (voices, the accompaniment including organ registration, or the lack of accompaniment).

An example of the less common through-composed tune (A B C D E F) is Samuel Sebastian Wesley's CORNWALL, which is also in the less common 886. 886 meter. The tune has a rich harmonic vocabulary, quick harmonic rhythm, a melody that carefully balances the rise and fall of the line, and interesting voice leading in each of the four voices. Routley describes Samuel Sebastian Wesley (1810–1876) as "the ablest church musician of the group [Victorian Composers]" and speaks of "the sheer artistry" of CORNWALL.[77] Samuel Sebastian Wesley's musical skills were well recognized. He began his musical career as a choirboy in the Chapel Royal and St. Paul's, became a noted organist at Hereford, Exeter, Leeds parish church, Winchester, and Gloucester, and beginning in 1850 taught at the Royal Academy. The tune is well suited to texts of some dignity and majesty. It was composed for his grandfather Charles's text "Thou God of glorious majesty," has been used for Christopher Smart's "We sing of God, the mighty source," and is suggested for Dudley-Smith's Christmas text, "To this our world of time and space" where Dudley-Smith says the "repetition of lines 3 and 6 ["our Saviour Christ has come"] in every verse is intended to emphasize a sense of destiny (cf. Galatians 4:4), the fulfilling of an eternal purpose, which is the central theme of the hymn, set forth in the opening verse."[78]

In addition to the elements of form in an individual hymn, more must be said later in the section on the practical dimension of hymnody about some consideration of "musical form" in the worship service as a whole. In addition to undergirding a particular word, textual phrase, stanza, or hymn, sensitive worship planning should give some attention to the musical flow of such matters as keys, meters, rhythms, tempi, melodies, harmonies, and timbres in the entire worship experience. Obviously, all the hymns in the same key or one meter might be musically boring. An appropriate flow of the larger musical matters may be subliminal for the average member of the congregation, especially if these are separated by intervening actions, but may sometimes be quite powerful. Primarily, the "musical form" of the service is dictated by the "liturgical form" with its contrasting moods of awe, praise, confession, affirmation, and dedication.

It must be emphasized yet again that the strophic form (the same music used for each stanza of text) of the hymn tune creates one of the major challenges to the music's fully complementing the entire text. The meanings of individual verses and the relationships between verses may be very different from one stanza to another. Complementing the text may then become more a matter of how the tune is "performed"—altering the tempo, timbre (media), or volume, adding a descant,[79] or providing a reharmonization, improvisation, or some combinations of these. The idea of a hymn tune simply being repeated for however many stanzas there are is contrary to any understanding of a text, to any intelligent expression of a text, and to any sense of musical aesthetics. There is the familiar story of a person playing for a certain American Guild of Organists audition being asked to play a certain hymn tune, and she perceptively asked, "To what text and to which stanza should I play it?" More is said about this issue in the section "Performance" in chapter 8, "Practice."

Interrelations of the Musical Aspects

While we have discussed the musical aspects largely in isolation, it is in the artistic interaction of the musical dimension that music has its full meaning. In music, those "various items of experience" are the basic elements of rhythm, melody, harmony, timbre, dynamics, and form, and these function not in isolation but in an "internal conformation." The various aspects are vitally interrelated and, in the case of hymn tunes, also vitally related to the textual "items of experience." Some brief observations about several hymn tunes from the thirteenth to the twenty-first century will help to demonstrate something of the "internal conformation of the various items of [the musical] experience" and their interrelatedness.[80]

WINDSOR appeared first in Damon's *Psalter* of 1591, and its metric and rhythmic vitality are typical of many of the sixteenth-century psalm tunes. It is an appropriate tune for texts of joyous affirmation such as Watts's "Come, let us join our cheerful songs" or Wesley's "O for a thousand tongues." There is much to commend this rhythmic and multimetric vitality in portions of our worship when the tunes are in support of such biblically, theologically sound texts. Watts's text is an ecstatic paraphrase of Revelation 5:12-13, speaking of the praise of "ten thousand thousand" tongues of angels and calling for us to join with them in the cry, "Worthy the Lamb." Watts's summon of the "ten thousand thousand," and the "thousands of thousands" of Revelation 5:11 (NASB) is likely more poetic meiosis or understatement than poetic hyperbole.

Each of the four phrases of WINDSOR has a different "meter" and rhythm and, sung at a brisk tempo, can be an almost ecstatic expression. The melody of the third phrase begins the same as the second phrase (a melodic anaphora expanding the textual ideas in each stanza), but then exerts its independence. The motion of the melody is primarily conjunct, and the four short phrases abound in repeated melodic figures. The harmonization by Thomas Este (1540–1609) is in the harmonic minor with a fascinating rhythmic independence in the four voices and ending in a bright Picardy third. Melodically, rhythmically, harmonically, and structurally, this can be a joyous tune. Chosen carefully for certain common meter texts and sung in the mood of the text and tune, this sixteenth-century psalm tune can contribute much to the liturgical experience of today's worshipers. (See Figure 5.)

LONDON NEW is an example of the "Common Tunes" (not associated with a "proper" text) that appeared in the Scottish psalm book *The Psalmes of David in Prose and Meeter* of 1635. It reappeared in altered form in Playford's *Psalms & Hymns in Solemn Musick of Foure Parts* (London, 1671) and since *Hymns Ancient and Modern* has been popularly sung to Cowper's "God moves in a mysterious way his wonders to perform." John Wilson notes that "a successful tune will maintain its *poise* as it moves, balancing rise and fall without spending too long on the heights or in the depths," that with a "leap in either direction the next note returned within it, so restoring the balance," and then calls attention to LONDON NEW's "leaping with great dignity and freedom, yet never losing its equilibrium."[81] The fresh five-pulse phrase answered by the four-pulse phrase nicely complements the angularity of the melody. This distinct melodic contour and rhythm with its poise, balance, dignity, freedom, and equilibrium make it particularly appropriate for Cowper's text of assurance and awe based on Psalm 77:19; Job 28:1-3; 38; and 2 Samuel 22:7-20. There is something in the majestic angular melody and rhythm that complement the "moves,"

Figure 5. Words: "Come, let us join our cheerful songs," Isaac Watts (1674–1748). Music: WINDSOR. Damon's Psalter (1591).

"plants," "rides," the "unfathomable," the "never failing," that assures in the face of "fear" and "dread," that calls us to "trust him for his grace," and that leads us to know "he will make it plain." (See Figure 6.)

DARWALL'S 148 illustrates many aspects of a good hymn tune and the relationship of the musical facet to other facets of hymnody. The melody and bass were composed by John Darwall (1731–1789) for Tate and Brady's 1696 *A New Version of the Psalms of David, Fitted to the Tunes used in Churches.* The rhythm, melody, harmony, and form in William Henry Monk's (1823–1889) harmonized version provide a fine expression of a majestic text such as Richard Baxter's "Ye holy angels bright" in its 6.6.6.6.4.44.4 meter. The text as it often appears[82] is a revision of the opening stanzas of Baxter's hymn and calls, in succession, for "ye holy angels," "ye blessed souls at rest," "ye saints who toil below," and finally "my soul" to join in praise of God. Biblical allusions include Revelation 7:9; Hebrews 12:1; Psalms 103:1, 20-22; 148:2, 14; and 150, which are common to the theological and liturgical expressions of many traditions. The title page of Baxter's *The Poor Man's Family Book* (London, 1672), from which the text

Figure 6. Words: "God moves in a mysterious way," William Cowper (1774). Music: LONDON NEW, Playford's Psalms (1671).

comes, reads "Forms of Prayer, Praise and Catechism for the use of Ignorant Families that need them" and indicates its liturgical intent. J. R. Watson calls attention to the comprehensive and integrated aspects of Baxter's text and emphasizes that

> the hymn text works through the metrical employment of syntax and imagery, and the pleasure of the text is found in the interaction of all these things, and especially the way in which the complexities of what the poet needs to say—theological, expressive, penitential exultant, biblical—are fitted in to the rhythmical and metrical structure, and expressed through the rhymes.[83]

As "the interaction of all these things" is crucial not simply to the pleasure of the text but to a thorough understanding of the text, so is "the interaction of all . . . [including the musical] things," and, ultimately, the interaction of all the literary, musical, biblical, theological, liturgical, historical, and practical matters taken together is crucial for a comprehensive and integrated interpretation of a hymn.

The carefully crafted melody with its opening, ascending, triumphant, fanfare-like angular shapes of broken chords announces in each stanza those addressed. This is followed by descending scalar passages that say more about those addressed. The broken chords of the third phrase again support the text, which adds still more about those addressed. The largely quarter-note rhythm is interestingly broken into half-note rhythms in the fourth phrase together with a transition to the dominant key, where the meter shifts from 6s to 4s, and where the key verbs appear in each stanza. The tune is through-composed and the phrases are finely contoured with clear structure. The final musical phrase is a scalar ascent of a 9th, providing a broad and majestic complement to the positive affirmations of the text in each stanza.

William Henry Monk's (1823–1889) harmonization of DARWALL'S 148 is interesting not only in its variety of harmonic rhythm especially where the transition to the dominant key appears, but in its harmonic vocabulary, its use of non-chord tones, and the voice leading in each of the four voices. The harmonic rhythm and transition to the dominant serve especially well the ideas of this text. Monk's contributions to the music of hymnody are significant. He served as organist in three London-area churches and was later appointed choir director and professor of vocal music at King's College, London. He was the music editor of several hymnals including the 1861, 1875, and 1889 editions of *Hymns Ancient & Modern* and composed some fifty hymn tunes. Sydney Hugo Nicholson's (founder of The Royal School of Church Music) descant from *Hymns Ancient & Modern Revised* (London, 1950) provides an enhancing bit of counterpoint and an additional emphasis to the triumphant praise of the final stanza. DARWALL'S 148 is another example of intertwined dimensions and opportunities for expression in subtle changes in dynamics, tempo, and timbres or media.

Figure 7. Words: "Ye holy angels bright," Richard Baxter (1615–1691); rev. John Hampden Gurney (1802–1862). Music: DARWALL'S 148, melody and bass by John Darwall (1731–1789); harmony by William Henry Monk (1823–1889), alt.; descant by Sydney Hugo Nicholson (1875–1947). Used by permission of Church Publishing Incorporated, New York.

The ELLACOMBE melody, a fine musical setting for Watts's "I sing the almighty power of God," has an interesting history in that it comes altered from the *Gesangbuch . . . der Herzogl. Wirtembergischen katolischen Hofkapelle* of 1784; appears in the *Volstandige Sammulung der gewöhnlichen Melodien zum Mainzer Gesangbuch* (Mainz, 1833) in a version that is closer to the present hymn tune;[84] was adapted in the *Katolisches Gesangbuch*, 1863; was harmonized by William Henry Monk (1823–1889); appeared in the 1868 appendix to *Hymns Ancient and Modern*; and appears in the *Hymnbook 1982*, provided with a descant by Cyril Winn (1884–1973).

The strong unison opening and sturdy harmonic movement perfectly match the general mood of Watts's text in its exultation of God's creative acts and providential care. The musical phrasing clearly delineates what Watts has set off as the creative acts of God (mountains, seas, skies, sun, moon, stars, food, and creatures) and the way in which he emphasized the nature of God as omnipotent ("almighty"), omniscient ("the wisdom that ordained"), omnipresent ("the Lord is forever nigh"), and a God of loving, providential care. Each of the creations and each of the attributes of God has a biblical basis. William Henry Monk has given the melody a traditional setting without a highly varied harmonic vocabulary, with limited use of non-chord tones, and with only a hint of transition to the dominant key in the contrasting B section. The A A B B'A form is easily grasped and facilitates memory. The B section with its new melodic motif and contrasting range and tessitura highlights the "I sing the wisdom" to follow the A section's "I sing the almighty power." The B section is forcefully repeated before returning to the A section and then to the second stanza that begins, "I sing the goodness of the Lord." The contrasting B section also forms an appropriate shift in the second stanza where Watts moves to the second person, addressing God. This form of address continues into the beginning of the third stanza but then returns to the third person, set off by the B section. Such grammatical shifts of person are common in the Psalms, and it has been suggested that this may have influenced the choice of media or manner of performance of the Psalms in Old Testament times, as indicated by the superscriptions to some of them. Modern readers/singers should at least know whom they are addressing in their utterances, and here the musical setting can help.

Figure 8. Words: "I sing the almighty power of God," Isaac Watts, 1715. Music: ELLA-COMBE, later form (1868) of melody in *Württemberger Gesangbuch* (1784).

Henry Smart's 1867 tune, REGENT SQUARE, conveys the form and triumphant mood of James Montgomery's Christmas hymn, "Angels, from the realms of glory." In successive stanzas, as it appears in many hymnals, the hymn calls for "Angels," "Shepherds," "Sages," and "Saints" to "come and worship Christ, the new-born King."[85] The melody expressing this is interesting, singable, and nicely balanced with disjunct and conjunct motion. The straightforward rhythm on every pulse of REGENT SQUARE is relieved just enough by three slight variants. The dotted-quarter/eighth-note variant provides agogic, tonic, and dynamic accent to important syllables and words and provides negation of unaccented syllables. A half-note variant also occurs at the three cadences on such key rhymed words as "earth"/"birth," "night"/"light." There is a modest but effective use of non-chord tones. The harmonic rhythm is relatively slow with its change of harmonies sometimes only every third or fifth beat, but there is a judicious variety in the harmonies and a brief but welcomed transition through the relative minor to the dominant propelling into the climatic phrases "come and worship Christ, the new-born King." The three exclamations, "come and worship," "come and worship," and "worship Christ, the new-born King" are powerfully set off in ascending melodic sequences, each with its own "tonal center" (F, E, B), similar to climax (κλὶμαξ) in rhetoric.[86] The culminating final stanza might be enhanced with a descant.[87]

Figure 9. Words: "Angels from the realms of glory," James Montgomery, 1816, 1825. Music: REGENT SQUARE, Henry Smart, 1867.

UNDE ET MEMORES, with its subtle melodic contours, unobtrusive rhythm, reserved harmony, and fresh A A' B C form undergirds the textual accents, the meaning, and the mood of William Bright's (1824–1901) "And now, O Father, mindful of the love," for which the tune was composed by William Henry Monk (1823–1889.)[88]

The tune has also been used effectively for Dudley-Smith's powerful "In the same night in which he was betrayed," where the author's sensitive placement of key words at the same point in each stanza allows (or captures) a salient aspect of the music to undergird those words. In the tenth full measure, the salient G# of the melody leading briefly to the dominant key is also the longest note in the measure and on the secondary accent of the measure, and it is here, in each of the four stanzas, that Dudley-Smith places the words "lamplight," "torches," "dawning," and, interestingly, "dark." For both the Dudley-Smith and Bright texts, Monk's contrastive use of the open position of the voices in the third musical phrase effectively enhances the ideas of the text and propels the tune into a transition to the dominant and the climax in the fifth phrase before settling in the final phrase again into the close position. (See Figure 10.)

Carl Schalk, composer of more than fifty hymn tunes and carols, brought Jaroslav J. Vajda's unusual and irregular text, "Now the silence," into a form for congregational singing in 1968 with his tune, NOW.[89] Schalk earned advanced degrees from the Eastman School of Music, is a Distinguished Professor of Music Emeritus at Concordia University, served as editor of the journal *Church Music,* and as a member of various boards and committees for the Hymn Society, the National Association of Pastoral Musicians, and the Inter-Lutheran Commission on Worship. Schalk notes regarding the hymn and tune,

> While suitable as a general Eucharistic hymn, the tune and text were originally intended to serve as an Entrance Hymn for the celebration of Holy Communion . . . . It should be sung deliberately, in a slow dance-like rhythm. Concluding as it does on the dominant, and with the repetition of the final word "Now" three times, the music attempts to evoke a feeling of expectancy and incompleteness which is satisfied only in the Eucharistic celebration which follows.[90]

The melody, harmony, and "phrase marks" (bar lines and short vertical marks) in Schalk's tune honor the six groups of three lines given in the

Figure 10. Words: "And now, O Father, mindful of the love," William Bright (1824–1901), alt. Music: UNDE ET MEMORES, William Henry Monk (1823–1889).

author's collected hymn texts.[91] The tune is basically an A A' B B' (a fourth above A) A'' C (c' ''), and the "deliberately," "expectancy," and "incompleteness" of which Schalk speaks are conveyed in part by these repetitions of melodic lines and harmonic patterns, by the pulsating, compound meter with the repeated quarter-note and eighth-note rhythm, and by its concluding on the dominant. In addition to the slight changes in harmony that transition to the B section that is a fourth above the A section and then return to the original key, there is a subtle but significant change from the pitch a' to c'' on the word "heart" in the last repeat of the A section. As mentioned earlier, Raymond Glover and Robin Leaver regard this as "truly one of the most remarkable hymns of the twentieth century" and one that "has been ranked by critics as one of the finest hymns to come out of the last half of the twentieth century."[92] Schalk's musical setting is part of the popularity of this hymn. (See Figure 11.)

Sister Suzanne Toolan's "I am the bread of life" "is arguably the most frequently sung communion piece in Roman Catholic repertory,"[93] but the hymn appears in Lutheran and Episcopal hymnals as well as in numerous contemporary songbooks and has been translated into more than twenty languages. The hymn appeared first in *Music for the Requiem Mass* (San Francisco, 1966). The author is also the composer of the tune that bears the same name as the text. Sister Suzanne is an advocate for the music and prayer of the Taizé ecumenical community and leads Taizé-type retreats. Elements of the Taizé style of worship can be seen in the text and tune. For some eight years she has traveled with others to minister to the inmates of San Quentin Penitentiary. The five verses of the hymn are adapted almost literally from John 6:35, 44, 51, 53, and the irregular text is accommodated to the steady pulse with a basic harmonic rhythm of one chord to a measure. In Taizé style, a variety of instruments are sometimes added in the gatherings in which the hymn is sung. A refrain concludes each stanza, and a descant is provided for stanzas 4 and 5. (See Figure 12.)

Figure 11. Words: "Now the silence," Jaroslav J. Vajda (1919–2008). Music: NOW, Carl Flentge Schalk (b. 1929). Words and music © 1969 Hope Publishing Company, Carol Stream, IL. 60188. All Rights Reserved. Used by permission.

Figure 12. Words: "I am the bread of life," Suzanne Toolan (b. 1927); adapt. of John 6. Music: I AM THE BREAD OF LIFE, Suzanne Toolan (b. 1927); arr. Betty Pulkingham (b. 1928). © 1971, 1993 by G.I.A. Publications, Inc. 7404 S. Mason Ave., Chicago, IL 60638 www.giamusic.com 800.442.1358. All rights reserved. Used by permission.

A (capo 2, (G). The descant may be sung after stanzas 4 and 5.

Karen Lafferty's "Seek ye first" and tune of the same name were composed in 1971 following a study of Matthew 6:33. The second stanza, based on Matthew 7:7, may have been created extemporaneously and then transmitted orally. The elegant simplicity and economy of the repeated melody and harmonic progressions allow the words to speak. The contrasting "Alleluia" refrain forms a fine descant or counter melody, or the tune may be sung as a two-part canon at the distance of eight measures.

Figure 13. Words: "Seek ye first the kingdom of God," St. 1, Matthew 6:33; adapt. Karen Lafferty (20th C.). st. 2, Matthew 7:7. Music: SEEK YE FIRST, Karen Lafferty (20th C.). This may be sung in two-part canon at the distance of eight measures.

There are evidences of the beginnings of healthy reciprocal influences between traditional hymnody and "praise and worship" texts and music. Some "traditional hymnody" is showing more spontaneity and freshness and increased varieties of rhythmic interest and media. Some "praise and worship" types are showing a broader spectrum of biblical and theological contents expressed in texts of better literary quality. Such mutual influences may well be advantageous to both types. The hermeneutics advocated in this book not only serves the interpretation and evaluation of existing hymns but also expresses concepts useful for the creation of texts and tunes in various styles.

An example of a popular, contemporary congregational song that has biblical, theological, and liturgical content with worthy literary and musical expression is Keith Getty and Stuart Townend's "In Christ alone my hope is found" that Bert Tosh, Senior Producer of Religious Programmes, BBC Northern Ireland, in a 1990 address to the Hymn Society of Great Britain & Ireland said "has been described as the most popular worship song ever."[94] As in their other collaborations, "In Christ alone" shows poetic influences of standard hymnody and contemporary song writing and musical influences of folk and hymn tunes.

Julian Keith Getty (b.1974), a Northern Ireland composer, orchestrator, performer, conductor, and producer, studied music at Durham University and conducting at the Tanglewood Music Center in Massachusetts. He studied classical guitar and participated in a summer master class under the Irish flautist, Sir James Galway. Stuart Townend (born 1963), son of a Church of England vicar in Halifax, West Yorkshire, started learning to play the piano at age seven, made his commitment to Christ at the age of thirteen, and began songwriting at age twenty-two. He studied literature at the University of Sussex. Townend has led worship services and performed in conferences and festivals across the world. His music often shows influences of Christian rock music and folk music as well as traditional hymnody.

The long-meter-doubled text of "In Christ alone" is replete with biblical allusions (Acts 4:12; 1 Tim 1:1; Pss 27:1; 18:2; Isa 12:2; 1 Pet 2:6; Isa 25:4; Eph 3:18; Mark 4:39; John 14:26; 1 Cor 15:28; Phil 2:7; Col 2:9; Matt 27:39-44; Isa 53:6; John 8:12; 1 Pet 1:19; 2 Cor 12:9; and John 10:29) and poetic features (anaphora, antithesis, assonance, and consonance) and reflects theological and liturgical insights that are not often seen in popular worship songs. Biblical metaphors and Pauline concepts of Christ flow in a natural, unpretentious manner. Attention is focused on the incarnation, the death, the resurrection, and the second coming of Christ, and the overall structure is held together with the concepts of "in Christ alone," "in the love of Christ," "in the death of Christ," and "in the power of Christ."

An interesting theological issue surfaced when a 2013 denominational hymnal committee decided not to include this hymn because the holders of the copyright would not grant permission for the line "Till on that cross as Jesus died the wrath of God was satisfied" to be altered to read, "Till on that cross as Jesus died the love of God was magnified."[95] This is a good example of attention being paid on both sides to the theological facet of hymnody that here is the difference between two theories of atonement. Actually, as explained in *A Dictionary of Theology*, four main theories of atonement have been presented through history, and there is much to commend James Atkinsons's suggestion that "No one theory should be allowed to be seen as antagonistic to another. In a very real sense they all belong to catholic truth; each expresses an element of the truth uniquely its own, and the wise man would seek to reconcile them knowing that no one theory, nor any combination of them all, is sufficient to contain the fullness of the reality."[96]

The AABA unison musical setting has intergenerational and interdenominational appeal, bearing the text in its own unpretentious way. The contrasting "B" section nicely undergirds the climactic fifth and sixths lines of each stanza. There is clear evidence that Getty and Townend collaborated on both text and tune. The text and tune lend themselves to congregational expressions of affirmation and testimony in a variety of liturgical contexts, and the natural, fresh expressions of this hymn and tune allow worshipers to encounter significant biblical, theological truths. (See Figure 14.)

The Musical "Voice" in a "Polyphonic" Hermeneutics

From the beginnings of corporate expression of the Christian faith, the musical "voice" has played a vital and powerful role in public worship. The earliest forms were continuations or modifications of the Jewish synagogue tradition. While well-conceived, well-chosen, and well-performed music can convey powerful thoughts and feelings on its own, it can also, when undergirding well-written biblical/theological/liturgical texts, contribute to understanding the texts, be felt with a surprising consensus across many cultures, and provide a memorable polyphony of experiences, as has been well attested throughout history.

While not all those who sing hymns will be equally interested in the myriad aspects mentioned here about the musical facet, the fact remains that the vital interaction of these aspects constitutes the beauty of hymn tunes and often contributes immeasurably (even if subliminally) to the

Figure 14. Words: "In Christ Alone." Music: IN CHRIST ALONE by Keith Getty and Stuart Townend, © 2002 Thank You Music (admin. by EMI Christian Music Publishing). All rights reserved. Used by permission.

literary expression of the biblical, theological, and liturgical contents of hymns. The metrical, rhythmic, melodic, harmonic, and formal aspects and the text/tune relationships are intricately intertwined, to say nothing of the more interpretative matters of tempo, dynamics, timbre, and phrasing that take place in performance. This simultaneity of the many aspects in music is impossible to describe fully in prose writing, but their importance must be emphasized and attended to if hymns are to be more thoroughly understood—the aim of a valid hermeneutics of hymnody—and if singing is to be all that it should be for the glory of God.

Two concessions must be made in concluding this chapter on the musical dimension of hymnody. First, the musical setting is neither the only nor always the best way to interpret the text. Some of the biblical and theological truths and some of the literary beauty may be missed in the rhythmic congregational singing, especially when the printed text is interlined with the music. It is profoundly important that we not only sing but that we also read silently and aloud and meditate on the hymn texts. Such meditative reading is important and will contribute immeasurably to a more meaningful corporate singing of hymns in worship. There is much to commend text or word editions of hymnals.[97] A worthy goal for those who plan and lead worship would be to provide individuals and families encouragement and ways that the hymn texts of worship may be used in the home for reading and meditation in times prior to services. There is the potential for a phenomenal synergy when private and family study, prayer, and meditation blossoms into the corporate expression of biblical, theological, and liturgical texts, expressed in beautifully conceived words and music that have been prayerfully and well chosen for the worship of God.

Second, following the analysis of the various inner workings of the music, we must then return to the actual hearing of it and be reminded of that perhaps apocryphal story we mentioned earlier: after Schumann played a new composition for a group of friends and when they excitedly asked him to tell them about the work, he sat down and played it again. In times of meditation and in preparation for corporate worship, hymns should be read aloud and then sung and/or played.

The biblical, theological, liturgical, and literary facets of hymns find potentially powerful expression in congregational singing when supplied with hymn tunes with the qualities discussed in this chapter. An example is Hubert Parry's tune JERUSALEM,[98] composed in 1916 as an anthem setting of William Blake's preface to his "Milton a Poem" printed about 1808. The tune serves well as a vehicle for Carl P. Daw's hymn, "O day of peace that dimly shines." Charles Hubert Hastings Parry (1848–1918) is recognized as one of the great twentieth-century English musicians. He was professor of music at the University of Oxford and later director of the Royal College of Music, authored books about music, and composed anthems, cantatas, oratorios, and a piano concerto. His hymn tunes REPTON,

RUSTINGTON, LAUDATE DOMINUM, INTERCESSION, and JERUSALEM are still in use today. JERUSALEM is a majestic and triumphant setting for Daw's text in general mood, word stress, and highlighting of key words. The text was actually written to fit Parry's tune. When sung well, it serves both the confident prayer based closely on Isaiah's vision (2:2–4) in stanza 1 and on the triumphant vision of the new Jerusalem in the last days in stanza 2 with the "peaceable kingdom" imagery of Isaiah 11:6–9. In a stately tempo, the rhythmic patterns flow over a variety of harmonic colors and transitions until in the third phrase the sequence-like rise climaxes on the word "grace" in stanza 1 and the word "peace" in stanza 2 before settling confidently in stanza 1 to the text, "shall see Christ's promised reign of peace," and in stanza 2 to the text, "for all the earth shall know the Lord." The carefully constructed contrary motion of the introduction with anticipation of the last phrase of the hymn tune establishes the confident, prayerful mood of the text. The interlude with its metrical shift and slight alterations of the melody and bass line of the introduction move the mood from the prayer for guidance to the vision of God's fulfillment of that day of peace that now only dimly shines.

The entire text rests solidly on Scripture and, in a general way, moves more and more into the biblical language. The hymn focuses on the positive theological aspects of eschatology, leaving negative aspects of judgment to another time. The "day of peace that dimly shines" looks to "Christ's promised reign of peace." There is in the closing line, "all the earth shall know the Lord," something of Philippians 2:10–11, when "at the name of Jesus every knee will bow, of those who are in heaven and on earth and under the earth, and that every tongue will confess that Jesus Christ is Lord, to the glory of God the Father."

The church will, over the years, be served by committed, experienced, skillful Christian hymn writers who can cast the great biblical and theological truths into clear, beautiful, forceful, and memorable expressions that have that almost impossible quality of speaking with an immediacy and yet can bear repetition, each one stimulating deeper thoughts and feelings. Carl Daw is an example of these writers with his ordination in the Protestant Episcopal Church, experience as rector and as vicar-chaplain, degrees (BA, MA, PhD) in English from major universities and teaching in that field, his hymn writing and translation, his service as Executive Director of the Hymn Society in the United States and Canada (1996 to 2009), and his service as curator of hymnological collections. In 2007 he was made a Fellow of the Hymn Society, and in 2011 he was made a Fellow of the Royal School of

Church Music. There is here a depth and breadth of experience to be respected in the field of hymnology.

The attentive reader/singer will recognize that Daw's use of imagery of "day," "swords," "wolf," "lamb," "beasts," "cattle," and "little child" is borrowed from Isaiah and sieze the opportunity to consider the relation of the Old Testament symbols to New Testament theology. The imagery calls to mind such visual representation as Edward Hicks's "Peaceable Kingdom," and the figures of speech and thought cause the mind to explore the larger theological meanings. "Day" is itself something of a metonymy and personification, and the alliteration of "warring worlds" and "learn of love" nicely emphasizes contrasting ideas. The unusual frequency of the liquid "l" and "m" sounds supports the peaceful mood. The two triads of "hopes and prayers and dreams," and "justice, truth, and love" relate and emphasize positive ideas.

The hymn moves in a stately iambic, long meter doubled, and cross rhymes focusing on the "Day of peace," "the Hope of peace," and "Christ's reign of peace," all nicely supported by Parry's hymn tune. This is not some placid peace but a triumphant gaining of what has been promised. Much of the literary beauty of the text can be lost in an interlinear reading and is better seen in its poetic form.

O day of peace that dimly shines
through all our hopes and prayers and dreams,
guide us to justice, truth, and love,
delivered from our selfish schemes.
May the swords of hate fall from our hands,
our hearts from envy find release,
till by God's grace our warring world
shall see Christ's promised reign of peace.

Then shall the wolf dwell with the lamb,
nor shall the fierce devour the small;
as beasts and cattle calmly graze,
a little child shall lead them all.
Then enemies shall learn to love,
all creatures find their true accord;
the hope of peace shall be fulfilled,
for all the earth shall know the Lord.

The historical/biographical background of the hymn is telling. Daw's inspiration came from his reading of *Turning to Christ: A Theology of Renewal and Evangelization* by Urban T. Holmes III, who had been a great influence on Daw during his seminary days and who had died suddenly a few months before Daw's reading of the book.

The hymn is especially appropriate when the Isaiah passages or the theological concepts of the last days of peace are part of the liturgy. Services with an emphasis on social justice would be well served by this hymn. The author of the hymn states, "Although this hymn affirms that peace is always God's gift, it also recognizes the importance of human responsibility in preparing an environment in which peace can flourish."[99] While the plural personal pronouns and prayerful mood of the first stanza are obviously congregational, the affirmation and absence of such pronouns in the second stanza allow its being sung chorally in a triumphant manner.

When a skillful writer frames a text with a carefully chosen, well-written tune in mind, there is great potential that the beauty and power of the text and of the music will combine in a remarkable synergy. A well-written text and tune and their wedding such as found in this hymn text and tune merit careful consideration of the biblical, theological, liturgical, literary, musical, practical, historical/biographical/sociocultural voices as suggested in this comprehensive and interrelated hermeneutics of hymnody.

Notes

1. Karl Barth, *Church Dogmatics*, ed. T. F. Torrance and G. W. Bromiley (Edinburgh: T & T Clark, 1956–1975), vol. 4, pt. 3, 2nd half, 867.

2. There are major indexes and databases devoted to hymn tunes. Hymnary.org is an online searchable database of hymns and hymnals containing over one million hymn tunes and texts and incorporates the *Dictionary of North American Hymnology*. Nicholas Temperley's *The Hymn Tune Index: A Census of English-language Hymn Tunes in Printed Sources from 1535 to 1820* is a melodic index that allows the reader to look up any of nearly 20,000 British and American hymn tunes without advanced knowledge of the composer, name, or text. Johannes Zahn's *Die Melodien der deutschen evangelischen Kirchenlieder* is a critical anthology of almost 9,000 hymn melodies developed and used in German Lutheran churches.

3. See the section on "The Objectivity of Truth and Beauty" in chapter 1.

4. Alfred North Whitehead, *Adventures of Ideas* (New York: Macmillan, 1933) 341.

5. Barth, *Church Dogmatics*, ed. Torrance and Bromiley, vol. 2, pt. 1, 650–66.

6. C. S. Lewis, *Perelandra* (New York: The Macmillan Company, 1944) 33. Edward Lockspeiser attributes a similar comment to Mendelssohn in 1841: "It is not that musical thought is too nebulous for verbal expression; on the contrary, by its nature it is too precise"

(Lockspeiser. *Music and Painting: A Study in Comparative Ideas from Turner to Schoenberg* [New York: Harper & Row, 1973] 9).

7. Susanne K. Langer, *Philosophy in a New Key: A Study of the Symbolism of Reason, Rite, and Art* (A Mentor Book published by The New American Library, 1951) 198–99.

8. Alfred North Whitehead, *Adventures of Ideas* (New York: Macmillan, 1933) 341.

9. It has been acknowledged that some of the texts Bach used in his chorales and cantatas were not of the highest literary merit. In these cases the musical merit does more than simply convey the text.

10. Christopher C. Hill, s.v. "Rhetoric," *The New Harvard Dictionary of Music*, ed. Don Randel (Cambridge MA: The Belknap Press of Harvard University Press, 1986).

11. See chapter 5, "Poetry" and the discussion on the "Distinctives of poetic language and its potential as religious language."

12. Hill, s.v. "Rhetoric."

13. Blake Wilson, George J. Buelow, and Peter A. Hoyt, "Rhetoric and Music," *Grove Music Online*, ed. L. Macy, http://www.grovemusic.com.

14. Ibid.

15. See chapter 5. Some of the more creative composers who write for specific texts may use aspects of these principles to subtly convey textual and musical meanings.

16. In music, this form is called "Arch Form," often referred to by the German term "*Bogenform*."

17. For example, the eleven movements of Bach's motet, "Jesu, meine Freude," are in chiasmus form with the first and last movements being the chorale or hymn and the sixth-movement center being the double fugue flanked on either side by settings of Scripture and choral variations.

18. See the discussion of these rhetorical devices in chapter 5, "Poetry."

19. Roger Scruton, *The Aesthetics of Music* (Oxford: Clarendon Press, 1997) 18.

20. Ibid., 216.

21. Humphrey Burton, *Leonard Bernstein* (New York: Doubleday, 1994) 421.

22. Quoted in Roger Hazelton, *New Accents in Contemporary Theology* (New York: Harper & Brothers, Publishers, 1960) 26.

23. Amos N. Wilder, "Art and Theological Meaning," *Union Seminary Quarterly Review* 18/1 (November 1962): 16.

24. Douglas R. Hofstadter, *Le Ton beau de Marot: In Praise of the Music of Language* (New York: Basic Books A Division of HarperCollins Publishers, 1997) xiii.

25. Ibid., 272.

26. Ibid., 165.

27. Douglas R. Hofstadter, *Gödel, Escher, Bach: an Eternal Golden Braid: A Metaphorical Fugue on Minds and Machines in the Spirit of Lewis Carroll* (New York: Basic Books A Member of the Perseus Books Group, 1999) xiii.

28. John Wilson, "Looking at Hymn Tunes: the Objective Factors," ed. Robin A. Leaver, James H. Litton, Carlton R. Young, *Duty and Delight: Routley Remembered* (Carol Stream IL: Hope Publishing Company, 1985) 127.

29. Erik Routley, *The Music of Christian Hymnody: A Study of the Development of the Hymn Tune since the Reformation, with Special Reference to English Protestantism* (London: Independent Press Limited, 1957).

30. Wilson, "Looking at Hymn Tunes."

31. J. R. Watson, *The English Hymn: A Critical and Historical Study* (Oxford: Oxford University Press, 1999) vii–viii.

32. Wilson, "Looking at Hymn Tunes," 125.

33. Ibid., 132.

34. Routley, *Music of Christian Hymnody*, 6.

35. Ibid., 64.

36. Ibid., 66.

37. Ibid., 71.

38. Ibid., 89–93.

39. Ibid., 143.

40. Ibid., 112.

41. K. L. Parry and Erik Routley, *Companion to Congregational Praise* (London: Independent Press, 1953) 80.

42. E.g., Routley, *Music of Christian Hymnody*; Paul Westermeyer, *Let the People Sing: Hymn Tunes in Perspective* (Chicago: GIA Publications, Inc., 2005); Harry Eskew and Hugh T. McElrath, *Sing with Understanding: An Introduction to Christian Hymnody*, 2nd ed. (Nashville: Broadman Press, 1995); William Jensen Reynolds, *A Survey of Christian Hymnody*, 5th ed. revised and enlarged by David W. Music and Milburn Price (Carol Stream IL: Hope Publishing Company, 2011); and, in a more summary fashion, in numerous surveys of hymnody.

43. Some general concepts about the history of hymnody are discussed in chapter 7.

44. See Robert G. McCutchan, *Hymn Tune Names* (Nashville: Abingdon Press, 1957). Such works as Katharine Smith Diehl, *Hymns and Tunes: An Index* (New York: The Scarecrow Press, Inc., 1966) have melodic indexes, and some are useful in locating tunes in various hymnals. See also David W. Perry, *Hymns and Tunes Indexed by First Lines, Tune Names, and Metres Compiled from Current Hymnbooks* (The Hymn Society of Great Britain & Ireland and The Royal School of Church Music, 1980).

45. William R. Taylor and W. Stewart McCullough, "Introduction," *Psalms*, vol. 4 of *The Interpreter's Bible* (New York: Abingdon Press, 1955) 8–10. The authors suggest that the following may be possible identifications of the music to which the Psalms were sung: "Alamoth" (Psalm 46), "Do not Destroy" (Psalms 57–59, 75), "Dove of Far-off Terebinths" (Psalm 56), "Gittith" (Psalm 8, 81, 84), "Hind of the Dawn" (Psalm 22), "Lilies" (Psalms 45, 69, 80), "Mahalath" (Psalm 53, 88), "Mahalath Lleannoth" (Psalm 88), "Muth-labben" (Psalm 9), and "Shushan Eduth" (Psalm 60).

46. Routley, *Music of Christian Hymnody*.

47. *A House of Praise*, 307.

48. Robert Louis Stevenson's remarks are discussed in chapter 1.

49. *The Hymnbook 1982: The Hymns together with Accompaniments from The Hymnal 1982* (New York: Church Hymnal Corporation, 1985) does provide metronomic markings for most hymn tunes, but is careful to note that "The size and resonance of the room, the number of singers, the accompanying instrument(s), the relative familiarity of the hymn, and the occasion may modify tempo in actual congregational performance" (1027). *The English Hymnal* also indicates specific metronomic markings, but Ralph Vaughan Williams, musical editor, in Percy Dearmer, ed., *The English Hymnal with Tunes* (London: Oxford University Press, 1933) xii, also notes that the suggested tempi "indicate the proper speed in a fairly large building with a congregation of average size."

50. Dearmer, ed., *The English Hymnal with Tunes*, xiii.

51. Curt Sachs, *Rhythm and Tempo: A Study in Music History* (New York: W. W. Norton & Company, Inc. 1953) 11.

52. Harold S. Powers, "Rhythm," *The New Harvard Dictionary of Music*, ed. Don Randel (Cambridge MA: The Belknap Press of Harvard University Press, 1986).

53. This is discussed in chapter 8.

54. Curt Sachs, *Rhythm and Tempo: A Study in Music History* (New York: W. W. Norton & Company, Inc., 1953) 16–17.

55. The important element of tempo is discussed in chapter 8.

56. John Wilson, "Looking at Hymn Tunes: the Objective Factors," ed. Robin A. Leaver, James H. Litton , and Carlton R. Young, *Duty and Delight: Routley Remembered* (Carol Stream IL: Hope Publishing Company, 1985) 144.

57. Michael Baughen, consultant ed., *Hymns for Today's Church* (London: Hodder and Stoughton, 1982) 60 (i).

58. *A House of Praise*, 447.

59. *Lutheran Book of Worship* (Minneapolis: Augsburg Publishing House and Philadelphia: Board of Publication, Lutheran Church in America, 1978) 61.

60. Ibid. 46.

61. *Hymnbook 1982* provides six such melodies, including those by Michael Praetorius and William Billings.

62. *Rejoice in the Lord: A Hymn Companion to the Scriptures*, lists 25 "Hymns with Descants" (p. 608).

63. *Hymns for Today's Church* (London: Hodder and Stoughton, 1982) 470.

64. *The Hymnal 1982* and its partner, *Hymnbook 1982*, 382.

65. Dynamics are discussed in more detail in chapter 8.

66. See Joseph P. Swain, *Harmonic Rhythm: Analysis and Interpretation* (Oxford: Oxford University Press, 2002) 5.

67. YORK is discussed in more detail in chapter 7 and Figure 23.

68. See below for further discussion of the tune, and see chapter 4 for a further discussion of the text. The Latin text is the basis of the hymn tune name.

69. John Wilson, "Looking at Hymn Tunes: the Objective Factors," in Robin A. Leaver, James H. Litton, and Carlton R. Young, eds., *Duty and Delight: Routley Remembered* (Carol Stream IL: Hope Publishing Company, 1985) 140.

70. Walter Piston, "Harmonic Rhythm," *Harvard Dictionary of Music*, ed. Willi Apel, 2nd ed. rev. and enlarged (Cambridge MA: The Belknap Press of Harvard University Press, 1969).

71. Joseph P. Swain, *Harmonic Rhythm: Analysis and Interpretation* (Oxford: University of Oxford, 2002) v.

72. Roger Sessions, *Harmonic Practice* (New York: Harcourt, Brace and Company, 1951) 77.

73. The arrangement in *Hymnbook 1982*, no. 621, is from the *English Hymnal* and is possibly by Vaughan Williams.

74. The third phrase of short meter (66.86) texts and tunes shows that the contrast inside of repetition provides both a satisfaction in form and an emphasis to the textual and musical ideas of the third phrase, e.g., the CARLISLE tune with its musical sequences in the third phrase emphasizes texts as in Dudley-Smith's "The darkness turns to dawn," "The God of grace is ours," and "The best of gifts is ours."

75. Richard F. French, "Psalter," *The New Harvard Dictionary of Music* (Cambridge MA: The Belknap Press of Harvard University Press, 1986).

76. F. F. Bruce, "The Poetry of the Old Testament," ed. D. Guthrie and J. A. Motyer, *The New Bible Commentary*, rev. ed. (Grand Rapids MI: Wm. B. Eerdmans Publishing Co., 1970) 41–47.

77. Routley, *Music of Christian Hymnody*, 125.

78. *A House of Praise*, 315.

79. *Hymnal 1982* provides in its partner, *Hymnbook 1982*, a number of alternate accompaniments and descants.

80. See the discussion of the thirteenth-century hymn tune DIVINUM MYSTERIUM in chapter 2.

81. John Wilson, "Looking at Hymn Tunes: the Objective Factors," in *Duty and Delight: Routley Remembered*, ed. Robin A. Leaver, James H. Litton, and Carlton R. Young (Carol Stream IL: Hope Publishing Company, 1985) 127–28.

82. *Hymnbook 1982*, no. 625; Raymond F. Glover, ed., and *The Hymnal 1982 Companion* (New York: Church Hymnal Corporation) IIIb, 625.

83. J. R. Watson, *The English Hymn: A Critical and Historical Study* (Oxford: Oxford University press, 1999) 36.

84. See Glover, ed., *The Hymnal 1982 Companion*, IIIa, 210.

85. The stanza addressed to "Sinners" is omitted in most hymnals because of its strong words and in spite of its allusion to the beautiful words of Psalm 85:10.

86. The tune was originally written for Horatius Bonar's "Glory be to God the Father," where a similar repetition occurs, as in the final stanza, "Glory, glory, glory, glory, Glory to the King of kings!"

87. Craig Sellar Lang's descant (*Hymnbook 1982*, no. 368) is a fine countermelody with rhythmic interest.

88. Bright and his text are discussed in chapter 4, "Liturgy."

89. Vajda's hymn, "Now," is discussed in chapter 4.

90. Schalk to Glover, 21 March 1984, "Church Hymnal Corporation Papers," New York, as quoted in Glover, ed., *The Hymnal 1982 Companion*, 626.

91. Jaroslav J. Vajda, *Now the Joyful Celebration: Hymns, Carols, and Songs* (St. Louis: Morning Star Music publishers, 1987) 27.

92. Glover, ed., *The Hymnal 1982 Companion*, 623, 625.

93. Fred Moleck of GIA Publications, Inc., http://www.giamusic.com/sacred_music/tabletalk/375.cfm.

94. Bert Tosh, "Producing 5,842 Hymns," *Hymn Society of Great Britain & Ireland Bulletin* 19/5 (January 2010): 161.

95. Mary Louise Bringle, "Debating Hymns," *The Christian Century*, 1 May 2013.

96. James Atkinson, s.v. "Atonement," in Allan Richardson, ed., *A Dictionary of Theology* (Philadelphia: Westminster Press, 1976).

97. See, for example, *Poems of Grace: Texts of the Hymnal 1982* (New York: Church Publishing Incorporated, 1998).

98. Church Hymnal Corporation, *Hymnbook 1982: The Hymns together with Accompaniments from The Hymnal 1982* (New York: The Church Hymnal Corporation, 1985) 597.

99. Carl P. Daw Jr., *A Year of Grace: Hymns for the Church Year* (Carol Stream IL: Hope Publishing Co, 1990) 166.

CHAPTER 7

History, Biography, and Socioculture

The Importance of Understanding the Historical, Biographical, and Sociocultural Voices of Hymnody

The three large disciplines referred to in this chapter (the historical, biographical, and sociocultural) are grouped with the considerations that they are vitally related, that the first two (historical, biographical) have been dealt with rather extensively in hymnological writings, and that the latter (the sociocultural) is less so but should be considered in conjunction with the former. Understanding the larger historical/biographical/sociocultural context of a hymn's origin and its uses past and present often yields valuable insights for interpreting the hymn and for appreciating the life experiences of individuals involved in its writing and subsequent uses. Well-written histories and biographies can sometimes help us understand meanings, relationships, and even secondary or indirect influences of the larger political, economic, artistic, religious, or sociocultural contexts.

J. R. Watson rightly affirms that "for a full understanding of an individual hymn it is necessary to see it in a historical context, which affects the hymn because it determines the hermeneutics by which the biblical material is explored, and the composition of the interpretive community for which it is written."[1] "A historical context" must, for an adequate hermeneutics of hymnody, not only trace the provenance and evolution of hymns, hymn tunes, and hymnals and the lives of the writers (as do most histories of hymnody and hymnal companions) but also provide some insight into the larger sociolocultural contexts in which the writings were born (as most histories of hymnody and hymnal companions do not usually do).

The social aspects of this dimension refer to people who share, in a continuous relationship, the same geographical area, the same basic political authority, laws, morals, complex of knowledge and beliefs, and some general cultural expectations. The cultural aspects of this dimension refer more specifically to groups within a society who consciously share with each other a common heritage of geographical origin, ancestry, language, traditions, customs, religion, art, food, dress, and ideology. Each group may share some general cultural values, but there are also subcultures that are to varying degrees different from each other and the larger culture.[2]

Historical and sociocultural understanding is necessary not only for the sound interpretation of hymns but also for the effective choice and use of hymns. For hymns or any art forms to speak effectively to their time and place, there must be some sensitivity to the culture that they seek to address. Amos Wilder observes that "in each new age and climate the theopoetic of the church is reshaped in inseparable relation to the general imagination of the time."[3] He puts great emphasis on a vital creativity and imagination with the church.

> It is at the level of the imagination that any full engagement with life takes place. It is not enough for the church to be on guard against the Philistine in the world. Philistinism invades Christianity from within wherever the creative and mythopoetic dimension of faith is forfeited. When this happens doctrine becomes a caricature of itself. Then that which once gave life begins to lull and finally to suffocate us.[4]

Wilder uses a metaphor to note that cultural sensitivity has been a mark of truly effective Christian witness from its beginning.

> When Paul and other missionaries to the Gentiles went out into the cities of Asia Minor and Greece they had to appeal to a different kind of culture. . . . The terms and categories of their witness had to be modulated to awaken response in a different theater with its own acoustics and its own imaginative repertoire. Their words and their ceremonies carried over into the hearts of men because they could do this.[5]

Missiology has increasingly recognized the importance of cultural understanding and indigenous leadership and thinking. Learning the language of the society was an obvious need, but learning and engaging the culture, the music, was often slow in coming. Such engagement in the interest of communication sometimes carried with it dangers of endorsing customs and meanings that were not in keeping with the Christian faith.

Finding that balance, learning the language of a society, is still true in our own culture and, in many cases, even more difficult given the multicultural character of many congregations.

Perspectives of Historiography

Historians have made interesting comments on their art of historiography. Will and Ariel Durant, in the first of the eleven monumental volumes of the series *The Story of Civilization*, confessed that "most history is guessing, and the rest is prejudice."[6] In the small volume, *The Lessons of History*, written after four decades of work on their ten volumes, they affirmed, "Our knowledge of any past event is always incomplete, probably inaccurate, beclouded by ambivalent evidence and biased historians, and perhaps distorted by our own patriotic or religious partisanship."[7]

The music historian Paul Henry Lang stated a purpose of his *Music in Western Civilization*: "I have endeavored to prevent the many-sided shimmering wealth of art from becoming mere abstraction by searching always for the overtones that accompany facts and accomplishments, trying to see behind every detail the whole of the creative soul struggling for articulation and expression."[8] In *A Short History of Opera*, music historian Donald Grout makes a similar remark: "The landscape of history is not alone the solid earth of fact; above must spread the rolling cloudbanks of imagination."[9] Grout was too fine a historian to suggest some free-wheeling, make-it-up-as-you-go approach to historiography or some unfounded "guessing." What he affirms is the need, after exploring the "solid earth of fact," to project one's self into the *Zeitgeist*, to experience the time, to understand the true nature, reasons, and meanings of events, to probe the thoughts and feelings of persons who inhabited an earlier time and a different area of space.

Yet another perspective on history requires us to consider the continuing flow of cultural, sociological, and even psychological contexts out of which people in our own day understand hymns of today and of many centuries earlier. T. S. Eliot reminds us that the past is "altered by the present as much as the present is directed by the past."

> . . . what happens when a new work of art is created is something that happens simultaneously to all the works of art which preceded it. The existing monuments form an ideal order among themselves, which is modified by the introduction of the new (the really new) work of art among them. The existing order is complete before the new work arrives; for order

to persist after the supervention of novelty, the *whole* existing order must be, if ever so slightly, altered; and so the relations, proportions, values of each work of art toward the whole are readjusted; and this is conformity between the old and the new. Whoever has approved this idea of order, of the form of European, of English literature, will not find it preposterous that the past should be altered by the present as much as the present is directed by the past.[10]

The interpretations we make of hymns based on history do affect at least our own understanding of "all the works of art which precede it." The need for readjustment may be true not only of our understanding and appreciation of the medium but perhaps also of our understanding and appreciation of the message. There is, then, a responsibility for applying a valid hermeneutics of history and a valid hermeneutics of hymnody. Each week millions of people sing hymns oblivious to the historical period of their writing, to say nothing of the historical, social, or cultural circumstances in which the authors or composers conceived the creation and expressed it for the people of their time and place. In many cases, an understanding of those circumstances could greatly enrich the experience of hymn singing.

Some Turning Points in the Evolution of Hymnody

The story of hymnody is a fascinating complex of biblical, theological, liturgical, literary, biographical, sociological, cultural, and musical facets that both reflect and influence multiple aspects of the lives of God's people. Almost every tradition of Christian believers in almost every part of the world has continued to cultivate a hymnody suitable to the language and doctrines of its own culture and faith. All through history and in every culture, these expressions of faith have assumed an amazing variety of forms, types, and styles. The fascinating and complex history of hymnody has been chronicled in numerous works.[11] Intensive studies have been written on aspects of hymnody.[12] Portions of books are devoted to historical surveys of the field.[13] Entire dictionaries and encyclopedias are devoted to the subject.[14] Articles on numerous aspects of hymnody appear in major dictionaries and encyclopedias,[15] and in journals dedicated to the field.[16] Books devoted to the larger subject of church music often include major sections on hymnody.[17] There are biographies and studies of individual hymn writers[18] as well as collections of their letters and other writings. Festschrifts have been prepared to honor some of the major figures in hymnology.[19] Major organizations are devoted to the study and practice of hymns.[20] Hymnology has become a recognized discipline in major universities and seminaries.[21] In addition to the almost inumerable hymnals are collections and catalogues of hymnody,[22] and much information is available in the numerous handbooks and companions to hymnals. There are indexes and concordances of the texts and tunes of hymns.[23] An increasing number of websites are devoted to aspects of hymnody.[24] In addition to these studies directly related to hymnody are a host of general studies related to the histories of periods, countries, groups, and individuals that often discuss hymnody. Chronologies referring to events and personages that are contemporary can contribute much to understanding the larger contexts.[25]

Given this abundance of research and writing, this chapter makes no attempt to provide a history of hymnody. It does seem wise to present what are generally accepted to be some of the turning points before focusing on related aspects that are often not a major concern in historical studies. The evolution of hymnody is a fascinating story involving peoples of almost every culture in every period of human history. Music and poetry, more specifically hymns, in the broadest definition of the term, have played major roles in the life of God's people as they have expressed their deepest thoughts and feelings. A significant feature in the evolution of hymnody, especially Christian hymnody, has been this increasing involvement of the people in actual singing.

As early as Genesis 4:21, the inspired Scriptures refer to music, identifying "the father of all those who play the lyre and pipe" and later recording the great songs of Moses and of Miriam and the lyric passages of the prophets. The Scriptures also devote a major section to the "hymnbook" of the Jewish nation. The Psalms remain one of the great spiritual documents of civilization, a collection of Hebrew religious poetry with memorable imagery and parallelism that was sung by the people of God at that time, by others through its translations into Greek and Latin, and then into virtually every known language of God's people. The Psalms continue to be a repository inspiring a variety of congregational expressions even to our day. Many scholars consider that the superscriptions to the Psalms give indications of the actual tones or melodies used to sing them. The content and literary form, especially in the litanies and similarly repeated sections, indicate the possibility that groups of people actually participated in singing.

The New Testament records the great canticles of Mary, Zacharias, and Simeon and the song of the angels at the birth of Jesus, all of which have been a part of Christian liturgy throughout history. The New Testament also gives challenging admonitions to the people of God to sing psalms, hymns, and spiritual songs, and even incorporates what authorities agree to be actual fragments of hymns of the early church. The Bible remains the primary source and inspiration for Christian hymnody.

In the time of Christ and in the first centuries, Greek culture permeated the Roman Empire, and early Christians with their Synagogue heritage used the Greek language not only to record what has come to be the New Testament but also to author some of the great hymns expressing the faith and combating early heresies. A number of Greek hymns of the early Christians (second and third centuries) still appear in various translations in many hymnals, as do some Syrian hymns. Gustave Reese emphasizes the importance of Syria in the early history of Christian Chant, noting, "Syria, a part of the Roman Empire, a neighbor of the Holy Land, and a scene of intense Christian activity, was an ideal center for the development of a Chant combining those basis elements that were to prove characteristic of Christian Chant generally."[26] Syrian Chant, he adds, "drew upon the Palestinian, and in turn influenced not only the Byzantine and Armenian, but bodies of Chant in Italy and Southern France. Syrian custom especially favored antiphony."[27]

Both Byzantine hymnody of the Eastern Church that began in the fourth and fifth centuries and the development of the Roman liturgy and the rise of Latin hymnody in the Western church in the same general period produced hymns that continue to be included in modern hymnals in fine translations. The liturgical chant, in addition to the Latin Roman Catholic, included the Old Roman, Ambrosian, Gallican, and Mozarabic chant, and, in the medieval Christian church, a body of hymns also arose in the liturgical chant traditions in the Armenian, Russian, and Slavonic rites. Portions of some of the biblical and non-biblical hymns from these traditions have been translated and become parts of congregational singing in various Christian traditions.

In some of these traditions, the chants were not truly congregational expressions, though they were significant in the later development of congregational hymns. The rise of responsorial and antiphonal chant increasingly involved not only the clergy and then selected and trained singers but also finally the congregation, and it is the congregational singing of hymns that most concerns us here.

In contrast to an emphasis on the elaborate polyphony and Latin texts of the Catholic Church that appeared in the later Medieval and early Renaissance periods, the Protestant tradition focused on hymnody. The

Lutheran chorales, in a growing number of hymnals, came to be more in the nature of vernacular sacred folk song, more homophonic in style, more strophic in form, more doctrinal and confessional in content, and more congregational in use. During this period were influences of the Moravians and the Anabaptists, and, in the seventeenth century, Pietism spurred a new type of hymnody. Each of these and the Reformed church with its rhymed translation of the Psalms (Psalters) influenced English and American hymnody.

The 1559 Injunction of Elizabeth gave authority for the singing of hymns in the Anglican service, and a series of Psalters ensued. The Sternhold and Hopkins Psalter ("Old Version") of 1562 had, in addition to the rhymed translations of the Psalms, nine "original" hymns. The Tate and Brady Psalter of 1696, *A New Version of the Psalms of David, Fitted to the Tunes Used in Churches*, with its more polished literary style of the Psalms, was nearer to the style of hymns. The 1708 supplement provided tunes and included paraphrases of other portions of Scripture.

As metrical versions of the Psalms gave way to paraphrases, then to paraphrases of other passages of Scripture, there came more acceptance of freely composed hymns. In *The Psalms of David Imitated in the Language of the New Testament* (1719), the nonconformist Isaac Watts did not simply translate Psalms but, as he said in his preface, "imitated" and paraphrased the Psalms, allowing the psalmist to "always speak the common sense and language of a Christian . . . and thus to compose a *Psalm-book for Christians* after the manner of the Jewish Psalter," giving us true English hymnody. Many of the hymn texts in the eighteenth century were in common (86.86), long (88.88), or short iambic meter (66.86), and there came to be a wealth of melodies in those meters for congregational singing. A long train of great English hymn writers followed Watts, and numerous writers in both "high" and "low" Anglican traditions continued to contribute to the growing stream of hymns. There was an influx of new hymnals in England (*Hymns Ancient and Modern*, 1861) and a rise of denominational hymnals in North America. The nineteenth century and the Oxford Movement saw new approaches to texts and music.

The English colonists brought to North America a variety of religious beliefs and practices, including a range of types and styles of hymnody that were adopted in or adapted to the new cultural contexts. Efforts at providing resources such as the Bay Psalm book of 1640 were early on met with serious challenges to an effective practice of hymnody. Because colonists in the various regions were often faced with a lack of experience in congregational singing and even illiteracy, there developed the practice of lining-out, in which each line was read or sung by the minister or another person before being sung by the congregation. While this facilitated congregational singing at the time, it often distorted the meanings of texts and hampered any intelligent performance of the music of the psalms and hymns. The problems were sometimes exacerbated by the lack of congregants who had musical skills or even the ability to read music, and compounded in some places by an inadequate number of capable musical leaders. In New England, singing schools arose to promote musical literacy, and in many places this encouraged and improved congregational singing and inspired the writing of new texts and tunes. Secular folk songs and religious texts joined with the white and black spirituals. The personal religious experience that was reflected in the spirituals had a counterpart in more urban, evangelical gospel songs.

In the following decades in England and America, a large body of hymnody continued to rise in the varied religious traditions and social cultures. A wide variety of types, forms, styles, and qualities of congregational song continues to evolve in many places in the world.

In our historical period, various emphases in theological thinking, liturgical movements, and cultural shifts in literary and musical styles have given rise to a flood of new forms of hymnody. Some have been fresh, needed, positive, and powerful additions, and others less so. During the 1950s in England, a new "pop" type of contemporary congregational singing began to emerge with members of the Twentieth-century Church Light Music Group. Geoffrey Beaumont and others provided Broadway-type tunes for traditional hymn texts. Similar styles emerged in America. This influence continued in the 1960s with the "Jesus Movement" and youth musicals. Some of these tunes and some folk/rock tunes began to have an influence on congregational singing. The group who met in Dunblane, Scotland, and produced the influential *Dunblane Praises* (1962) and *Dunblane Praises II* (1964) set off profound influences on subsequent hymnody. In the 1960s, there began, in what has been called the "hymn explosion," a new wave of hymn writing, hymn singing, hymnals, hymnal supplements, and a new emphasis on hymnology. The writing of hymns, composing of tunes, collecting, studying, and writing about hymns at that time and in the years following have often been done by highly skilled, trained, and experienced persons and have contributed immeasurably to the worship experiences of Christians and to a growing respect for hymnody.

During this time, Gelineau Psalmody and the music of the Taizé community were exerting great influence. The Taizé community with its multicultural, multilingual, ecumenical nature brought a new sociocultural dimension to hymnody. In the seventies there was a new influx or revival, especially in America, of the "praise choruses" and "Scripture songs" that were relatively short textual passages sung to popular melodies, often highly repetitive and not requiring a hymnal.

In the late 1960s and the 1970s, several major hymnals produced supplements that contained both old and new materials, some from other countries, for use in churches in England, Canada, Australia, and the United States. Such collections as *Hymns and Songs* appeared as a supplement to the *Methodist Hymn Book*, and *100 Hymns for Today* was published by the proprietors of *Hymns Ancient and Modern*. In 1971 the *New Catholic Hymnal* was published with contributions by several internationally recognized composers, including Edmund Rubbra, Jean Langlais, and Benjamin Britten. In 1975 there appeared such works as *English Praise: A Supplement to the English Hymnal* and *New Church Praise*, which was a supplement for both *The Church Hymnary* and *Congregational Praise*. The hymns of Timothy Dudley-Smith, Fred Pratt Green, Fred Kaan, and Brian Wren gave a new impetus to hymn writing. The increased use of hymns and tunes from the British hymn renaissance motivated the creation of new texts and music in North America, especially in the 1980s and 1990s. Significant texts came from such writers as Thomas H. Troeger, Jaroslav Vajda, Omer Westendorf, Margaret Clarkson, Carl P. Daw Jr., Gracia Grindal, Sylvia Dunstan, and many others in the United States and Canada. Many of these gave creative expression to the biblical, theological, literary, and liturgical dimensions of hymnody. Tunes came from David Hurd, Carol Doran, Calvin Hampton, Alfred V. Fedak, Carl F. Schalk, Austin Loveless, Carlton R. Young, and a host of others.

The last decades have seen a significant rise in ethnomusicology, the study of music in cultures, and in the study of the social psychology of music.[28] Hymnals have shown an increase in the inclusion of hymns from other nations, cultures, and ethnic groups. The cultural differences within a society are often reflected not only in the writing of the texts, the composition of the music, and the compilation of hymnals but also in the selection of texts and tunes for worship, and in the way hymns are sung and understood by people in a single congregation.

Almost every area of the arts and of many other fields of study has generally been divided into a series of periods set off by significant changes in the styles and forms, and these periods have changed with increasing frequency: the Middle Ages, often considered to be from about 500 to 1450 (almost a thousand years); the Renaissance from about 1430 to 1650 (some

200 years); the Baroque from about 1600 to 1750 (some 150 years); the Classical period from about 1720 to 1820 (some 100 years); the Romantic period from about 1820 to 1900 (some 80 years); while the twentieth century has seen a flood of even more rapid changes in styles and forms. In the last century, music has seen the rise of impressionism, expressionism, atonal, serial/twelve-tone, aleatory, microtonal, futurism, neoclassicism, electro-acoustic, computer, minimalism, and varieties of subcategories and forms of eclecticism. While the more conservative areas of twentieth-century hymn texts and hymn tunes did not experience such radical and rapid change, they did experience and continue to experience significant and relatively rapid changes brought about to a great extent by historical, social, cultural, and technological changes as well as by specific theological and denominational events.

Though we classify periods of art history and identify movements, the artistic creations of any period or movement do not always fall so neatly into our pigeonholes. There are usually multiple currents of thoughts that bear on both the creation and the interpretation of the creations. We sometimes fail to consider the appreciation and often deep love that the most knowledgeable people of other times and places had for the hymn texts and tunes of their day. We may also fail to understand how both the older hymns and the recent creations can speak to us today in very new ways and how difficult it often is for church members to accept new and different church music.

In any "period," there were and are creative thinkers and artists who drew from or "belonged" to earlier or even later periods, and we must not always force people or events to fit some preconceived classifications. Once we have "pigeonholed" some period, person, or work, there will likely be some person, action, or creation that is completely out of character, an anomaly that defies traditional classification and circumstances. We may then be forced to consider either a much larger historical, sociological, or cultural context or perhaps explore a much smaller, even (to the extent possible) a very personal, biographical, and even psychological context to understand some works.

In a sort of Hegelian dialectic, many of the new hymns have been reactions antithetical to prevailing styles, forms, and emphases addressing issues that are new or at least current and striving for fresh and meaningful expressions of the Christian faith. Many of the new expressions resulted from or resulted in some fusion or synthesis with current or even earlier expressions. Few if any of the textual or musical expressions grow in a vacuum, without any relation to the larger historical, sociocultural environment. While the better hymns stand on their own, many are better understood by probing into the temporal and spatial contexts of their origin and use and, in some cases, probing into those narrower dimensions of local and even personal circumstances.

There is no illusion that the preceeding mention of a few of the turning points has been a history or balanced presentation of the complex evolution of this profoundly important body of Christian literature. It was simply thought necessary to identify a few of the more obvious parts of the story and to provide some points of reference for those who may not have looked at something of the larger unfolding evolution of hymnody.

Multicultural Music

A sound interpretation of hymnody must consider the degree to which the music complements the biblical, theological, liturgical content and serves the literary expression of that content, and it often requires an understanding of the historical and sociocultural facets, especially as societies are becoming more multicultural.

The attention to multicultural[29] (ethnic, international, global) music that surfaced especially in the nineteenth and early twentieth centuries in secular circles affected the Christian church. A renewed interest in the folk music of many countries and the work of recording, transcribing, and collecting it by such people as Cecil Sharp in England, Béla Bartók in Hungry, Alan Lomax, and George Pullen Jackson in the United States has influenced hymnody. In the United States alone, there was a rich and varied heritage of folk hymnody including the Negro spirituals and the works found in Jackson's *White Spirituals in the Southern Uplands: The Story of the Fasola Folk, Their Songs, Singings, and Buckwheat Notes,* as well as some charming melodies, many with fresh modal characteristics, in the Appalachian folk music, much of which was brought by European immigrants. John Wyeth's *Repository of Sacred Music, Part Second,* William Walker's *Southern Harmony,* and B. F. White and E. J. King's *Sacred Harp* were influenced by folk music, and a whole movement of Sacred Harp singing continues, often using the texts of Watts and Wesley.

As indigenous music became more accepted on the mission fields, traditional (or "traditional style") music from the mission fields began to make its way into European and North American cultures, and in recent decades these hymn texts and hymn tunes are increasingly appearing in denominational hymnals.[30] Admittedly, music from the mission fields has sometimes been westernized to some degree in harmony, rhythm, melody, or media.

In some major denominational hymnals in the United States, traditional texts from other cultures (especially Spanish-language texts) have even been printed in their original language. The traditional Mexican folk hymn, widely known by the name "Somos del Señor" taken from the first Spanish words of the refrain and title, is used for the text "Pues Si Vivimos" ("When we are living") and appears in some hymnals with the text in both Spanish and English. The anonymous first stanza closely follows Romans 14:8 and the profound theological affirmation that "whether we live or whether we die, we are the Lord's." The final three stanzas reflect on the saying of Jesus in John 15:8, "My Father is glorified by this, that you bear much fruit and become my disciples," adding the teaching, "whether we suffer, or sing rejoicing" and affirming that we can always find persons whom we can help and feed. Given this biblical/theological base, the *Companion to the United Methodist Hymnal* (1989) suggests that liturgically "the hymn is suitable for times of remembrance and new beginnings, for example graveside commit-tals, baptisms, or weddings."[31] The text expresses the message in beautiful, simple, and clear statements that are easy to memorize. This traditional Spanish melody is plaintive, singable, and memorable. The first musical phrase is repeated, the third phrase is treated sequentially, and the final four measures form the refrain, which is to be repeated after the final stanza to iterate the basic idea, "We belong to God." The arpeggiated accompaniment, in the setting probably by Elise S. Eslinger,[32] is in the style of the Spanish guitar, and Hal Hopson's setting[33] reflects a Spanish rhythm. The stanzas might be sung by soloists accompanied by guitar, and the simple, repetitive refrain ("somos del Señor") can be sung by the congregation. This traditional Spanish text and music is an example of multicultural hymnody born out of its own time that, in a simple, fresh, and compelling way, combines the biblical, theological, liturgical, literary, musical, and practical facets of hymnody.

Figure 15. Words: "Pues vivimos," stanza 1 anon., trans. Elise S. Eslinger, 1983; stanzas 2, 3, and 4 by Roberto Escamilla, 1983, trans. George Lockwood, 1987. © 1989 The United Methodist Publishing House, admin. by The Copyright Company, Nashville, TN. All rights reserved. Used by permission. Music: SOMOS DEL SEÑOR. Traditional Spanish melody; harmonization from *Celebremos*, 1983.

The Ghana folk song now known in many hymnals in the United States as "Jesu, Jesu" was adapted by Tom Colvin and harmonized by Charles H. Webb and is used for the text based on John 13:11-17 and Luke 10:27, written by Tom Colvin, missionary in Africa, for a meeting of evangelists at Chereponi in northern Ghana. The hymn tune begins with the refrain melody, which opens with a rising minor third followed by the descending minor third, calling "Jesu, Jesu." The remainder of the refrain is made up of a descending figure in descending sequences imploring "fill us with your love, show us how to serve the neighbors we have from you." The melody of the contrasting stanzas is made up of a phrase of a melodic arch in descending sequences noting the act of Jesus washing the feet of the apostles and expressing ways in which we can minister to neighbors rich and poor, near and far. As with many folk songs, the stanzas may be sung by soloists and the refrain by the congregation. The *Companion to the United Methodist Hymnal* (1989) suggests, "The hymn is particularly appropriate for Holy Week services including those that observe Jesus' washing the feet of his disciples, recalling his words: 'Very truly, I tell you, servants are not greater than their master, nor are messengers greater that the one who sent them' (John 13:16.)"[34] The hymn also draws on the words of Jesus recorded in Luke 10:27, "You shall love . . . your neighbor as yourself," the theological significance of which can be seen in Jesus's identifying this as the second great commandment. The elements of good hymnody are present in this profoundly simple hymn from another culture. (See Figure 16.)

Africans who came to the North American continent brought their melodic, rhythmic, and harmonic styles and specific songs that have helped sustained them even in our present day. New songs were created: shouts, moans, chants, psalms, hymns, and the Afro-American spirituals[35] that continue to inspire believers in many cultures. An example of one style of the spirituals is "I will trust in the Lord" with its pentatonic melody, occasional flatting of the third degree of the scale, and, though they can hardly be notated, its rhythmic vitality in a moderately slow tempo and melodic bending. William Farley Smith, consultant in African American music and worship to the Hymnal Revision Committee of *The Hymns of the United Methodist Hymnal* (1989), who arranged the spiritual, has pointed out the similarities it bears to the shaped-note tune[36] PISGAH. He notes that both melodies may come from "Camp meetings of frontier U. S. A. [that] allowed interracial attendance, resulting in many shared, borrowed, and adapted tunes and texts. . . . [It should be] sung moderately slowly with heavy rhythmic accents [accompanied by] . . . a swaying body motion."[37]

Figure 16. "Jesu, Jesu, fill us with your love." Words: Tom Colvin, 1968. Music: CHERE-PONI, Ghana folk song from Chereponi, northern Ghana. Harmony by Charles W. Webb 1988. © 1969 and 1989 Hope Publishing Company, Carol Stream, IL 60188. All rights reserved. Used by permission.

Figure 17. Words: Afro-American spiritual (Ps 37:3). Music: I WILL TRUST, Afro-American spitirual; adapt. and arr. By William Farley Smith, 1987. © 1989 The United Methodist Publishing House. All rights reserved. Used by permission.

Asian hymns and hymn tunes have also made their way into denomination hymnals in the United States. "God created heaven and earth" (*Chin Chú Sióng-té chó thin tóe*) is a popular Taiwanese hymn about the creation. The traditional words, based on Genesis 1:1-5 and Acts 4:24, have been translated by Boris and Clare Anderson, missionaries who served in the Tainan Theological College, a seminary for the Presbyterian Church of

Taiwan. Stanza 1 is a call to praise the God who created heaven and earth, all perfect things, darkness, and light. Stanza 2 is a call to praise the God of great mercy and love who meets our needs and gives blessing to each one of us. Stanza 3 is an important theological statement in light of the religious pluralism of Taiwan, affirming that God is one, that idols are mere vanity, that handmade gods of wood and clay cannot help us. Stanza 4 speaks of the saving grace of the creator God and the thankfulness due him by his creatures, small and great, who enjoy the blessed state of salvation. This author cannot evaluate the accuracy of the translation and its faithfulness to the original, but the biblical theology of the translated hymn is expressed in a worthy literary way appropriate in many liturgical contexts. The pentatonic melody, said to be a Pin-po melody from Taiwanese Sèng-si, has been harmonized by I-to Loh, who was educated at Tainan Theological College, Taiwan; Union Theological Seminary, New York; and the University of California, Los Angeles, and who committed himself to the contextualization of church music of Taiwan and other Asian countries. I-to Loh has provided interesting counterpoints and counter rhythms while still retaining the tune's traditional nature. Native instruments, flutes, or recorders may contribute to the distinctiveness of the melody. Stanzas 1 and 3 might be sung by soloists as affirmations about the nature of God. Stanzas 2 and 4 that speak of "us" and "our" might be sung by the congregation. Again, we have a hymn born out of its own culture, a hymn with biblical, theological, liturgical, literary, musical, and practical significance that can speak to multiple cultures in simple, fresh, and compelling ways.

Figure 18. Words: "God created heaven and earth," *Chin Chú Sióng-té chó thi ⁿtóe* traditional Taiwanese hymn. Trans. Boris and Clare Anderson. © 1983 G.I.A. All rights reserved. Used by permission. Music: TOA-SIA, traditional Taiwanese melody, harm. I-to Loh. © 1983 The United Methodist Publishing House. All rights reserved. Used by permission.

Folk Hymnody

Nineteenth-century romanticism placed an emphasis on nationalism that gave rise to a new attention to the folk music of many cultures, and this had a significant impact on hymnody that continues to our own day. Ralph Vaughan Williams's appreciation for folk music and his adaptation of it for hymn tunes is well known. George Pullen Jackson, one of the leading musicologists of American folk songs, shared that love of folk music and noted that some American folk hymns may have been adapted from secular folk melodies that came from Great Britain. These Anglo-American folk songs often included modal melodies or gapped scales, especially pentatonic scales. These folk hymns began to be written down and were taught in the singing school movement using the four-shape sol-fa solmization that the colonists brought from England. *The Sacred Harp* was a popular shaped-note collection published in 1844 and was widely used in the southern part of the United States.

The tune PROSPECT from that collection has the pentatonic melody in the tenor, frequent open or parallel fifths and fourths, and occasional four-part harmony. The long-meter melody is in a typical A A B A form. The repeat of the opening phrase is indicated by a repeat sign rather than being written out, which affects the underlay of text as is typical in the collection. There is a recurring rhythmic figure that is nicely relieved by the "scotch snap" in the contrasting B section at the apex of the melody. Any proper interpretation of shaped-note hymnody requires an understanding of the clefs and shapes used in this form. It is interesting that this tune seems to have come originally from the collection known as *Southern Harmony* of 1835; appeared in the *Sacred Harp*, a popular shaped-note collection published in 1844; was widely used in the southern part of the United States; made its way into the *Lutheran Book of Worship*, 1978 (and other hymnals); was referred to Timothy Dudley-Smith by an American musician; and is the tune for which Dudley-Smith, in England in October 1994, wrote the text, "From life's bright dawn to eventide." This is mentioned simply as an example of how the appreciation of folk hymnody has grown and how it has been disseminated.

Figure 19. B. F. White and E. J. King, eds, *The Sacred Harp: A Collection of Psalm and Hymn Tunes, Odes, and Anthems*. Philadelphia: S. C. Collins, 1860. Words: "Why should we start, or fear to die?" Graham. Music: PROSPECT.

The Gospel Song

While rural camp meetings and revivalism influenced the singing school movement and the American folk hymn in the early nineteenth century, an urban revivalism later in the century gave rise to its own popular hymnody—the gospel song. Fanny Crosby's "To God be the glory"[38] is one example of the gospel song with the typical chorus, though the text is atypical, being more objective than most gospel songs. William Doane has provided a setting that in melody, rhythm, harmony, and form carefully match the mood of the stanzas and the chorus of Crosby's text. The term "chorus" is used here in the technical sense to describe the appended music and text that is not a continuation of the thoughts of the stanzas in gospel songs in contrast to the "refrain" in hymns, where the appended music and text are a continuation of the thoughts of the stanzas. (See Figure 20.)

Taizé

An inspiring and significant phenomenon in multicultural hymnody and ecumenicity is the Taizé community in Taizé, Saône-et-Loire, Burgundy, France. This community has brought a new sociocultural dimension to hymnody. The ecumenical monastic order founded in 1940 of some 100 brothers from 30 countries is committed to peace and justice, prayer, music, meditation, kindness, and simplicity. The music, originally conceived and composed by Jacques Berthier, is sung in a wide variety of languages and frequently consists of simple phrases of Scripture, especially the Psalms, often repeated and sometimes sung in canon, and often improvised with a variety of instrumental accompaniments. The community has become a major site for Christian pilgrimage, and its style of congregational song has become widely influential. One example of the many styles can be seen in the simple setting of the "Gloria in excelsis Deo" fragment sung to GLORIA CANON. The Luke 2:14 text records these words that the angels sang announcing to the shepherds the birth of Jesus. The emphasis here is on giving glory to God in heaven for what he has done on earth in inaugurating a new era of peace, of *shalôm*, of salvation. The roots of the more complete liturgical text of what is now known as the Greater Doxology go back to the third and fourth century and the great controversies about the nature of Christ. The biblical, theological, liturgical significance of this text is simply but elegantly expressed in the sequential treatment of the opening "Gloria," followed by

Figure 20. Words: "To God be the glory," Fanny J. Crosby, 1875. Music: TO GOD BE THE GLORY, William H. Doane, 1875.

a contrasting melodic arch for "in excelsis Deo," then an "inverted" "Gloria" treated sequentially, and concluding with a sequential "Alleluia" as a completion of the opening sequence. Singing this canon over and over, beginning softly, gradually increasing the volume, and adding instruments, can make it an inspiring, multilingual, multicultural hymn of praise.

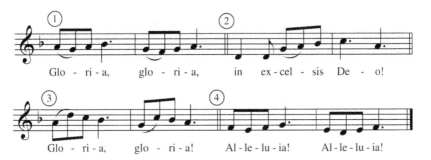

May be sung as a canon

Figure 21. Words: "Gloria, Gloria," Luke 2:14. Music: GLORIA CANON. Jacques Berthier and the community of Taizé. © 1979 Les Presses de Taizé by permission of G.I.A. Publications, Inc. All rights reserved. Used by permission.

Gelineau

Gelineau Psalmody, a distinctive congregational form, is based on a translation of the Psalms made from the Hebrew and intending not only to reflect the meaning but also to retain the poetic rhythm and verse structure. Each line has a specific number of accented syllables and a varying number of unaccented syllables to be sung in natural rhythm of careful speech. The accented syllables are in a fairly slow tempo. A soloist sings the verses, and the antiphons may be sung responsorially or antiphonally and can be sung in harmony and with accompaniment. "How great is your name" (Ps 8) is one example of Gelineau of Psalmody.

Figure 22. Words: "How great is your name," Psalm 8. Music: Joseph Gelineau. © 1958. G.I.A. Publications, Inc. All rights reserved. Used by permission.

Responsibilities to the Original Intent of a Hymn and to the Multicultural Aspects in Today's Churches

Those who interpret hymn texts have the responsibility of respecting the intents of the author or composer, and this may be more difficult to understand in the works from other cultures. Being bound in a denominational hymnal, selected by worship leaders, sung in a context of a liturgy, deprived of certain stanzas, to say nothing of thoughtless singing, have all not infrequently given a hymn a meaning quite removed from the historical context of its origin and the intention of the author. There are varying degrees of responsibility, but creators of works may at least be disappointed to see their creations used in way that are in opposition to their original intent. This may be more likely the case in matters of theology rather than the arts. Recognizing a responsibility to the original intent might at least foster a better understanding and interpretation of the work.

The intents, contexts, associations, and traditions of subsequent users often take precedence over the intent of the creator. There is a responsibility of church leaders to make informed interpretations and decisions about hymns and to help expand the thinking of parishioners, at least the more receptive and certainly the children, in ways that allow them to appreciate the dimensions of hymnody in order that they may, in time, interpret and evaluate hymns in ways that are more sound and contribute to their more meaningful worship and discipleship.

Sound interpretations of texts and music require not only an understanding of the multiple historical, biographical, and sociocultural contexts at the time of origin but also an understanding of the diverse sociocultural contexts in which hymns are used today. Within many (even small) congregations, there may be a surprising variety of subcultures—not only of what we normally conceive of as multiethnic, multicultural (national/linguistic) diversity but also diversity of generational, educational, professional, and economic levels as well as varieties of aesthetic tastes in literature and music and very different understandings and appreciations about religion, Christianity, and hymns. Hymns are most often corporate, congregational expressions and function differently in such complex and interactive contexts. Spiritual leaders must try to be aware of the cultural differences that are the results of the particular configurations of experiences in the lives of individuals, families, and congregations. A comprehensive and integrated hermeneutics should accommodate those differences, suggest how hymnody may thrive and serve in these difference contexts, and offer a more objective basis for dealing with the use of hymns in these diversities.[39]

The larger and perhaps even more the immediate social, educational, political, religious, and economic environments influence the personal, psychological, emotional, and spiritual perspectives of the individual writer, composer, reader/singer, and even a congregation. Timothy Dudley-Smith's sensitivity to the larger sociocultural context yields an interesting insight into his own concerns as a hymn writer. In a review and reflection on

Stephen Sondheim's book *Finishing the Hat: Collected Lyrics (1954–1981), with Attendant Comments, Principles, Heresies, Grudges, Whines and Anecdotes,* Dudley-Smith notes that

> Sondheim describes himself as having been irritated by the convention which held sway when he began, that a chorus of peasants, soldiers, convicts—whoever they may be—"apparently all have exactly the same thought at the same time" (345). For "chorus," read "congregation"; and the hymn writer's task is to give them words (the same words for each, of course) that will allow two distinct things to happen. The text will allow their common shared faith, and their love for Christ, to find united expression; but it will also give enough room for individuals, perhaps at very different stages of their Christian journey, to find something in the words to make specially their own.[40]

It is not the responsibility only of the author "to give enough room for individuals . . . to find something in the words to make specially their own," but also the responsibility of individuals to mature "at very different stages of their Christian journey" and "to find something in the words to make specially their own." Moreover, it is the responsibility of ministers to provide avenues for Christian maturity and even for developing an understanding of hymnody, which, after the Scriptures themselves, is one of the most basic forms of Christian literature and helps shape a Christian's thinking.

We have referred to T. S. Eliot's remark, "the poet is occupied with frontiers of consciousness beyond which words fail, though meanings still exist. A poem may appear to mean very different things to different readers, and all of these meanings may be different from what the author thought he meant . . . there may be much more in a poem than the author was aware of."[41] It is at the level of individual congregations that addressing the sociocultural differences is perhaps most immediate and challenging for ministers. The demands of preaching the word of God are truly manifold, but many congregants will concede to a minister some degree of objectivity, even authority, in theology and biblical interpretation. However, regarding the texts and especially the music of hymns, many congregants consider taste to be a matter of preference, not a matter of discernment, and they approach the music subjectively rather than objectively. It is certainly open to both approaches but is too often purely subjective. The matter of preference is easy to affirm, but the matter of guiding individuals toward discernment is more challenging. Here again, a comprehensive and integrated hermeneutics offers a broader and more objective approach.

It is crucial that the aspiration for betterment, refinement, learning, and increased sensitivity be an avenue for a deeper understanding of the things of God and for a more thorough expression of our thoughts and feelings about these things and not simply an aesthetic concern. An individual's or a congregation's understanding of a hymn or a hymn tune may often be deepened or even changed when consideration is given to the interrelatedness of the biblical, theological, liturgical, literary, musical, and historical dimensions of a hymn as well as considerations of the larger sociocultural and personal influences (religious, denominational, theological, psychological) in the life and works of the author or composer.

The Reciprocal Impacts of Culture and Hymnody

The history of hymnody in English-speaking countries alone is a complex drama of the mutual influences between hymnody and the Christian faith as played out in a surprising variety of social and cultural settings. The sociocultural dimensions of hymnody refer not only to geographical areas and political authority, to distinctive cultural values—the knowledge, beliefs, attitudes, and behavior that people within a society share—but also to their diverse capacities for creative activity, symbolic thinking, discrimination of taste, and aspiration for betterment, refinement, and learning. Religions, denominations, and individual churches are not only groups of people who share religious beliefs; they are social phenomena and cultural expressions of the people, their language, music, literature, and even socioeconomic and educational aspects.

C. Michael Hawn has remarked about the cultural insensitivity that early on characterized too many missionaries and quotes an analogy by D. T. Niles.

> Missionaries have often been criticized for importing Western culture along with the gospel. Asian ecumenist D. T. Niles (1908–1970), a Ceylon (now Sri Lanka) native, described the relationship between the gospel and culture.
>
> > "The gospel is like a seed and you have to sow it. When you sow the seed of the gospel in Palestine, a plant that can be called Palestinian Christianity grows. When you sow it in Rome, a plant of Roman Christianity grows. You sow the gospel in Great Britain and you get British Christianity. The seed of the gospel is later brought to America and a plant grows of American Christianity. Now when missionaries came to our lands they brought

not only the seed of the gospel, but their own plant of Christianity, flower pot included! So, what we have to do is to break
the flower pot, take out the seed of the gospel, sow it in our own
cultural soil, and let our own version of Christianity grow."[42]

Understanding the sociocultural context is not simply an inroad for
evangelism or missions; it grows out of sensitivity to other cultures and languages. This sensitivity has greatly enriched many twentieth-century
hymnals that have been including hymns from Africa, Asia, South and Central America, Native American Indian cultures, and folk hymnody of the
United States that reflects regional and cultural differences in our own country. Some hymnals have included not only texts (both translated and left in
their original language) but also tunes reflecting the musical style. In addition to the hymns and tunes that have been brought from other cultures,
the phenomenal influx of cultures into the diverse English-speaking cultures
has brought new ways of thinking about and expressing the Christian faith.

Hymns are influenced by the larger cultural milieu (the language, arts,
literature, religious thinking, government, and traditions of a people) in
which hymns are conceived and used, and hymns frequently influence the
larger historical, social, and cultural contexts. Hymns have been and continue to be both expressions of the Christian faith and, for many church
members, the strongest force in actually shaping their religious thinking,
and for those outside the church hymns sometimes shape their concepts of
the church and of the Christian faith. Church music in general has had a
phenomenal impact on culture. The music of Bach (especially the choral
music that is so bound up with the hymnody of his day) continues to have
an extraordinary impact on many aspects of culture. This is true of the
"church" music of many other composers as well.

A valid hermeneutics of hymnody requires some concept of the sociocultural influences on the writing, composition, compilation, selection,
understanding, appreciation, and singing of hymns. The very concepts of
"English hymnody," "American hymnody," "African-American hymnody,"
"Eighteenth-century hymnody," "Twentieth-century English hymnody,"
"Protestant hymnody," "Catholic hymnody," "Eighteenth-century Anglican
hymnody," and "Lutheran hymnody" are not only historical, chronological,
geographical, ethnic, and denominational, but also, to some extent, involve
sociocultural distinctions growing out of educational and religious backgrounds, financial status, and occupational/professional positions. Many
congregations have become increasingly intercultural and multilingual, and

those who write, edit, select, and use hymns should be aware of these cultural differences.

One indication of the cultural impact of hymns is the hundreds of quotations from hymns that are included in the *Oxford Dictionary of Quotations.* William Cowper alone has been one of the most quoted persons in the dictionary. In the 2001 *Oxford Dictionary of Quotations,* eighty-three quotations from William Cowper continue to be a part of the culture of the English-speaking world. Erik Routley noted in his 1952 *Hymns and Human Life* fifty-two hymns that "are hymns which the ordinary Englishman knows, whose tunes he can immediately place and which have a place in his common life more assuredly perhaps than any other religious literature, the Bible not excluded."[43] That number has certainly diminished significantly, but there are likely still many hymns or lines from hymns known to English-speaking citizens, though some may not realize that they are lines from hymns. J. R. Watson notes that some one in four of the chosen contributors to the 1981 edition of the *Oxford Book of Christian Verse* are hymn writers.[44] The cultural impact is also true of hymn tunes. As noted earlier, some of the greatest composers including Bach, Buxtehude, Beethoven, Mendelssohn, Wagner, Debussy, Stravinsky, Ives, Vaughan Williams, Britten, Copland, and others have drawn on chorales, psalm tunes, and hymn tunes in their compositions. Hymnody continues to hold a large and influential presence in many aspects of our cultures.

The influence of hymnody on culture can be seen in literary forms that abound in references to hymn singing and to specific hymn texts as seen in such writers as George Eliot, D. H. Lawrence, Iris Murdock, Thomas Hardy, John Betjeman, and Margaret Drabble, to name a few. The Pulitzer Prize-winning American writer William Saroyan quotes a startling seventy-four lines from some forty-seven different hymns in just six paragraphs from the heart of his autobiographical short story, "Resurrection of a Life," in which he remembers the great paradoxes that he faced in growing up as a boy during the Depression.[45] This probably unparalleled number of quotes from hymn lines from an unparalleled number of hymns in such literature comes from an intimate acquaintance with the hymns. Saroyan's father was an Armenian immigrant who had been educated as a Presbyterian minister, and Saroyan does not seem to have chosen randomly either the content or the sequence of the hymns. He writes of "the music, so good and clean, so much of the best in man."[46] These were "the songs he loved and he sang them with all his might."[47] Yet the ambivalence in his life is shown in an interruption of the rude "Spat" occurring fifteen times, increasing and then decreasing in frequency between the hymn lines, and in the three intentional "misquotes": "Onward unchristian soldiers" "O blessed nothingness," and "For the Bible tells you so." There are numerous statements of "he could not believe," but one statement of "he could not disbelieve." His poetic, impressionistic, optimistic autobiographical style came to be known as "Saroyanesque." This one short story is a brilliant study of immigrant Armenian-American culture in California during the Great Depression, a wrestling with the theological dilemma of theodicy, and an example of how much hymns are part of and even influence the sociocultural mileau.

The thoughts of a contemporary theologian and dedicated, skilled hymn writer give us more hope regarding the continuing reciprocal impacts of hymnody with society and culture. In his enlightening article, "Personal, Cultural and Theological Influences on the Language of Hymns and Worship," Thomas Troeger identifies his purpose and then shares his personal response to the profound changes occurring in our cultures. His purpose was

> . . . to clarify the larger issue of tension between the received faith and the changing culture and experience of the hymn writer. When structural history changes, when the architectonic plates of language move to a breaking point, when the ontological metaphors are transformed—then how do we respond as hymn writers, editors and liturgists? That is the fundamental issue before us.
>
> My response has been to pray for the transfigurative spirit, a form of consciousness that is alive to the cloud of witnesses from the past and that honors the intention of their interpretive traditions without mimicking their style.[48]

His conclusion addresses again the reciprocal influence of hymns and theology with a special emphasis on "the passion of the believing heart."

> . . . the creation of a vital contemporary hymnody is an act of ministry that may energize future theology even as contemporary theology is challenging and vitalizing our current efforts as poets for the church. This is especially true of hymnody when it blends together the rigor of theology with the passion of the believing heart.[49]

Personal and Psychological Aspects of Hymns

While hymns do reflect the larger historical and cultural contexts of society and are usually considered to be corporate expressions in worship, they are, in their inception and often in their later singing, very personal expressions of the heart, soul, and mind of individuals, especially for those most sensitive to the biblical, theological, liturgical, literary, and musical expression in hymns. Christian hymnody demands that we glean from the texts and tunes everything possible that will strengthen our worship, discipleship, proclamation, ministry, and fellowship. Understanding the historical and sociocultural dimensions can contribute significantly to a more complete hermeneutics. However, some of the "overtones" that a sensitive hermeneutics of hymnody should listen for are in the personal lives of authors, composers, ministers, and members of the congregation.

J. R. Watson, in his study of the English hymn, devotes space to the biographical, personal, and even psychological dimension of hymnody when he speaks of the events in the life of Henry Francis Lyte. He notes that "the unusual circumstances justify a reference to biography: for Lyte's work can be seen to have features that a psychoanalyst might attribute to the early loss of his mother and remarriage and distancing of his father. . . . Lyte was psychologically preconditioned to this kind of dependence by his unstable childhood."[50] Watson also observes that "hymns are . . . the expression of all the varieties of human religious experience, the dark places of the soul, the exaltation, the sense of penitence, and the sense of joy."[51] Much remains to be done in the study of psychological influences in the lives of those who write hymns and the psychological impact of hymnody on the lives of those who read and sing hymns. The present writer certainly claims no authority in matters psychological and has only little formal study in the area, but biographical studies of a number of hymn writers refer to situations that seem to have had significant bearings on their psychological outlook. Such references are certainly not confined to the darker moods (e.g., Henry Francis Lyte and William Cowper); often mentions are made of family, friends, religious experiences, and educational situations that provide a positive environment for their writing as is the case with Charles Wesley.

A fascinating and growing facet of the psychology of music is music therapy, which is increasingly contributing to our understanding of the enduring power of music and of hymn texts and tunes in people's lives. Persons who have lost much of their cognitive powers are still able to recall, perhaps meaningfully, great amounts of hymn texts and tunes, and it is documented that the stimulation of this facet of their memory can affect other facets of memory as well as the person's attitude and sense of well-being. For those trained in music and medicine, music therapy has proven to be an important area of ministry. Every lover of fine hymns should find comfort and encouragement in realizing the powerful associations that are imbedded in the hymnic experiences of those who create hymns and those who read and sing them.

Sometimes understanding a hymn writer's background will negatively affect one's appreciation or even acceptance of a text or tune, especially if some relevant aspect of the historical context or the character or thinking of the author or composer is considered troublesome. If an author's theological perspective on issues other than that expressed in a specific hymn is contrary to that of the reader or singer, should that cancel any appreciation of the hymn? How informed and carefully thought out is the theological position of the reader or singer? To what extent, for example, is the anti-Semitism of Wagner or the moral character of Coleridge or Caravaggio relevant in the acceptance and appreciation of their art? One must decide to what extent such issues are relevant. One may also decide against a hymn in which the theological position on the stated issue is in keeping with the reader or singer's perspective, but the literary or musical expression is of dubious quality. Again, it may be asked how well informed and thought out is the reader's or singer's insights for making judgments about the rightness of theology or the quality of literary or musical expressions. In such cases, a comprehensive and integrated hermeneutics provides a more objective base for such judgments.

The Historical, Biographical, and Sociocultural "Voices" in a "Polyphonic" Hermeneutics

The rich polyphony of the biblical, theological, liturgical, literary, musical, and practical dimensions of hymns moves within the vibrant historical and sociocultural counterpoint of their time and place. The great English poet John Milton (1608–1674), for example, lived and worked in the time of or under the continuing influence of such people as Shakespeare, Cervantes, El Greco, Sir Walter Raleigh, Francis Bacon, Galileo, Kepler, John Donne, Caravaggio, Frescobaldi, Schütz, Descartes, Monteverdi, John Bunyan, and John Locke. He also wrote during the time of the spread of the King James version of the Bible, the English Commonwealth and Restoration, and the settling of the colonies in America. Out of the multitude of varying historical, sociocultural conditions in his day, Milton made significant contributions to English psalmody. In the 1640s, out of his strong theological convictions, Milton supported efforts by the Presbyterians to reform the Church of England, and with pamphlets he attacked the Episcopal form of church government. He later broke with the Presbyterians, supported the independents, who had imprisoned Charles I, and received a Latin secretaryship in Cromwell's Commonwealth government. At this point he became blind, but during his retirement after the Restoration (1660), he produced *Paradise Lost* (1667), which many consider to be the greatest epic in the English language.

In 1648, Milton had translated, paraphrased, and verse by verse cast into common meter nine Psalm texts (Psalms 80 through 88), and in marginal explanatory phrases he supplied the original Hebrew and inserted his own words in italics. These efforts show both his high regard for Scripture and his concern for its corporate expression by worshipers. The text "The Lord will come and not be slow" that still appears in many hymnals was selected from several of his paraphrases from Psalms 82, 85, and 86. The hymn, in spite of its brevity, its strictness, and its being in the most common of hymn meters, is not without literary beauty. This particular cento appeared first in the *New Congregational Hymn Book* (London, 1859) more than two hundred years after Milton's metric translation of the nine Psalms, and then it appeared in hymnals of the Methodist, Anglican, Episcopal, and other theological and liturgical traditions across the English-speaking world.

Milton's text is often sung to the hymn tune YORK, of which we spoke briefly in our discussion of the musical dimension regarding the melodic, harmonic, rhythmic, timbral, and formal qualities of the tune. This "simple," four-measure (and one of the four is a repetition) hymn tune has a rich history of its own, and an understanding of at least some of the interactions of those parts of its history can contribute to our appreciation of the tune and enhance our singing of the text. The tune appeared first with the name STILT in the 1615 Scottish psalm book as one of "The XII Common Tunes, to which all Psalmes of eight syllables in the first line, and sixe in the next may be sung." Thomas Ravenscroft selected the tune for his 1621 psalter as one of the most popular tunes and gave it the name YORK. One of the arrangements that Ravenscroft commissioned for the tune was by John Milton's father and at some point became used for the son's text. The tune found its way into numerous psalters and hymnals, including the 1698 *Tate and*

Brady New Version of the Psalms of David. The setting by Milton's father later became the basis of the tune as found in *The English Hymnal.* Simon Wright in his insightful study of the "soundscape" of *The English Hymnal* says "the use of YORK in *The Pilgrim's Progress* is somehow the most musically significant manifestation of an *English Hymnal* soundscape component in Vaughan Williams's own work." He adds,

> The great hymn tune YORK . . . is possibly the item that meant more to Vaughan Williams than any other in the book [*The English Hymnal*]. It is a fine, traditional hymn tune, taken from the Scottish Psalter of 1615, with slightly later harmony. It is broad, robust, and diatonic, but with distinct modal inflection in the harmony. . . . For Vaughan Williams, that cheerful agnostic, the tune became a motto, one associated with his own musical pilgrimage, his own life pilgrimage. Having selected it for the hymnal, YORK was then used by him in the Epilogue to music he wrote for a dramatized version of *Pilgrim's Progress* . . . , used again by him in 1924 as a carillon in Hugh the Drover, and in 1942 in music for a BBC radio adaptation of *Pilgrim's Progress.* Finally, it became the splendid opening music for Vaughan Williams's great Morality, *The Pilgrim's Progress* of 1951, and was also used elsewhere at key points in that score. Edward Dent [the famous English (Cambridge) musicologist] wrote to Vaughan Williams that "YORK is the making of the whole opera . . . . I find it indescribably uplifting, every time it comes in, and more and more; it sets the whole mood of the opera at the start (and how beautifully you have orchestrated the wind there) and I felt I should never have got to Paradise if I didn't hear YORK there!"[52]

Here again we see in this short text and tune the dimensions that are basic to a comprehensive and integrated hermeneutics of hymnody. As a versified biblical (Psalm) text, the hymn has been associated with a variety of theological positions and various liturgical traditions. The text was given its literary form by one of the greatest figures in the history of English literature, and, of the music, Sir John Hawkins wrote in his *History of Music* (London, 1776), "This tune is so well known that within memory half the nurses of England were used to sing it by way of lullaby, and the chimes of many country churches have played it six or eight times in 24 hours from time immemorial."[53] The vigorous tune has retained its vitality through the centuries and has been the basis of numerous instrumental and choral settings. Its use in congregational form has been embellished with descants.[54]

The polyphony of dimensions that characterizes fine hymnody is again intertwined in this short example.

Figure 23. Words: "The Lord will come and not be slow," John Milton (1608–1674), alt.
Music: YORK, melody from The CL Psalmes of David, 1615; adapt. The Whole Booke of
Psalmes, 1621; harm. John Milton Sr. (1563?–1647).

James Montgomery's (1771–1854) "In the hour of trial," is from a very
different historical period, cultural context, and personal experience, and is
thus a very different type of text.

> In the hour of trial, Jesus, plead for me,
> Lest by base denial I depart from Thee.
> When Thou seest me waver, with a look recall,
> Nor for fear or favor suffer me to fall.
>
> With forbidden pleasures should this vain world charm,
> Or its tempting treasures spread to work me harm,
> Bring to my remembrance sad Gethsemane,
> Or, in darker semblance, cross-crowned Calvary.
>
> Should Thy mercy send me sorrow, toil and woe,
> Or should pain attend me on my path below,

Grant that I may never fail Thy hand to see;
Grant that I may ever cast my care on Thee.

If with sore affliction thou in love chastise,
pour thy benediction on the sacrifice:
then upon the altar freely offered up,
though the flesh may falter, faith shall drink the cup.

When my last hour cometh, fraught with strife and pain,
When my dust returneth to the dust again,
On Thy truth relying, through that mortal strife,
Jesus, take me, dying, to eternal life.[55]

An understanding of the historical and biographical background of this hymn contributes to an interpretation of what the hymn says and how it says it. Some insight into the biblical, theological, and literary thinking of James Montgomery (1771–1854) is gained by knowing that he spent his early life in the home of a Moravian Brethren pastor and missionary to the West Indies and that he flourished in the early years of the Romantic movement. These immediate and larger contexts are reflected in the devotional and evangelical nature of many of his hymns. Erik Routley regarded Montgomery as "the typical English hymnwriter" of the nineteenth century and "the greatest of Christian lay hymnwriters." From a writer about hymns, Montgomery's introductory essay to *The Christian Psalmist* is thought to be the first work in hymnology by an English author and a work that J. R. Watson considers "the finest essay that has ever been written on hymns."[56]

The sociocultural context of Montgomery's British Isles in 1834 was characterized by the nineteenth-century Romantic movement in the arts with its emphasis on subjective, personal, and emotional qualities as in the poetry of William Wordsworth, Samuel Taylor Coleridge, and the continued influence of Lord Byron, Percy Bysshe Shelley, and John Keats; in the paintings of Joseph Mallord William Turner and John Constable; and in the continued popularity of the novels of Sir Walter Scott.

In 1834, at the time of the writing of this hymn, the British Isles were still in a time of domestic reform and a time of trial and testing in many areas. There had been improvements in criminal law relating to severity (more than two hundred offenses prescribed the death penalty), and reforms had been enacted allowing wage workers to organize and receive reasonable hours and proper wages. Though slave trade in Great Britain had been abolished in 1807, the law of 1834 decreed that living slaves be apprenticed and gradually freed and descendants be born free. The Poor Law of 1834 sought to correct abuses of the system by forbidding able-bodied persons to receive aid except in poor houses and allowed them to find work in other communities. It was in this context that Montgomery as a newspaper editor addressed humanitarian causes, including the abolishment of slavery and child labor, as well as being a prolific hymn writer and significant hymnologist, poet, reviewer, lecturer on poetry in Sheffield and in London at the Royal Institution, critic, and a person committed to the Bible Society and Foreign Missions.

Some appreciation of the hymn tune is gained from knowing that Ralph Vaughan Williams (1872–1958), composer of KING'S WESTON, was a major figure in twentieth-century music and is known for his composition, conducting, lecturing, collecting, and editing. His compositions include symphonies, chamber music, opera, choral music, and film scores. He conducted the performances of many of his compositions and was conductor at the Leith Hill Music Festival. He gave lectures in England and America. He traveled the English countryside collecting English folk music and used some of those melodies in his own compositions. This interest also influenced him as musical editor of *The English Hymnal* and can be seen in his hymn tune KING'S WESTON.

The rich biblical allusions of Montgomery's text refer to the trial of our Lord, to the "trial" and denial of Peter, and to our own times of testing and trial. The word and concept "trial" in this hymn refer both to the legal, courtroom context and to instances of trouble and hardship. Both meanings are common in the Bible and often share in the testing of one's ability to endure. The courtroom scenes with accusations, defense, and witnesses occur in the Psalms and the prophetic writings of Amos, Micah, Isaiah, and Jeremiah. The phrase "with a look recall" is an allusion to Luke 22:61-62 that records how Christ, at his trial, turned to look at Peter who, in his own trial and testing, had thrice denied Jesus. Christ's look not only recalled a weakness but also brought a gripping sense of shame, a wrenching guilt that Peter felt for his denial and that caused him to go out and weep bitterly. The clause "Jesus, plead for me" alludes in a general way to the numerous cries of believers for intercession. The phrases "With forbidden pleasures should this vain world charm" and "dust returneth to the dust" allude to Genesis 3. The clause "Grant that I may ever cast my care on Thee" is a clear reference to 1 Peter 5:7. The phrase "If with sore affliction thou in love chastise" draws on Hebrews 12:6, which is based on Proverbs 3:12 and

Revelation 3:19. The phrase "the sacrifice: then upon the altar freely offered up" might suggest Genesis 22 with Abraham's willingness to freely offer his own son and the presage of Christ's sacrificial death. Montgomery calls forth the pivotal event of biblical and human history with biblical references to "Gethsemane," "drink the cup" (Matt 26:39, 42, and 44), and "Calvary" (Luke 23:33 KJV), bringing into focus the self-emptying (*kenosis*) of Christ (Phil 2:58) and his sacrificial death for the sins of humanity, a central tenant of the Christian faith.

The biblical allusions and references call forth the theological doctrine of Christ's redeeming act and of his intercession for humanity. The allusions are to Jesus's saving act on "cross-crowned Calvary" and to Jesus as our advocate: "he ever liveth to make intercession" (Heb 7:25), "to appear in the presence of the Father for us" (Heb 9:24), an "Advocate with the Father, Jesus Christ the righteous" (1 John 2:1). The anxiety of possible "denial," "waver," and "fall" are not here a confession but a plea for intercession and deliverance from these. While there may not be here James's perspective, "Consider it all joy, my brethren, when you encounter various trials . . ." (Jas 1:2), there is the acknowledgment that trial and testing are borne out of God's love, "knowing that the testing of your faith produces endurance. And let endurance have its perfect result, so that you may be perfect and complete, lacking in nothing" (Jas 1:3-4).

There is also here a theology of prayer. The hymn is a prayer, and each stanza centers on a verb or entreaty—"plead for me," "with a look recall," "bring to my remembrance," "Grant that I may never fail Thy hand to see; Grant that I may ever cast my care on Thee," "pour thy benediction on the sacrifice," and "take me, dying, to eternal life." J. R. Watson opines that "Montgomery is the greatest hymn-writer on the difficult subject of prayer."[57] He is the author of some of the great prayers in hymnody.[58]

The biblical theology of the hymn makes it appropriate in numerous liturgical contexts, especially as part of confession in public liturgy or in private meditation in Lent and other times of penance and renewal. It would serve well as the conclusion of a sermon on temptation and intercession. Liturgical readings of any of the biblical passages referred to in the hymn may make appropriate the singing of the hymn. The corporate and private acknowledging that hours of trial and temptation are possibilities in our nature may serve to call the Christian to deeper discipleship, evangelism, and ministry to others, which are all part of the historical and etymological meaning of liturgy.[59]

The literary expressions of the biblical, theological, and liturgical content of the hymn are achieved through imaginative, creative language that shapes words, sounds, meanings, patterns of rhyme, meter, rhythm, tones, imagery, ideas, and allusions that help worshipers express their thoughts and feelings in ways that soar above discursive prose. The adjectives are carefully chosen and powerfully descriptive: "base denial," "forbidden pleasures," "tempting treasures," "sore affliction," "sad Gethsemane," and "cross-crowned Calvary." The mood of entreaty is heightened by the rhythm and frequency of the rhyme scheme—by the three-fold anaphora of "or" to enumerate the extremes of temptation and the pleading anaphora of "Grant" as well as the concluding pair of "when" and its ring of finality. The five-fold alliteration in the phrase "Nor for fear or favor suffer me to fall" and its contrast of "fear" and "favor" form a powerful prayer for deliverance from both extremes. The three-fold alliteration and the paradox in "though the faith may falter, faith shall drink the cup" is a beautiful inversion of "I do believe; help my unbelief" in Mark 9:24. The second and third stanzas form something of an extended antistrophe to the ideas of "fear" and "favor," developing first the second threat of "favor" in the lines "With forbidden pleasures would this vain world charm, / Or its sordid treasures spread to work me harm," immediately pitted against the reminders of "sad Gethsemane" and "in darker semblance, cross-crowned Calvary." The stanzas that follow develop the first threat of "fear" in the words, "sorrow, toil and woe," "pain," "sore affliction," "my last hour," "strife and pain." The closing paradoxical plea of "Lord, receive me, dying, to eternal life" is a fitting conclusion to the hymn.

Ralph Vaughan Williams's KING'S WESTON is a worthy musical undergirding of the literary expressions of the biblical, theological, and liturgical content of the hymn. The simple, unison, sequential, plaintive, folk-like melody with its repetitive rhythm is appropriate for the entreaty of this text. The rising melodic line in the third phrase, its transition to the dominant of the relative major, and the climax at the beginning of the fourth phrase with its "reversal" of the rhythm and melodic direction all match precisely the mood and meaning of the text in each stanza. From that apex, the melodic line descends in resignation again to its lowest pitch level. The melody is supported by interesting harmonic progressions, a harmonic rhythm that changes almost every beat, and non-chord tones in every measure, especially the effective passing and double passing tones.

As with any hymn, attention must be given to the practical aspects of selecting and singing the hymn. The distinctive use of Scripture and theological concepts of this hymn would be ill-served without careful consideration of placement in the liturgy. The congregation should be carefully prepared for a meaningful singing of the hymn. A sharing of some of the information given in this summary prior to singing could be ten minutes well spent before the service or in the service—not only as preparation but also as an act of worship itself. Each of the five stanzas printed here calls for some variety in singing, though the third and fourth stanzas are similar in idea. The hymn is decidedly subjective (thirteen personal pronouns) and may well be sung as a solo. With proper preparation, a solo singing of the hymn could be more "congregational" than some thoughtless singing by the congregation. (See Figure 24.)

Hymns such as those discussed in this chapter call for a comprehensive and integrated hermeneutics that contributes to an understanding of the polyphony of facets in fine hymnody, to an ever increasing appreciation of fine hymnody, to a broader and more objective evaluation of hymns, and to a more sensitive experience of hymn singing.

Figure 24. Words: "In the Hour of Trial," James Montgomery (1771–1854). Music: KING'S WESTON, Ralph Vaughan Williams (1925). All rights reserved. Used by permission.

Notes

1. J. R. Watson, *The English Hymn: A Critical and Historical Study* (Oxford: Clarendon Press, 1997) 41.

2. See Anna Tomasino, *Music and Culture* (Burnt Mill, Harlow, Essex, England: Longman, 2005); Jeff Todd Titon (gen ed.), James T. Koetting, David P. McAllester, David B. Reck, and Mark Slobin, *Worlds of Music: An Introduction to the Music of the World's People* (New York and London: Schirmer Books and Collier Macmillan Publishers, 1984); and Susan S. Tamke, *Make a Joyful Noise Unto the Lord: Hymns as a Reflection of Victorian Social Attitudes* (Athens: Ohio University Press, 1978).

3. Amos Niven Wilder, *Theopoetic: Theology and the Religious Imagination* (Philadelphia: Fortress Press, 1976) 4.

4. Ibid., 2.

5. Ibid., 27.

6. Will and Ariel Durant, *Our Oriental Heritage* (New York: Simon and Schuster, 1954) 12.

7. Will and Ariel Durant, *The Lessons of History* (New York: Simon and Schuster, 1968) 11–12.

8. Paul Henry Lang, *Music in Western Civilization* (New York: W. W. Norton and Company, Inc., 1941) xxii.

9. Donald Grout, *A Short History of Opera* (New York & London: Columbia University Press, 1965) preface, xi.

10. T. S. Eliot, "Tradition and the Individual Talent," in *The Sacred Wood: Essays on Poetry and Criticism* (New York: Barnes and Noble, 1920) 49–50.

11. E.g., Louis F. Benson, *The English Hymn* and his *The Hymnody of the Christian Church*; Harry Eskew and Hugh T. McElrath, *Sing with Understanding: An Introduction to Christian Hymnody*; William Jensen Reynolds, Milburn Price, and David Music, *A Survey of Christian Hymnody*; Albert Edward Bailey, *The Gospel in Hymns: Backgrounds and Interpretations*; F. J. Gillman, *The Evolution of the English Hymn*; A. S. Gregory, *Praises with Understanding*; Samuel Willoughby Duffield, *English Hymns: Their Authors and History*. Listed here and in the following notes are only a few examples of an enormous body of works in the various categories. The full bibliographic information on each of the works referred to in this section is found in the bibliography.

12. E.g., J. R. Watson, *The English Hymn: A Critical and Historical Study;* Erik Routley, *The Music of Christian Hymnody: A Study of the Development of the Hymn Tune since the Reformation, with Special Reference to English Protestantism*; Friedrich Blume, *Protestant Church Music; A History*; Leonard Ellinwood, *The History of American Church Music*; Robert Stevenson, *Protestant Church Music in America*; and Austin C. Lovelace, *The Anatomy of Hymnody*.

13. E.g., Carlton R.Young, *My Great Redeemer's Praise: An Introduction to Christian Hymns*; Donald P. Hustad, *Jubilate! Church Music in the Evangelical Tradition*.

14. E.g., *The Canterbury Dictionary of Hymnology* and the *Dictionary of North American Hymnology*.

15. E.g., *The New Harvard Dictionary of Music; Die Musik in Geschichte und Gegenwart;* and http://www.grovemusic.com; *Encyclopædia Britannica* Online, http://www.britannica.com.

16. E.g., *The Hymn*, which is the journal of The Hymn Society in the United States and Canada; *The Hymn Society of Great Britain and Canada Bulletin;* and the *Internationalen Arbeitsgemeinschaft für Hymnologie Bulletin.*

17. E.g., Paul Westermeyer, *Te Deum: The Church and Music;* Andrew Wilson-Dickson, *The Story of Christian Music from Gregorian Chant to Black Gospel: An Illustrated Guide to All the Major Traditions of Music in Worship.*

18. E.g., Frank Baker, *Charles Wesley's Verse;* Bernard L. Manning, *The Hymns of Wesley and Watts;* Amelia Heber, *The Life of Reginald Heber,* D.D.; Bill Hutchings, *The Poetry of William Cowper.*

19. E.g., Robin A. Leaver and James H. Litton, eds., *Duty and Delight: Routley Remembered.*

20. E.g., The Hymn Society in the United States and Canada, The Hymn Society of Great Britain and Canada, and the Internationalen Arbeitsgemeinschaft für Hymnologie.

21. Regional accrediting agencies and the Association of Theological Schools evaluate university and seminary programs with courses devoted to hymnology.

22. E.g., Philipp Wachernagel, *Das deutsche Kirchenlied von der ältesten Zeit bis zum Anfang des 17. Jahrhundert;* Johannes Zahn, *Die Melodien der deutschen evangelischen Kirchenlieder;* and Nicholas Temperley, *The Hymn Tune Index: A Census of English-language Hymn Tunes in Printed Sources from 1535 to 1820.*

23. E.g., Katharine Smith Diehl, *Hymns and Tunes: An Index;* Thomas B. McDormand and Frederic S. Crossman, *Judson Concordance to Hymns.*

24. E.g., *The Canterbury Dictionary of Hymnology,* http://www.hymnology.co.uk/; the *Dictionary of North American Hymnology;* the *Hymn Tune Index* http://hymntune.music.uiuc.edu and http://hymntune.library.uiuc.edu/hti1/default.asp; and Hymnary, http://www.hymnary.org/.

25. E.g., Peter N. Stearns, *The Encyclopedia of World History,* and Neville Williams, *Chronology of the Modern World 1763 to the Present Time.*

26. Gustave Reese, *Music in the Renaissance,* rev. ed. (New York: W. W. Norton & Company, Inc., 1959) 68.

27. Ibid.

28. E.g., David Hargreaves and Adrian North, *The Social and Applied Psychology of Music* (Oxford: Oxford University Press, 2008); John A. Sloboda and Patrik N. Juslin, "Psychological Perspectives on Music and Emotion," in *Music and Emotion: Theory and Research,* ed. Patrik N. Juslin and John A. Sloboda (Oxford: Oxford University Press, 2001); Jeff Todd Titon, James T. Koetting, David P. McAllester, David B. Reck, and Mark Slobin, *Worlds of Music: An Introduction to the Music of the World's People* (New York and London: Schirmer Books and Collier Macmillan Publishers, 1984); Paul R. Farnsworth, *The Social Psychology of Music* (New York: Holt, Rinehart and Winston, 1970); and Everett Helm, *Music and Tomorrow's Public: An Intercultural Survey* (New York: Heinrichshofen Edition, 1981).

29. The impact that the music and texts (translated and untranslated) from other cultures has had on hymnody is significant and growing. It is a complex phenomenon, and the few examples that follow only hint at the rich diversity.

30. *The United Methodist Hymnal* (1989) includes 26 traditional hymns, melodies, and prayers from 16 non-European and non-North American countries and includes in its *Companion to the Methodist Hymnal* sections that discuss "Asian American Hymns" and "Hispanic American Hymns."

31. Carlton Young, ed., *Companion to the United Methodist Hymnal* (Nashville: Abingdon Press, 1993) 564.

32. *United Methodist Hymnal* (Nashville: The United Methodist Publishing House, 1989) 356.

33. *Celebrating Grace* (Macon GA: Celebrating Grace, Inc., 2010) 265.

34. *United Methodist Hymnal,* 437.

35. James Weldon Johnson's "O Black and Unknown Bards" is an inspiring poem about those who wrote the powerful and beautiful words and music of the Afro-American spirituals.

36. See below for comments on shaped-note singing.

37. In Diana Sanchez, ed., *The Hymns of the United Methodist Hymnal (1989)* (Nashville: Abingdon Press, 1989) 161.

38. The text is discussed in chapter 4.

39. One perceptive study of hymnody that gives attention to the larger historical context is Henry Bett, *The Hymns of Methodism*, 3rd ed., rev., recast, and greatly enlarged (London: The Epworth Press, 1913, 1945), which devotes a chapter to "The Hymns and Contemporary Events."

40. Timothy Dudley-Smith, "What Can a Hymn Writer Learn from a Lyricist? A Review and Reflection on Sondheim's Finishing the Hat," *The Hymn Society Bulletin* 19/11 (July 2011): 450; Stephen Sondheim, *Finishing the Hat: Collected Lyrics (1954–1981), with Attendant Comments, Principles, Heresies, Grudges, Whines and Anecdotes* (London: Virgin Books; New York: Alfrled A. Knopf, 2010).

41. T. S. Eliot, *On Poetry and Poets* (London: Faber, 1957) 30.

42. C. Michael Hawn, http://www.gbod.org/resources/history-of-hymns-god-created-heaven-and-earth. See also C. Michael Hawn's article "Global Hymnody" in the *Canterbury Dictionary of Hymnology*, http://www.hymnology.co.uk/g/global-hymnody. The SIL International (formerly the Summer Institute of Linguistics) website, http://www.sil.org, contains nearly 150 ethnomusicological monographs on specific cultural groups.

43. Erik Routley, *Hymns and Human Life* (London: John Murray, 1952) 288.

44. J. R. Watson, ed., *An Anthology of Hymns* (Oxford: Oxford University Press, 2002) vii.

45. William Saroyan, "Resurrection of a Life," from *Story*, ed. John Updike, in *The Best American Short Stories of the Century* (New York: Houghton Mifflin Company, 1999) 159–68.

46. Ibid., 165.

47. Ibid., 166.

48. Thomas H. Troeger, "Personal, Cultural and Theological Influences on the Language of Hymns and Worship," *The Hymn: A Journal of Congregational Song* 38/4 (October 1987): 14.

49. Ibid., 15.

50. J. R. Watson, *The English Hymn: A Critical and Historical Study* (Oxford: Oxford University Press, 1999) 346, 351.

51. Ibid., 4.

52. Simon Wright, "'Pale Green of the English Hymnal!'—A Centenary Retrospective," *Brio: Journal of the United Kingdom And Ireland Branch of the International Association of Music Libraries* 43/1, Archives and Documentation Centres (Spring/Summer 2006): 17–18. Edward Dent's quote is from Michael Kennedy, *A Catalogue of the Works of Ralph Vaughan Williams, 2nd ed.* (Oxford: Oxford University Press, 1996) 200.

53. J. Hawkins. *A General History of the Science and Practice of Music* (London, 1853; repr., New York: Dover Publications, 1963) 502.

54. Such as the one adapted from S. Stubbs in Routlely's *Rejoice in the Lord: A Hymn Companion to the Scriptures*, no. 102.

55. Altered, see http://www.hymnary.org/text/in_the_hour_of_trial.

56. J. R. Watson, *The English Hymn: A Critical and Historical Study* (Oxford: Clarendon Press, 1997) 305.

57. J. R. Watson, *The English Hymn: A Critical and Historical Study* (Oxford: Oxford University Press, 1999) 308.

58. His great hymn on prayer, "Prayer is the soul's sincere desire," concludes with the prayer, "O, thou by whom we come to God, The Life, the Truth, the Way, The path of prayer thyself hast trod: Lord teach us how to pray." Other prayer hymns include "Shepherd of souls, refresh and bless thy chosen pilgrim flock"; the stanza "Jesus, Lord, our Captain glorious" from "Praise the Lord through every nation"; "O Spirit of the living God"; "Lord, for ever at Thy side"; "O God, Thou art my God alone"; "Lord God, the Holy Ghost"; his prayer based on our Lord's prayer, "Our Heav'nly Father hear"; and his prayer hymn, "Lord, teach us how to pray aright."

59. The larger historical and etymological meaning of liturgy is discussed in more detail in chapter 4.

CHAPTER 8

Practice

The primary purposes of a holistic hermeneutics are to understand as thoroughly as possible the multiple and interrelated facets of hymnody and to interpret this understanding for those who use hymns. The goal is to help people realize as fully as possible the vast potentials of hymns in the various aspects of the Christian life. We sought to establish earlier[1] that those various aspects of the Christian life, the ministries of the individual Christian and the fellowship of Christian believers (the church), may, in their broadest possible classification, be grouped into four areas, each of which can be manifested in numerous ways: worship (private, family, and corporate/public), discipleship (growing in the Christian faith—prayer, Bible study, tenants of faith), proclamation (sharing the message of Christ), and service (ministering to the temporal needs of people). Hymns have played and must continue to play a major role in each of these aspects of the Christian life.

How the vast potentials of hymnody are to be realized in the ministries of the Christian church requires attention to matters that might be grouped under five broad headings: (1) commitment to helping individuals and churches realize the fullest potential of the hymn-singing experience; (2) education of the congregation to the importance, possibilities, and manner of hymn singing; (3) planning of worship and the choice of hymns and hymn tunes; (4) logistics and matters of physical facilities; and (5) performance, the actual singing and playing of hymns and hymn tunes giving attention to the tempo, dynamics, media, and phrasing. Erik Routley once suggested, "A hymn . . . is not really a good hymn until it has been well written, well chosen, and well sung."[2] In previous chapters, we have discussed the "well written" in terms of the biblical, theological, and liturgical contents and the literary and musical forms of expressing the contents. How the "well chosen" and "well sung" is achieved is the practical "voice" in the polyphonic hermeneutics.

Spiritual Commitment

Hymn singing is an intellectual, emotional, aesthetic, physical, social, but primarily spiritual experience. A sound practice of hymnody (writing, editing, compiling, interpreting, teaching, planning, selecting, leading, playing, reading, or singing hymns) must begin with the recognition that hymnody, at its core, is a spiritual experience. The most artistic, lively performance of a hymn absent a deep spiritual commitment to the divine purposes of hymnody is an empty achievement, "full of sound and fury, signifying nothing."[3]

The practical matters of hymnody are intricately intertwined and grow out of and express the maturing spiritual life of individuals and congregations. Paul admonished the early Christians to "be filled with the Spirit, speaking to one another in psalms and hymns and spiritual songs, singing and making melody with your heart to the Lord; always giving thanks for all things in the name of our Lord Jesus Christ to God, even the Father" (Eph 5:18-19). Paul seems here to be referring to the use of hymns not only in acts of worship, nor perhaps even in "teaching and admonishing" (Col 3:16), but as part of the everyday lives of spirit-filled believers. Also, Paul uses the verbs "speaking" (λαλοῦντες) and "singing" (ᾄδοντες) perhaps suggesting that, in the context of everyday life, one might very well speak (talk to, tell, converse with) fellow believers using the texts of psalms, hymns, or spiritual songs. One certainly might sing a hymn of praise and make melody in the context of daily life, but it was likely possible in Paul's day, as in our own day, that one can be more involved in the singing and making melody than in the message and meaning of the text.

Paul affirmed his own commitment to pray and sing with the spirit: "I will pray with the spirit and I will pray with the mind also; I will sing with the spirit and I will sing with the mind also" (1 Cor 14:15). By capitalization, versions of Scriptures make a distinction between "be filled with the Spirit" and "I will pray with the spirit . . . and sing with the spirit."[4] The former refers to the Holy Spirit and the latter refers to the human spirit—not simply human faculty but one's deepest religious thoughts, feelings, and moral conscience, or "the divine *pneuma* which dwells in the baptized believer and enables him to pray."[5] In both senses, hymnody is a spiritual experience, a matter related to the Holy Spirit and to the Christian's spiritual nature or what the Bible often refers to as the heart,[6] the seat of the deepest religious thoughts, feelings, and moral conscience. Christ also declared that "the true worshipers will worship the Father in spirit and truth; for such people the Father seeks to be His worshipers" (John 4:23).

John Wesley, in his seven directions for singing hymns, emphasized that hymn singing is a spiritual experience.

> Above all sing spiritually. Have an eye to God in every word you sing. Aim at pleasing Him more than yourself, or any other creature. In order to [do] this attend strictly to the sense of what you sing, and see that your Heart is not carried away with the sound, but offered to God continually; so shall your singing be such as the Lord will approve of here, and reward [you] when he cometh in the clouds of heaven.[7]

Hymnody, at its root and core, is a matter of the "heart," a spiritual experience, and the best hope for realizing the potentials of hymnody is from the spiritually mature. George Herbert spoke of this in his lines from "A True Hymn": "The fineness which a hymn or psalm affords, / Is, when the soul unto the lines accords."

Hymn singing is an opportunity for obeying what Christ identified as the first and great commandment, "you shall love the Lord your God with all your heart, and with all your soul, and with all your mind, and with all your strength" (Mark 12:30). True devotion and deep commitment to the real purposes of hymnody are primary, practical prerequisites to hymn singing.

There is the potential of a beautifully ever-increasing cycle for maturing Christians in their experience with fine hymns. The practical matters of commitment, education, planning, logistics, and performance are intricately intertwined and grow out of and express the maturing spiritual lives of individuals and congregations. Those who have truly experienced hymns, studied hymns, enjoyed hymns are those who seem most devoted to the most meaningful, practical aspects of true hymn singing—for themselves and for others. This may be most obvious in corporate worship, but it often begins in the most private contexts. Those most committed to hymns, those who have experienced the multiple facets of this basic and familiar form of Christian literature, must be sensitive to those who have less experience with and less appreciation of hymns, those who rarely or never experience any significant degree of the breadth or depth of hymns.

We must confess, to our disappointment, that hymns are not always appreciated even by some of the spiritually mature, some whom we would most expect, certainly hope, to share our appreciation. One of these, C. S. Lewis, has given us a crucial lesson regarding the practice of hymn singing. In one of his letters, he wrote, "I naturally loathe nearly all hymns; the face and life of the charwoman in the next pew who revels in them, teach me that good taste in poetry and music are not necessary to salvation."[8] In his essays on theology and ethics, Lewis later iterated his conviction.

> When I first became a Christian, about fourteen years ago, . . . I disliked very much their hymns, which I considered to be a fifth-rate poems set to sixth-rate music. But as I went on I saw the great merit of it. . . . I realized that the hymns (which were just sixth-rate music) were, nevertheless, being sung with devotion and benefit by an old saint in elastic-side boots in the opposite pew, and then you realize that you aren't fit to clean those boots. It gets you out of your solitary conceit.[9]

Lewis's essay, "On Church Music" in *Christian Reflections*, is a familiar and powerful lesson for both those who most appreciate hymns and for those who have little or no appreciation at all. With keen insight, he suggests, "the problem is never a merely musical one."

> There are two musical situations on which I think we can be confident that a blessing rests. One is where a priest or an organist, himself a man of trained and delicate taste, humbly and charitably sacrifices his own (aesthetically right) desires and gives the people humbler and coarser fare than he would wish, in a belief (even, as it may be, the erroneous belief) that he can thus bring them to God. The other is where the stupid and unmusical layman humbly and patiently, and above all silently, listens to music which he cannot, or cannot fully, appreciate, in the belief that it somehow glorifies God, and that if it does not edify him this must be his own defect. Neither such a High Brow nor such a Low Brow can be far out of the way. To both, Church Music will have been a means of grace: not the music they have liked, but the music they have disliked. They have both offered, sacrificed, their taste in the fullest sense. But where the opposite situation arises, where the musician is filled with the pride of skill or the virus of emulation and looks with contempt on the unappreciative congregation, or where the unmusical, complacently entrenched in their own ignorance and conservatism, look with the restless and resentful hostility of an inferiority complex on all who would try to improve their taste—there, we

may be sure, all that both offer is unblessed and the spirit that moves them is not the Holy Ghost.[10]

It is worth emphasizing Lewis's observation, "the problem is never a merely musical one. . . . Discrepancies of taste and capacity will, indeed, provide matter for mutual charity and humility."[11] A practical solution is often one of education.

Education

Effective congregational singing is greatly enhanced when ministers and congregants understand the importance, the possibilities, the manner, and the joy of meaningful hymn singing. The congregation is obviously not a choral society, but given the profound potentials of hymn singing, the popularity of hymn singing, and the amount of time given in most services to hymn singing, more must be done in the education of leaders in the choice of hymns and in the education of people for the singing of hymns.

Due to an all too prevalent neglect of effective music and worship education of ministers and congregations, there has frequently been a lamentable poverty where, given the wealth of texts and tunes, there should be a rich experience. Hymn texts and tunes are too often chosen (and consequently sung) out of the ignorance or apathy of worship leaders. Too often there has been the assumption that congregations cannot really sing hymns intelligently and sensitively. The clergy as well as church musicians need to be knowledgeable about the multiple and interrelated dimensions of hymnody and, to some limited degree, even "skilled" in the use of music in the church.

Biblical scholars, sound theologians, literary critics, trained liturgists, skilled musicians, and concerned worshipers have noted the current crisis of congregational singing. Beginning especially in the last decades of the twentieth century, those who by default most strongly influenced church music (editors, pastors, and "musicians") became committed to a type of congregational song that is more "contemporary" and more immediately appealing than the way in which some traditional hymns are sung. There has rushed into the lamentable vacuum texts and music that often have more immediate appeal than the more worthy texts and tunes poorly sung by people who for years have been uninformed of their truth and beauty.

This seems to have happened in some cases as a result of poor training provided by those of us in theological education; of careless worship planning that led admittedly to uninteresting and meaningless singing of a relatively limited and overused number of traditional hymns; of the serious weakening of music education in many public schools and churches; and of radically changing social contexts in which new forms of entertainment and more passive types of music enticed people to become less aware of the importance of profound biblical teachings, insightful theological concepts, meaningful liturgical contexts, beautiful literary expressions, and truly significant musical settings. Many children, youth, and even adults have consequently inherited texts and music that are actually more temporary than contemporary, leaving them with the concept of a shallow and faddish Christian faith.

J. R. Watson considers that there is much in our present culture to "suggest that the older generations now living may well be the last for whom the traditional hymn is an integral part of their emotional and spiritual culture. The English hymn is in danger of becoming a subject for academic study rather than a living form of worship."[12] He wrote his book, *The English Hymn*, because he felt bound to record his sense of the English hymn "before it disappears in the name of progress."[13] We must avoid this danger, not for the sake of the great tradition of hymnody but because of what fine hymnody can continue to provide to individual Christians, to the Christian church, and to those who will or should become part of the church. Church music must not succumb to uninteresting and meaningless singing of a limited repertoire of either traditional or contemporary hymns and must not abandon the great practice of God's people expressing the profound truths of the Christian faith and praising God through fine hymns of every era and style.

Some aspects of contemporary texts and tunes for congregational singing are admirable and must not only be retained but also be replicated. There is a freshness to much of the current music and a new sense of involvement. There are traditional texts and tunes for congregational singing that are less than worthy and should probably be retired. There are often texts and tunes that are too stale and staid to offer inspiration for mental or spiritual involvement. The issue is not really "traditional" or "contemporary," but the presence of biblical theology, liturgical appropriateness, literary and musical value, and spiritual maturity in the people. A significant step toward avoiding the weakness and enhancing the strengths is in education.

Those who create the hymns, edit them, choose them, sing them, and experience them in many ways must not let congregational singing continue to slip into the abyss of mediocrity. Fine hymnody can be, must be, relevant, "contemporary," and profoundly meaningful and involving. The hope for hymnody rests in those who value profound biblical teachings, insightful theological concepts, meaningful liturgical contexts, beautiful literary expressions, and truly significant musical settings of fine hymnody of every era. The realization of those values rests largely on leaders who cultivate a congregation's ever-deepening spiritual life, who have a commitment to a continuing education, who are in a constant pursuit of fine new hymns from the past and the present to express the faith, and who are insistent that the singing of hymns be interesting, involving, relevant, and meaningful with the expressed purpose of deepening and broadening the ministries of worship, discipleship, evangelism, and service.

For those who are most aware and seeking, the finest hymns display more and more truth and appreciation each time they are sung. The finest texts and music continually stimulate new thoughts and feelings as Christians mature and as new circumstances and contexts provide new perspectives. Church leaders must supply resources, opportunities, and encouragement for believers to develop continually in spiritual maturity, in a deepened sensitivity, and in a better understanding and skill in the use of the hymns and texts. With good guidance by church leaders and with diligent commitment of church members, this enriching cycle can be set in motion.

The finest education in hymnody often comes through providing meaningful experiences of hymn singing—fine texts and tunes chosen prayerfully and carefully, well sung in the context of truly spiritual worship services.[14] As organists must understand music theory, registration, fingering, and pedaling, and possess a wealth of skills to interpret music for the listeners; as pastors should understand pastoral ministry, some Greek and Hebrew, and principles of homiletics, and possess skills of interpreting Scripture; as choir masters must understand music theory and vocal technique, and possess skills of conducting and interpreting the music, so must those responsible for congregational singing possess a holistic understanding of hymns, a comprehensive and integrated hermeneutics of the literature of their field. Those responsible for the singing of hymns will often broaden and deepen a congregation's understanding and appreciation of hymns more by interpreting them in the singing than by explaining the intricacies of all the facets. Opportunities should be provided regularly for the congregation to hear the sensitive interpretations of hymns by solo, ensemble, or choral singing or certain verses of hymns, as well as opportunities, especially for those interested, for deeper study. For some congregants, hearing a sensitive interpretation of a verse may encourage more careful singing.

Encouragement should be made for worshipers to read or sing hymns in their home, especially ones that will be sung the following Sundays. Public worship is often less meaningful than it should be because private worship is absent. The individual Christian's private use of hymns in devotion should be marked by a personal, prayerful, and careful choice of hymns; by the best possible "performance" of the hymn (even if only remembered silently or read silently or aloud, or sung even by a less than musical person); by some effort to probe more deeply into the meaning of the hymn; and by some attention to the physical surroundings, if nothing more than an effort to remove distractions.

The reading and singing of hymns in family and private worship will not only enrich family and private worship but will also contribute immeasurably to public worship. Many of the texts hold profound truths that require time for careful reading, rereading, and true meditation. It is unfortunate that the tune often dominates the text (with some hymn writers, this may not be unfortunate), and a person may become more involved in the act of singing than in what is sung and to whom it is sung. In both private and congregational worship, the music/text issue is compounded in many hymnals by the interlinear placement of the hymn texts. This aids in the singing of texts but frequently hampers the understanding of their biblical and theological truths and often destroys an appreciation of many literary aspects of the hymn as poetry. Seeing the hymn in poetic form and reading it aloud as poetry often contribute much to the understanding and improve meaningful singing. Both the musical and literary experiences can contribute to the spiritual experience. The reverse is profoundly true. A fuller understanding of the text (including its literary, biblical, theological, liturgical dimensions) can often come in times of home and private devotion and will contribute to an understanding of what the music should be and how it should be performed—all as expressions of the spiritual experience.

The multiple facets of hymns are rich sources for sermon illustrations. Entire worship services can incorporate hymns either following the liturgy[15] or built around certain themes or biblical passages. From those experiences there frequently comes a willingness or even desire to know more about hymns. The leadership should then provide occasions for meaningful instruction about hymns such as special study sessions, congregational rehearsals (prior to services or as special services), graded choirs, Sunday school devotionals, prayer services, fifth Sunday evening sings, and hymn festivals.

Many congregants have little understanding about their hymnal—neither the information that usually appears on the page nor the hymnal indexes. Too few have been challenged to consider the biblical basis, theological meanings, literary beauty, liturgical significance, historical context, or biographical backgrounds of hymns. Section headings to portions of the worship service and texts printed in the order of worship may help guide worshipers, and labeling hymns according to their purpose in the service (hymn of adoration, confession, proclamation, service, prayer, intercession, or petition) may contribute to more meaningful experiences. Occasionally, a sentence or Scripture before the listing of a hymn calls attention to its biblical basis, meaning, and purpose. Directions might be printed in orders of service for the singing by stanzas—solo, choir, congregation, men, women, unison, or in parts. This is not for some clever "sing-along" but should serve to undergird the meanings, to provide opportunities for listening, and to realize more fully the wealth of experiences in hymn singing. Articles in the church paper can sometimes be used as effective teaching. An attractive, prominently located hymn bulletin board or library display window can be used to inform people. A sermon or series of sermons can make extensive use of hymn texts to present theological concepts and doctrinal beliefs and provide interesting illustrations and poetry. The full text or the number of a hymn might be suggested for meditation and preparation for the service. Surveys should be made from time to time to determine which hymns are meaningful to the congregation and why. Fresh, new texts or tunes may be introduced to congregations through a hymn-of-the-month plan where information can be shared with graded choirs and the congregation. Sometimes new meanings of hymns can be discovered by singing them to new tunes, through reharmonizations, by varying the tempo and rhythm, and by different media including "hymn concertatos."[16] Some hymns or groups of hymns can be arranged for congregation, choir, soloists, small ensembles, organ, and instruments.

Perhaps what is most important for the future of meaningful hymnody is that children and young people have the opportunity to be meaningfully involved with fine hymns and tunes.[17] Sunday schools, childrens' choirs, youth organizations, and other educational activities provide numerous opportunities for the involvement of children and youth. Ballad hymns can be used in conjunction with Bible stories, and well-done hymn dramatizations and monologues can be effective with children and youth. Some hymnals include an "Index of Hymns for use with Children."[18]

Most Christian congregations are accustomed to exhortation and to exegesis of Scripture and generally receptive to sermonic explanations and challenges. Church leaders must find convincing, interesting, and relevant ways of educating those in their care to the importance, the possibilities, the manner, and the joy of meaningful hymn singing that engages the heart, soul, mind, and body.

Planning

For a hymn to be truly well chosen for worship,[19] there must be thoughtful, prayerful consideration of a complex of interrelated matters. John D. Witvliet wrote of the "important and terrifying priestly task" of choosing hymns, placing on the lips of worshipers words and "the melodies that interpret those words and give them affective shape."[20] Choosing hymns should involve all worship leaders and be done far enough in advance for music leaders to prepare accompaniments and choral presentation, and for the development of devotional materials to be used by families in preparation for worship.[21]

In choosing hymns for worship (or for any ministry of the church), consideration should be given to the larger biblical, theological content of the text; to the original historical and cultural context of the hymn; to the literary quality of the texts; to the musical quality of the tune; and to the relationship of the tune to the text. This concern for quality is not simply an aesthetic consideration. It is a concern for what most effectively expresses thoughts and feelings to and for the congregation and will do so over a long period. Consideration should be given to the liturgical appropriateness in the progression of revelation, adoration, conviction, confession, absolution, thanksgiving, proclamation, affirmation, call, and dedication and to how each hymn relates to the Scripture readings, sermon, and other hymns. Considerations for the season of the year, the church year, and the time of day are not simply liturgical considerations; they are practical. Activities, physical vitality, attitudes, and moods of people prior to worship influence their receptivity and involvement in a whole range of matters. The time of day may affect "mundane" musical matters of range, tessitura, and tempi.

The choice of hymn tunes should consider the sequence and relationship of such musical matters as keys, meters, tempi (within stanzas, between stanzas, and between hymns), styles, moods, ranges, tessituras, textures, and media (vocal and instrumental). These matters may be subtle, and the perceptions of the flow of many musical aspects will probably be subliminal, but they are potentially significant. Preparation may involve the use of available resources such as scriptural indexes, topical indexes, lectionaries, and Internet resources.[22]

The acoustics, size, and configuration of the room should be considered carefully in choosing the tune as well as the media. Consideration should be given to choosing the best media (choir, congregation, men, women, instruments) for each of the various stanzas in the acoustical environment. The acoustics are significant determinants of tempo and volume in the singing of hymns. It is critical that whatever distracts from the quality of sound be minimized and whatever enhances the sound be maximized. This is important not simply for the quality of sound itself but also for what acoustics contribute to helping worshipers feel comfortable and supported.

Making choices in these interrelated matters is especially complicated when trying to give consideration to the possible appreciation, understanding, and capabilities that a diverse congregation may have for any or all of the matters. This is further compounded when there is something of a different congregation each week and a concern for guiding congregations into a constantly developing maturity in their appreciation, understanding, and capabilities. This usually means that some variety must be considered in each service and in services over time. To the extent possible, consideration should be given to the makeup (age, cultural backgrounds) of the congregation and of the presence of visitors and non-Christians in the service. Consideration should also be given to a balance of the familiar and the unfamiliar, the traditional and the new. Some thought should be devoted to the recentness and frequency of the use of texts and tunes not only to avoid overuse but also, by frequent enough use, to contribute to the understanding and appreciation of a growing body of hymns that are familiar and meaningful to the congregation.

Many of the considerations discussed here not only apply to worship but must also be given to the use of hymns in the ministries of discipleship, proclamation, and social service that may occur in places and times and with people very different from those of the ministry of worship. In every case, choices must be made prayerfully.

When choosing hymns for public worship, one would do well to bear in mind Erik Routley's glowing remarks about Benjamin Britten's use of congregational hymn singing in his opera, *Noye's Fludde*. In the most positive terms, Routley affirms the ideas that make the selection of hymns in this dramatic work "a sufficient education in how to choose hymns for public worship."

> A study of the use of these three hymns ["Lord Jesus, think on me," "Eternal Father, strong to save," and "The Spacious Firmament"] in *Noye's Fludde* is a sufficient education in how to choose hymns for public worship. Basically, and making every allowance for the need to get a sufficient number of hymns known to a congregation to make this possible, this is how hymns should be chosen: with a sensitive ear to their allusions (especially to cross-references like that to the flood in the first of these), a neighborly concern that they shall be practically singable, and a very careful use of the hymns that people regard as "their own," and that make it possible for them really to bring part of themselves into the drama of worship. A hymn is not "their own" until it is really well known, almost hackneyed. During the earlier stages a new hymn is part of the drama that is coming across from the pulpit-end of the church—when it is really a folk song, it is part of the drama that comes from the pew-end. That is the secret that ministers and directors of worship and organists must master before the choosing of hymns becomes a real part of the drama of worship.[23]

Routley says of this dramatic presentation of a single biblical story,

> . . . this is how to present the Bible, and it is therefore a pattern of how Protestant Bible-centered worship should be conceived. If we would preach, we would drive the Bible home into the real lives of the worshipers. Even if all we do is read the Bible rather than acting it, and expound it rather than put it on stage, the drama need never be absent. . . . the central genius of it is exactly what every worship director who knows his business has been trying to apply through all the generations of Protestantism.[24]

Logistics

For congregational singing to be most effective, it is important that proper attention be given to physical facilities such as lighting, air conditioning, seating, musical instruments, and sound system, and to the availability of hymnals and orders of worship. Some of these matters require attention just hours before the service. Other matters, such as acoustics, require attention in the earliest stages of architectural design. Properly prepared for, many of these long-term and more immediate matters should never cross the worshipers' minds, but the lack of proper attention to them can, unfortunately, be highly disruptive. Much has rightly been written on the acoustics of worship spaces because the suppression of unwanted sound and the enhancement of wanted sound are of great importance to effective congregational singing and to the entire worship experience.[25]

As much can be learned from Britten's opera, *Noye's Fludde*, about choosing of hymns, much can also be learned from Howard and Moretti's fascinating study, *Sound and Space in Renaissance Venice*,[26] about logistics and the vital, practical relationships among the areas of liturgy, architectural design, acoustics, and music in worship. We do well to give serious attention to the logistical matters regarding the visual, aural, artistic, and ritual facets of worship, the most basic act of the Christian faith.

Performance

For a hymn to be sung and played sensitively, consideration must be given to understanding the possibilities and limitations of the congregation regarding tempo, dynamics, phrasing, and media. The congregation is not a choir and cannot be expected to express the subtleties of music that characterize a fine performance. However, worshipers should not be denied the possibilities of deeper artistic and spiritual experiences and the intelligent and sensitive expression of the texts and music that are possible with the leadership of an accomplished organist and choir. The musical potential of most congregations is probably vastly underestimated or even grossly neglected to the great hindrance of their having a better understanding of textual meaning, of their experiencing literary and musical beauty more fully, and of their realizing a deeper meaning and even enjoyment from a more sensitive involvement in worship through hymn singing.

The vital musical elements of tempo, dynamics, phrasing, and media (timbre) are rarely explicitly indicated in hymnals and are left to the discretion of those who in some way plan, direct, or accompany the singing.[27] Much in these interpretive matters of "performance" is frequently assumed to be beyond the interest or abilities of congregations, and, consequently, congregations are denied a more meaningful experience with either the music or the text. It is strongly maintained here that much can and should be done in matters of interpretation that would contribute to the congregation's understanding, expression, and even enjoyment. This is not to claim that congregational singing is a "performance," nor to claim that congregations can or should be expected to sing as a finely rehearsed choir, but it is to insist that in the singing of meaningful texts set to music that has some artistic value, congregations, which often have some degree of aesthetic sophistication and, more important, some depth of Christian maturity, should be given more opportunities to express themselves more fully than is often the case.[28] This can often be achieved by the leadership of the organ and the choir, by careful attention to the selection of hymns and to the preparation of the worship space, and certainly by educating the congregation. Brief pre-service rehearsals of the congregation that focus, more by demonstration than by "lecture," on the tempo, dynamics, phrasing, media (congregation, men, women, solo, choir), and manner of singing (direct, responsorial, antiphonally) can create sensitivity to expressive singing, develop skills in appropriate singing to convey better the meaning of the hymn texts, and be enjoyable for the congregation. Training events especially for children and young people can be enjoyable experiences and contribute much to the experience of hymn singing.

The hymn tune shares some basic features with folk songs and even with some of the simpler strophic, syllabic, nineteenth-century art songs (the *Lied*). In these are possible models for interpreting the varieties of meanings in the stanzas of hymns. The renewed interest in folk and folk-like music in the mid-twentieth century and the singing of some performers and some groups offered, in various ways, models for congregational singing. The very "singableness" and freshness of the rhythms and melodies of these songs make them engaging. The strophic form, the ballad style, the solo singer, the repeated choruses or refrains giving opportunities of enjoyable participation, the light-hearted nature, and the possibility of identification with some of the incidences mentioned in the texts invite participation. All of these qualities of folk songs may, at certain times, be part of the singing of congregations.

These same qualities are evident in some of the great art songs. The most famous of the art song (*Lied*) composers was Franz Schubert, who composed numerous strophic and modified-strophic songs. Given the musicality of both Franz Schubert and the great baritone, Johann Michael Vogl, whom Schubert accompanied in singing his compositions, the stanzas or strophes of even Schubert's purely strophic *Lieder* were certainly not all sung in exactly the same way. Congregations and accompanists today are not expected to have the musical gifts or sensitivity of a Schubert or a Vogl, but the important biblical, theological, liturgical, and literary differences between the stanzas of many hymns require at least some musical differences in singing. Not to respond musically to the differences in and between stanzas is a violation of the meaning and mood of the text similar to reading mechanically and without expression. As Schubert did in his "modified strophic" songs, an organist, by slight changes in dynamics, tempo, phrasing, registration, and even changes in keys or modes, can help congregants express the important differences in the meanings of hymn stanzas.[29] There is much to commend the use of solo voices and choral singing for appropriate stanzas of hymns both to give the congregation the opportunity to listen to the text sung in expressive ways and to have a model of some of the musical dimensions that can be varied to express more clearly the meaning of the text.

Tempo

The important aspects of tempo and its modifications of ritard, accelerando, and rubato, as well as such related matters as tenuto and fermata are, if done at all in hymnody, usually matters of practice and tradition rather than a composer's markings. Vaughan Williams, musical editor of the 1906 *English Hymnal with Tunes*, considered that in his day, "The custom in English churches is to sing many hymns much too fast . . . . Metronome marks are added to each hymn, which, the editor believes, indicate the proper speed in a fairly large building with a congregation of average size."[30] However, the moods and meanings of texts require that tempos should not always be the same for every stanza of a hymn. Significant, even if very moderate changes in tempo might be made between stanzas or even within a stanza to convey meanings. Practice and tradition in hymn singing too often ignore these aspects, and congregations plod thoughtlessly through hymn tunes with little realization of what could and often should be done musically for the interpretation of the text. If done, these variations are usually conveyed to the congregation by the organist and choir. Sensitive interpretation in these matters requires skill and careful education of the congregation to heighten awareness. The purpose is not for musical accuracy or some aesthetic, "concert" experience; rather, the purpose is for the best possible understanding and expression of the text whatever the level of musicality of the congregation.

Dynamics

Dynamics, like tempo, are not usually indicated in hymnals and are matters of performance. While a congregation is not a skilled, rehearsed choir with capabilities of subtle dynamic gradations, it is capable of following the leadership of the organ and choir in performing or at least responding to certain appropriate degrees of dynamics that best interpret the text.

Phrasing

Phrasing is both a musical and textual matter and is perhaps best conveyed by the organist. Congregations that are truly sensitive to the meaning of the text are more inclined to observe the phrasing and breathing. Phrasing and breathing include attention to the textual phrase, the musical phrase, and the relationship between these. If congregational rehearsals are used as a special event or prior to a service, attention should be called to these matters of phrasing and breathing that make for the intelligent expression of texts. Enjambments of text are often obscured by the musical phrase or by the breath capacities of untrained singers. There are even larger, structural matters of phrasing—antecedent and consequent phrases, periods, and double periods, that may not be beyond the capacities of congregations.

Media and Timbre

The most obvious expressions of timbre or tone color are the media (congregation, choral, solo, men's voices, women's voices, organ with its varieties of registration, non-keyboard instruments, a cappella singing, etc.), but timbre also refers to range, tessitura, keys, and pronunciation. There are distinctive qualities regarding tone, timbre, or sound in the hymn text itself, and when the text is actually set to music and sung, the complexities are compounded—for good or for ill. The hymn tune and the singing of it may enhance, complement, distract from, or even contradict what the hymn writer intended when choosing certain words for their sounds in general and in rhyme in particular. Again, the congregation is not a choir, but some modifications of timbre at least by media may heighten sensitivity to the meaning of the text, provide appropriate variety in the hymn-singing experience, and encourage sensitive listening to the singing of others.

Antiphonal, Responsorial, and Direct Singing

The basic ways in which hymns and other liturgical texts may be sung or read are ancient and can today be profoundly important in expressing the texts. The "direct" method of performance (one person or group singing or reading the text without alternation) is the most basic and in the liturgies is seen most obviously in the medieval psalmody of Gregorian chant, with the cantor singing the Psalm verses. The basic "solo" idea was, of course, continued in the *Historia* of Schütz and in the cantatas, oratorios, and passion music of Bach and others. This "solo" manner of performance could be especially appropriate in hymnody for the narrative, "ballad-like" hymns discussed in chapter 5. Hymns that are cast in a narrative form, such as "While shepherds watched their flocks," and those written in the first person singular, such as "Come, O Thou traveler unknown," could be sung directly, at least in part, by a soloist. Hymns and stanzas in the form of a prayer or affirmation could be sung by the congregation or choir. Soloists, choir, or the congregation may perform a text "directly" when there is no response or antiphony.

Responsorial singing (one or more soloists or readers reading or singing and being responded to by the choral or congregational singing or reading of a refrain or response) can be an appropriate way to sing hymns that are written in a dialogical form such as "Art thou weary, art thou languid?" or "Watchman, tell us of the night." Antiphonal singing or reading (sung or read alternately by two halves of a choir or congregation) such as "What child is this?" is rooted in Old Testament worship and is a logical manner of expressing many texts. The antiphonal rendering of certain Psalms (e.g., 24:7-10) is well known. These different manners of singing provide opportunities for listening, and the variation of timbres, the spatial separation, the alternation of media, and the interaction of individual to group and group to group may reflect differences in personal or corporate expression and may relate to shifts between the grammatical person or the person or group being addressed. Vaughan Williams says of antiphonal singing between the choir and the congregation, "By this means the people are given a distinct status in the services, and are encouraged to take an intelligent interest in the music they sing."[31]

Descants, Hymn Anthems, Hymn Concertati, and Hymn Cantatas

Solo, choral, or instrumental descants can often provide a powerful enhancement to certain stanzas. Some hymnals provide descants to certain hymns, and some include an index to the descants.[32] It is significant that some of the indexes refer to specific hymns and stanzas and not simply to the hymn tune, because the descant is a descant above the specific *text*, not simply an obbligato part soaring above the melody.

Anthems based on hymn texts and hymn tunes may follow historical precedents of "full anthems" (a choral setting) or "verse anthems," with sections for solo voices alternating with sections for full chorus, may have two choirs ("decani" and "cantoris"), may be a cappella, may have organ or orchestral accompaniment, or may have combinations of these. Some such settings move toward the form of a cantata. The chorale cantatas of J. S. Bach, based on texts and melodies of the great German Protestant chorales, are models for "hymn cantatas" and "hymn concertatos"[33] in our day based on the words and/or music of hymns. Such works, by exploiting a wider range of musical ideas, may create significant musical experiences and, more important, significant worship experiences especially when there is the meaningful involvement of the congregation.

Experiencing and expressing ("performing") hymns through descants, hymn anthems, hymn concertati, and hymn cantatas is not simply an aesthetic experience, though it should be that. The purpose is to facilitate a more total experience and to express more clearly the meaning of hymns. These matters of performance are not necessarily difficult or time-consuming and must not call attention to themselves. If incorporated prayerfully, thoughtfully, and incrementally the performance will be perceived as natural and appropriate.

Each of the four traditional stanzas of Isaac Watts's great hymn, "When I survey the wondrous cross,"[34] takes some forty-five seconds to sing in a traditional manner, and yet the thoughts and feelings expressed in those four stanzas range through contempt of pride, rejection of unworthy things, sacrifice of self, pity for the dying Christ, awe of the love of Christ, joy for the unspeakable gift, and surrender to the love of God. Such a text and tune must not be demeaned by some inappropriate, overly dramatic "performance," nor by a casual or routine singing that grows out of a lack of understanding of the hymn's basic biblical truths of Christian theology or out of insensitivity to the meaningful poetic expression of those truths. The spectrum of thoughts and feeling would certainly allow some, even if subtle, variety of tempi, volume, and media. Such a text might call for a carefully executed instrumental prelude, interludes, or transitions to provide time for meditation. There might well be periods of silence to facilitate meditation. The first and second stanzas might be sung as a solo (the second stanza could be sung by the congregation). The third stanza could be sung by the choir and the final stanza by the congregation. An instrumental or choral descant might enhance the majestic thoughts of the final stanza. Appropriate tempi, volume, and accompaniment could contribute to a suitable interpretation of the text. The eleven personal pronouns could justify an unaccompanied (and unseen?) solo singing of the text and, properly done, could inspire a profoundly "congregational" involvement with the text and singing of the final stanza.

> When I survey the wondrous cross
> On which the Prince of glory died,
> My richest gain I count but loss,
> And pour contempt on all my pride.

> Forbid it, Lord, that I should boast,
> Save in the death of Christ my God!
> All the vain things that charm me most,
> I sacrifice them to His blood.

> See from His head, His hands, His feet,
> Sorrow and love flow mingled down!
> Did e'er such love and sorrow meet,
> Or thorns compose so rich a crown?

> Were the whole realm of nature mine,
> That were a present far too small;
> Love so amazing, so divine,
> Demands my soul, my life, my all.

The Practical "Voice" in a "Polyphonic" Hermeneutics

Hymnody is an applied art form. The academic, theoretical, historical studies of hymns come to full fruition in functional, practical applications. The great counterpoint of the biblical, theological, and liturgical content, the literary and musical expressions of that content, and the historical, biographical, and sociocultural contexts can be fully realized only when attention is given to the spiritual maturity of individuals, families, and congregations andto their involvement in the ministries of the church; to the education of the congregation about the importance, possibilities, and manner of hymn singing; to worship planning and the choice of hymns and hymn tunes; to the logistical matters of the physical facilities; and to the "performance" of the hymn, especially matters of tempo, dynamics, media, phrasing, and breathing.

The finest hymn writers have been gifted and committed Christians writing for other Christians committed to the church. An example is the varied roles in which Thomas Troeger continues to be an active witness to both his scholarly and his applied or "practical" sides. A Professor of Christian Communication at Yale Divinity School, Yale University, he is an active minister in and dually aligned with the Presbyterian and Episcopal churches. He has served as national chaplain to the American Guild of Organists, president of the Academy of Homiletics (the North American guild of scholars in homiletics), and President of *Societas Homiletica* (the international guild of scholars in homiletics). He is a flutist, author, lecturer, worship leader, and one of the finest hymn writers that the United States has produced in our generation. It is no mean tribute that Brian Wren, one of the finest English hymn writers in our generation, describes Troeger as "a front-rank theological poet, hymnic theologian, and poetic hymnist, whose words delight the imagination, inspire with new insights, and move us at the deepest level."[35]

Troeger's hymns are based in biblical theology and Christian history, rich in the imagery and devices of poetry, and written for practical, evangelical use with believers and "peripheral believers." He has explained, "I am also writing these hymns for evangelical reasons: to reach peripheral believers, those who encounter the holy through common experience but who feel awkward claiming that experience through traditional hymnic language because of its distance from contemporary idiom."[36] He has been able to exploit some of the subtle dimensions of poetry and yet appeal to "average" believers and "peripheral believers."

His hymn, "View the present through the promise," was written for the Advent season with application to numerous lections for Advent. In richly poetic and yet clear language he deals with the biblical, theological concept of eschatology, the Parousia, Christ's second coming. That basic idea is clearly and emphatically conveyed in the litany/refrain/epimone "Christ will come again" that chimes nine times through the hymn. A series of forceful verbs further strengthens the vigorous affirmation—"View," "Trust," "Lift," "Probe," "Match," "Make," and "Pattern" at the beginning of verses or lines. The driving trochaic meter is reinforced, even accelerated through a judicious use of alliteration—"present/promise," "despite deepening darkness," "probe/present/promise," "let/loving," and "present/promise/premise." The tempo is further accelerated with the triad of words in double or feminine rhyme in the last verses of each stanza—"grieving/believing/conceiving," "giving/forgiving/living," and "calculating/creating/waiting" that provide a dramatic foil before the final "Christ will come again" in each stanza. The rhyme scheme is abcbdddb, with a delightful consonant rhyme in the third stanza ("promise" and "premise"). It is a hymn that calls for use, for practical application in the worship of today's church.

> View the present through the promise,
>   Christ will come again.
> Trust despite the deepening darkness,
>   Christ will come again.
> Lift the world above its grieving
>   through your watching and believing
> in the hope past hope's conceiving:
>   Christ will come again.
>
> Probe the present with the promise,
>   Christ will come again.
> Let your daily actions witness,
>   Christ will come again.
> Let your loving and your giving
>   and your justice and forgiving
> be a sign to all the living:
>   Christ will come again.
>
> Match the present to the promise,
>   Christ will come again.
> Make this hope your guiding premise,
>   Christ will come again.
> Pattern all your calculating
>   and the world you are creating
> to the advent you are waiting:
>   Christ will come again.[37]

Herbert Murrill's 1951 tune CAROLYN[38] is a fine vehicle for Troeger's text. Murrill served various positions as organist and choral director, was organ scholar at Worcester College, Oxford, served as BBC Head of Music, and, at the time of his death, was Professor of Composition at the Royal Academy of Music. Routley says this tune "has a substantial claim to be the most pregnant utterance in the book [the *B.B.C. Hymn Book*] and the finest tune written since [Ralph Vaughan Williams's] DOWN AMPNEY."[39]

It is appropriate to call attention to some of the unusual features of this tune, how these features emphasize the text and its relation to the other dimensions, and how the practical application may be made of the text and tune. The tune is in an A A' B C form, and though it begins and ends in C minor there are interesting and convincing tonal shifts. The A section moves toward the dominant of the relative major but cadences "deceptively" on a G-major chord with an appoggiatura in the alto emphasizing the refrain, "Christ will come again," which is the biblical/theological/liturgical theme of the text. The A' section is largely a sequence of the first section (beginning with the "melody" in the bass), and this time does cadence in the dominant of the relative major key (with an accented passing tone in the alto), calling attention again to "Christ will come again." The B section begins in the minor form of that dominant of the relative major key, evolves into the major form of the chord, and transitions into the relative major; the apex of the melody is on a G-flat major chord (!) on the word "hope" in the first stanza, "sign" in the second stanza, and "advent" in the final stanza. Beginning in the B section are three two-measure sequential figures that propel the text through its three eight-syllable lines and Troeger's trio of feminine-rhymed gerunds. It then returns to the original key of C minor. After fourteen measures of simple quadruple time, the closing cadence slips into a fresh 6/4 meter with a rather standard authentic cadence, the subdominant with a dissonant appoggiatura in the soprano (7th of the chord) and tenor (9th of the chord), followed by the minor dominant 7th followed by the tonic chord again with its dissonance (this time a 4–3 suspension in the tenor) emphasizing the words, "Christ will come again." This belabored prose description only hints at the richness of the hymn tune. The form of the music beautifully complements in each stanza the meter, rhyme, form, ideas, wording, and mood of the text.

One practical approach in the singing of this text would be for the congregation to sing the "litany/refrain," "Christ will come again," in response to the choir's singing of the other verses or lines. In the context of the Advent season or of any focus on the second coming of Christ and sung in association with appropriate Scripture readings, this hymn can be a powerful statement on this major doctrine of the Christian faith.

A hermeneutics that contributes to a comprehensive and interrelated understanding of a hymn is a major responsibility of worship planners and leaders. Interpretations of the hymn could be provided, in a variety of ways so that the practice of hymn singing may be a truly biblical, theological, liturgical, literary, musical, sociocultural experience.

Figure 25. Words: "View the present through the promise," Thomas H. Troeger (b. 1945), *Borrowed Light: Hymn Texts, Prayers, and Poems* (New York: Oxford University Press, 1994) 123. Used by permission. Music: CAROLYN © Herbert Murrill (1909–1952). Reproduced by kind permission of the Continuum International Publishing Group, a Bloomsbury Company.

Notes

1. See chapter 4.

2. Erik Routley, *Hymns and Human Life* (Grand Rapids MI: Eerdmans, 1967) 299.

3. From William Shakespeare's *Macbeth*, Act 5, Scene 5.

4. This distinction was addressed by Brian Wren in comments about his hymn, "There's a spirit in the air," saying "heard and sung speech can't rely on visual, typographical clues" ("Hymn Interpretation: 'There's a spirit in the air,'" *The Hymn* 47/2 [April 1996]: 43).

5. Clarence Tucker Craig, "The First Epistle to the Corinthians," *The Interpreter's Bible* (New York: Abingdon-Cokesbury Press, 1953) 10:201.

6. See Carlton R. Young, *Music of the Heart: John and Charles Wesley on Music and Musicians: An Anthology* (Carol Stream IL: Hope Publishing Company, 1995) 9–18.

7. John Wesley, *Select Hymns with Tunes Annext; Designed chiefly for the USE of the People Called Methodists*, 1761, ed. 1770.

8. C. S. Lewis, *Letters of C. S. Lewis*, ed. W. H. Lewis (New York: Harcourt Brace Jovanovich, 1966) 7 December 1950, p. 224. When we read "nearly all hymns," we long to know which hymns Lewis did not loathe.

9. C. S. Lewis, *God in the Dock: Essays on Theology and Ethics*, "Answers to Questions on Christianity" (1944), ans. 16., ed. Walter Hooper (Grand Rapids MI: Eerdmans, 1978) 61–62. We find comfort in Lewis's comment, ". . . as I went on I saw the great merit of it."

10. C. S. Lewis, "On Church Music" (1949, para. 9–10), in *Christian Reflections*, ed. Walter Hooper (Grand Rapids MI: Eerdmans, 1967) 96–97.

11. Ibid.

12. J. R. Watson, *The English Hymn: A Critical and Historical Study* (Oxford: Oxford University Press, 1999) ix.

13. Ibid., x.

14. See Hal Hopson. *100+ Ways to Improve Congregational Hymnsinging: A Practical Guide for All Who Nurture Congregational Singing* (Carol Stream IL: Hope Publishing Company, 2002) and Hal Hopson, "Ways to Improve Congregational Singing," *The Hymn* 55/1 (January 2004): 11–16.

15. See chapter 4.

16. A hymn concertato is an arrangement indicating media (choir, congregation, solo, instruments, organ, unison, parts, a cappella, etc.), tempo, dynamics, and perhaps involving reharmonization and varied types of accompaniment for the performance, including the congregation, of the stanzas of a hymn.

17. See Mary Nelson Keithahn, "Engaging Children and Youth in Congregational Song: Twelve Suggestions," *The Hymn: The Journal of The Hymn Society in the United States and Canada* 61/3 (Summer 2010): 17.

18. *Hymnbook 1982: The Hymns together with Accompaniments from The Hymnal 1982* (New York: Church Hymnal Corporation, 1985) 1028–29.

19. While the discussion at this point focuses on the acts of worship, many of the same principles relate to making choices in the other ministries of discipleship, proclamation, and social concern in which individual Christians and communities of Christians may be involved.

20. John D. Witvliet, *Worship Seeking Understanding: Windows into Christian Practice* (Grand Rapids MI: Baker Publishing, 2003) 232.

21. See Anne Harrison. "Choosing Hymns—Some Reflections," *Hymn Society of Great Britain & Ireland Bulletin* 18/5 (January 2007): 166–70.

22. Online sources such as *HymnQuest CD-ROM*; the Worship Matrix accompanying the hymnal *Celebrating Grace; Cyberhymnal*; and denominational websites may be useful.

23. Erik Routley, *Words Music and the Church* (New York: Abingdon Press, 1968) 163–64.

24. Ibid., 164.

25. Some of the useful works on acoustics are John Backus, *The Acoustical Foundations of Music* (New York: W. W. Norton & Co., 1977); Arthur H. Bednade, *Fundamental of Musical Acoustics*, 2nd rev. ed. (New York: Dover Publications, Inc., 1990); Murray Campbell and Clive Greated, *The Musician's Guide to Acoustics* (Oxford: Oxford University Press, 1994); and Donald E. Hall, *Musical Acoustics, 3rd ed.* (Florence KY: Cengage Learning, 2001).

26. Deborah Howard and Laura Moretti, *Sound and Space in Renaissance Venice* (New Haven: Yale University Press, 2010).

27. Some hymnals, such as the *Hymnbook 1982* (New York, 1982) 1026–1027, offer "General Performance Notes."

28. Hopson, *100+ Ways to Improve Congregational Hymnsinging* and Hopson, "Ways to Improve Congregational Singing," 11–16.

29. Walther Durr, the German musicologist and Schubert authority, notes in his article, "Schubert and Johann Michael Vogl: A Reappraisal," ". . . there is no doubt that strophic songs require some alterations—not real embellishments, but variants between the several stanzas . . . . Goethe's recommendations to Eduard Genast [the director of Weimar's court theater] are well known [Heinrich W. Schwab, *Sangbarkeit: Popularität und Kunstlied* (Regensberg, 1965) 69; *Studien zür Musikgeschichte des 19. Jahrhunderts*, Band 3]. When Genast sang to the poet Reichardt's composition of his *Jägers Abendlied*, Goethe sat on his armchair, covering his eyes with his hand. At the end of the song he sprang up, exclaiming: 'It is a bad way of singing this song,' and then, striding up and down the room, he hummed and continued: 'The first and third stanza should be sung pithily with a certain fierceness, the second and fourth softer, because there a new sentiment is to be felt.'"

At the end of the second stanza of Goethe's "Der Gott und die Bajadere," Schubert himself notes, "NB. Bei diesen Strophen sowohl als bei den ubrigen muß der Inhalt derselben das Piano und Forte bestimmen [In these stanzas, as well as the others, the contents must determine whether they are to be sung piano or forte]" (Franz Schubert's Werke: Kritisch durchgesehen Gesamtausgabe, ed. Eusibius Mandyezewski [Leipzig, 1895], ser. 20, vol. 3, p. 33; Walther Durr. "Schubert and Johann Michael Vogl: A Reappraisal," *19th-Century Music* 3/2 [November 1979]: 126–140).

30. Ralph Vaughan Williams, musical ed., "Preface, The Music," *The English Hymnal with Tunes* (London: Oxford University Press, 1933) xii.

31. Ibid., xi–xii.

32. Erik Routley, *Rejoice in the Lord: A Hymn Companion to the Scriptures* (Grand Rapids MI: Wm. B. Eerdmans Publishing Company, 1985) 608.

33. The American Choral Directors Association website, http://choralnet.org/resources/viewResource.phtml?id=2437&lang=en&category=1, provides a compilation of hymn concertatos.

34. See David W. Music, "'When I Survey the Wondrous Cross': A Commentary," *The Hymn* 65/2 (Spring 2014): 7–13.

35. Brian Wren, "Praise God and Pound the Typewriter—A Critical Appreciation of Thomas Troeger," *The Hymn*, Journal of Congregational Song 37/3 (October 1986): 18.

36. Thomas H. Troeger, *Borrowed Light: Hymn Texts, Prayers, and Poems* (New York: Oxford University Press, 1994) 188.

37. Ibid., 123.

38. Routley, *Rejoice in the Lord*, 42.

39. Erik Routley, *The Music of Christian Hymnody: A Study of the Development of the Hymn Tune Since the Reformation, with Special Reference to English Protestantism* (London: Independent Press Limited, 1957) 170.

CHAPTER 9

Postlude: The Necessity of Interdisciplinary Conversations in a Comprehensive and Integrated Hermeneutics of Hymnody

"The many are better judges than a single man of music and poetry;
for some understand one part, and some another,
and among them they understand the whole."[1]

—Aristotle, *Politics*, 1281b7

This book has attempted to present a comprehensive and integrated hermeneutics of hymnody that contributes to understanding the complex polyphony of biblical, theological, liturgical, literary, musical, historical, biographical, sociocultural, and practical facets of fine hymnody. The hope has been to raise a new awareness of these multiple and interrelated voices that will deepen understanding, increase appreciation, provide a more objective basis for evaluation, and contribute to the meaningful singing of hymns. An emphasis has been that what is said biblically, theologically, and liturgically in a hymn is intricately bound with how it is said literarily, musically, and practically and that understanding the context of the creation, history, and current uses of a hymn is vital.

Probing the breadth and depth of this multifaceted art form, this polyphony of voices, requires a variety of knowledge and skills. It is hoped that there will emerge new and vital dialogues between and conversations among those knowledgable and skilled in the various disciplines that are essential parts of hymnody. It is the contention of this author that a true understanding of the breadth and depth of hymnody requires a comprehensive and integrated hermeneutics, and that is possible only with a new and vital interdisciplinary approach because none of us has the necessary knowledge and skills in each of the disciplines involved.

Hymnody, at its finest, is a complex art form that deals with the profound issues of human existence. As devout, knowledgeable, and skilled persons in those disciplines related to hymnology share with one another and find ways to share with laypersons appropriate aspects of that learning, the experience of hymn singing can be enriched. If given opportunities to explore intelligently the many facets of fine hymnody, those who are less experienced with this basic form of Christian literature, or even in the Christian faith, can begin to encounter similar thoughts and feelings that will grow deeper and broader through continued involvement with fine hymns and the Christian experience.

A total experience with hymns is basically spiritual (responding to God's revelation of himself) but also mental (engaging the mind), aural (hearing the sounds of words and music), oral and physical (singing words), historical (rooted in significant events in lives of Christians of many eras), social and cultural (relating to groups of people who share values, knowledge, beliefs, attitudes, and behavior), and psychological (involving personal and corporate mental and emotional aspects). Hymn singing at its finest is in keeping with our Lord's command to love our God with all our heart, and with all our soul, and with all our mind, and with all our strength (Mark 12:30).

A comprehensive and integrated hermeneutics of hymnody is the responsibility of the authors, composers, hymnal editors, educators, worship leaders, and, with proper help, the worshipers. While it is not reasonable to expect that each of these have the same kind or depth of understanding, skills, or appreciation of every dimension, it seems reasonable to expect that a deeply committed Christian should constantly desire a more meaningful involvement in this part of the Christian experience. From the beginning of Christianity through our own day, hymns have been a rich source of biblical understanding and theological insight, and a powerful medium for the expression of our worship of God. Part of the duty and delight of a more comprehensive and integrated hermeneutics is a continual growing in awareness of the facets of hymnody and a richer experiencing of the beautiful interaction of these facets in expressing our worship of God.

It must be emphasized again that the facets of hymnody are not to be thought of independently nor simply as related layers. Hymnody at it finest is a vital, linear, simultaneous, "polyphonic" interaction of multiple aspects. Each hymn is a different configuration of the dimensions, and each reader, singer, and congregation brings to each hymn different configurations of understanding, experiences, and feelings. Fine hymns are vibrant, contrapuntal artworks moving in time, with multiple facets occurring simultaneously. The simultaneity of these multiple facets provides much of the powerful impact of the beautiful quality of fine hymnody and creates great difficulty in discussing it. A truly comprehensive and integrated hermeneutics of hymnody requires more than simply talking about each dimension or even a cumulative layering of the dimensions. It begs for an evasive "polyphony in prose" to show the vital interaction and simultaneity of the aspects. Because every dimension of hymnody is at play in the rich "polyphony" of well-written, well-chosen, and well-sung hymns, numerous different ways must be explored to bring these dimensions and their vital interplay into fullest realization.

A brief look at two very different hymns may help again shed light on what this hermeneutics considers to be the dimensions of hymnody and their vital interrelatedness.

⬛◆⬛

The "Voices" in a "Polyphonic" Hermeneutics

The multiple and interrelated dimensions of fine hymnody may be illustrated in the hymn "O Love, how deep, how broad, how high" (*O Amor quam ecstaticus*), taken from a longer Latin hymn (*Apparuit benignitas*) in a perhaps fifteenth-century manuscript found at Karlsruhe, Germany.[2] The hymn is sometimes attributed to Thomas à Kempis (c. 1380–1471). In the six stanzas that appear in many hymnals as translated by Benjamin Webb (1819–1895) and altered by his lifelong friend, John Mason Neale (1818–1866), there is a burst of biblical, theological, liturgical, and literary profoundness and beauty. The hymn begins with turns of phrases expressing awe of the love that "God, the Son of God, should take our mortal form for mortals' sake"—"how deep, how broad, how high, high passing thought and fantasy" as expressed in Ephesians 3:14-19, 1 John 3:1, Philippians 2:6-7, and Romans 8:38-39. The four middle stanzas chime the life and atoning death of Christ with twelve ringing "for us" phrases proclaiming Christ's incarnation, baptism, temptation, teachings, miracles, betrayal, scouring, mocking, death, resurrection, ascension, and sending of the Holy Spirit! The final Trinitarian stanza gives "All glory to our Lord and God / for love so deep, so high, so broad." The chronological/logical development form embraces the anaphoric "for us" phrases. There is in this hymn a rare spectrum of biblical events, theological implications, and liturgical possibilities.

The hymn evokes the same historical, biographical, social, and cultural visions connected with Thomas à Kempis's *The Imitation of Christ* and the devotional life in fifteenth-century Netherlands. This hymn is something of a companion to Kempis's *Imitation* that is still today one of the most widely read devotional works.

Figure 26. Words: "O Love, how deep, how broad, how high," Latin, 15th century; trans. Benjamin Webb (1819–1885), alt. Music: THE EIGHTH TUNE, Thomas Tallis (1505–1585). At least the last stanza should be sung in canon.

O love, how deep, how broad, how high,
how passing thought and fantasy,
that God, the Son of God, should take
our mortal form for mortals' sake!

For us baptized, for us He bore
His holy fast, and hungered sore;
for us temptations sharp He knew,
for us the tempter overthrew.

For us He prayed; for us he taught;
for us his daily works he wrought;
by words and signs and actions, thus
still seeking not Himself, but us.

For us to wicked men betrayed,
scourged, mocked, in purple robe arrayed,
he bore the shameful cross and death,
for us gave up His dying breath.

For us He rose from death again;
for us He went on high to reign,
for us He sent His Spirit here
to guide, to strengthen, and to cheer.

All glory to our Lord and God
for loved so deep, so high, so broad;
the Trinity whom we adore
for ever and for evermore.

The text frequently appears with the tunes DEO GRACIAS (AGIN-COURT SONG) and DEUS TUORUM MILITUM. Another appropriate tune is THE EIGHTH TUNE by Thomas Tallis (1505–1585), one of the most distinguished composers in the history of English music. In its majestic simplicity, Tallis's tune is a fine vehicle for this text. Its completely unintrusive rhythm allows each finely carved phrase of the melody to bear the flow of words and provide in the third phrase the climax of thought that occurs in each stanza. The first and sixth stanzas might be sung by the congregation, while stanzas two through five might be sung by soloists or groups reminding the congregation of Christ's redeeming work. Singing the sixth stanza in three-voice canon with brass and organ can be a superb expression of praise of the Trinity.

The multiple and interrelated dimensions involved in the interpretation of a hymn may also be illustrated in the more contemporary hymn, "There's a spirit in the air," by Brian Wren (b. 1936). Here again, a more thorough understanding of the hymn requires consideration of the interrelated facets, and, interestingly, each of these interrelated facets is, as we shall see, referred to almost casually by the author in one short article.[3] While the hymn might appear to be deceptively "simple," it is actually a carefully crafted literary statement of theology with biblical bases, written for a specific liturgical season, now usually paired with a most appropriate musical setting with interesting, practical performance possibilities—all growing out of the author's historical context.

Wren's theology regarding what God through Christ and the Holy Spirit has done and is doing is, as he says of one of his other hymns, based on "the Bible as the 'classic model' of and for the Christian faith" and, as he says in that hymn, "the Bible that we know, . . . the working model for our faith, alive with hope for all."[4] He first wrote "There's a spirit in the air" for Whitsunday or Pentecost (Acts 2) in 1969 for the English church he served as minister. The hymn grew out of the theological concern that "our hymnal had several hymns about the Holy Spirit's (usually seven-fold) gifts to the believer [Rom 12; two lists in 1 Cor 12; 2 Cor 12; and Eph 4], a smaller number suggesting that the Spirit might be doing something in the church, but almost none speaking of the Spirit's work in the world or in creation."[5] In his notes in *Faith Renewed* (1995), Wren explains, "at a time when hymnody focused mainly on the Holy Spirit's individual gifts and animating presence in the church, this hymn celebrates the Spirit 'living, working in our world.'"[6]

In an immediate context and practical way, he spoke of "Our work [that of Brian's congregation] for world development through Oxfam and Christian Aid, and for the homeless through the equally forthright charity, Shelter, was the backdrop to the hymn," and in the larger historical context and practical application of the hymn, Wren notes "The time was ripe; all the churches felt a reawakening sense of God's work in society, and needed to connect Sunday worship with Monday morning."[7]

The carefully crafted structure of the hymn with its complementing first and last stanzas, its double refrain, and its enumeration of ministries in the middle stanzas combine to bear forcefully its biblical theology. Regarding his literary expression of the theology, Wren writes, "Wanting a hymn which young and old could enjoy together, I opted for a refrain and tried for simple language." While the language is "simple," there is a wealth of biblical allusions and hints to current social needs. Wren notes that, "For added interest," he used a double refrain[8] "modeled on Isaac Watts, whose 'Give to our God immortal praise' has alternating refrains, each crafted to complete its preceding lines." In both Watts and Wren there is more than simple "added interest." Each uses the double refrain to emphasize two different but complementary ideas. Wren emphasizes that the refrain for stanzas 1, 3, 5, and 7—"living, working in our world!"—"states that God's love has been revealed in Christ. Leaving open how far others might also reveal it, yet affirming that 'the love that Christ revealed' is at work in the whole world." His second refrain for stanzas 2, 4, and 6 "speaks of Emmanuel, God with us ('has come to stay'), calling us to anticipate God's coming reality by 'living tomorrow's life today.'"

> There's a spirit in the air,
> telling Christians ev'rywhere:
> > "Praise the love that Christ revealed,
> > living, working in our world!"

> Lose your shyness, find your tongue;
> tell the world what God has done:
> > God in Christ has come to stay.
> > Live tomorrow's life today!

> When believers break the bread,
> when a hungry child is fed:
> > praise the love that Christ revealed,
> > living, working in our world.

> Still the Spirit gives us light,
> seeing wrong and setting right:
> > God in Christ has come to stay.
> > Live tomorrow's life today!

> When a stranger's not alone,
> where the homeless find a home,
> > praise the love that Christ revealed,
> > living, working in our world.

May the Spirit fill our praise,
guide our thoughts and change our ways.
    God in Christ has come to stay,
    Live tomorrow's life today!

There's a Spirit in the air,
calling people everywhere:
    praise the love that Christ revealed,
    living, working in our world.

The first stanza proclaims that the *Spirit* is *telling Christians* everywhere, "Praise the love that Christ revealed, living, working in our world today!" The second stanza is a call to evangelism, a call for Christians, like the first disciples, to find their tongue to "tell the world what God has done," to witness to the power of Christ who is at work today and who has come to stay. The next three stanzas proclaim the ways in which the Holy Spirit is present in the church's concern for the social issues of hunger, injustice, the stranger, and homelessness (issues that Christ referred to in Matt 25:34-46). Wren's reference to worship, evangelism, and social ministry is consistent with the use of the term "liturgical" (λειτουργία, ας) in its broader, etymological, historical, and biblical sense to refer to the whole range of individual and corporate ministry. The sixth stanza is a call for the Spirit to "fill our praise, guide our thoughts and change our ways" and again an affirmation that through the Spirit, God in Christ has come to stay. In the last stanza, complementing the first, the *Spirit* is *calling people* everywhere, "Praise the love that Christ revealed, / living, working in our world today!"

In his 1996 comments on the interpretation of the hymn, Wren makes an interesting confession regarding his literary expression of the theological concept: "Looking back, my attempt to move from an indefinable 'something' felt by many to the Holy Spirit, known in Christ, by moving from lower case to upper case ("spirit" in number one to "Spirit" in number four, number six, and number seven) was a failure, because heard and sung speech can't rely on visual, typographical clues." Out of his concern for the practical aspects of understanding the hymn, Wren suggests,

To broaden the hymn's uses, ask a youth or adult retreat or class what the above phrases ["when believers break the bread," "where the homeless find a home / a hungry child is fed / a stranger's not alone"] call to mind for different peoples. . . . Or display stanza three replacing its first two lines with spaces for their seven syllables, and inviting people to write new couplets which lead into "praise the love that Christ revealed, / living, working in our world." The couplet can begin with "if," "as," "when," or "where." "When the lonely find a friend" would be logical, but "God, forgive our greed and wrong" would not.[9]

Stanzas 1, 6, and 7 may best be sung by the full congregation in unison. Each of stanzas 2, 3, 4, and 5, addressing different situations, could be sung by soloists or different groups (e.g., youth, women, men, choir). The choir sopranos should sing the descant on stanzas 4 and 7.

Regarding the musical setting of the text, Wren notes,

> John W. Wilson's 1970 pairing of the text with his tune LAUDS is an inspired match, wisely followed by most hymnals. If your tune is ORIENTIS PARTIBUS, avoid singing it as slowly as you sing "The friendly beasts." Here as elsewhere, if you read the text, it will tell you how it wants to be sung. . . . Flute and drum go well with ORIENTIS PARTIBUS, which also sounds well unaccompanied.[10]

John Wilson's LAUDS affirms the lilting, joyous praise of this hymn through a singable, folk-like, compound-meter melody in well-rounded phrases, supported by a quick harmonic rhythm, and a descant to be sung on the fourth and seventh stanzas. The music is in keeping with Wren's "simple language" and his desire for a hymn "which young and old could enjoy together." One is reminded of Wren's "I come with joy, a child of God" and the lilting American folk melody to which it is often sung, LAND OF REST. (See Figure 27.)

The fine polyphony that characterizes the comprehensive and interrelated hermeneutics advocated in this book and the very purposes at the heart of congregational singing are beautifully presented in Fred Pratt Green's "When in our music God is glorified." The hymn, written in 1972 in response to John Wilson's request for a new text for Stanford's tune ENGELBERG, has, because of the profound expression of its message, become one of the twentieth century's internationally accepted hymns.

With its biblical basis in Psalm 150, Mark 14:26, and Matthew 26:30, the hymn reflects a historical/biblical theology of worship, and its theme of congregational expression in worship makes its liturgical uses manifold. The

Figure 27. Text: "There's a spirit in the air," Brian Wren (b. 1936). Music: LAUDS, John Wilson (1905–1992). © 1969, 1979, 1995 Hope Publishing, Company. Carol Stream IL 60188. All rights reserved. Used by permission.

tightly constructed one-sentence stanzas (two on stanzas four and five) of 10 10 10.4 meter and three rhymed lines plus an "alleluia!" employ alliteration, contrast, and metaphor, and its inevitable flow and convincing logic causes thought and feeling to soar together borne on the wings of Stanford's exultant hymn tune.

> When in our music God is glorified,
> and adoration leaves no room for pride,
> it is as though the whole creation cried
> Alleluia!
>
> How often, making music, we have found
> a new dimension in the world of sound,

as worship moved us to a more profound
Alleluia!

So has the Church, in liturgy and song,
in faith and love, through centuries of wrong,
borne witness to the truth in every tongue,
Alleluia!

And did not Jesus sing a psalm that night
when utmost evil strove against the Light?
Then let us sing, for whom he won the fight,
Alleluia!

Let every instrument be tuned for praise!
Let all rejoice who have a voice to raise!
And may God give us faith to sing always
Alleluia! Amen.[11]

What is expressed here about the church's hymns through centuries of wrong and about the ideal for hymn singing should shape our continuing prayer that God will bless our singing, that God will be glorified, that we might find a new dimension in sound and worship, that we might bear in faith and love a witness to the truth, that we might sing for him who won the fight, and that God might give us faith to always sing "Alleluia."

Notes

1. Some translations read "the general public" rather than "many." While Aristotle is speaking here in the larger context of politics and democracy, there are many areas in which the "many" might well be less than the general public. A few lines later, Aristotle acknowledges, "It is not indeed clear whether this collective superiority of the many compared with the few good men can possibly exist in regard to every democracy and every multitude," and "This arrangement of the constitution is however open to question in the first place on the ground that it might be held that the best man to judge which physician has given the right treatment is the man that is himself capable of treating and curing the patient of his present disease, and this is the man who is himself a physician." It might, then, be argued that the many who have the necessary knowledge, skills, and commitment are better judges "of music and poetry" than a single person.

2. J. R. Watson. "O Love, how deep, how broad, how high," Canterbury Dictionary of Hymnology, http://www.hymnology.co.uk/. See http://lorem-ipsum.wikispaces.com/amor-quam for an English translation (largely the Webb/Neale) compared to the original Latin.

3. Brian Wren, "Hymn Interpretation: 'There's a spirit in the air,'" *The Hymn* 47/2 (April 1996): 43.

4. Brian Wren, "Deep in the Shadows of the Past," *Faith Looking Forward* (Carol Stream IL: Hope Publishing Company, 1983), no. 5, notes and stanza 4.

5. Wren, "Hymn Interpretation: 'There's a spirit in the air,'" 43.

6. Brian Wren, *Faith Renewed* (Carol Stream IL: Hope Publishing Company, 1995) notes to hymn 22.

7. Wren, "Hymn Interpretation: 'There's a spirit in the air,'" 43.

8. It should be noted that in Psalm 107 there is a biblical precedent for the double refrain in each of the Psalm's four strophes. The first refrain notes that the people, each time in a different crisis, "cried out to the Lord in their trouble; he delivered them out of their distresses." The second refrain admonishes the people, "Let them give thanks to the Lord for His lovingkindness, and for His wonders to the sons of men!"

9. Wren, "Hymn Interpretation: 'There's a spirit in the air,'" 43.

10. Ibid. Wren even suggests specific tempi for the singing of each hymn tune, but it is difficult to be too specific with tempi since much depends on the size and acoustics of the space in which a hymn is sung, on the size of the congregation singing, and on which instruments are involved.

11. Hope Publishing Company, Carol Stream IL 60188. © 1972. All rights reserved.

Bibliography

Adey, Lionel. *Class and Idol in the English Hymn*. Vancouver: University of British Columbia Press, 1988.

———. *Hymns and the Christian "Myth."* Vancouver: University of British Columbia Press, 1986.

Aland, Kurt; Matthew Black, Carlo M Martini, Bruce M. Metzger, and Allen Wikgren, editors. *The Greek New Testament*. 3rd ed. New York: United Bible Societies, 1978.

Apel, Willi, editor. *Harvard Dictionary of Music*. 2nd ed. Cambridge: The Belknap Press of Harvard University Press, 1969.

Aristotle. *Politics*. 1281b7.

Backus, John. *The Acoustical Foundations of Music*. New York: W. W. Norton & Co., 1977.

Bailey, Albert Edward. *The Gospel in Hymns: Backgrounds and Interpretations*. New York: Charles Scribner's Sons, 1952.

Baker, Frank. *Charles Wesley's Verse: An Introduction*. 2nd ed. London: Epworth Press, 1968.

———, ed. *Representative Verse of Charles Wesley*. London: The Epworth Press, 1962.

Baldick, Chris. *The Concise Oxford Dictionary of Literary Terms*. Oxford: Oxford University Press, 1990.

Barnett, Lincoln. *The Universe and Dr. Einstein. With a foreword by Albert Einstein*. New York: The New American Library, 1964.

Barth, Karl. *Church Dogmatics*. T. F. Torrance and G. W. Bromiley, editors. Edinburgh: T. & T. Clark, 1962.

Baughen, Michael, editor. *Hymns for Today's Church*. London: Hodder and Stoughton, 1982.

Bebbington, David. "Evangelicalism in Its Settings; The British and American Movements since 1940." In Mark A. Noll, David W. Bebbington, and George A. Rawlyk, editors. *Evangelicalism: Comparative Studies of Popular Protestantism in North America, the British Isles, and Beyond, 1700–1990*. New York: Oxford University Press, 1994.

Bednade, Arthur H. *Fundamentals of Musical Acoustics*. 2nd rev. ed. New York: Dover Publications, Inc., 1990.

Begbie, Jeremy S., and Steven R. Guthrie, editors. *Resonant Witness: Conversations between Music and Theology*. Grand Rapids MI: William B. Eerdmans Publishing Company, 2011.

Begbie, Jeremy S. *Theology, Music, and Time*. Cambridge: Cambridge University Press, 2000.

Benson, Louis F. *The English Hymn*. London, 1915.

———. *The Hymnody of the Christian Church*. Richmond VA: John Knox Press, 1956.

Berkhof, Louis. *Principles of Biblical Interpretation*. Grand Rapids MI: Baker Pub Group, 1950.

Bernstein, Leonard. "The Unanswered Question" 1. *Musical Phonology* [1973 at Harvard] Norton Lectures, No. 1 of 6. http://avaxhome.ws/music/classical/Leonard_Bernstein_The_Unanswered_Question_Musical_Phonology.html.

Bett, Henry. *The Hymns of Methodism*. London: Epworth Press, 1945.

Bishop, Selma L. *Isaac Watts Hymns and Spiritual Songs 1707–1748: A Study in Early Eighteenth Century Language Changes.* London: The Faith Press, 1962.

Black, C. Clifton. *The Rhetoric of the Gospel.* St. Louis: Chalice Press, 2001.

Bloom, Allan. *"Our Ignorance," pt. 2. The Closing of the American Mind.* New York: Simon and Schuster, 1987.

Bloom, Harold. *Genius: A Mosaic of One Hundred Exemplary Creative Minds.* New York: Warner Books, 2002.

Bonhoeffer, Dietrich. *Letters and Papers from Prison.* Enlarged edition, Eberhard Bethge; translated by Reginald Fuller et al. New York: Macmillan, 1972.

Book of Common Prayer and Administration of the Sacraments and other Rites and Ceremonies of the Church Together with the Psalter or Psalms of David According to the use of The Church of England. Cambridge: Cambridge University Press, 1968.

Book of Common Prayer and Administration of the Sacraments and other Rites and Ceremonies of the Church Together with the Psalter or Psalms of David According to the use of The Episcopal Church. New York: Oxford University Press, 1990.

Boslough, John. *Stephen Hawking's Universe.* New York: Avon Books, 1985.

Bradley, C. Randall. "Congregational Song as a Shaper of Theology: A Contemporary Assessment." *Review and Expositor: A Consortium Baptist Theological Journal* 100/3 (Summer 2007): 351–73.

Brooks, Cleanth, and Robert Penn Warren. *Understanding Poetry.* 4th ed. New York: Holt, Rinehart and Winston, 1976.

Bruce, F. F. "The Poetry of the Old Testament." In D. Guthrie and J. A. Motyer, editors. *The New Bible Commentary.* Grand Rapids MI: Wm. B. Eerdmans Publishing Co., revised edition 1970. 41–47.

Bullinger, E. W. *Figures of Speech Used in the Bible: Explained and Illustrated.* Grand Rapids MI: Baker Book House, 1898, reprinted 1968.

Burton, Humphrey. *Leonard Bernstein.* New York: Doubleday, 1994.

Campbell, Murray, and Clive Greated. *The Musician's Guide to Acoustics.* Oxford: Oxford University Press, 1994.

Canterbury Dictionary of Hymnology. J. R. Watson and Emma Hornby, editors. Music editor: Jeremy Dibble; Australasian editor: Colin Gibson; Canadian editor: Margaret Leask; USA editor: Carlton R. Young; IT consultant: James V. Jirtle. www.hymnology.co.uk/.

Celebrating Grace. http://www.celebrating-grace.com.

Celebrating Grace. Macon GA: Celebrating Grace, Inc., 2010.

Chester, Timothy. *Awakening to a World of Need: The Recovery of Evangelical Social Concern.* Leicester: IVP, 1993.

Ciardi, John, and Miller Williams. *How Does a Poem Mean?* Boston: Houghton Mifflin Company, 1975.

Craig, Clarence Tucker. "The First Epistle to the Corinthians." *The Interpreter's Bible.* New York: Abingdon-Cokesbury Press, 1953.

Cyberhymnal. http://www.cyberhymnal.org/index.htm; http://www.hymntime.com/tch/.

Daw, Carl P. Jr. *A Year of Grace: Hymns for the Church Year.* Carol Stream IL: Hope Publishing Co., 1990.

Dearmer, Percy, editor. *The English Hymnal with Tunes.* London: Oxford University Press, 1933.

Dearmer, Percy. *Songs of Praise Discussed.* Oxford: Oxford University Press, 1933.

De-la-Noy, Michael. *Michael Ramsey: A Portrait.* London: Collins, 1990.

Deutsche Bibelgesellschaft. "Nachwort, Die Prinzipien dieser Übersetzung." *Die Bibel in heutigem Deutsch.* Stuttgart: Deutsche Bibelgesellschaft, 1982.

Dictionary of North American Hymnology. http://www.hymnary.org/dnah.

Diehl, Katharine Smith. *Hymns and Tunes: An Index.* New York: The Scarecrow Press, Inc., 1966.

Drabble, Margaret, editor. *The Oxford Companion to English Literature.* Oxford: Oxford University Press, 1985.

Dudley-Smith, Timothy. *A Flame of Love: A Personal Choice of Charles Wesley's Verse.* London: Triangle SPCK, 1987.

———. *A House of Praise: Collected Hymns 1961-2001.* Oxford: Oxford University Press; Carol Stream IL: Hope Publishing Company, 2003.

———. "Hymns and Songs in Christian Worship: Past, Present—and Future?" *Hymn Society of Great Britain & Ireland Bulletin* 19/5 (January 2010).

———. *John Stott: A Biography: The Later Years.* Downers Grove IL: InterVarsity Press, 2001.

———. "What Can a Hymn Writer Learn from a Lyricist? A Review and Reflection on Sondheim's *Finishing the Hat.*" *The Hymn Society Bulletin* 19/11 (July 2011): 450.

Duffield, Samuel Willoughby. *English Hymns: Their Authors and History.* New York: Funk & Wagnalls Company, 1894.

Dunstan, Sylvia. *In Search of Hope and Grace: 40 Hymns and Gospel Songs.* Chicago: GIA, 1991.

Durant, Will, and Ariel Durant. *The Lessons of History.* New York: Simon and Schuster, 1968.

Durant, Will. *Our Oriental Heritage.* New York: Simon and Schuster, 1954.

Durr, Walther. "Schubert and Johann Michael Vogl: A Reappraisal." *19th-Century Music* 3/2 (November 1979): 126–140.

Eliot, T. S. "A Dialogue on Dramatic Poetry." *Selected Essays.* New York: Harcourt, Brace and Company, 1950.

———. *On Poetry and Poets.* London: Faber, 1957.

———. "Tradition and the Individual Talent." *The Sacred Wood: Essays on Poetry and Criticism.* New York: Barnes and Noble, 1920.

Ellinwood, Leonard. *The History of American Church Music.* rev. ed. New York: Da Capo Press, 1970.

English Hymnal with Tunes. London: Oxford University Press, 1906.

Epstein, Edmund L. *Language and Style.* London: Methuen, 1978.

Eskew, Harry, and Hugh T. McElrath. *Sing with Understanding: An Introduction to Christian Hymnody.* 2nd edition. Nashville: Broadman Press, 1995.

Evans, John, editor. *Journeying Boy: The Diaries of the Young Benjamin Britten 1928–1938*. London: Faber and Faber, 2009.

Farnsworth, Paul R. *The Social Psychology of Music*. New York: Holt, Rinehart and Winston, 1970.

Fenton, J. C. *Saint Matthew*. Hopkinton MA: Penguin Press, 1963.

French, Richard F. "Hymn." In *The New Harvard Dictionary of Music*. Edited by Don Randel. Cambridge: Belknap Press of Harvard University Press, 1986.

———. "Psalter." *The New Harvard Dictionary of Music*. Edited by Don Randel. Cambridge: Belknap Press of Harvard University Press, 1986.

Frost, Maurice, editor. *Historical Companion to Hymns Ancient & Modern*. London: William Clowes & Sons, Limited, 1962.

Gesangbuch. http://www.Gesangbuch.org.

Gillman, F. J. *The Evolution of the English Hymn*. London, 1927.

Glover, Raymond F., editor. *The Hymnal 1982 Companion, i–v*. New York: Church Hymnal Corporation, 1994.

Graves, John. *Goodbye to a River*. Houston: Gulf Publishing Company, 1960.

Green, Fred Pratt. *The Hymns and Ballads of Fred Pratt Green*. Carol Stream IL: Hope Publishing Company, 1982.

Gregory, A. S. *Praises with Understanding*. London, 1936.

Grout, Donald J. *A Short History of Opera*. 1-volume edition. New York & London: Columbia University Press, 1965.

Grove Music Online. Edited by L. Macy, http://www.grovemusic.com.

Guthrie, D., and J. A. Motyer. *The New Bible Commentary*, revised edition. Grand Rapids MI: Wm. B. Eerdmans Publishing Co., 1970.

Hall, Donald E. *Musical Acoustics*. 3rd ed. Florence KY: Cengage Learning, 2001.

Halmo, Joan. "Hymn Interpretation," 'You, Lord, Are Both Lamb and Shepherd.'" *The Hymn* 53/2 (April 2002): 46.

Hargreaves, David J., and Adrian C. North, editors. *The Social Psychology of Music*. Oxford: Oxford University Press, 1997.

Harrison, Anne. "Choosing Hymns—Some Reflections." *Hymn Society of Great Britain & Ireland Bulletin* 18/5 (January 2007): 166–70.

Hartje, Gesa F. "Keeping in Tune with the Times—Praise & Worship Music as Today's Evangelical Hymnody in North America." *Dialog: A Journal of Theology* 48/4 (Winter 2009), Gettysburg: Lutheran Theology Seminary.

Hastings, Adrian. *A History of English Christianity, 1920–1990*. 3rd edition. London: SCM Press, 1991.

Hatchett, Marion J. *Commentary on the American Prayer Book*. San Francisco: HarperSanFrancisco (An Imprint of HarperCollins Publishers), 1995.

Hawking, Stephen W. *A Brief History of Time: From the Big Bang to Black Holes*. New York: Bantam Books, 1988.

Hawkins, John. *A General History of the Science and Practice of Music*. London: T. Payne and Son, 1776.

Hawn, C. Michael. "Global Hymnody." *The Canterbury Dictionary of Hymnology.* http://www.hymnology.co.uk/g/global-hymnody.

————. "History of Hymns: 'God Created Heaven and Earth,'" http://www.gbod.org/resources/history-of-hymns-god-created-heaven-and-earth.

Hazelton, Roger. *New Accents in Contemporary Theology.* New York: Harper & Brothers, Publishers, 1960.

Heaney, Seamus. *Beowulf: A New Verse Translation.* New York: Farrar, Straus and Giroux, 2000.

Heber, Amelia. *The Life of Reginald Heber, D.D.* London: 1830.

Helm, Everett. *Music and Tomorrow's Public: An Intercultural Survey.* New York: Heinrichshofen Edition, 1981.

Hepburn, R. W. "Religious Language." *Oxford Companion to Philosophy.* Edited by Ted Honderich. Oxford: Oxford University Press, 1995.

Hick, John, editor. "The Myth of God Incarnate." *100 Hymns for Today.* London: SCM Press, 1977.

Hill, Christopher C. "Rhetoric." In Don Michael Randel, editor. *The New Harvard Dictionary of Music.* Cambridge: The Belknap Press of Harvard University Press, 1986.

Hofstadter, Douglas R. *Le Ton beau de Marot: In Praise of the Music of Language.* New York: Basic Books (A division of HarperCollins Publishers). 1997.

————. *Gödel, Escher, Bach: an Eternal Golden Braid: A Metaphorical Fugue on Minds and Machines in the Spirit of Lewis Carroll.* New York: Basic Books (A member of the Perseus Books Group), 1999.

Hollander, John. *The Untuning of the Sky: Ideas of Music in English Poetry, 1500–1700.* New York: W. W. Norton & Company, Inc., 1970.

Holman, C. Hugh. *A Handbook to Literature.* 3rd edition. New York: The Odyssey Press (A division of The Bobbs-Merrill Company, Inc., Publishers), 1972.

Hopson, Hal. *100+ Ways to Improve Congregational Hymnsinging: A Practical Guide for All Who Nurture Congregational Singing.* Carol Stream IL: Hope Publishing Company, 2002.

————. "Ways to Improve Congregational Singing." *The Hymn* 55/1 (January 2004): 11–16.

Horgan, Paul. *Great River: The Rio Grande in North American History.* Hanover, New England: The University Press of New England and Wesleyan Press, 1984.

Horne, Thomas Hartwell. *An Introduction to the Critical Study and Knowledge of the Holy Scripture.* London, for T. Cadell by A. & R. Spottiswoode, 1828. Vol. 1.

Houts, Margo G. "Feminine Images for God: What Does the Bible Say?" http://clubs.calvin.edu/chimes/970418/o1041897.htm.

Howard, Deborah and Laura Moretti. *Sound and Space in Renaissance Venice.* New Haven: Yale University Press, 2010.

Hügel, F. von. *Selected Letters.* J. M. Dent & Sons ltd., 1928.

Hurtado, Larry W. *At the Origins of Christian Worship: The Context and Character of Earliest Christian Devotion.* Grand Rapids, Michigan/Cambridge, UK: William B. Eerdmans Publishing Company, 1999.

Hustad, Donald P. *Jubilate! Church Music in the Evangelical Tradition.* 2nd edition. Carol Stream IL: Hope Publishing Company, 1981.

Hutchings, Bill. *The Poetry of William Cowper.* London: Croom Helm, 1983.

Hymnary. http://www.hymnary.org.

Hymnbook 1982: The Hymns together with Accompaniments from The Hymnal 1982. New York: The Church Hymnal Corporation, 1985.

HymnQuest (CD-ROM published on behalf of the Pratt Green Trust), London: Stainer & Bell Ltd., 1997. http://www.stainer.co.uk/hymnquest/demo2011.html.

Inwood, M. J. "Hermeneutics." *The Oxford Companion to Philosophy.* Edited by Ted Honderich. Oxford: Oxford University Press, 1995. Inwood's quote is from Friedrich Ast's Grundlinien der Grammatik, Hermeneutik und Kritik (Landshut: Thomann, 1808).

Joint Commission on the Revision of the Hymnal of the Protestant Episcopal Church in the United States of America. The *Hymnal 1940 Companion.* 3rd revised edition. New York: The Church Pension Fund, 1951.

Julian, John, editor. A *Dictionary of Hymnology.* New York: Dover Publications, 1907.

Juslin, Patrik N., and John A. Sloboda, editors. *Music and Emotion: Theory and Research.* Oxford: Oxford University Press, 2001.

Keble's Lectures on Poetry, 1832–1841. Translated by Edward Kershaw Francis. Oxford: At the Clarendon Press, 1912.

Keithahn, Mary Nelson. "Engaging Children and Youth in Congregational Song: Twelve Suggestions." *The Hymn: The Journal of the Hymn Society in the United States and Canada.* Vol. 61, No. 3 (Summer, 2010): 17.

Kennedy, George A. "Foreword" to Heinrich Lausberg. *Handbook of Literary Rhetoric: A Foundation for Literary Study.* Boston: Brill, 1998.

Kidner, Derek. *Psalms 1–72.* Leicester: InterVarsity Press, 1973.

Kinzie, Mary. *A Poet's Guide to Poetry.* Chicago: The University of Chicago Press, 1999.

Lang, Paul Henry. *Music in Western Civilization.* New York: W. W. Norton and Company, Inc., 1941.

Langer, Susanne K. *Philosophy in a New Key: A Study of the Symbolism of Reason, Rite, and Art* A Mentor Book published by The New American Library, 1951.

Lanier, Sidney. *The Science of English Verse.* Volume 16. "Early National Literature, Part II; Later National Literature, Part I," of *The Cambridge History of English and American Literature: An Encyclopedia in Eighteen Volumes.* Edited by A. W. Ward, A. R. Waller, W. P. Trent, J. Erskine, S. P. Sherman, and C. Van Doren. New York: G. P. Putnam's Sons; Cambridge, England: University Press, 1907–1921.

Laughlin, Robert B. *A Different Universe: Reinventing Physics from the Bottom Down.* New York: Basic Books, 2005.

Lausberg, Heinrich. *Handbook of Literary Rhetoric: A Foundation for Literary Study.* Translated by Matthew T. Bliss, Annemiek Jansen, and David E Orton. Edited by David E. Orton and R. Dean Anderson. Boston: Brill, 1998.

Lawrence, D. H. *The Evening News* (London) 13 October 1928. In Anthony Beal, editor, *Selected Literary Criticism: D. H. Lawrence.* Portsmouth NH: Heineman, 1956.

Leaver, Robin A., and James H. Litton, editors. *Duty and Delight: Routley Remembered*. Carol Stream IL: Hope Publishing Company and Norwich: Canterbury Press, 1985.

Leith, John H., editor. *Creeds of the Churches: A Reader in Christian Doctrine from the Bible to the Present*. Chicago: Aldine Publishing Company, 1963.

Lenti, Vincent A. "Of the Father's Love Begotten." *The Hymn* 60/3 (Summer 2009) 7–15.

Lewis, C. S. *God in the Dock: Essays on Theology and Ethics*. "Answers to Questions on Christianity" (1944), answer 16. Edited by Walter Hooper. Grand Rapids MI: Eerdmans, 1978.

———. *Letters of C. S. Lewis*. Edited by W. H. Lewis. New York: Harcourt Brace Jovanovich, 1966.

———. "On Church Music," (1949 para. 9-10) in *Christian Reflections*. Edited by Walter Hooper. Grand Rapids MI: Eerdmans, 1967.

———. *Perelandra*. New York: The Macmillan Company, 1944.

———. *Studies in Medieval and Renaissance Literature*. Edited by Walter Hooper. Cambridge: Cambridge University Press, 1966.

Lockspeiser, Edward. *Music and Painting: A Study in Comparative Ideas from Turner to Schoenberg*. New York: Harper & Row, 1973.

Longford, Lord. *Pornography: The Longford Report*. London: Coronet, 1979.

Lovelace, Austin C. *The Anatomy of Hymnody*. New York: Abingdon Press, 1965.

Manning, Bernard L. *The Hymns of Wesley and Watts: Five Informal Papers*. London: The Epworth Press, 1942.

Marty, Martin E. "The Phenomenology of Hymnody: What Is Going On When Christians Sing Hymns in Congregation?" *The Hymn* 59/3 (Sumer 2008): 8–14.

Maxwell, William D. *An Outline of Christian Worship: Its Developments and Forms*. London: Oxford University Press, 1936.

McCutchan, Robert G. *Hymn Tune Names*. Nashville: Abingdon Press, 1957.

McDonald, William. "Søren Kierkegaard (1813–1855)." *Internet Encyclopedia of Philosophy: A Peer-reviewed Academic Resource*. www.iep.utm.edu/kierkega/.

McDormand, Thomas B. and Frederic S. Crossman. *Judson Concordance to Hymns*. Valley Forge: Judson Press, 1965.

Milligan, G. "The Greek Papyri with Special Reference to their Value for N. T. Study" (n.p., 1912). In A. T. Robertson, *A Grammar of the Greek New Testament in the Light of Historical Research*. Nashville: Broadman Press, 1934.

Moleck, Fred. GIA Publications, Inc. www.giamusic.com/sacred_music/new_releases.cfm.

Montgomery, James. *The Christian Psalmist*. London and Glasgow: Richard Griffin & Co., 1825.

Moody, Dale. *The Word of Truth: A Summary of Christian Doctrine Based on Biblical Revelation*. Grand Rapids MI: William B. Eerdmans Publishing Company, 1981.

Music, David W. "'When I Survey the Wondrous Cross': A Commentary," *The Hymn*. 65/2 (Spring 2014): 7–13.

New American Standard Bible. Anaheim GA: Foundation Publications, Inc., 1995.

Newport, John P. *Life's Ultimate Questions: A Contemporary Philosophy of Religion.* Dallas: Word Publishing, 1989.

Niles, John Jacob. *Songs of the Hill Folk.* Set 14 of Schirmer's Folk Song Series: Twelve Ballads from Kentucky, Virginia and North Carolina. New York: G. Schirmer, 1934.

Noll, Mark A., David W. Bebbington and George A. Rawlyk, editors. *Evangelicalism: Comparative Studies of Popular Protestantism in North America, the British Isles, and Beyond. 1700–1990.* New York: Oxford University Press, 1994.

O'Connor, Michael. "The Singing of Jesus." In Jeremy S. Begbie and Steven R.Guthrie, editors, *Resonant Witness: Conversations between Music and Theology.* Grand Rapids MI: William B. Eerdmans Publishing Company, 2011.

Oremus Hymnal. http://www.oremus.org/hymnal.

Osborn, G., editor. *The Poetical Works of John and Charles Wesley,* 13 volumes. London: Wesleyan Methodist Conference Office, 1868–72.

Oxford Dictionary of Scientific Quotations. Edited by W. F. Bynum and Roy Porter. Oxford: Oxford University Press, 2006. Oxford Reference Online. www.oxfordreference.com/views/ENTRY.html?subview=Main&entry=t218.e72.

Parker, Alice. *Creative Hymn-Singing.* Chapel Hill: Hinshaw Music, Inc., 1976.

Parry, K. L., and Erik Routley. *Companion to Congregational Praise.* London: Independent Press, 1953.

Perrine, Laurence. *Literature: Structure, Sound, and Sense.* 4th edition. New York: Harcourt Brace Jovanovich, Inc., 1983.

Perry, David W. *Hymns and Tunes Indexed by First Lines, Tune Names, and Metres Compiled from Current Hymnbooks.* The Hymn Society of Great Britain & Ireland and The Royal School of Church Music, 1980.

Pinsky, Robert. *The Inferno of Dante: A New Verse Translation.* New York: Farrar, Straus & Giroux, 1994.

Piston, Walter. "Harmonic Rhythm." In *Harvard Dictionary of Music.* 2nd ed. Willi Apel, editor. Cambridge: The Belknap Press of Harvard University Press, 1969.

Plato. *Laws.* II, 658B.

Poems of Grace: Texts of the Hymnal 1982. New York: Church Publishing Incorporated, 1998.

Pope, Alexander. "Essay on Criticism." <http://poetry.eserver.org/essay-on-criticism.html>.

Powers, Harold S. "Rhythm." In *The New Harvard Dictionary of Music.* Don Randel, editor. Cambridge: The Belknap Press of Harvard University Press, 1986.

Raby, F. J. E. "The Poem 'Dulcis Iesu Memoria.'" *Bulletin of the Hymn Society* 33 (October 1945): 1–6.

Ramm, Bernard. *Protestant Biblical Interpretation.* Revised edition. Boston: W. A. Wilde Company, 1956.

Randel, Don Michael, editor. *The New Harvard Dictionary of Music.* Cambridge MA: The Belknap Press of Harvard University Press, 1986.

Reese, Gustave. *Music in the Renaissance.* Revised edition. New York: W. W. Norton & Company, Inc., 1959.

Reynolds, William Jensen. *A Survey of Christian Hymnody.* 5th ed. revised and enlarged by David W. Music and Milburn Price. Carol Stream IL: Hope Publishing Company, 2011.

Richards, I. A. "Principles of Literary Criticism." *Encyclopædia Britannica.* 2010.

Richards, I. A., and C. K. Ogden. *The Meaning of Meaning: A Study of the Influence of Language upon Thought and of the Science of Symbolism.* Magdalene College, University of Cambridge, 1923; Orlando: Harcourt Brace Jovanovich, Publishers, 1989.

———. *Principles of Literary Criticism.* London: Routledge Publishing Co., 1924; Taylor & Francis e-library, 2004.

Richards, I. A. *The Philosophy of Rhetoric.* New York: Oxford University Press, 1936, 1964.

———. *Practical Criticism: A Study of Literary Judgment.* Orlando: Harcourt Brace & Company, 1929.

———. "Principles of Literary Criticism." *Encyclopædia Britannica.* 2010. http://www.britannica.com/.

Richardson, Alan, editor. "Language, Religious." *A Dictionary of Christian Theology.* Philadelphia: The Westminster Press, 1969.

Robertson, A. T. *A Grammar of the Greek New Testament in the Light of Historical Research* Nashville: Broadman Press, 1934.

Routley, Erik. "A Collection of Hymns by Timothy Dudley-Smith." *The Hymn* 33/4 (October 1982): 262.

———. *Hymns and Human Life.* Grand Rapids MI: Eerdmans, 1967.

———. *Hymns Today and Tomorrow.* New York: Abingdon Press, 1964.

———. *The Music of Christian Hymnody: A Study of the development of the hymn tune since the Reformation, with special reference to English Protestantism.* London: Independent Press Limited. 1957.

———. *A Panorama of Christian Hymnody.* Collegeville MN: Liturgical Press, 1972.

———, editor. *Rejoice in the Lord: A Hymn Companion to the Scriptures.* Grand Rapids MI: Wm. B. Eerdmans Publishing Company, 1985.

———. *Words, Music, and the Church.* New York: Abingdon Press, 1968.

Routley, Erik and Peter Cutts. *An English-speaking Hymnal Guide.* Chicago: GIA Publications, 2005.

Sachs, Curt. *The Commonwealth of Art.* New York: W. W. Norton & Company, Inc., 1946.

———. *Rhythm and Tempo: A Study in Music History.* New York: W. W. Norton & Company, Inc. 1953.

Sanchez, Diana, editor. *The Hymns of the United Methodist Hymnal.* Nashville: Abingdon Press, 1989.

Saroyan, William. "Resurrection of a Life," from Story, edited by. John Updike. *The Best American Short Stories of the Century.* New York: Houghton Mifflin Company, 1999. 159–68.

Schiller, Friedrich. *Schillers Werke. Nationalausgabe.* Nobert Oellers, Julius Petersen, Lieselotte Blumenthal, Benno von Wiese, Siegfried Seidel. Stiftung Weimarer Klassik; Schiller-

Nationalmuseum. Weimar: Hermann Bohlaus Nachfolger, 2000- ISBN: 3740000317. Volume 17. Page 362.

Schilling, S. Paul. *The Faith We Sing*. Philadelphia: The Westminster Press, 1983.

Schubert, Franz. *Werke: Kritisch durchgesehen Gesamtausgabe*, Edited by Mandyezewski, Eusibius. Leipzig, 1895. Series 20, volume 3, page 33.

Scruton, Roger. *Aesthetics of Music*. Oxford: Clarendon Press, 1997.

———. *An Intelligent Person's Guide to Philosophy*. New York: Penguin Books, 1996.

Sessions, Roger. *Harmonic Practice*. New York: Harcourt, Brace and Company, 1951.

Sidney, Sir Phillip. "The Defense of Poesy." *English Essays from Sir Philip Sidney to Macalay*. Volume 29 of *The Harvard Classics*. Edited by Charles Eliot. New York: P. F. Collier & Son, 1910.

Sloboda, John A., and Patrik N. Juslin. "Psychological Perspectives on Music and Emotion," in *Music and Emotion: Theory and Research*, edited by Patrik N. Juslin and John A. Sloboda. Oxford: Oxford University Press, 2001.

Sondheim, Stephen. *Finishing the Hat: Collected Lyrics (1954–1981), with Attendant Comments, Principles, Heresies, Grudges, Whines and Anecdotes*. New York: Alfred A. Knopf, 2010.

Spencer, Donald A. *Hymn and Scripture Selection Guide: A Cross Reference of Scripture and Hymns with over 12,000 References for 380 Hymns and Gospel Songs*. Valley Forge: Judson Press, 1977.

Stearns, Peter N, editor. *The Encyclopedia of World History*. Rev. of the work originally edited by William L. Langer. 6th ed. New York: Houghton Mifflin Company, 2001.

Steiner, George. *Real Presences*. Chicago: University of Chicago Press, 1989.

Stevenson, Robert. *Protestant Church Music in America: A Short Survey of Men and Movements from 1564 to the Present*. New York: W. W. Norton & Company, Inc., 1966.

Stevenson, Robert Louis. "The Art of Writing." *Contemporary Review* (April 1885).

Stulken, Marilyn Kay. *Hymnal Companion to the Lutheran Book of Worship*. Philadelphia: Fortress Press, 1981.

Swain, Joseph. P. *Harmonic Rhythm: An Analysis and Interpretation*. Oxford: Oxford University Press, 2002.

Sydnor, James R. *Hymns and Their Uses*. Carol Stream IL: Hope Publishing Company, 1982.

Taizé Community: Meditative Singing. http://www.taize.fr/en_article338.html; http://www.taize.fr/en_article681.html. "Meditative Singing," "MP3 and Podcasts," and "Learning the Songs."

Tamke, Susan S. *Make a Joyful Noise unto the Lord: Hymns as a Reflection of Victorian Social Attitudes*. Athens: Ohio University Press, 1978.

Taylor, William R., and W. Stewart McCullough. "Introduction," *Psalms*. Volume 4 of The Interpreter's Bible. New York: Abingdom Press, 1955.

Temperley, Nicholas. *The Hymn Tune Index: A Census of English-language Hymn Tunes in Printed Sources from 1535 to 1820*. Oxford: Clarendon Press, 1998.

Thayer, Joseph H. *Thayer's Greek-English Lexicon of the New Testament*. New York: Baker Book House, 1977.

Tillich, Paul. *The Religious Situation*, translated by Richard H. Niebuhr. New York: Henry Holt & Company, Inc., 1931. New York: Meridian Books, Inc., 1956.

Titon, Jeff Todd, James T. Koetting, David P. McAllester, David B. Reck, and Mark Slobin. *Worlds of Music: An Introduction to the Music of the World's People*. New York and London: Schirmer Books and Collier Macmillan Publishers, 1984.

Tolkien, J. R. R. *The Monsters and the Critics*. London: Harper Collins, 1997.

Tomasino, Anna. *Music and Culture*. Burnt Mill, Harlow, Essex, England: Longman, 2005.

Tosh, Bert. "Producing 5,842 Hymns," *Hymn Society of Great Britain & Ireland Bulletin* 19/5 (January 2010).

Troeger, Thomas. *Borrowed Light: Hymn Texts, Prayers, and Poems*. Oxford: Oxford University Press, 1994.

————. "Personal, Cultural and Theological Influences on the Language of Hymns and Worship." *The Hymn: A Journal of Congregational Song* 38/4 (October 1987): 7–19.

Trueblood, Elton. *Philosophy of Religion*. New York: Harper & Brothers, 1957.

Unger, Merrill F. *Principles of Expository Preaching*. Grand Rapids MI: Zondervan Publishing House, 1955.

United Methodist Hymnal. Nashville: The United Methodist Publishing House, 1989.

Updike, John, editor. *The Best American Short Stories of the Century*. New York: Houghton Mifflin Company, 1999.

Vajda, Jaroslav J. *Now the Joyful Celebration*. St. Louis: MorningStar Music Publishers, 1987.

Vaughan Williams, Ralph, Musical Editor. "Preface, The Music." *The English Hymnal with Tunes*. London: Oxford University Press, 1933.

Wackernagel, Philipp. *Das deutsche Kirchenlied von der ältesten Zeit bis zum Anfang des 17. Jahrhundert*. 5 vols. Leipzig, 1864–1877.

Wainwright, Geoffrey, and Karen B. Westerfield Tucker, editors. *The Oxford History of Christian Worship*. Oxford: Oxford University Press, 2006.

Wallace, Robin Knowles. "Hymns as a Resource for the Language of Worship." *The Hymn* 58/3 (Summer 2007): 33–37.

Watson, J. R., editor. *An Annotated Anthology of Hymns*. Oxford: Oxford University Press, 2002.

————. *Awake My Soul: Reflections on Thirty Hymns*. London: SPCK, 2005.

————. *The English Hymn: A Critical and Historical Study*. Oxford: Oxford University Press, 1999.

————. "Hymns and Literature: Form and Interpretation." *Hymn Society of Great Britain & Ireland Bulletin* 238, 17/5 (January 2004): 126–32.

Watson, J. R. and Emma Hornby, editors. *Canterbury Dictionary of Hymnology*. www.hymnology.co.uk/.

Watts, Isaac. *Hymns and Spiritual Songs*. London: Printed by J. H. for John Lawrence at the Angel in the Poultrey, 1709.

Welch, John W., editor. *Chiasmus in Antiquity: Structures, Analyses, Exegesis*. Hildesheim: Gerstenberg Verlag, 1981.

Wells, Marcus. "Translating Hymns." *Hymn Society of Great Britain & Ireland Bulletin* 239, 17/6 (April 2004).

Wesley, Charles. *The Journal of Charles Wesley.* http://wesley.nnu.edu/charles-wesley/the-journal-of-charles-wesley-1707-1788/the-journal-of-charles-wesley-may-1-august-31-1738/.

Westermeyer, Paul. "A Hymnal's Theological Significance." *Dialog: A Journal of Theology* 48/4 (Winter 2009): 313–19. Gettysburg: Lutheran Theology Seminary.

———. *Let the People Sing: Hymn Tunes in Perspective.* Chicago: GIA Publications, Inc., 2005.

———. *Te Deum: The Church and Music.* Minneapolis: Fortress Press, 1998.

———. *With Tongues of Fire: Profiles in 20th-Century Hymn Writing.* St. Louis: Concordia Publishing House, 1955.

White, B. F., and E. J. King, editors. *The Sacred Harp: A Collection of Psalm and Hymn Tunes, Odes, and Anthems.* Philadelphia: S. C. Collins, 1860.

Whitehead, Alfred North. *Adventures of Ideas.* New York: Macmillan, 1933.

Wilder, Amos N. "Art and Theological Meaning." *Union Seminary Quarterly Review* 18/1 (November 1962).

———. *New Testament Faith for Today.* New York: Harper & Brothers, Publishers, 1955.

———. *Theopoetic: Theology and the Religious Imagination.* Philadelphia: Fortress Press, 1976.

Williams, Neville. *Chronology of the Modern World 1763 to the Present Time.* New York: David McKay, Inc., 1966.

Wilmart, A. *Le "Jubilus" dit de Saint Bernard.* Rome, 1944.

Wilson-Dickson, Andrew. *The Story of Christian Music from Gregorial Chant to Black Gospel: An Illustrated Guide to all the Major Traditions of Music in Worship.* Minneapolis: Fortress Press, 1992.

Wilson, Blake, George J. Buelow, and Peter A. Hoyt, "Rhetoric and Music." *Grove Music Online.* Edited by L. Macy. http://www.grovemusic.com.

Wilson, Edward O. *Consilience: The Unity of Knowledge.* New York: Alfred A. Knopf, 1998.

Wilson, John. "Looking at Hymn Tunes: the Objective Factors." In Robin A. Leaver and James H. Litton, editors, and Carlton R. Young, executive editor, *Duty and Delight: Routley Remembered.* Carol Stream IL: Hope Publishing Company and Norwich: Canterbury Press, 1985.

Witvliet, John D. *Worship Seeking Understanding: Windows into Christian Practice.* Grand Rapids: Baker Academic, 2003.

Wordsworth, William. "Expostulation and Reply and The Tables Turned," as quoted in *The Norton Anthology of English Literature.* New York: W. W. Norton & Company, Inc., 1968, 1262.

———. *Lyrical Ballads with Pastoral and Other Poems in Two Volumes.* London: Longman, Hurst, Rees, and Orme, 1805. Preface, L [page 50]. www.bartleby.com/39/36.html.

Wren, Brian. *Faith Looking Forward.* Carol Stream IL: Hope Publishing Company, 1983.

———. *Faith Renewed.* Carol Stream IL: Hope Publishing Company, 1995.

———. "Hymn Interpretation: 'There's a spirit in the air.'" *The Hymn* 47/2 (April 1996): 43.

———. "Praise God and Pound the Typewriter—A Critical Appreciation of Thomas Troeger." *The Hymn: Journal of Congregational Song* 37/3 (October 1986): 13–19.

Wright, David R. "The Many Mysteries of Meter." *Hymn Society of Great Britain & Ireland* 232, 16/11 (June 2002): 266–69.

———. "What Do Hymns Say About Daily Work." *Hymn Society of Great Britain & Ireland Bulletin Occasional Paper.* Third series, number 2.

Wright, Simon. "'Pale Green of the English Hymnal!'—A Centenary Retrospective." *Brio: Journal of the United Kingdom and Ireland Branch of the International Association of Music Libraries, Archives and Documentation Centres* 43/1 (Spring/Summer 2006).

Young, Carlton, editor. *Companion to The United Methodist Hymnal.* Nashville: Abingdon Press, 1993.

———. *Music of the Heart: John and Charles Wesley on Music and Musicians: An Anthology.* Carol Stream IL: Hope Publishing Company, 1995.

———. *My Great Redeemer's Praise: An Introduction to Christian Hymns.* Akron OH: OSL Publications, 1995.

Zahn, Johannes. *Die Melodien der deutschen evangelischen Kirchenlieder.* 6 volumes. Gütersloh, 1888-1893.

Index of Hymns

Index of Hymn Tunes

Index of Scripture

Index of Persons

Index of Topics

CPSIA information can be obtained
at www.ICGtesting.com
Printed in the USA
LVHW041923230822
726685LV00001B/51